the *Lyle*
official
ANTIQUES
review

All prices quoted in this book are obtained from a variety of auctions in various countries during the twelve months prior to publication and are converted to dollars at the rate of exchange prevalent at the time of sale.

DRAWINGS BY

PETER KNOX
GEORGE HOGG
W. YOUNG
PAMELA GRANT
J. PAGE
ALISON MORRISON

the Lyle
official
ANTIQUES
review
1980

COMPILED BY MARGOT RUTHERFORD
EDITED BY TONY CURTIS

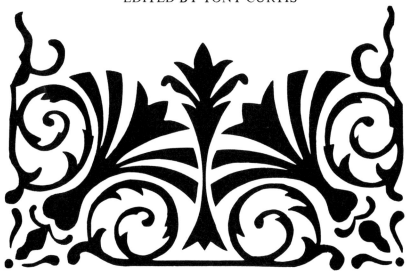

The publishers wish to express their sincere thanks
to the following for their kind help and assistance
in the production of this volume:

MARGARET ANDERSON
LYNN HALL
CARMEN MILIVOYEVICH
JANICE MONCRIEFF
MAY MUTCH
NICOLA PARK

SBN 0-902921-90-8

Copyright © Lyle Publications '79
Glenmayne, Galashiels, Scotland.
10th year of issue.

Printed by Apollo Press
Dominion Way, Worthing, Sussex, England.
Bound by Newdigate Press, Vincent Lane,
Dorking, Surrey, England.

Distributed in the U.S.A. by
Apollo, 391 South Road (U.S.9)
Poughkeepsie, New York 12601.

CONTENTS

Acknowledgements

Abbott's, *The Hill, Wickham Market, Suffolk.*
Linden Alcock, *8-9 Bridge Street, Hereford.*
Alfie's Antique Market, *13-15 Church Street, London.*
Allen & May, *18 Bridge Street, Andover, Hamps.*
Anderson & Garland, *Anderson House, Market Street, Newcastle.*
Andrew Hilditch & Son, *19 The Square, Sandbach, Cheshire.*
T. Bannister & Co., *Market Place, Haywards Heath, Sussex.*
Barber's, *12 Shoplatch, Shrewsbury, Salop.*
Barber's Fine Art Auctions, *6 Walton Road, Woking, Surrey.*
Biddle & Webb, *Enfield House, Islington Row, Edgbaston.*
Boardman's, *Clare, Suffolk.*
Messrs. Boisgirard and De Heeckeren, *Paris.*
Bonham's, *Montpelier Galleries, Montpelier Street, London.*
Bonsor Penningtons, *82 Eden Street, Kingston-upon-Thames.*
Bradley & Vaughan, *59 Perrymount Road, Haywards Heath, Sussex.*
British Antique Exporters, *206 London Road, Burgess Hill, W. Sussex.*
E. J. Brooks, *39 Park End Street, Oxford.*
Wm. H. Brown, *33 Watergate, Grantham, Lincs.*
Bruton, Knowles & Co., *The Hill, Upton-on-Severn, Worcs.*
Buckell & Ballard, *1a Parsons Street, Banbury, Oxon.*
Bukowskis, *Arsenalsgatan 2, Stockholm.*
Burrows & Day, *39/41 Bank Street, Ashford, Kent.*
Burtenshaws Walker, *66 High Street, Lewes, Suffolk.*
Butler & Hatch Waterman, *86 High Street, Hythe, Kent.*
A. G. Byrne & Co., *Co. Wicklow, Ireland.*
Champetier de Ribes, *Ribeyre, Millon, France.*
Chancellors & Co., *31 High Street, Ascot, Berks.*
H. C. Chapman & Son, *North Street, Scarborough, Yorks.*
Christie's, *8 King Street, St. James', London.*
Christie's, *Geneva. Per Agent.*
Christie's New York, *502 Park Avenue, New York City, New York.*
Christie's S. Kensington, *85 Old Brompton Road, London.*
Chrystal Brothers, Stott & Kerruish, *Bowring Road, Ramsey, Isle of Man.*
Churchman's Auction Galleries, *Church Street, Steyning, W. Sussex.*
Clarke Gammon, *45 High Street, Guildford, Surrey.*
Coles, Knapp & Kennedy, *Palace Pound, Ross-on-Wye, Herefords.*
Cubitt & West, *Millmead, Guildford, Surrey.*
Clifford Dann & Partners, *43 South Street, Eastbourne.*
Alonzo Dawes & Hoddell, *Sixways, Clevedon, Avon.*
Dee & Atkinson, *The Exchange, Driffield, Yorks.*
Dickinson, Davy & Markham, *10 Wrawly Street, Brigg.*
Robert Dowie, *Leven, Fife.*
Drewatt, Watson & Barton, *22 Market Place, Newbury, Berks.*
Drewery & Wheeldon, *Gainsborough, Lincs.*
Hy. Duke & Son, *40 South Street, Dorchester, Dorset.*
Eadon, Lockwood & Riddle, *2 St. James Street, Sheffield.*
J. & R. Edmiston, *164-166 Bath Street, Glasgow.*
Edwards, Bigwood & Bewlay, *78 Colmore Row, Birmingham.*
Weller Eggar, *74 Castle Street, Farnham, Surrey.*
Ellis, *44/46 High Street, Worthing.*
Frank H. Fellows, *Bedford House, 88 Hagley Road, Edgbaston.*
Alan Fitchett & Co., *28 Gloucester Street, Brighton, Sussex.*
John Francis, Thomas Jones, *King Street, Carmarthen, Dyfed.*
F. le Gallais, *Bath Street, Jersey, Channel Islands.*
Garrod Turner, *50 St. Nicholas Street, Ipswich, Suffolk.*
P. J. Garwood, *Ludlow, Shropshire.*
Geering & Colyer, *Highgate, Hawkhurst, Kent.*
Rowland Gorringe, *15 North Street, Lewes, Sussex.*
Andrew Grant, *Cookshill, Salwarpe, Droitwich, Worcs.*
Graves, Son & Pilcher, *38 Holland Road, Hove, Sussex.*
Grays Antique Market, *58 Davies Street, London.*
Grays Antique Mews, *1-7 Davies Mews, London.*
Green's, *Wantage, Oxon.*
Gribble, Booth & Taylor, *West Street, Axminster, Devon.*
James Harrison, *35 West End, Hebden Bridge, W. Yorks.*
Heathcote Ball & Co., *47 New Walk, Leicester.*
Hexton & Cheney, *3 Pier Road, Littlehampton, Sussex.*
Hobbs Parker, *9 Tufton Street, Ashford, Kent.*
John Hodbin, *53 High Street, Tenterden, Kent.*
Humberts, Grace & Chasemore, *Magdalene House,*
Magdalene Street, Taunton, Somerset.
Hussey's, *Alphinbrook Road, Alphington, Exeter.*
Jackson-Stops & Staff, *Town Hall, Chipping Camden, Glos.*
Jolly's, *The Auction Rooms, Old King Street, Bath.*
Jordan & Cook, *High Street, Worthing.*
G. A. Key, *Market Place, Aylsham, Norfolk.*
King & Chasemore, *Station Road, Pulborough, Sussex.*
G. Knight & Son, *West Street, Midhurst, Sussex.*
Lacy Scott, *3 Hatter Street, Bury St. Edmunds.*
Laidlaw's, *Wakefield, Yorkshire.*

Lalonde Bros. & Parham, *Station Road, Weston-Super-Mare, Avon.*
W. H. Lane & Son, *Morrab Road, Penzance, Cornwall.*
Langlois Ltd., *Don Street, Jersey, Channel Islands.*
T. R. G. Lawrence & Son, *19b Market Street, Crewkerne, Somerset.*
James & Lister Lea, *11 New Hall Street, Birmingham.*
Lewes Auction Rooms, *Lewes, Sussex.*
Leys, *Kipdorpvest 46, Antwerp.*
Locke & England, *1-2 Euston Place, Leamington Spa, Warwickshire.*
R. L. Lowery & Partners, *24 Bridge Street, Northampton.*
Mallam's, *26 Grosvenor Street, Cheltenham.*
Mallam's, *24 St. Michael's Street, Oxford.*
Manchester Auction Mart, *3-4 Atkinson Street, Manchester.*
Frank Marshall & Co., *Marshall House, Church Hill, Knutsford.*
Thomas Mawer & Sons, *Lincoln Auction Rooms, Lincoln.*
May, Whetter-Grose, *Cornubia Hall, Par, Cornwall.*
McCartney, Morris & Barker, *25 Corve Street, Ludlow, Shrops.*
Meads of Brighton, *St. Nicholas Road, Brighton.*
Messenger, May & Baverstock, *93 High Street, Godalming.*
Thomas N. Miller, *18-26 Gallowgate, Newcastle-upon-Tyne.*
John Milne, *9 North Silver Street, Aberdeen.*
Moore, Allen & Innocents, *33 Castle Street, Cirencester, Glos.*
Morphet's of Harrogate, *4-6 Albert Street, Harrogate.*
Morton's, *New Orleans, America.*
Moss, *13 Whitehorse Street, Baldock, Herts.*
Neales of Nottingham, *192 Mansfield Road, Nottingham.*
D. M. Nesbit & Co., *7 Clarendon Road, Southsea, Hants.*
Nock Deighton, *52 Whitburn Street, Bridgenorth, Shrops.*
Nottingham Auction Mart, *Byard Lane, Bridlesmith Gate, Nottingham.*
Olivers, *23-24 Market Hill, Sudbury, Suffolk.*
Osmond, Tricks & Son, *The Auction Rooms, Regent Street, Bristol.*
Outhwaite & Litherland, *Kingsway Galleries, Fontenoy Street, Liverpool 3.*
Parsons, Welch & Cowell, *129 High Street, Sevenoaks, Kent.*
Pearsons, *Walcote Chambers, High Street, Winchester.*
Phillips, *7 Blenheim Street, New Bond Street, London.*
Phillips, *New York Gallery.*
John H. Raby, *St. Mary's Road, Bradford, W. Yorks.*
Ragg, Travis & Isherwood, *12 Princes Drive, Colwyn Bay, Clwyd.*
Samuel Rains & Son, *17 Warren Street, Stockport.*
Renton & Renton, *16 Albert Street, Harrogate.*
Riddett's, *23 Richmond Hill, The Square, Bournemouth.*
Russell, Baldwin & Bright, *Ryelands Road, Leominster.*
Andrew Sharpe & Partners, *Ilkley, Yorkshire.*
Silvester's, *2 & 4 High Street, Warwick, Warwickshire.*
C. T. & G. H. Smith, *Lanark House, New Street, Ledbury, Herefordshire.*
Smith-Woolley & Perry, *5 West Terrace, Folkestone.*
Sotheby's, *34-35 New Bond Street, London.*
Sotheby Bearne, *3 Warren Road, Torquay, Devon.*
Sotheby's Belgravia, *19 Motcomb Street, London.*
Sotheby's, *Monaco. Per Agent.*
Sotheby's Parke Bernet, *New York.*
Sotheby's, *Zurich. Per Agent.*
Spark & Rogerson, *Matlock Auction Gallery, Matlock, Derbyshire.*
Spear & Sons, *The Hill, Wickham Market, Woodbridge, Suffolk.*
Henry Spencer & Sons, *20 The Square, Retford, Yorkshire.*
Stooke, Hill & Co., *3 Broad Street, Leominster, Herefordshire.*
Stride's, *Southdown House, St. John's Street, Chichester.*
Swetenham's, *Bold Place, Chester, Cheshire.*
Sworder's Salerooms, *19 North Street, Bishops Stortford, Herts.*
Christopher Sykes, *11 Market Place, Wobum, Milton Keynes.*
David Symonds, *High Street, Crediton, Devon.*
Charles Taylor & Sons, *2 Mason Street, Sidney Street, Salford.*
Laurence & Martin Taylor, *63 High Street, Honiton, Devon.*
Garrod Turner, *50 St. Nicholas Street, Ipswich, Suffolk.*
Vernon's of Chichester, *1 Westgate, Chichester.*
Vidler & Co., *Rye Auction Galleries, Rye, Sussex.*
Vincent & Vanderpump, *24 Greyfriars Road, Reading.*
V. & V. Chattel Auctioneers, *6 Station Road, Reading.*
Vosts, *Lower Mamey Tower, Colchester, Essex.*
Walker, Barrett & Hills, *Wolverhampton, Staffs.*
Wallis & Wallis, *Regency House, 1 Albion Street, Lewes, Sussex.*
Warner, Sheppard & Wade, *16-18 Halford Street, Leicester.*
Thomas Watson, *27 North Street, Bishop Stortford, Herts.*
Way, Riddett & Co., *Town Hall Chambers, Lind Street, Ryde.*
J. M. Welch & Sons, *The Town Hall, Dunmow, Essex.*
West London Auctions, *Sandringham Mews, High Street, Ealing.*
Peter Wilson, *50 Hospital Street, Nantwich, Cheshire.*
P. F. Windibank, *18 Reigate Road, Dorking, Surrey.*
Wingett & Son, *29 Holt Street, Wrexham.*
Woolley & Wallis, *Castle Auction Mart, Salisbury, Wilts.*
Worsfolds, *40 Station Road West, Cantebury, Kent.*

9

ANTIQUES REVIEW

Seconds out! This is the year of conflict in the antiques world. Battle lines are drawing up for a big fight between Dealers and salerooms and tempers are running high.

The competition between the two branches of the trade has been hardening for some time, with murmurs of discontent among Dealers about what they consider to be the unfair advantages enjoyed by salerooms in capturing the lion's share of the business. The last twelve months has seen a tremendous escalation in this. Till now Dealers feel justified in claiming that the salerooms are enjoying a monopolistic situation which could well drive the private Dealer out of business.

What concerns Dealers is that small salerooms all over the country are falling like ninepins before the takeover policies of the big three – Christie's, Sotheby's and Phillips. Hardly a month passes without yet another old firm having an extra graft on its name and an injection of cash and modern selling know-how brought into their operations. The latest to fall are King and Chasemore – now part of the Sotheby empire – and Edmiston's of Glasgow, an old established family firm which has recently been taken over by Christie's.

All this causes a good deal of concern among Dealers because, as one Midland Dealer said –

"The big salerooms, like Christie's and Sotheby's, are taking all the trade. They will sell anything, even the most ordinary stuff that used to be left for the smaller Dealers. In the old days they were very snobby and would only touch Rembrandts but they take anything now and, as a consequence, stock is very hard to find."

The evidence of shortness of stock is immediately obvious to anyone doing a trade survey of Britain – thin window displays, poorly stocked shops, a regrettable proliferation of low quality or gimmicky items, shops that are too often closed while the proprietor is 'on the road' because profits do not allow extra staff to be a commercial proposition.

The problems of the Dealers are being earnestly taken up by LAPADA whose spokesman, Philip Broadbridge, is having a long, hard look at the world of the Dealer.

"The trade is seriously worried about this saleroom takeover," said Mr Broadbridge, "but what too many of the Dealers still ignore is that this new development is a combination of cleverness by the auction houses and the trade not looking after their own affairs as well as they might."

For too long it seems business has been a boom thing for Dealers and they stopped having to worry about it – trade came in growing volume as the years went by. Now trade is going elsewhere – both private buyers and sellers are flocking to the salerooms and it is the concern of people like Mr Broadbridge to ask why and to try to reverse the trend before all but the biggest specialist Dealers are driven completely out of business.

Philip Broadbridge has part of the answer.

"The trade must learn to make itself more attractive to the general public. When the boom years were on, too many Dealers felt they did not need the man in the street and there was a proliferation of 'Trade Only' signs. These will now have to go. Shops ought to open regularly, at decent hours and if the proprietor has to be out on the road all the time, he will have to make his shop available to passing trade somehow. People soon tire of calling at a shop which is never open. If they want to buy something or have something to sell, they then go to the salerooms. Another thing that the trade has to live down is that in the past there have been far too many reports about the public being ripped off. Dealers have been given a bad image by this and that impression must now be lived down."

Mr Broadbridge also wants Dealers to be more concerned about their public relations. It is well acknowledged that part of the success of all the big salerooms is due to their adroit use of the media — they have adopted the 'hard sell' with great impact and have never missed an opportunity to bring to public notice any examples of saleroom surprises or unusual achievements. People, all over the country, are well aware of the activities of Christie's, Sotheby's, Phillips, Bonham's and other big auction houses when they do not know the whereabouts of their own local Dealers or what sort of things they specialise in selling. This, says LAPADA, must be changed. Dealers will have to project themselves more if they are to survive.

"They ought to take advertisements in the local press and never miss an opportunity of bringing their names to the public notice," said Mr Broadbridge.

What all Dealers feel must be emphasised in their bid to survive, is that if people sell at auction, they rarely receive more than eighty per cent of the price the item is knocked down for. Almost all big salerooms now charge a ten per cent seller's fee, a ten per cent buyer's fee, a cataloguing fee and other sundry charges. The seller has to wait, sometimes for several months, on his money because goods are held up awaiting specialist sales and there are delays over cataloguing and appraising. Then, after the item has been sold, salerooms usually have a month gap before paying out.

A Dealer in Woburn, who has seen private trade shrink alarmingly over the past twelve months, said with emphasis "We will not only give a fair price to a private seller but we pay on the nail. In cash." Another enterprising Dealer, who is putting his mind to surviving, is an antiquarian bookseller from Guildford who takes out newspaper advertisements putting his case —

"I am prepared to pay as much by private treaty as I would pay in the saleroom," he said. "By dealing directly with me, owners can therefore realise more and there are the added benefits of immediate CASH PAYMENT and the avoidance of sundry extra charges. But the greatest advantage in direct sale to me is speed. I am prepared to buy for spot cash."

All reputable Dealers now are anxious to make the point that people with something to sell should try them first because the prices offered in a private sale might even be in excess of what is finally realised at auction. The proprietor of a big London antiques market said ruefully —

"What amazes me is that I have

seen goods sold in auction houses for more than they are priced in shops in really very expensive areas. This does not mean the seller gets more — you must remember to deduct the hidden charges. Yet the public flock to sales. We are in the happy position of being situated near the salerooms and so we get the spin off from people going there. If we were sitting in some market town in the middle of England we would really be worried. Trade has been very bad over this winter and it is doubtful if some of the more isolated shops will be able to survive."

So survival is the name of the Dealing game. With both buyers and sellers being seduced away from them by the razzmatazz tactics of the big auction houses, they will either have to compete in the same field and with the same determination or disappear.

"The trade must learn to make itself more attractive in every way to the general public," said Mr Broadbridge. "The public must know that if they are selling, a fair price will always be given. They must also know that if they are buying, the goods will be covered with the safeguard of the Dealer being prepared to take them back if the buyer is dissatisfied. Another thing that is too often forgotten, is that the public is far better protected if they buy from a Dealer because the law helps them. Auction houses are absolved from this legal restraint as you cannot take back to them something that turns out to be a disappointment."

Battle plans being drawn up for the future do not prevent the trade being seriously worried now. When the big salerooms first introduced the buyer's ten per cent premium, there was an enraged outcry but the premium has spread and though the Dealers' associations have tried to bring a lawsuit saying that this levy is illegal, there seems little likelihood of them being successful.

The concerted hostility on the part of the Dealers against the blanket activities of the salerooms is increased when they look at developments abroad. In Sweden, auction houses have taken to conducting sales on television with "phone in" bids. If this takes on in Britain, private Dealers will be even more hard hit than they are at the moment. Another sign of the times is a recent report from America that the big salerooms are beginning to dabble in that strange American phenomenon, the "Tag" sale.

"Tag" sales are conducted in private houses by people who have something to sell. Goods are priced with tags and the sellers advertise their sale all over the locality with hand written little signs. These sales have, naturally, not been popular with the American Dealers but now they are even more dangerous because Sotheby's are beginning to show interest in managing them. They are not yet, of course, taking a hand in selling old washing machines or garden tools but tend to specialise in selling off the contents of larger houses — rather like the still popular house sales in Britain. The auction houses put the prices on the tags, collect the money and then pay the seller after deducting their commission. The price tags will be estimated according to the latest saleroom prices. At "Tag" sales the seller pays twenty-five per cent of the gross and no buyers' premiums are charged. Dealers, hearing of all this, sweated even more with justified alarm.

While the Dealers are in the doldrums, the salerooms are very much on a successful upgrade. Apart from expansion all over Britain, they are spreading into America and onto the Continent of Europe as well. Both Christie's and Sotheby's now have two New York salerooms. Christie's second was opened this summer specifically to sell "middle range" items. This is to be a carbon copy of their "middle range" South Kensington Saleroom, the profits from which were staggeringly into the millions last year.

During the calendar year 1978 Sotheby's growth of turnover was thirty-nine per cent and Christie's was thirty-six per cent for their operations throughout the world. Total cash figures worked out at £182.3 million and £101.8 million for Sotheby's and Christie's respectively. Phillips, who have been trying very hard in London, the provinces and abroad, trailed a distant third behind the big two monoliths with a nineteen per cent increase and a turnover of £27.5 million . . . still a respectable profit however. London was where the biggest business was transacted and Sotheby's at Bond Street were sixty-two per cent ahead with a £26 million total profit. This is even more surprising when it is remembered that the previous year they had the blockbusting sale of the Von Hirsch collection. Christie's biggest success was made in their South Kensington rooms which was up sixty per cent with a turnover of £10 million. The fourth London saleroom, Bonham's, also shared in the saleroom boom and during last year they turned over £8.3 million, an increase of thirty per cent. Phillips do not give figures for London operations alone but it is estimated to be in the region of £20 million and their sales were up by thirty per cent on last year's figures. It is, therefore, no surprise that one of the darlings of Stock Exchange investors are Sotheby's shares which rose from 150p in 1977 to 368p earlier this year. Christie's shares which were first offered at 70p in November 1973 reached 158p this year.

Even smaller salerooms around the country have benefitted from the new public interest in auctions. The growth of business is such that firms no longer bother to report to the trade press when they cross the million pound turnover mark. Inflation of prices has, of course, been a contributory factor in reaching this figure. The increased volume of goods handled is also responsible and many provincial houses have found it necessary to extend or improve their premises in the past year. Some of them, who still do not charge a buyer's premium, are finding a rush to buy from local Dealers is swelling their business.

Another interesting development in the past year is the final laying of the old fear that Britain was suffering from an art and antiques "drain" because of the activity of foreign buyers. In 1978, figures now show, total exports of antiques, defined as objects more than one hundred years old and of fine art of any age was £259 million − but imports into the country totalled almost as much at £223 million. It is stressed that items imported from abroad for sale in Britain are logged both coming in and, if they are subsequently bought by foreign buyers, going out. The Von Hirsch collection, for example, must account for large figures in both imports and exports because German buyers bought heavily at these sales.

The customers coming from abroad to Britain continue to be led by the Americans and exports of antiques and pictures from the United Kingdom to U.S.A. stand at £40.2 million and £44.6 million respectively, increases of thirteen per cent and twenty per cent over the previous year. The biggest increase, however, has been marked up by Swiss buyers and this trend has been noticed by Dealers all over the country, who have consistently named Swiss, German and Dutch as their best customers from abroad. The Germans imported sixty per cent more antiques from

Britain in 1978 than they had done before and fifteen per cent more paintings.The Swiss, however, increased their antiques imports by an impressive one hundred and twenty-five per cent and paintings imports by thirty-three per cent. The Dutch popularity as customers with Dealers is not borne out by the figures which show them down by four per cent in antiques exports and by a sad seventy-four per cent in the field of pictures. Other interesting trends that have shown up in the annual Department of Trade figures are the emergence of Australia as a buying power in Britain and the falling away of Canada which has been caused by the recent decline in the dollar there. Spain too has declined as a customer in the past months and their figures were down by fifty-five per cent. The up and down Japanese yen however, held up well enough in 1978 for Japanese customers to be back in strength buying both pictures and antiques in Britain. Italy, however, has gone down almost to negligibility because of the sad state of the lira. One Dealer in the South of England said sadly —

"We used to have three or four Italians in here every week. I do not think I have seen one for months now." However, enterprising Dealers have taken the fight into their enemy camp and are finding Italy an ideal place for buying, especially pictures. More surprisingly, Sweden is also expanding as an art source and in the past year Britain imported more than £2.1 million pounds of pictures from there.

Although American still tops the buying and selling tables, Dealers all over the country have found recently that American buyers no longer make up their best customers. "The age of the almighty dollar is past, past, past," said one Dealer in the North of England. "The people who come into the antique shops are usually horrified at the rate

things here have increased in price. This is not the happy hunting ground for them that it once was. My best customers are the Germans and the Dutch. The French and the Italians as buyers are almost non-existent." A London Dealer agreed with him — "The French are nowhere," he said. "The Americans are out too, their inflation has hit them hard. In fact, America is the place to go to buy now." Although some Dealers in this country say, in short, "America is finished," this statement has to be qualified because auction houses like Sotheby's and Christie's are expanding their business there and they are not people to put money into a loss area. Christie's believe that America is a developing market and are now looking to the West Coast, San Francisco and Los Angeles. Already they have two New York salerooms and believe that it would be possible to string a line of reputable salerooms right across the Continent of America by their already established practice of taking over existing businesses. "We would not be going to America if it was a dead market," said a Christie's man. This view of the U.S.A. was shared by an American Dealer who now sees the antique trade in his country as being in a similar situation as it was in Britain ten years ago — a sellers' rather than a buyers' market. He looks forward to buyers from all over the world coming to America to buy. "Astute traders will always make a buck," he said confidently.

In spite of the ups and downs of foreign markets and business, Britain still stands supreme in the world of art and antiques. A Sotheby's lady said — "Britain has been the centre of the art and antiques world for several years now — a position that it has been building up to since 1954 when various restrictions on art imports and foreign currency transactions were removed by the Government.

So Britain leads the world and should continue to do so for yet another decade at least.

Finally, as is the Lyle Official Review's custom, we asked Dealers and salerooms all over the country for their tips on what should make money in 1980.

A London Dealer said without hesitation — "Victorian Gothic items have increased enormously in price and should continue to make money. In fact the demand for church furniture in Japan is absolutely insatiable. We thought we had soaked it up last year but that was far from the truth. Other things that go like hot cakes are stained glass, scientific instruments and old tools. For the past ten years there has been an amazing escalation in the price of old oak but I feel that buyers ought to be looking at fine 18th and 19th century mahogany furniture which has not shared in the oak boom at all. The crudest oak makes a bomb, so avoid it and go for satinwood and inlaid fine furniture. Similarly, it is a mug's game now to try to buy fine paintings and English porcelain — the prices are sky high. They are no longer a trading commodity from the Dealers' point of view. Instead, people should look for samplers, early textiles like fine bedspreads and wall hangings — that's where the big profits could be made."

Another provincial Dealer from the Midlands agreed with him and stressed that scientific instruments should make good buys in the coming months — "They have gone up in price steadily, keeping well ahead of inflation," he said. "They are also a good investment because you can't fake them, they are much too intricate and it would cost more to make a fake than it would to buy an antique instrument."

Other Dealers all had their favourite tips — some said they were being patronised by people in search of fakes as collecting good fakes is becoming quite a cult. Other people are looking for stuffed birds, walking sticks, toys, fairings, bond and share certificates and playing cards. Perhaps the strangest of the new items to come into the market is street furniture — lamps, manhole covers and street signs. This spring there was an exhibition in East London's Geffrye Museum of a collection of street furniture built up by two collectors, Chris Baglee and Andrew Morley. The exhibition was such a success that it went on tour to Edinburgh, Glasgow and other centres like Alton and Basingstoke before going on to Holland in early 1980. Wherever the exhibition goes it starts an interest in people making their own street furniture collections — so watch that manhole cover. It may not be there the next time you walk along the street.

The most noticeable trend in 1979 however, is that it has been the Year of the Chair. Prices of good quality antique chairs have simply zoomed ahead. At King and Chasemore's ten Regency chairs were sold this spring for £2,400; a pair of George I walnut chairs sold at Drewatt, Watson and Barton's of Newbury for £1,600 and six Hepplewhite dining chairs realised £2,200 at Neales of Nottingham.

New interest is being shown in cast iron, wood and solid fuel burning stoves, perhaps because of the escalating price of heating oil and electricity. Sotheby's recently held a sale of cast iron stoves and were surprised to sell one for £3,800 and an Art Nouveau stove dated 1910 for £950. A sale of old tools at Christie's South Kensington saleroom made a surprising total of £62,789 this spring.

So the field of antique finds continues to expand into hitherto unknown areas. That is perhaps one of the chief interests in the world of antiques today.

LIZ TAYLOR

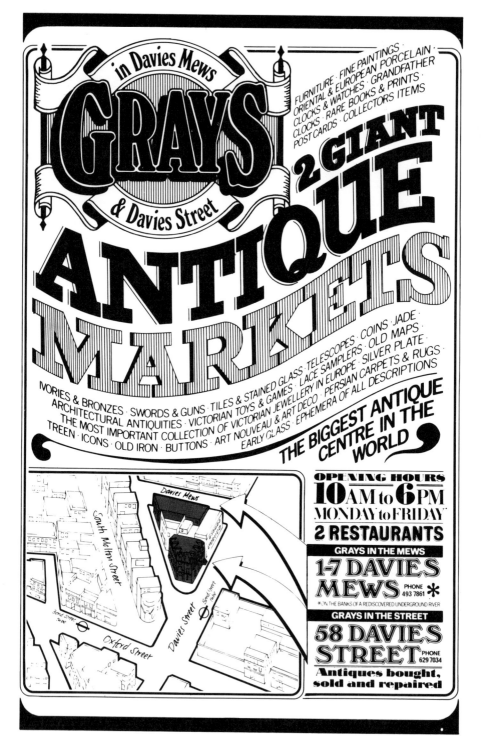
16

BRITISH ANTIQUE EXPORTERS LTD

WHOLESALERS   EXPORTERS   PACKERS   SHIPPERS

HEAD OFFICE: 206 LONDON ROAD, BURGESS HILL, WEST SUSSEX, RH15 9RD   ENGLAND
CABLES BRITISHANTIQUES BURGESS HILL   TELEX 87688
TELEPHONE BURGESS HILL (04446) 45577

To: Auctioneers, wholesalers and
retailers of antique furniture,
porcelain and decorative items.

Dear Sirs,
We offer the most comprehensive service available in the U.K.
As wholesale exporters, we sell 20ft. and 40ft. container-loads of
antique furniture, porcelain and decorative items of the Georgian
Victorian, Edwardian and 1930's periods. Our buyers are strategically
placed throughout the U.K. in order to take full advantage of
regional pricing. You can purchase a container from us for as little
as £5,000. This would be filled with mostly 1870 to 1920's furniture
and chinaware; you could expect to pay approximately £7,000 to
£10,000 for a quality shipment of Georgian, and Victorian furniture
and porcelain. Our terms are £1,000 deposit, the balance at time
of arrival of the container. If the merchandise should not be to
your liking, for any reason whatsoever, we offer you your money
back in full, less one-way freight.

If you wish to visit the U.K. yourself and purchase individually
from your own sources, we will collect, pack and ship your
merchandise with speed and efficiency within 5 days. Our rates
are competitive and our packing is the finest available anywhere
in the world. We operate a weekly service to both New York and
New Orleans, and a monthly service to Australia. Our courier-
finder service is second to none and we have knowledgeable couriers
who are equipped with a car and the knowledge of where the best
buys are.

If your business is buying English antiques, we are your contact.
We assure you of our best attention at all times.

Yours faithfully
BRITISH ANTIQUE EXPORTERS LTD.

N. Lefton
Chairman and Managing Director.

DIRECTORS : N. LEFTON (Chairman & Managing),   P. V. LEFTON,   G. LEFTON,   THE RT. HON. THE VISCOUNT EXMOUTH,   A. FIELD, MSC FBOA DCLP FSMC FAAO.
REGISTERED OFFICE 12/13 SHIP STREET, BRIGHTON   REGISTERED NO 893406 ENGLAND
BANKERS NATIONAL WESTMINSTER BANK LTD 155 NORTH STREET, BRIGHTON, SUSSEX   THE CHASE MANHATTAN BANK, N.A., 410 PARK AVENUE, NEW YORK

17

THERE ARE A GREAT MANY ANTIQUE SHIPPERS IN BRITAIN

but few, if any, who are as quality conscious as Norman Lefton, Chairman and Managing Director of British Antique Exporters Ltd. of Burgess Hill, Nr. Brighton, Sussex. Seventeen years' experience of shipping goods to all parts of the globe have confirmed his original belief that the way to build clients' confidence in his services is to supply them only with goods which are in first class saleable condition. To this end, he employs a staff of over 50, from highly skilled, antique restorers, polishers and packers to representative buyers and executives. Through their knowledgeable hands passes each piece of furniture before it

BRITISH ANTIQUE EXPORTERS LTD

Member of L.A.P.A.D.A

206 LONDON ROAD
BURGESS HILL
WEST SUSSEX, RH15 9RD, ENGLAND
Telex 87688
Cables BRITISH ANTIQUES BURGESS HILL

Telephone BURGESS HILL (04446) 45577

leaves the B.A.E. warehouses, ensuring that the overseas buyer will only receive the best and most saleable merchandise for their particular market. This attention to detail is obvious on a visit to the Burgess Hill warehouses where potential customers can view what must be the most varied assortment of Georgian, Victorian, Edwardian and 1930's furniture in the UK. One cannot fail to be impressed by, not only the varied range·of merchandise but also the fact that each piece is in showroom condition awaiting shipment. As one would expect, packing is considered somewhat of an art at B.A.E. and David Gilbert, the director in charge of the works, ensures that each piece will reach its final destination in the condition a customer would wish. B.A.E. set a very high standard and, as a further means of improving each container load David Gilbert, who also deals with customer/container liaison, invites each customer to return detailed information on the saleability of each

BRITISH ANTIQUE EXPORTERS LTD

206 LONDON ROAD   Member of L.A.P.A.D.A.
BURGESS HILL
WEST SUSSEX, RH15 9RD, ENGLAND
Telex 87688
Cables BRITISH ANTIQUES BURGESS HILL

Telephone BURGESS HILL (04446) 45577

19

piece in the container thereby ensuring successful future shipments. This feedback of information is the all important factor which guarantees the profitability of future containers. "By this method" Mr. Lefton explains, "we have established that an average £7000 container will immediately it is unpacked at its final destination realise in the region of £10000 to £14000 for our clients selling the goods on a quick wholesale turnover basis". When visiting the warehouses various container loads can be seen in the course of completion. The intending buyer can then judge for himself which type of container load would best be suited to his market. Initial enquiries are dealt with by Tracy Pert who also ensures that the documentation is correct in all its detail. She guarantees the container a smooth passage until its final destination.

BRITISH ANTIQUE EXPORTERS LTD

206 LONDON ROAD   Member of L.A.P.A.D.A.
BURGESS HILL
WEST SUSSEX, RH15 9RD, ENGLAND
Telex 87688
Cables BRITISH ANTIQUES BURGESS HILL

Telephone BURGESS HILL (04446) 45577

Burgess Hill is located
7 miles from Brighton, 39 miles from London.

BRITISH ANTIQUE EXPORTERS LTD

206 LONDON ROAD   Member of L.A.P.A.D.A.
BURGESS HILL
WEST SUSSEX, RH15 9RD, ENGLAND
Telex 87688
Cables BRITISH ANTIQUES BURGESS HILL

Telephone BURGESS HILL (04446) 45577

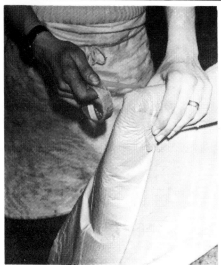

In an average 20-foot container B.A.E. put approximately 150 to 200 pieces carefully selected to suit the particular destination. There are always at least 10 outstanding or unusual items in each shipment, but every piece included looks as though it has something special about it.

Based at Burgess Hill 7 miles from Brighton and on a direct rail link with London 39 miles (only 40 minutes journey) the Company is ideally situated to ship containers to all parts of the world. The showrooms, restoration and packing departments are open to overseas buyers and no visit to purchase antiques for re-sale in other countries is complete without a visit to their Burgess Hill premises where a welcome is always found.

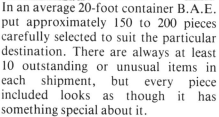

BRITISH ANTIQUE EXPORTERS LTD

206 LONDON ROAD   Member of L.A.P.A.D.A.
BURGESS HILL
WEST SUSSEX, RH15 9RD, ENGLAND
Telex 87688
Cables BRITISH ANTIQUES BURGESS HILL
Telephone BURGESS HILL (04446) 45577

23

A selection of antiques

Georgian Mahogany Bureau bookcase

Victorian Card Table

1920 Queen Anne High-backed Chair

Georgian Mahogany Chest of Drawers

Edwardian Oak Bureau

Victorian Duchess Marble-top Wash Stand

Victorian Windsor Chair

American Wooton Desk

Victorian Walnut Queen Anne High-backed Chair

24

from a container load

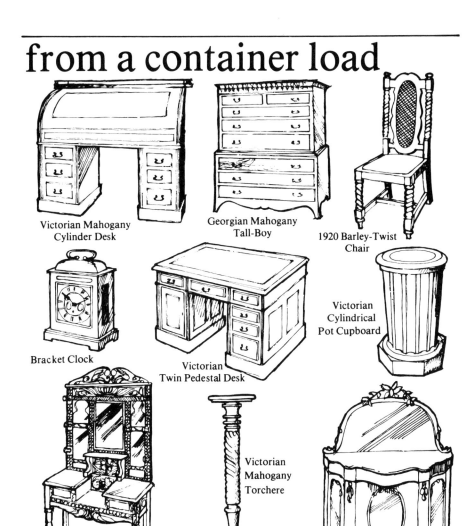

Victorian Mahogany
Cylinder Desk

Georgian Mahogany
Tall-Boy

1920 Barley-Twist
Chair

Bracket Clock

Victorian
Twin Pedestal Desk

Victorian
Cylindrical
Pot Cupboard

Victorian
Carved Oak Hall-stand

Victorian
Mahogany
Torchere

Victorian Walnut Marble Top and
Mirrored- back Credenza

25

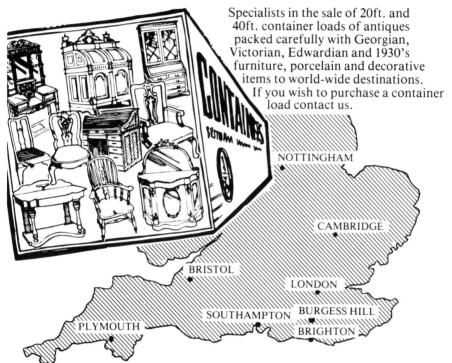

26

FREIGHT FORWARDING AND SHIPPING DEPT.

Guarantee

SPEED

Collections nationwide packed and shipped within 5 days.

EFFICIENCY SAFE ARRIVAL

We only employ skilled packers who have undergone extensive B.A.E.L. training. Our packing is the finest available in England. Your purchases will arrive safely.

We ship 20 ft and 40 ft container loads and route to your door. 20 ft container packing charge including collections within 60/75 mile radius £465.

Single items special low cost deliveries to:
NEW ORLEANS • NEW YORK

BRITISH ANTIQUE EXPORTERS LTD

Member of L.A.P.A.D.A.

206 LONDON ROAD
BURGESS HILL
WEST SUSSEX, RH15 9RD, ENGLAND
Telex 87688
Cables BRITISH ANTIQUES BURGESS HILL

Telephone BURGESS HILL (04446) 45577

Our new showroom
is now open where you
can buy individual pieces
or a container load
at competitive
wholesale prices.

Always at least
10 Wooton Desks in
stock in first class
condition.

The Finest Available
in the U.K.

20 ft container loads of wholesale antique furniture and decorative
items (all in good condition) Georgian, Victorian and Edwardian
periods. £7,500 delivered to your door — full unconditional money
back guarantee if not completely satisfied. (It may be an unseen
container but you cannot lose).

We also offer container packing for overseas buyers. Express collection
packing and 20 ft containerisation service £465 + lowest freight rates
to the USA — purchases collected, packed and shipped within 5 days. We
only employ specially trained packers therefore your purchases arrive
safely.

British Antique Exporters Ltd.
206 London Road,
Burgess Hill,
West Sussex RH15 9RD,
England.

Burgess Hill is
7 miles from Brighton
39 miles from London
15 minutes -
Gatwick Airport

Telephone
Burgess Hill
(04446) 45577

Telex 87688

MEMBER OF
LAPADA

Guild of
Master Craftsmen

33

Terry Antiques
(TH Murphy)

Fine English Furniture
and Antiques of all descriptions

Continental Carriers

Importers and Exporters

175 Junction Road, London N19

Tel. 01-263 1219

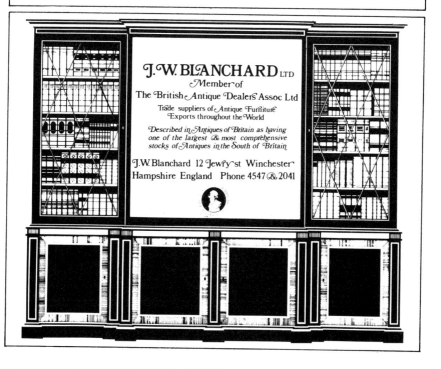

Millions of Antiques in Bermondsey

Five minutes from Tower Bridge

Bermondsey Antique Warehouses Consortium

Millions of Antiques

Roger and Lyn Hampshire Antiques*
1 Newhams Row
Bermondsey Street
London SE1
Tel: 01 403 1496

Antique mahogany and oak, Victorian
and 'Jazz Age' furniture, Naval style
decorated furniture and reproduction
trade signs.

Open Weekdays only
Thursday till 8pm   6000 Square feet.

MacNeill's Art and Antique Warehouse
Newhams Row
175 Bermondsey Street
London SE1
Tel: 01 403 0022   Telex 883177

Twelve Dealers

Victorian, Edwardian and Period
furniture, Porcelain, Jewellery
and Silver etc.,

Open weekdays 9.30am to 5.30pm
Thursday to 8pm

Fine and Rare
Top Floor
MacNeills Warehouse
Newhams Row
175 Bermondsey Street
London SE1 3UW
Tel: 01 407 5602

Specialists in supplying and
manufacturing hitherto
unobtainable facsimilies of
cabinet fittings. Ivory
Escutcheons and Drawer Pulls,
Brassware, marquetrie and
limited editions of furniture.
Enquiries and special orders
welcomed.

Bermondsey Antique Warehouse
173 Bermondsey Street
London SE1 3UW
Tel. 01 407 2040

Five floors of general Antiques with
an emphasis on Victorian and
Edwardian trade furniture at
competitive prices.

Top and 2nd Floor	P H Forrest and Son*
	J Stewart
	John Sturton (Mr Pickwick)
	D B Cater
	(formerly of Camden Passage)
1st Floor	London Antique Dealers*
	Proprietor Robert Whitfield
Ground Floor	Bronzegate
	R Haw
	Ron Andrews and Ken G Pratt
	P Nash
Basement	P Nash

Open weekdays 9am to 5pm
Thursday to 8pm
Friday at 7am

in Bermondsey

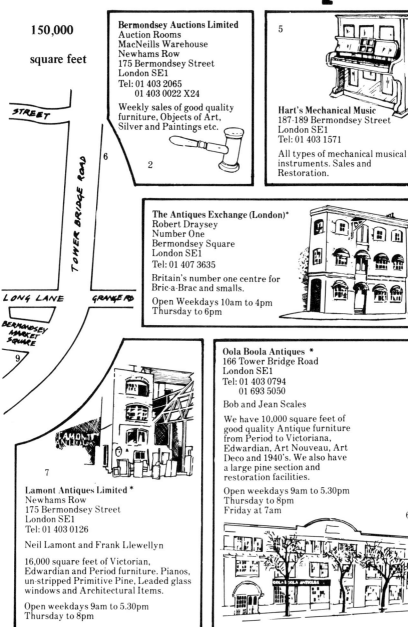

150,000

square feet

STREET

TOWER BRIDGE ROAD

6

LONG LANE *GRANGE RD*

BERMONDSEY MARKET SQUARE

9

Bermondsey Auctions Limited
Auction Rooms
MacNeills Warehouse
Newhams Row
175 Bermondsey Street
London SE1
Tel: 01 403 2065
01 403 0022 X24

Weekly sales of good quality
furniture, Objects of Art,
Silver and Paintings etc.

2

5

Hart's Mechanical Music
187-189 Bermondsey Street
London SE1
Tel: 01 403 1571

All types of mechanical musical
instruments. Sales and
Restoration.

The Antiques Exchange (London)*
Robert Draysey
Number One
Bermondsey Square
London SE1
Tel: 01 407 3635

Britain's number one centre for
Bric-a-Brac and smalls.

Open Weekdays 10am to 4pm
Thursday to 6pm

9

Oola Boola Antiques *
166 Tower Bridge Road
London SE1
Tel: 01 403 0794
01 693 5050

Bob and Jean Scales

We have 10,000 square feet of
good quality Antique furniture
from Period to Victoriana,
Edwardian, Art Nouveau, Art
Deco and 1940's. We also have
a large pine section and
restoration facilities.

Open weekdays 9am to 5.30pm
Thursday to 8pm
Friday at 7am

6

7

Lamont Antiques Limited *
Newhams Row
175 Bermondsey Street
London SE1
Tel: 01 403 0126

Neil Lamont and Frank Llewellyn

16,000 square feet of Victorian,
Edwardian and Period furniture. Pianos,
un-stripped Primitive Pine, Leaded glass
windows and Architectural Items.

Open weekdays 9am to 5.30pm
Thursday to 8pm

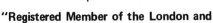

Late 19th century ala-
baster figure of an eagle,
by W. Gebler, 17½in.
high. (Sotheby's Belgravia)
$213 £110

Alabaster figure of a
Bohemian girl, 1890's,
34½in. high.
(Sotheby's Belgravia)
$1,393 £700

Italian alabaster group,
1880-1900, 27½in.
high. (Sotheby's Bel-
gravia) $995 £500

ANIMALIA

Very rare passenger pigeon,
mounted on branch, 22in.
high, in glass dome.
(Sotheby's Belgravia)
$873 £450

Scottish ram's head table
snuff, dated 1843, with
snuff scoop and ivory
mallet, 17½in. long.
(Christie's S. Kensington)
$525 £250

Victorian mounted stag's
head. $40 £20
(Vernons of Chichester)

19th century snuff mull,
10½in. wide. (Sotheby's
Belgravia) $594 £300

Crocodile handbag with
stuffed crocodile on the
front flap. (Sotheby's
Belgravia) $605 £300

Fine stuffed peregrine
falcon in glass case,
20½in. high.(Sotheby's
Belgravia) $407 £210

Unusual late 19th century monkey musician trio automaton, 1ft.1in. high. (Sotheby's Belgravia) $4,776 £2,400

Late 19th century French singing bird automaton, 17in. high. (Sotheby's Belgravia)$1,492 £750

Tea party musical automaton, German, circa 1914, 11½in. wide. (Sotheby's Belgravia) $915 £460

Grizzly bear automaton who moves his legs and bends forward. (Manchester Auction Mart) $257 £130

'Screaming' Jumeau bisque-headed musical automaton doll. (Christie's N. York) $8,500 £4,359

Victorian musical automaton of a rabbit emerging from a cabbage. (Manchester Auction Mart) $663 £335

Late 19th century French negro accordion player musical automaton, 11½in. high. (Sotheby's Belgravia) $597 £300

English barrel organ grinder automaton, circa 1920, 2ft.2in. high. (Sotheby's Belgravia) $1,492 £750

Amusing French musical automaton, circa 1900, 1ft.2in. high. (Sotheby's Belgravia) $1,094 £550

Late 19th century American clockwork dancing doll toy, 9¾in. high. (Sotheby's Belgravia) $318 £160

Pierrot serenading the Moon, late 19th century automaton, 20in. high. (Sotheby's Belgravia) $4,565 £2,300

Late 19th century French monkey drummer automaton, 1ft.6in. high.(Sotheby's Belgravia) $696 £350

Mid 19th century English dancing dolls toy, 10½in. high. (Sotheby's Belgravia) $278 £140

19th century French musical automaton. (Phillips) $3,636 £1,800

Late 19th century French composition headed musical automaton. (Christie's S. Kensington) $1,940 £1,000

Unusual French nightingale singing bird automaton, 1ft. 9½in. high, circa 1900. (Sotheby's Belgravia) $1,293 £650

Late 19th century French clown and horse musical automaton, 1ft.2½in. wide. (Sotheby's Belgravia) $557 £280

Doll automaton with bisque head and shoulders, circa 1860-80, 2ft.2in. high.(Sotheby's Belgravia)$5,572 £2,800

Rosewood wheel barometer, 8in. dial, circa 1830, 39in. high.(Christopher Sykes)
$386 £195

Mahogany stick barometer by Dollond, London, 102cm. high. (King & Chasemore)$776 £400

Late 18th century French barometer. (Drewatt, Watson & Barton)
$1,373 £680

Georgian bow fronted mahogany stick barometer, 38½in. high.(Parsons, Welch & Cowell)
$1,090 £540

Walnut stick barometer with brass register plate, 2ft. 11½in. high. (Sotheby's)
$1,782 £900

Attractive wheel/ banjo barometer in rosewood, circa 1840, 40½in. high. (Christopher Sykes)
$366 £185

-Early 18th century walnut pillar barometer, 3ft.3in. high. (Sotheby's)
$1,386 £700

Finely figured and inlaid Sheraton wheel barometer. (Moss)
$445 £225

George III mahogany stick barometer by J. Lunn, Edinburgh, 3ft.3in. high. (Sotheby's)
$882 £450

Victorian oak cased barometer.(British Antique Exporters)
$50 £25

Oak cased mercury stick barometer, 49in. high.(Christopher Sykes)
$693 £350

Oak barometer and timepiece, 1880's, 44in. high.(Sotheby's Belgravia)
$343 £170

William and Mary walnut marquetry stick barometer, circa 1880, 49in. high.(Sotheby's Belgravia)
$1,782 £900

Fine rosewood cased stick barometer, 38in. high. (Christopher Sykes)
$782 £395

Very rare George II column barometer, 2ft.11in. high. (Sotheby's)
$2,178 £1,100

George III mahogany stick barometer, 3ft.2¼in. high, D. Stampa, Edinburgh. (Sotheby's)
$470 £240

Late 19th century combined clock, thermometer, barometer and barograph, 2ft.3in. wide. (Sotheby's Belgravia)$537 £270

Rare 6½in. dial rose-wood barometer by James Somelvico. (Christopher Sykes) $757 £390

Mahogany cased angles barometer, circa 1770, 35½in. high.(Lawrence's) $3,990 £2,100

Inlaid mahogany stick barometer by Negrety, 1850, 44in. long.(Gray's Antique Mews) $1,287 £650

Mother-of-pearl in-laid rosewood baro-meter, circa 1850, 44¾in. high. (Sotheby's Belgravia) $834 £430

Walnut marque-try barometer, 3ft.2½in. high, with brass regi-ster plate. (Sotheby's) $1,683 £850

George III maho-gany banjo baro-meter, 38in. high. (Parsons, Welch & Cowell)$648 £360

Good George I walnut barometer, circa 1720, 3ft. 5½in. high. (Sotheby's) $2,178 £1,100

Bronze of Paul Elouard's face, 15in. high, on marble base.(Gray's Antique Mews) $2,424 £1,200

Art Deco bronze 'Chasing the Hind' by Aurore Onu. (R. L. Lowery & Partners) $1,494 £740

Chinese sleeve weight in the form of a locust.(Alfie's Antique Market) $40 £20

Large 19th century bronze study, signed Myrver, 60cm. high. (King & Chasemore) $895 £450

Pair of spelter figures signed Louis Moreau, circa 1900, 18in. high. (Sotheby's Belgravia) $278 £140

Bronze statuette by Varlese Napoli, 24½in. high.(Christie's S. Kensington) $565 £280

Art Deco bronze 'Arab Mother' by D. Chiparus. (R. L. Lowery & Partners) $4,040 £2,000

Art Deco bronze figure signed Dyson Smith, 1927. (Gray's Antique Market) $803 £390

Art Deco ivory and gilt bronze figure, 13¼in. high, signed L. Sosson. (Parsons, Welch & Cowell) $633 £320

Stylish WMF polished bronze stemmed dish, circa 1910, 19cm. high. (Sotheby's Belgravia) $594 £300

Franz Bergmann cold-painted bronze figure, circa 1910, 5in. high.(Sotheby's Belgravia) $627 £320

Late 19th century Seimin bronze cucumber, 8½in. long.(Sotheby's Belgravia)$480 £250

One of a pair of 19th century bronze ewer ornaments.(Russell, Baldwin & Bright) $1,227 £620

Bronze group of five children, signed Jaeger, circa 1910, 3¾in. high. (Sotheby's Belgravia) $551 £290

Mid 19th century French bronze of Bacchanalian group. (Sotheby's Belgravia) $1,710 £900

19th century Italian bronze by Girba Franti. (Alfie's Antique Market) $544 £275

Art Deco metal figure by Rischmann, 22¾in. high. (Christie's) $388 £200

Raoul Larche bronze bust, circa 1900, 47cm. high. (Sotheby's Belgravia) $776 £400

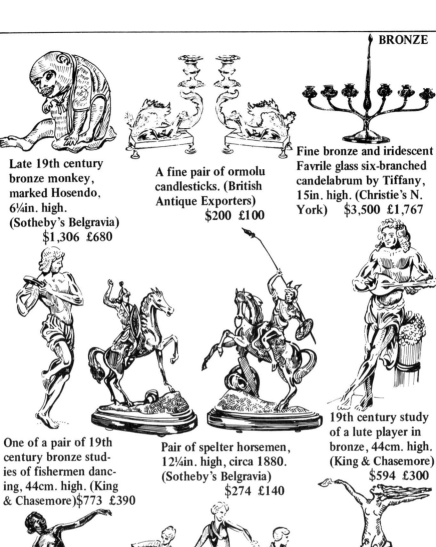

Late 19th century bronze monkey, marked Hosendo, 6¼in. high. (Sotheby's Belgravia) $1,306 £680

A fine pair of ormolu candlesticks. (British Antique Exporters) $200 £100

Fine bronze and iridescent Favrile glass six-branched candelabrum by Tiffany, 15in. high. (Christie's N. York) $3,500 £1,767

One of a pair of 19th century bronze studies of fishermen dancing, 44cm. high. (King & Chasemore) $773 £390

Pair of spelter horsemen, 12¼in. high, circa 1880. (Sotheby's Belgravia) $274 £140

19th century study of a lute player in bronze, 44cm. high. (King & Chasemore) $594 £300

Bronze figure by Lucien Alliot, 1920's, 24½in. high. (Sotheby's Belgravia) $329 £170

Good Philippe bronze and ivory group, 1920's, 48cm. high. (Sotheby's Belgravia) $7,524 £3,800

Silvered bronze, Generelli 1926. (Gray's Antique Mews) $5,050 £2,500

BRONZE

Pair of cold-painted bronze and ivory figures, signed Omerth, 6½in. high, 1920's. (Sotheby's Belgravia) $480 £250

One of a pair of Leon Jallot Art Deco bronze appliques, 19.3cm. high, circa 1925. (Sotheby's Belgravia) $297 £150

Pair of bronze putti, circa 1880, 9in. high.(Sotheby's Belgravia) $417 £210

Rare bronze group, signed Gilbert Bayes, dated 1904.(Sotheby's Belgravia)$970 £500

A pair of bronze candelabra, 1850. (Sotheby's Belgravia) $24,750 £12,500

Bronze figure of a woman by Luca Madrassi, circa 1900, 19¾in. high.(Sotheby's Belgravia) $475 £250

One of a pair of Charles X ormolu and bronzed metal table candelabra, 22in. high, circa 1825. (Sotheby's)$1,019 £520

A set of five Art Nouveau bronze plaques. (King & Chasemore) $117 £60

Chiparus figure in bronze and ivory. (Spencer's) $3,267 £1,650

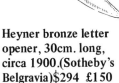

19th century bronze group, 14in. wide.(Nottingham Auction Mart)$388 £200

Heyner bronze letter opener, 30cm. long, circa 1900.(Sotheby's Belgravia)$294 £150

Bronze figure of a jaguar, 22¼in. long, 1920's. (Sotheby's Belgravia) $213 £110

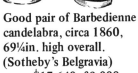

Bronze figure of Perseus Arming by Sir Alfred Gilbert, 1880's, 14¼in. high. (Sotheby's Belgravia) $3,234 £1,650

Good pair of Barbedienne candelabra, circa 1860, 69¼in. high overall. (Sotheby's Belgravia) $17,640 £9,000

Late 19th century bronze by W. Szczblewski.(King & Chasemore) $1,188 £600

One of a series of 'Scarf Game' dancers, circa 1901. (Christie's N. York) $12,100 £6,454

Late 18th/early 19th century bronze figure of The Athlete, 13¼in. high.(Sotheby's Belgravia) $358 £180

Mid 16th century Venetian bronze figure of Venus Marina, 7¾in. high. (Sotheby's) $1,178 £620

BRONZE

One of a pair of spelter urns, circa 1870, 12¼in. high.(Sotheby's Belgravia) $237 £120

Art Deco bronze group by Gemaretti, 22in. wide. (Christie's) $679 £350

Late 19th century inlaid bronze vase, one of a pair, 13in. high. (Sotheby's Belgravia) $883 £460

Late 19th century German bronze figure, 12¾in. high. signed Prof. Ernst Seger. (Sotheby's Belgravia) $422 £220

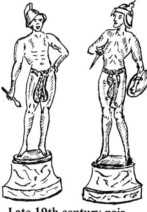

Late 19th century pair of bronze gladiators, signed Prof. Tuch. (Sotheby's Belgravia) $307 £160

One of a pair of late 19th century gilt and patinated bronze urns, 15¾in. high.(Sotheby's Belgravia) $518 £270

Ijoken Joun bronze vase and cover, circa 1880, 7in. high. (Sotheby's Belgravia) $845 £440

Late Ming dynasty bronze figure, 11¾in. high. (Christie's)$1,210 £623

Important 19th century bronze model of a seated tiger, 24½in. high. (Manchester Auction Mart) $4,242 £2,100

Early 19th century bronze incense burner, one of a pair, 10½in. high.(Christie's) $800 £412

Large Art Deco spelter group, 32in. wide, Paris. (Christie's) $504 £260

One of a pair of late 19th century inlaid bronze vases, 13¾in. high.(Sotheby's Belgravia) $1,440 £750

Mid 19th century bronze figure of Jason, 25in. high. (Sotheby's Belgravia) $403 £210

A pair of 19th century bronze figures, 17¾in. high, on marble bases. (Geering & Colyer's) $912 £480

One of a pair of mid 19th century bronze ewers, 25½in. high. (Sotheby's Belgravia) $883 £460

Unusual late 19th century bronze arhat, 12in. high. (Sotheby's Belgravia)$2,016 £1,050

13th century Pagan figure of the Buddha in bronze, 10¾in. high. (Christie's) $2,640 £1,360

Late 19th century bronze group, 16in. long. (Sotheby's Belgravia) $1,306 £680

BRONZE

Large Murakami bronze jardiniere, circa 1900, 14½in. high.(Sotheby's Belgravia) $346 £180

Late 19th century bronze eagle, 19¾in. high.(Sotheby's Belgravia) $1,114 £580

Weiner Werkstatte bronze vase, circa 1910, 8cm. high.(Sotheby's Belgravia) $620 £320

Bronze figure, circa 1900, of Handaka Sonja, 10in. high. (Sotheby's Belgravia) $499 £260

Pair of spelter figures of Duellists, circa 1910, signed Ch. Masse, 24½in. high. (Sotheby's Belgravia) $336 £170

Late 19th century bronze figure, 38¼in. high.(Sotheby's Belgravia) $922 £480

One of a pair of late 19th century bronze vases, 24¼in. high. (Sotheby's Belgravia) $1,440 £750

19th century bronze figure of an old man, 9in. long. (Christie's) $1,210 £623

Late 19th century inlaid bronze vase, 13¾in. high. (Sotheby's Belgravia) $1,248 £650

Late 19th century
bronze koro and
cover, 13¼in. high.
(Sotheby's Belgravia)
$557 £290

Chiparus bronze and ivory figure,
10½in. long, 1920's. (Sotheby's
Belgravia) $3,104 £1,600

Late 19th century
Nakao bronze in-
cense burner and
cover, 15½in. high.
(Sotheby's Belgravia)
$480 £250

Early 18th century gilt
bronze seated figure of
Kuan Yin, 9½in. high.
(Christie's)
$1,760 £907

Colinet bronze and
ivory figure of a
dancer, 1920's, 43.5cm.
high.(Sotheby's Bel-
gravia) $5,432 £2,800

German bronze model
of a lion. (Christie's S.
Kensington) $233 £120

5th/3rd century B.C.
bronze chih, 5¾in.
high.(Christie's)
$1,045 £538

Bronze lion cast in the
T'ang style, 10in. long.
(Christie's) $935 £481

Large late 19th cen-
tury Komin bronze
vase, 19¼in. high.
(Sotheby's Belgravia)
$614 £320

BRONZE

Bronze figure of a tribesman, 41cm. high, (King & Chasemore) $364 £190

Large 19th century bronze study by P. J. Mene, 70cm. high. (King & Chasemore) $2,784 £1,450

Late 19th century bronze Samurai, 15in. high. (Sotheby's Belgravia) $730 £380

19th century bronze model of a panther, Paris, 18¾in. wide. (Christie's) $1,125 £580

One of a pair of bronze vases, circa 1900, 7¼in. high. (Sotheby's Belgravia) $269 £140

Late 19th century bronze model of a bison, 12¼in. wide. (Christie's) $660 £340

One of a pair of 19th century French bronze urns, 36¼in. high.(Christie's) $5,820 £3,000

Mid 19th century bronze model of a foal, Russian, 9¼in. wide. (Sotheby's) $970 £500

Late 19th century Seiunsai koro and cover, 34½in. high. (Sotheby's Belgravia) $1,382 £720

56

One of a pair of bronze models of Temple Guardians, 67cm. high, Tibetan. (King & Chasemore) $1,075 £560

Late 19th century incense burner, 23¾in. high. (Sotheby's Belgravia) $864 £450

Late 19th century bronze vase, 20¾in. high. (Sotheby's Belgravia) $1,190 £620

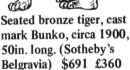

19th century bronze model of a panther, Paris, 16in. wide. (Christie's) $931 £480

Unusual bronze vase, circa 1900, 12in. high. (Sotheby's Belgravia) $288 £150

Seated bronze tiger, cast mark Bunko, circa 1900, 50in. long. (Sotheby's Belgravia) $691 £360

One of a pair of mid 19th century bronze urns and covers, 9¼in. high. (Sotheby's Belgravia) $180 £95

Late 19th century cast bronze jardiniere, 14in. high. (Sotheby's Belgravia) $499 £260

Late 19th century Harachika Hiraishi Chikanaga bronze vase, 22in. high. (Sotheby's Belgravia) $2,112 £1,100

BRONZE

Late 19th century bronze vase, 10½in. high. (Sotheby's Belgravia) $269 £140

Bronze archer, circa 1900, 11¾in. high. (Sotheby's Belgravia) $557 £290

One of a pair of late 19th century bronze vases, 14½in. high.(Sotheby's Belgravia) $1,190 £620

One of a pair of late 19th century bronze vases, 21¾in. high. (Sotheby's Belgravia) $346 £180

Unusual tsuba made of Sentoku, perhaps by Somin. (Sotheby's) $505 £250

Late 19th century inlaid bronze and iron flaming nimbus, 7¾in. high. (Sotheby's Belgravia) $1,152 £600

Limousin bronze figure, 1930's, 56cm. high. (Sotheby's Belgravia) $252 £130

Pair of bronze figures of young women, signed Bouret, 14¾in. high, circa 1880. (Sotheby's Belgravia) $614 £320

Rigot bronze and ivory figure, 35cm. high, 1920's. (Sotheby's Belgravia) $582 £300

6th/8th century gilt bronze house shrine, 6½in. high.(Christie's) $715 £368

Bronze figure of a young girl, signed Jaeger, 21¼in. high, circa 1915.(Sotheby's Belgravia) $634 £330

One of a pair of bronze ewers, circa 1870's, 12¾in. high. (Sotheby's Belgravia) $209 £110

One of a pair of late 19th century bronze koros and covers, 24in. high.(Sotheby's Belgravia) $422 £220

Late 19th century bronze dish inlaid in gold, silver and bronze, 12in. diam.(Sotheby's Belgravia) $480 £250

Late 19th century bronze vase, 17¼in. high.(Sotheby's Belgravia) $922 £480

Palmer and Co. gilt bronze and glass candlestick, circa 1870, 27¾in. high.(Sotheby's Belgravia) $133 £70

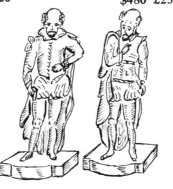

Pair of bronze figures of Elizabethan gentlemen, 15½in. high, circa 1880's. (Sotheby's Belgravia) $634 £330

One of a pair of Japanese patinated bronze ovoid vases, 10in. high. (Phillips)$1,090 £540

59

Bronze bust signed Macgillivray, 11¼in. high, dated 1915. (Sotheby's Belgravia) $588 £300

Early 20th century bronze group signed T. Campaiola, 24in. high. (Sotheby's Belgravia) $352 £180

Bronze bust by Alfred Drury, 16in. high, dated '09. (Sotheby's Belgravia)$352 £180

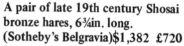

A pair of late 19th century Shosai bronze hares, 6¾in. long. (Sotheby's Belgravia)$1,382 £720

Barbedienne bronze and marble encrier, circa 1860, 15¾in. long. (Sotheby's Belgravia) $513 £270

Spelter lampstand, after Bouret, circa 1890, 28in. high. (Sotheby's Belgravia) $135 £70

Mechanical bronze figure 'Bare on Bear'. (Andrew Grant) $1,029 £520

Bronze figure of David, circa 1880, 29in. high, signed F. Barbedienne. (Sotheby's Belgravia) $1,482 £780

19th century bronze seated figure of Mercury. (King & Chasemore) $792 £400

Bronze figure of a horse, circa 1880, 6in. wide. (Sotheby's Belgravia) $548 £280

Bronze and ivory figure by H. Chiparus Etling, Paris, circa 1920, 7¾in. high. (Sotheby's Belgravia) $725 £370

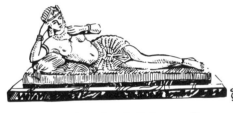

Chiparus silvered and gilt bronze figure, 1920's, 46cm. long. (Sotheby's Belgravia) $1,940 £1,000

Pair of bronze figures of a nanny-goat and a panther, 11in. and 7in., circa 1900. (Sotheby's Belgravia) $268 £140

Bronze figure signed L. Alliot, circa 1920. (Sotheby's Belgravia) $285 £150

Late 19th century Samurai in bronze, 11¾in. high. (Sotheby's Belgravia) $768 £400

Bronze two-branched candelabrum, circa 1900, 19¼in. high.(Christie's N. York) $1,500 £757

61

BRONZE

Bronze study of a woman on a horse by Louis Tuaillon, circa 1900, 14½in. long.(Sotheby's Belgravia) $318 £160

Unique three-light candelabrum, London, 1911, 14½in. high. (Sotheby's)$901 £460

Watanabe group of lion and tiger, 20in. long. (Sotheby's Belgravia) $864 £450

Late 19th century bronze and champleve enamel koro and cover, 17½in. high. (Sotheby's Belgravia) $538 £280

Austrian Hagenauer chrome lady with ebony panther, 1930. (Gray's Antique Market) $1,544 £780

Rare bronze figure of the Gooseboy by Wm. Reid Dick, dated 1936, 34in. high. (Sotheby's Belgravia)$2,587 £1,300

Mid 19th century bronze urn and cover, 14¼in. high.(Sotheby's Belgravia) $192 £100

Late 19th century gilt bronze and marble figure, after J. Causse, 20in. high.(Sotheby's Belgravia) $378 £190

Bronze figure by Elkington, circa 1870, 17¾in. high.(Sotheby's Belgravia) $705 £360

Late 19th century
bronze jardiniere,
16in. high.(Sotheby's
Belgravia)$576 £300

One of a pair of Scottish
Regency candelabra,
circa 1830, 9in. high.
(Sotheby's) $232 £120

Gilt metal encrier,
circa 1880, 5½in.
high.(Sotheby's
Belgravia)$352 £180

Austrian Art Nouveau
bronze mirror, 35.5cm.
high, circa 1900.
(Sotheby's Belgravia)
$465 £240

1930's aeroplane ash-
tray.(Alfie's Antique
Market) $47 £24

One of a set of six
early 20th century
gilt metal wall-lights,
27in. high.(Sotheby's
Belgravia) $741 £390

Bronze group of two
dogs, circa 1880, 9in.
long, signed Lalouette.
(Sotheby's Belgravia)
$298 £150

Early 16th century
Florentine bronze
of Hercules, 13½in.
high.(Sotheby's)
$82,320 £42,000

Gilt bronze figure of
a lioness, circa 1920,
11in. long.(Sotheby's
Belgravia)$318 £160

American bronze figure, signed Paul Herzel, circa 1910. (Sotheby's Belgravia) $194 £100

Pair of bronze figures of Royal tennis players, circa 1880, 10in. high. (Sotheby's Belgravia) $326 £170

Italian bronze stallion on marble base, 42cm. high. (Phillips) $19,208 £9,800

Bronze figure by Eugene Laurent, 14¾in. high, circa 1870. (Sotheby's Belgravia) $509 £260

Early 20th century bronze group, 10¾in. wide, sold with another bird. (Sotheby's) $384 £200

Bronze figure by Francis Derwent Wood, circa 1900, 17¼in. high. (Sotheby's Belgravia) $329 £170

Early 19th century French bronze group of three putti, 59in. high. (Christie's) $10,670 £5,500

One of a pair of 19th century Empire ormolu and bronze candelabra, 30in. high. (Jolly's) $1,900 £1,000

Bronze model of a nef, mid 19th century, 18¼in. high. (Bonham's) $411 £210

Small Egyptian bronze, 10in. high, circa 1090 B.C. (Christie's) $99,000 £50,000

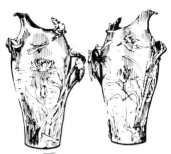

A pair of Art Nouveau gilt bronze jardinieres, circa 1900, 16½in. high. (Christie's N. York) $1,500 £757

Art Nouveau bronze, 21in. high. (Smith-Woolley & Perry) $950 £480

Bronze figure of Icarus, by Alfred Gilbert, 48.5cm. high.(Christie's) $23,520 £12,000

Silvered bronze plaque by Edward William Wyon, 1850's, 19 x 23¾in. (Sotheby's Belgravia) $352 £180

Bronze figure of a young girl, circa 1920, 67 x 33½in. (Sotheby's Belgravia) $235 £120

One of a pair of late 19th century bronze vases, 9½in. high. (Sotheby's Belgravia) $365 £190

Korschann bronze vase, 31.5cm. high, circa 1900. (Sotheby's Belgravia) $784 £400

Bronze vase and cover, circa 1900, 15½in. high.(Sotheby's Belgravia) $730 £380

Late 19th century Okome Kitataka inlaid bronze incense burner, 16½in. high. (Sotheby's Belgravia) $1,382 £720

Bronze 'Head of a Girl' by Emilio Greco, 1951. (Gray's Antique Market) $5,656 £2,800

Gilt bronze and ivory group of a Camelier, signed A. Leonard, circa 1910, 10¾in. high. (Sotheby's Belgravia) $736 £370

French bronze and ivory figure of a girl, signed A. Carrier-Belleuse, 22ins. high. (Phillips) $1,656 £820

Good bronze figure of a Taureg Camelier, circa 1900, 22in. wide. (Sotheby's Belgravia) $9,950 £5,000

Art Deco bronze and ivory figure of a Hungarian Dancer by Chiparus, 13in. high. (Phillips)$1,414 £700

Bronze and ivory figure by A. Gaudez, circa 1885, 14in. high. (Sotheby's Belgravia) $1,432 £720

Bronze figure of a heron by Jules Moigniez, circa 1860, 21¼in. high. (Sotheby's Belgravia) $2,089 £1,050

Unusual bronze figure of a knife grinder, circa 1880, 25¼in. high. (Sotheby's Belgravia) $1,990 £1,000

Bronze figure of a grazing ewe, by Rosa Bonheur, circa 1860, 6in. wide. (Sotheby's Belgravia) $417 £210

Art Deco kneeling figure on a marble base, 8in. high. (Alfie's Antique Market) $90 £45

Very large Geniyusai Seiya bronze figure, circa 1900, 40in. long. (Sotheby's Belgravia) $3,360 £1,750

Art Deco figure of a Hindu dancer, 14in. high, by C. J. R. Colinet. (Phillips) $1,252 £620

Pair of bronze figures by Henry Fugere, circa 1900, 8½in. high. (Sotheby's Belgravia) $1,094 £550

Art Deco figure of an Egyptian dancer, by C. J. R. Colinet, 10in. high. (Phillips) $1,212 £600

Bronze dog by P. J. Mene, circa 1870, 5in. high. (Sotheby's Belgravia) $278 £140

Bronze figure of a dancing girl, signed Lorenzl, circa 1920, 16in. high.(Sotheby's Belgravia) $499 £260

20th century Italian bronze figure of a fawn, 34¼in. high. (Sotheby's Belgravia) $1,472 £740

Early 20th century
bronze group of two
lovers, 55in. long.
(Sotheby's Belgravia)
$1,241 £640

Hagenauer bronze
vase, circa 1910,
11.5cm. high.
(Sotheby's Belgravia)
$336 £170

19th century bronze
group of an elephant
and tigers by Ruishin
Sano. (Sotheby's N.
York) $4,000 £2,030

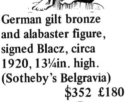

German gilt bronze
and alabaster figure,
signed Blacz, circa
1920, 13¼in. high.
(Sotheby's Belgravia)
$352 £180

Art Deco coloured bronze
figure, mounted on an
ashtray, 9in. high.(Geering
& Colyer) $303 £150

Renaud gilt bronze fig-
ure of a fairy, 1901,
27cm. high.(Sotheby's
Belgravia)$3,430 £1,750

Bronze figure by E.
Laurent, circa 1880,
14in. high.(Sotheby's
Belgravia) $722 £380

19th century Japanese
bronze, 4ft.4in. long.
(King & Chasemore)
$7,524 £3,800

Bronze figure of Eve
by Thos. Brock, circa
1910, 15¾in. high.
(Sotheby's Belgravia)
$582 £300

Gilt bronze group of
three putti, 1850's,
10¾in. wide.
(Sotheby's Belgravia)
$213 £110

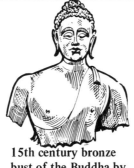

15th century bronze
bust of the Buddha by
Sukh'o'tai, 28½in. high.
(Christie's)$5,280 £2,721

19th century Japanese
bronze group. (Gray's
Antique Market)
$1,683 £850

Bronze figure by M.
Morton, circa 1910,
18in. high.
(Sotheby's Belgravia)
$232 £120

19th century classical
bronze figure group,
41cm. high. (King &
Chasemore)$730 £380

Mid 19th century bronze
group by Charles Cum-
berworth, 13½in. high.
(Sotheby's Belgravia)
$659 £340

Bronze bust of a young
woman, circa 1890,
signed E. Villanis, 24¼in.
high.(Sotheby's Belgravia)
$950 £500

Gilt bronze display cabi-
net, circa 1880, 11½in.
wide. (Sotheby's Belgravia)
$352 £180

Modern bronze bust
of an Indian, 14in.
high.(Sotheby's Bel-
gravia) $659 £340

Late 19th century bronze tiger, 12¾in. high.(Sotheby's Belgravia)　$518 £270

Art Deco bronze figurine by F. Preiss on marble base. (Alfie's Antique Market)　$757 £375

Regency period gilt bronze Sphinx. (Alfie's Antique Market)$131 £65

Bronze statue of George and the Dragon, by A. Turner, 1922. (Alfie's Antique Market)$272 £135

Early 20th century bronze figure, signed Gerschutzt. (Sotheby's Belgravia)　$365 £190

Dancing nymph car mascot, circa 1935, 7½in. high. (Sotheby's Belgravia)　$49 £25

19th century bronze, 18in. high, circa 1860. (Gray's Antique Mews)　$919 £455

One of a pair of Regency ormolu and gilt candelabras. (Alfie's Antique Market)　$363 £180

French ormolu and etched glass urn, 4½in. high.(Alfie's Antique Market)　$56 £28

Mid 19th century bronze model of a setter, signed J. Moigniez, 13in. wide. (Christie's) $679 £350

19th century Japanese globular bronze incense burner and cover.(Alfie's Antique Market) $128 £65

19th century bronze group of three terriers, 14¾in. high. (Christie's) $970 £500

Gilt and bronze figure of a dancer, signed Lorenzl, circa 1920, 20in. high.(Sotheby's Belgravia)$627 £320

Pair of bronze Marley horses, signed Coustou, circa 1900, 15¾in. long.(Sotheby's Belgravia) $716 £360

Bronze figure of Mercury, by Bologna, circa 1880, 32in. high. (Sotheby's Belgravia) $358 £180

One of a pair of mid 19th century ormolu candelabra, 13¼in. high.(Sotheby's Belgravia) $384 £200

Gilt bronze figure with ivory face and hands, 24in. high, by A. Carrier-Belleuse. (John H. Raby) $3,201 £1,650

One of a pair of mid 18th century Louis XV ormolu chenets, 15in. high.(Sotheby's) $4,180 £2,200

71

Tortoiseshell tea caddy with engraved plate on front. (Phillips) $444 £220

Tunbridgeware rectangular box, 3½in. long.(Parsons, Welch & Cowell) $29 £15

Chinese lacquer box, circa 1820, 3½in. wide. (Gray's Antique Mews)
$33 £16.50

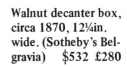

Tunbridgeware rectangular glove box, 10in. long. (Parsons, Welch & Cowell)
$70 £36

Persian lacquer pen box, 1853, 24.7cm. long. (Sotheby's)
$27,720 £14,000

Walnut decanter box, circa 1870, 12¼in. wide. (Sotheby's Belgravia) $532 £280

Three bottle tantalus, circa 1900, with playing card section. (Alfie's Antique Market) $757 £375

Early 19th century apothecary's cabinet, 8in. high. (Sotheby's Belgravia)
$543 £280

Mahogany decanter box, circa 1900, 12in. wide. (Sotheby's Belgravia) $361 £190

Carved sandalwood, ivory and bone chess set, circa 1890. (Sotheby's Belgravia) $588 £300

Primavera 'Longwy' crackle-glazed pottery box and cover, 9.5cm. diameter, 1920's. (Sotheby's Belgravia) $133 £70

Unusual satinwood, mahogany and ebony sewing case, 9½in. long.(Sotheby's Belgravia) $135 £70

George III woodworker's tool chest in a pine case, 3ft.6in. wide.(Messenger, May & Baverstock) $1,293 £650

Red and black Persian lacquered box. (Christopher Sykes) $63 £32

One of a set of six English mid 19th century tobacco containers, 1ft.5in. high.(Sotheby's Belgravia) $1,692 £850

Regency rosewood tea caddy with original mixing glass, circa 1810. (Gray's Antique Market) $222 £110

Early 20th century mahogany travelling writing box, 11¾in. high. (Sotheby's Belgravia) $368 £190

Late 19th century Chinese lacquered writing box with roll top.(Gray's Antique Market) $353 £175

Mosaic and tortoiseshell snuff box, circa 1820, 9cm. wide. (Sotheby's) $737 £380

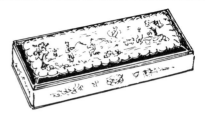

Sceaux Penthievre casket, circa 1750. (T. Bannister) $376 £190

Mid 19th century English apothecary's chest, 11in. high. (Sotheby's Belgravia) $737 £380

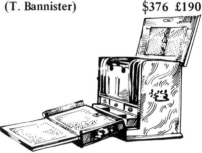

Walnut writing box, circa 1890, 11½ x 16¾in. (Sotheby's Belgravia) $310 £160

Early 18th century tortoiseshell and mother-of-pearl box, 16½in. wide. (Christie's S. Kensington) $1,089 £550

Victorian papier mache stationery box, 8½in. wide. (Burrows & Days) $87 £44

Early 19th century English apothecary's cabinet, 15in. high. (Sotheby's Belgravia) $1,261 £650

George III mahogany and kingwood three division tea caddy, 31cm. wide. (King & Chasemore) $258 £130

17th century oak bible box with scrolling decoration, 24in. wide. (Churchman's) $99 £52

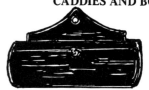

18th century black painted candle box, 11in. wide. (Christopher Sykes) $70 £35

Early 19th century mahogany chemist's chest complete with fittings. (Locke & England) $380 £200

Small Victorian tantalus. (W. H. Lane & Son) $196 £100

Coffee container, circa 1875. (Alfie's Antique Market) $108 £55

20th century sandalwood and ivory Indian games box, 18in. wide. (Sotheby's Belgravia) $422 £220

Early 19th century oak bible box, 24in. wide. (Manchester Auction Mart) $235 £120

Mid 19th century English apothecary's chest, 11in. high. (Sotheby's Belgravia) $737 £380

'Directore' mahogany decanter box, 19½in. high, circa 1912. (Sotheby's Belgravia) $543 £280

Circular pollard wood snuff box, circa 1820, 8.5cm. diameter. (Sotheby's) $116 £60

Victorian coromandel-wood box by Baxter, London, 1856, 8½in. wide.(Geering & Colyer) $151 £75

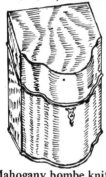

Mid 17th century oak spice cabinet, 15in. wide. (King & Chase-more) $504 £260

Unusual 19th century Chinese black lacquer tea caddy. (Christie's S. Kensington) $806 £420

Mahogany bombe knife box, shell handle and satinwood stringing. (Nottingham Auction Mart) $291 £150

Mahogany and inlaid decanter box with four cut-glass decan-ters, 8½in. high. (Christie's S. Kensington) $343 £170

Oak spice box, 17th century. (Drewatt, Watson & Barton) $1,358 £700

Early 19th century English apothecary's chest, 26in. high. (Sotheby's Belgravia) $1,164 £600

Late 18th century octagonal lacquer Kojubako, signed Zohiko. (Christie's)$1,320 £680

Unusual carved oak offertory box with iron lock and chain. (Phillips)$888 £440

Early 19th century tortoiseshell tea caddy, inlaid with mother-of-pearl. (Gray's Antique Market) $346 £175

Table cabinet in black, gilt and red lacquer, circa 1880, 26½in. high. (Sotheby's Belgravia) $250 £130

Crocodile skin travelling dressing case with gold mounted fittings. (Sotheby's Belgravia) $5,529 £2,850

One of a pair of George III mahogany and fruitwood banded knife boxes. (King & Chasemore) $1,089 £550

Reco Capey carved box and cover, 18cm. high. (Sotheby's Belgravia)$465 £240

Rare George II japanned tea caddy, circa 1740, 10¼in. wide. (Sotheby's) $764 £390

Edwardian C.W.S. biscuit tin. (Gray's Antique Market) $29 £15

Circular pollard wood snuff box, circa 1820, 8.2cm. diameter. (Sotheby's)$106 £55

'Intarsia' brass mounted and inlaid wood casket, circa 1900, 14cm. long. (Sotheby's Belgravia) $504 £260

Circular pollard wood snuff box, circa 1820, 8.2cm. diameter. (Sotheby's)$126 £65

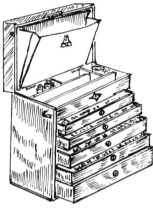

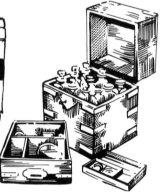

Late 19th century C. Ash & Sons dentist's case, 10½in. high. (Sotheby's Belgravia) $232 £120

Biscuit tin in the shape of a Mail van. (Christie's S. Kensington) $336 £170

Georgian apothecary's box. (Alfie's Antique Market) $782 £395

Tortoiseshell and mother-of-pearl inlaid tea caddy. (King & Chasemore) $574 £290

Early 19th century French musical necessaire, 7.5cm. wide.(Sotheby's) $854 £440

Late 19th century rect-angular box, 4¼in. long. (Sotheby's Belgravia) $211 £110

Circular pollard wood
snuff box, circa 1820,
9cm. diameter.
(Sotheby's)$213 £110

Mid 19th century tor-
toiseshell and silvered
metal mounted box.
(King & Chasemore)
$207 £105

Early 18th century
English oval tortoise-
shell snuff box, 8.5cm.
wide.   (Sotheby's)
$369 £190

Late 19th century
portable writing
desk, 18½in. wide.
(Sotheby's Belgravia)
$125 £65

Charles I oak bible box,
circa 1630, 2ft.3in.
wide.   (Sotheby's)
$3,135 £1,600

Oak decanter box,
circa 1880, with
Bramah lock, 13¾in.
wide. (Sotheby's
Belgravia)$368 £190

Coromandel travelling
dressing box, circa 1860,
with fitted interior.
(Sotheby's Belgravia)
$310 £160

Reco Capey carved
ebony box and cover,
21cm. high.
(Sotheby's Belgravia)
$504 £260

Oak candle box, circa
1790, 13in. wide.
(Christopher Sykes)
$126 £65

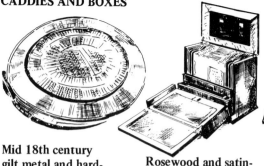

Mid 18th century
gilt metal and hard-
stone snuff box,
6.5cm. wide.
(Sotheby's)$388 £200

Rosewood and satin-
wood portable writ-
ing box, circa 1900,
12in. wide.(Sotheby's)
$705 £360

Tunbridgeware needle-
work box, 9½in. wide,
with lined interior.
(Parsons, Welch &
Cowell) $225 £115

Oak decanter box by
H. H. Dobson & Sons,
London, circa 1850,
9¾in. long.(Sotheby's)
$1,010 £500

Early 19th century
English apothecary's
chest, 8in. high.
(Sotheby's Belgravia)
$517 £260

Edwardian oak three
bottle tantalus with
plated mounts, 13in.
wide.(Nottingham
Auction Mart)
$274 £140

Victorian Tunbridge-
ware stamp box.
(Gray's Antique
Market) $33 £17

Small Victorian rosewood
tea caddy, inlaid with
mother-of-pearl.(Alfie's
Antique Market)$69 £35

19th century lacquer
Suzuribako, 9¼in.
wide.(Christie's)
$440 £226

Tunbridgeware box, decorated with a reindeer, 6in. square. (Parsons, Welch & Cowell) $47 £24

Walnut and marquetry humidor, circa 1880, 14 x 19½in.(Sotheby's Belgravia) $588 £300

19th century painted satinwood Sheraton design velvet lined box.(King & Chasemore) $198 £100

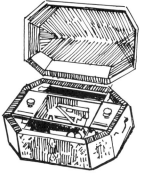

Black papier mache needlework box, circa 1840, 14in. long. (Gray's Antique Market) $282 £140

Dome topped tea caddy in Tunbridgeware, 6in. wide.(Parsons, Welch & Cowell) $137 £70

19th century Goanese ivory and silver sewing box.(McCartney, Morris & Barker) $574 £290

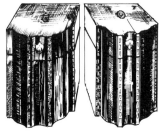

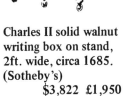

A pair of Sheraton knife boxes in mahogany.(Vidler's) $1,120 £560

Charles II solid walnut writing box on stand, 2ft. wide, circa 1685. (Sotheby's) $3,822 £1,950

Good Galle marquetry casket, 1890's, 28.5cm. high.(Sotheby's Belgravia) $3,920 £2,000

Late Victorian rosewood and marquetry travelling writing box, circa 1890, 14¼in. wide.(Sotheby's Belgravia) $594 £300

Madurell gilt metal casket, circa 1900, 37.5cm. long. (Sotheby's Belgravia) $792 £400

Mid 19th century amboyna wood oval shaped tea caddy, 14.5cm. wide. (King & Chasemore) $159 £80

Late 19th century oak cased calendar. (British Antique Exporters) $30 £15

Augsburg ivory jewellery cabinet, 17th century, 7½in. high. (Sotheby's) $5,130 £2,700

Large lacquered wood and jewelled box and cover, circa 1900, 110cm. high.(Sotheby's Belgravia) $744 £380

19th century lacquered box and cover, Japanese, 22cm. wide. (King & Chasemore) $464 £230

Victorian satinwood and crossbanded square shaped tea caddy, 13.5cm. wide. (King & Chasemore) $139 £70

Milanese casket with bone frieze, 8½in. wide, 15th century. (Sotheby's) $2,755 £1,450

Late Victorian pine
specimen chest.
(British Antique Ex-
porters) $60 £30

Regency rosewood tea
caddy inlaid with
mother-of-pearl, 12in.
long. (Gray's Antique
Market) $242 £120

Victorian papier mache
and mother-of-pearl
jewellery cabinet, 28cm.
wide. (King & Chasemore)
$525 £260

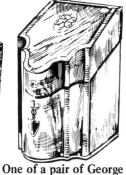

George III mahogany
decanter box, fully
fitted. (Bonham's)
$824 £400

19th century mahogany
and brass coal box.
(British Antique Expor-
ters) $40 £20

One of a pair of George
III mahogany and satin-
wood knife boxes,
22.5cm. wide. (King &
Chasemore)
$1,990 £1,000

Rosewood vanity case,
circa 1860, 6¾in. wide.
(Sotheby's Belgravia)
$282 £140

Victorian satinwood
square shaped tea
caddy, 11cm. wide.
(King & Chasemore)
$139 £70

Japanese gold lacquer
kwashi bako, or picnic
box, 7in. long.
(Phillips) $343 £170

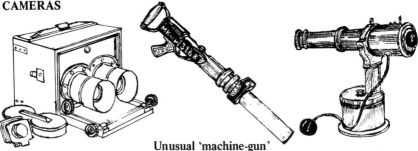

James How wet-plate stereoscopic camera, English, circa 1880. (Sotheby's Belgravia) $4,074 £2,100

Unusual 'machine-gun' Thornton Pickard camera, circa 1942, 39in. long.(Sotheby's Belgravia) $291 £150

'The Telephot' ferrotype button camera, circa 1900, English. (Sotheby's Belgravia) $1,125 £580

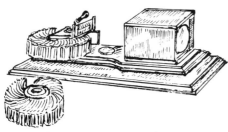

English Kinora, hand-cranked viewer, circa 1900, sold with two reels of photographs.(Sotheby's Belgravia) $853 £440

W. Watson & Sons Ltd., full-plate tailboard studio camera, circa 1930. (Sotheby's Belgravia) $378 £190

Reddings Luzo mahogany roll-film camera in ever ready case.(Christie's S. Kensington) $2,020 £1,000

A model, gem and enamel, plate camera, signed Cartier, 4in. high. (Christie's S. Kensington) $5,096 £2,600

Large J. H. Dallmeyer tailboard studio camera, circa 1880.(Sotheby's Belgravia) $995 £500

Marion type tropical
reflex camera, circa
1920, in leather case.
(Sotheby's Belgravia)
$1,455 £750

Ensign tropical roll-
film reflex camera,
circa 1925.
(Sotheby's Belgravia)
$398 £200

Fine quarter-plate field
camera by Sanderson.
(Alfie's Antique Market)
$316 £160

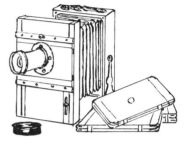

Good Van Neck & Co. tailboard whole-
plate camera, circa 1895, in original
case.(Sotheby's Belgravia) $378 £190

Good tailboard folding field camera,
circa 1920, with three double sided
plate holders.(Sotheby's Belgravia)
$174 £90

'The Telephot' ferro-
type button camera,
circa 1900, 1ft.2½in.
wide.(Sotheby's Bel-
gravia) $1,194 £600

J. Lancaster half-plate
'instantograph' collap-
sible camera, circa 1905.
(Sotheby's Belgravia)
$115 £58

Ferrotype 'mug' camera
with spare developing
tank, German, circa
1895, 11½in. high.
(Sotheby's Belgravia)
$1,067 £550

English ivory handled walking stick, circa 1830. (Sotheby's)
$272 £140

English ivory cane handle, circa 1780, 6.5cm. long. (Sotheby's)
$233 £120

Late 18th century gilt metal cane handle, 4.5cm. long, sold with two others. (Sotheby's)
$175 £90

Malacca walking stick, handle 4cm. high, circa 1770, sold with another. (Sotheby's)
$107 £55

Early 19th century Italian parcel gilt cane handle, 9.5cm. long. (Sotheby's)
$427 £220

Rhinoceros horn and silver pique cane handle, circa 1700, 12.5cm. long. (Sotheby's)
$310 £160

Early 19th century English ivory and horn walking stick, 84cm. long. (Sotheby's)
$252 £130

17th century silver gilt tubular spice box, 7.5cm. high. (Sotheby's)
$349 £180

18th century ivory and Narwhal walking stick, 96.5cm. long. (Sotheby's)
$349 £180

Long ivory cane with tapering shaft, circa 1780, 126cm. long. (Sotheby's)
$543 £280

Late 19th century Meissen parasol handle, 4.3cm. high. (Sotheby's Belgravia)
$118 £60

Late 19th century gilt metal cane handle, sold with two others. (Sotheby's)
$155 £80

17th century carved wood figure of a saint, 28½in. high. (Burrows & Day) $929 £460

19th century German carved ivory and boxwood figure group, 10½in. long.(Messenger, May & Baverstock)
$4,120 £2,000

Early 19th century lignum vitae string box, 5½in. high. (Gray's Antique Mews)
$64 £32

Franconian limewood relief of the Virgin and Child, circa 1520, 64½in. high.(Sotheby's) $47,500
£25,000

19th century Oriental gong with carved hardwood stand. (British Antique Exporters)
$130 £65

Late 19th century bronze bell on hardwood stand, 38in. high. (Sotheby's Belgravia) $230 £120

Early 18th century German boxwood flagon, 14in. high. (Sotheby's)
$5,510 £2,900

Lower Rhine oak group, circa 1500, 12in. long. (Sotheby's)
$3,040 £1,600

North Netherlandish limewood figure of a female saint, 41½in. high, circa 1460-80. (Sotheby's)
$14,250 £7,500

CARVED WOOD

Stylised human face mask of an ancestor, 13½in. high.(Christopher Sykes's)
$552 £285

Mid 19th century gilt wood door frame, 64in. wide. (Sotheby's Belgravia) $403 £210

Fine carved cartouche in the manner of Matthias Locke. (Sotheby's)
$2,525 £1,250

Inlaid hardwood panel, circa 1900, 29¾in. long. (Sotheby's Belgravia)
$192 £100

Late 17th century figure of Putai, in lacquered wood, 22in. high. (Christie's)$1,540 £793

Late 19th century compressed wood panel of General Gordon, 26¼in. high.(Sotheby's Belgravia)
$105 £55

One of a pair of 18th century Venetian blackamoor torcheres, 55in. high.(Christie's)
$1,552 £800

Unusual late 19th century carved softwood dias. (Sotheby's Belgravia)
$729 £380

South German wood carving, early 16th century.(Christie's S. Kensington)
$11,640 £6,000

Rare mask, from South Eastern Congo, of the Jokwe tribe.(Christopher Sykes's)
$727 £375

North African octagonal hardwood table, circa 1930. (Sotheby's Belgravia)
$806 £420

Turned dark fruitwood 'Cat' bowl stand.(Christopher Sykes's) $112 £58

17th century Dutch or German carved boxwood knife handle, 8.2cm. high. (Sotheby's) $310 £160

Figure of Amida from the Edo period, in giltwood, 28¼in. high. (Christie's)
$1,430 £737

17th century Italian carved figure of an angel, 32in. high. (Christopher Sykes's)
$727 £375

12th/13th century carved wood figure of Amida Buddha, 29cm. high.(King & Chasemore)$1,152 £600

Late 19th century gesso and carved wood group, 21in. high.(Sotheby's Belgravia) $1,114 £580

Swiss or Austrian carved walnut plaque of a hunter, circa 1870, 39½in. high.(Sotheby's Belgravia) $285 £150

CARVED WOOD

Pair of Baroque German carved wood cherubs, 10in. high. (Worsfolds) $935 £470

Late 19th century New Guinea wood crest. (Christie's) $18,180 £9,000

Spanish giltwood altar, circa 1700, 502cm. high. (Christie's) $2,134 £1,100

Early 20th century painted wood blackamoor, 67in. high. (Sotheby's Belgravia) $1,293 £650

18th century pair of Dutch dummy board figures, 45in. high. (Christie's) $1,746 £900

Large 18th century lignum vitae cup, 19in. high. (Butler & Hatch Waterman) $808 £400

Late 19th century Italian painted wood bird cage, 122in. high. (Sotheby's Belgravia) $2,786 £1,400

A pair of carved walnut candlesticks, circa 1900, 18in. high. (Gray's Antique Market) $242 £120

19th century cinnabar lacquer vase, 51cm. high. (Sotheby's Belgravia) $411 £210

Mid 19th century Scandinavian painted pine butter tub and cover. (Phillips) $380 £200

Late 19th century Indian polychrome fantasy bird, 64½ x 55in. (Sotheby's Belgravia) $3,582 £1,800

Early 20th century rosewood table shrine, 33in. high.(Sotheby's Belgravia) $849 £440

Early 19th century tobacconist's sign of a Highlander. (Edmiston's) $1,656 £820

Painted wood picture frame, circa 1900, 40½in. wide. (Sotheby's Belgravia) $525 £260

Unusual pagoda, circa 1880, 85½in. high. (Sotheby's Belgravia) $1,190 £620

Hagenauer carved wood and bronze figure, 23.5cm. high, 1910/20.(Sotheby's Belgravia) $774 £400

Pair of 17th century German carved wood statuettes, 24in. high. (Worsfolds) $3,582 £1,800

Hagenauer wood and bronze group of mother and child, 1910-20, 32.5cm. high.(Sotheby's Belgravia) $392 £200

91

CARVED WOOD

Early 17th century
yew wood mortar,
6¼in. high.
(Sotheby's)$931 £480

Mid 17th century Dutch
or German maplewood
spoon, 17.5cm. long.
(Sotheby's) $1,125 £580

Balsa wood mask made
for the 'Goelede' soci-
ety, Yoruba tribe.
(Gray's Antique Market)
$188 £95

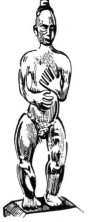

Maori carved wooden
house post, before
1840, 4ft.2½in. high.
(Christie's)
$99,000 £50,000

Late 18th century Oban
woodblock print,
Japanese. (King & Chase-
more)   ·$705 £360

Carved and painted
wooden mask from
West Africa.(Christie's)
$9,700 £5,000

18th century English
yew wood rushlight
nip, 11½in. high.
(Sotheby's)$543 £280

Carved walnut hunting
plaque, circa 1870, 47in.
high, Swiss. (Sotheby's
Belgravia) $608 £320

Rowley Gallery gilt-
wood low relief,
circa 1925, 71cm.
high.(Sotheby's Bel-
gravia) $99 £50

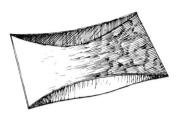

Wooden dish from
Matty Island, 19½
x 12in. (Sotheby's)
$24,250 £12,500

18th century turned
cherrywood tobacco
jar, 5½in. high.
(Sotheby's)$155 £80

Scandinavian carved
wood butter box.
(Christopher Sykes)
$74 £38

Hawaiian wooden
image, 10¼in.
high. (Sotheby's)
$485,000 £250,000

Rare pair of Charles
I bellows in elm and
fruitwood, circa 1640,
2ft. long.(Sotheby's)
$2,376 £1,200

Bas relief wood sculp-
ture, by Norman For-
rest, 1930's, 93cm.
high.(Sotheby's Bel-
gravia) $588 £300

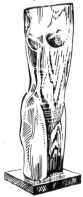

17th century Ming
wooden figure,
16in. high. (Gray's
Antique Mews)
$1,386 £700

Tlingit circular wood
face mask, 10in. diam.
(Sotheby's N. York)
$23,000 £11,165

Wood sculpture on
slate base, 1930's,
93cm. high.(Sotheby's
Belgravia)$1,176 £600

93

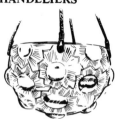

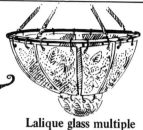

Glass chandelier by
Rene Lalique, 12in.
diameter. (Christie's
N. York)
$1,200 £606

Rare green glass and
bronze chandelier by
Tiffany, 46in. high.
(Christie's N. York)
$12,000 £6,060

Lalique glass multiple
panel hanging shade,
1920's, 49cm. diam.
(Sotheby's Belgravia)
$588 £300

Regency gilt brass Kolza
oil lantern, 2ft.1in. diam.,
circa 1820. (Sotheby's)
$470 £240

One of a pair of late
19th century giltwood
chandeliers, 39in. high.
(Sotheby's Belgravia)
$684 £360

Restoration hanging
Kolza lamp, circa
1820, 2ft.6in. diam.
(Sotheby's)
$1,089 £550

One of a pair of Art Deco
moulded glass and metal
wall lights, circa 1925,
42cm. high. (Sotheby's
Belgravia) $342 £180

Gilt bronze and Favrile
glass ceiling fixture by
Tiffany, 17in. high.
(Christie's N. York)
$3,000 £1,515

Fine and rare alaman-
der leaded glass chan-
delier by Tiffany, 48in.
high. (Christie's N. York)
$30,000 £15,151

Fine glass ceiling fixture by Rene Lalique, circa 1925, 10¾in. diam. (Christie's N. York)$2,000 £1,010

'Acanthus' brown-stained glass chandelier by Rene Lalique, circa 1925, 17¾in. diam. (Christie's N. York) $2,000 £1,010

Double overlay glass chandelier by Daum freres, 15½in. diam. (Christie's N. York) $2,500 £1,262

George II giltwood chandelier of fifteen lights, circa 1750, by Matthias Locke. (Sotheby's) $96,040 £49,000

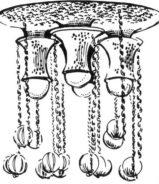

Good Wiener Werkstatte electroplated metal and glass ceiling light, circa 1905, 26cm. high. (Sotheby's Belgravia) $3,686 £1,900

Early 19th century bronze chandelier of eighteen lamps, 2ft. 3½in. diam.(Sotheby's) $1,235 £650

Iridescent Favrile glass chandelier by Tiffany, shade 14in. high. (Christie's N. York) $2,420 £1,247

Art Nouveau brass chandelier, circa 1900. (Sotheby's Belgravia) $184 £95

Favrile glass and bronze chandelier by Tiffany Studios, 20in. high. (Christie's N. York) $990 £510

20th century gilt metal hall lantern, 31½in. high. (Sotheby's Belgravia) $606 £300

Favrile glass turtle-back and leaded glass chandelier by Tiffany, 34½in. high. (Christie's N. York) $12,000 £6,060

Mid 19th century Scandinavian moulded glass chandelier, 32in. diam. (Sotheby's Belgravia) $388 £195

One of a pair of George III wall sconces, 10¼in. wide, London 1796, sold with two small brackets. (Sotheby's) $3,600 £1,800

One of a pair of cast iron gas chandeliers, circa 1870, 77in. high. (Sotheby's Belgravia) $363 £180

Art Deco wrought iron and Schneider glass chandelier, 1930's, 67cm. wide. (Sotheby's Belgravia) $392 £200

Large German Art Nouveau gilt metal chandelier, circa 1900, 128cm. high. (Sotheby's Belgravia) $633 £320

Yellow rose bush leaded glass hanging lamp by Tiffany, 24¾in. diam. (Christie's N. York) $17,600 £9,462

Large Dutch brass chandelier, circa 1900, 33in. diam. (Sotheby's Belgravia) $514 £260

One of a pair of Ans-
bach faience wall
vases, 8.5cm. wide.
(Sotheby's)$980 £500

18th century Ans-
bach faience tankard
with pewter footrim,
1791, 24.5cm. high.
(Sotheby's)
$1,960 £1,000

A pair of Ansbach eques-
trian figures, circa 1730,
24.5cm. high.(Sotheby's)
$1,568 £800

ARITA

Large Japanese Arita
vase, 70½in. high
overall.(Parsons,
Welch & Cowell)
$8,712 £4,400

Japanese Arita plate,
circa 1850, 16in.
diam. (Gray's Anti-
que Mews) $929 £460

19th century Arita
polychrome vase,
77.5cm. high. (May,
Whetter & Grose)
$282 £140

BELLEEK

Belleek croaking
frog, circa 1900,
5½in. high.
(Sotheby's Belgravia)
$392 £200

Belleek honey pot
in the form of a
beehive, 6¼in. high.
(Sotheby's Belgravia)
$343 £170

Part of a Belleek tea
service of forty-six
pieces, 1891-1855.
(Sotheby's Belgravia)
$470 £240

Berlin porcelain plaque, mid 19th century, 12 x 15in. (Sotheby's N. York) $16,000 £7,940

One of a pair of Berlin porcelain cabinet cups and saucers with gilt decoration. (Locke & England) $2,090 £1,100

Berlin enamel snuff box, circa 1746, 8cm. wide. (Sotheby's) $495 £250

Late 19th century Berlin group of Telemachus and Mentor, 33.5cm. high. (Sotheby's Belgravia) $352 £180

Berlin rectangular plaque, 5½in. wide, in giltwood frame. (Christie's) $1,067 £550

One of a pair of Berlin covered chocolate pots, 7¾in. and 5½in. high, circa 1830.(Warner, Sheppard & Wade) $588 £300

Berlin oval plaque, 10¾in. high. (Christie's) $620 £320

Berlin porcelain cabaret set of exhibition quality. (Russell, Baldwin & Bright) $1,287 £650

One of a pair of Berlin rectangular plaques, 13in. high. (Christie's) $8,148 £4,200

Bow miniature suc-
rier and cover, circa
1760. (Sotheby's)
$831 £420

Bow teapot, painted with
a dragon pattern, circa
1760. (Christie's)
$969 £480

One of a pair of rare
Bow miniature tea-
bowls and saucers,
circa 1760.
(Sotheby's)
$752 £380

Rare set of Bow figures of the Continents,
5¼in. high, circa 1762-65. (Sotheby's)
$3,960 £2,000

Bow porcelain
group of a Har-
lequin and his
Lady. (King &
Chasemore)
$673 £340

Superb Bow figure of
a 'Dismal' hound,
8.2cm. high.(Phillips)
$4,900 £2,500

Pair of Bow figures of
a monk and a nun, circa
1755-60, 4¼in. and
4¾in. high. (Sotheby's)
$554 £280

Early Bow cream
jug, 3in. high, circa
1753. (Sotheby's)
$509 £260

Porter cup by Edward
Prince. (Neales)
$1,365 £704

Good pair of cold-painted clay
figures of negroes, circa 1900,
22in. high. (Sotheby's Belgravia) $2,574 £1,300

One of a pair of
Wilton vases.
(Alfie's Antique
Market)
$111 £55

Villeroy and Boch vase,
circa 1910, 45.5cm.
high.(Sotheby's Bel-
gravia) $198 £100

Harry Parr figure of a seated
woman, 10in. high, Chelsea,
1924. (Sotheby's Belgravia)
$235 £120

Walton type figure
jug, Rodney's Sai-
lor, 11½in. high.
(Neales)$254 £130

Hand painted china
kettle, circa 1876, by
Powell & Bishop.
(Alfie's Antique Mar-
ket) $81 £40

Black Victorian urn
with glazed flowers.
(Alfie's Antique Mar-
ket) $90 £45

'Arctic' footwarmer in
Denby stoneware,
circa 1910. (Gray's
Antique Market)
$30 £15

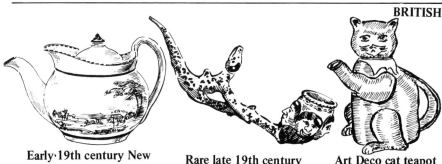

Early 19th century New Hall teapot from a thirty three-piece tea and coffee service. (H. C. Chapman & Son) $399 £210

Rare late 19th century Yorkshire pipe, 10¼in. long. (Sotheby's) $316 £160

Art Deco cat teapot in perfect condition. (Alfie's Antique Market) $58 £29

Issy high-fired porcelain figure, 1913, 44cm. high. (Sotheby's Belgravia) $396 £200

Unusually shaped apothecary's pill slab, decorated in blue and pink.(Sotheby's) $4,158 £2,100

Stoneware ginger beer bottle. (British Antique Exporters) $6 £3

Classical revival jug, circa 1860. (Alfie's Antique Market) $81 £40

Late 17th century slipware charger by Wm. Talor, 17½in. diam. (Sotheby's) $26,600 £14,000

Copeland Edward VII memorial vase, 1910, 7in. high.(Sotheby's Belgravia) $207 £105

Rye pottery Sussex
Rustic ware jug,
7in. high. (Burrows
& Day) $79 £40

Nantgarw saucer dish.
(Russell, Baldwin &
Bright) $495 £250

Large marbled jug with
pewter lid, circa 1850.
(Alfie's Antique Market)
$95 £48

One of a pair of urn
shaped covered vases,
circa 1770, 10½in.
high.(Warner, Shep-
pard & Wade)$784 £400

Victorian jug and basin set
of five pieces with floral
decoration. (Alfie's Antique
Market) $70 £35

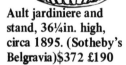

Ault jardiniere and
stand, 36¼in. high,
circa 1895. (Sotheby's
Belgravia)$372 £190

Rare fairing 'How's
Your Poor Feet?',
4¼in. high, circa
1890.(Sotheby's
Belgravia)$217 £110

Billingsley Mansfield
canary yellow oval
teapot. (Neales)
$2,027 £1,045

Stoneware urn, circa
1860, 36in. high.
(Sotheby's Belgravia)
$349 £180

Lowestoft blue and white sparrow beak cream jug, circa 1780, 3¼in. high.(Nottingham Auction Mart) $74 £38

'Bizarre' painted glazed pottery breakfast set, 1930's.(Sotheby's Belgravia) $386 £200

Goat cream jug, circa 1910, 5½in. high, in very good condition. (Alfie's Antique Market) $50 £25

Yorkshire pottery group, 9in. high, circa 1780-90. (Sotheby's) $548 £280

Scottish pottery Glasgow cup, saucer and plate. (Phillips) $56 £28

Pilkington's Royal Lancastrian lustre vase, 1910, 10in. high. (Sotheby's Belgravia) $294 £150

Victorian jug and basin set. (British Antique Exporters) $40 £20

Rare and amusing Yorkshire equestrian figure, 8¾in. high, circa 1780. (Sotheby's)$1,724 £880

Toby jug by Carrathurs Gould, 1917. (Gray's Antique Market) $252 £125

Late 19th century faceted Canton jardiniere, 11in. high. (Sotheby's Belgravia) $307 £160

Late 19th century Canton bowl, 10¼in. high.(Sotheby's Belgravia) $384 £200

One piece from a set of nine late 19th century Canton dessert dishes. (Sotheby's Belgravia)$653 £340

One of a pair of Cantonese vases, circa 1860, 23in. high. (Gray's Antique Mews) $1,732 £875

One of a pair of late 19th century Canton altar candlesticks, 7½in. high. (Sotheby's Belgravia) $1,498 £780

One of a pair of Cantonese porcelain vases. (Russell, Baldwin & Bright) $831 £420

Mid 19th century Canton vase, 24in. high.(Sotheby's Belgravia)$422 £220

Late 19th century Canton vase, 17in. high. (Sotheby's Belgravia)$595 £310

One of a pair of late 19th century Cantonese vases, 17in. high. (Sotheby's Belgravia) $1,382 £720

One of a pair of
Canton vases, circa
1870, 44.5cm. high.
(Sotheby's Belgravia)
$1,528 £780

Mid 19th century Canton bowl with slight
crack, 53cm. diam.
(Henry Spencer & Sons)
$970 £500

Mid 19th century
Canton garden seat,
48cm. high.
(Sotheby's Belgravia)
$1,470 £750

One of a pair of late
Canton baluster form
vases, 24in. high.
(Osmond Tricks)
$1,235 £650

One of a pair of yellow
ground Canton porcelain
moon flasks, 47cm. high,
mid 19th century.(King
& Chasemore)$1,623 £820

One of a pair of late
19th century Canton porcelain vases.
(King & Chasemore)
$588 £300

Large late 19th century Canton vase, 35in.
high.(Sotheby's Belgravia) $2,304 £1,200

One of a pair of late
19th century Canton vases, 26.2cm.
high.(Sotheby's Belgravia) $372 £190

Late 19th century Canton vase, one of a pair,
24¼in. high.(Sotheby's
Belgravia)$1,920 £1,000

Rare Caughley eye-
bath, 2in. high,
circa 1785-90.
(Sotheby's)
$633 £320

Caughley teabowl and
saucer painted in under-
glaze blue, circa 1785.
(Sotheby's) $215 £110

Caughley jug, 2in.
high, in underglaze
blue. (Sotheby's)
$215 £110

Rare Caughley inscribed
and dated 'cabbage-leaf'
jug, 1789, 7½in. high.
(Sotheby's)$445 £225

Caughley shell-shaped
dish, circa 1778-82, 8in.
diameter. (Sotheby's)
$376 £190

Very rare Caughley
commemorative jug,
circa 1799, 8in. high.
(Sotheby's)
$1,067 £560

Caughley coffee pot in
underglaze blue, 3½in.
high. (Sotheby's)
$294 £150

Caughley 'cabbage-leaf'
jug, 8in. high, circa
1785-90. (Sotheby's)
$1,029 £520

Caughley porcelain
mask jug. (Russell,
Baldwin & Bright)
$415 £210

Rare Chelsea set of fitted boxes, circa 1765, 6½in. wide. (Sotheby's)
$705 £360

Chelsea candlestick group of birds, circa 1762, 7in. high, repaired.(Sotheby's)
$529 £270

Good Chelsea sauce-boat of oval form, 7¾in. long, circa 1752-56. (Sotheby's)
$705 £360

Rare Chelsea plate, circa 1765, 8½in. diam. (Sotheby's)
$313 £160

A pair of Chelsea porcelain figures, 10½in. high. (Geering & Colyer)
$808 £400

One of a rare pair of Chelsea plates, circa 1765, 8½in. diam. (Sotheby's)
$588 £300

Rare oval Chelsea dish, 10¾in. wide, circa 1752-56.(Sotheby's)
$803 £410

Rare Chelsea vase of square section, 11in. high, circa 1765. (Sotheby's)$431 £220

Rare Chelsea dove tureen and cover, 7in. high, circa 1752-56, cover re-paired. (Sotheby's)
$2,574 £1,300

One of a pair of Ch'ien Lung famille rose bowls, 4¼in. diam. (Christie's) $800 £412

Ch'ien Lung period scalloped edge famille rose dish, 28cm. diam. (King & Chasemore) $585 £290

One of a pair of Ch'ien Lung green ground porcelain bottles with ivory stoppers. (Christie's) $120 £61

A garniture of five Ch'ien Lung famille rose porcelain vases, two of beaker form the remaining three of baluster form with covers, each painted in enamels and gilding. (King & Chasemore) $931 £450

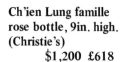

Ch'ien Lung famille rose bottle, 9in. high. (Christie's) $1,200 £618

Ch'ien Lung blue and white bidet, 24¼in. long. (Christie's) $1,330 £700

Famille verte figure of a hawk, Ch'ien Lung period, 20¾in. high. (Sotheby's) $15,680 £8,000

Ch'ien Lung bulbous vase enamelled in green, red and blue, 12½in. high. (Burrows & Day) $1,515 £750

One of a pair of Ch'ien Lung famille rose oval soup tureens with rare silver covers, circa 1770, 14oz. silver.(Sotheby's Ireland) $5,940 £3,000

One of a pair of Ch'ien Lung Chinese taste eggshell wine cups, 2¼in. diam. (Christie's) $600 £309

Ch'ien Lung famille rose bottle vase, 10¼in. high. (Christie's)$935 £481

Famille rose porcelain export jug and cover, Ch'ien Lung, 24cm. high. (King & Chasemore) $291 £150

Ch'ien Lung copper-red glazed bottle vase, 11¾in. high. (Christie's) $1,650 £850

Late 19th century Ch'ien Lung famille rose vase, one of a pair, 16¼in. high. (Sotheby's Belgravia) $1,075 £550

One of a pair of Ch'ien Lung plates decorated in gilt and grisaille. (Christie's) $431 £220

Rare Ch'ien Lung moulded famille rose bottle with rose quartz stopper. (Christie's) $150 £77

Chou dynasty cloth moulded bowl, 3½in. diameter.(Christie's) $715 £368

Late 19th century blue and white globular jar and cover, 13¾in. high. (Sotheby's Belgravia) $518 £270

Fine blue and white circular box and cover, 12½in. diameter. (Christie's) $7,150 £3,685

Transitional period blue and white beaker vase, 17in. high.(Christie's) $1,600 £824

One of a pair of 19th century yellow-ground fish tanks, 21in. diam. (Neales) $5,572 £2,800

Late 19th century blue and white vase, 42½in. high. (Sotheby's Belgravia) $1,114 £580

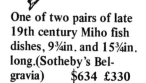

One of a pair of late 19th century blue and white vases and covers, 15in. high. (Sotheby's Belgravia) $461 £240

One of two pairs of late 19th century Miho fish dishes, 9¾in. and 15¾in. long.(Sotheby's Belgravia) $634 £330

One of a pair of Kyoto late 19th century candlesticks, 12¾in. high.(Sotheby's Belgravia)$288 £150

19th century pottery Kataleuchi bowl, 6¾in. diameter. (Christie's) $660 £340

15th century Chinese white porcelain stem cup, 3¾in. high. (Bonham's) $50,440 £26,000

One of ten Chinese wine tasting cups, 2½in. diameter. (Christie's) $120 £61

Late 16th century Fa Hua bottle mounted in ormolu, 14½in. high. (Christie's) $2,200 £1,134

Sui dynasty straw-glazed equestrian tomb figure, 13in. high. (Christie's) $1,870 £963

18th century blue and white rouleau vase, 22¼in. high.(Christie's) $1,700 £876

One of a pair of late 19th century blue and white jars, 13in. high.(Sotheby's Belgravia) $849 £440

Chinese porcelain frog jardiniere, 18th century, 11in. long. (Sotheby's) $714 £360

18th century Kuan type vase, 6in. high. (Christie's) $150 £77

Early 19th century
Chinese armorial
sauceboat and dish.
(A. G. Byrne & Co.)
$277 £140

Chinese bottle
shaped vase.
(Burrows & Day)
$170 £88

18th century Chinese
export porcelain punch-
bowl, 12¼in. diameter.
(Smith-Woolley & Perry)
$589 £310

18th century blue
and white pear
shaped bottle, 18¾in.
high. (Christie's)
$2,000 £1,030

Chinese white glazed
figure of the Bodhis-
attva Avalokitesvara,
12½in. high.(Christie's)
$79,200 £40,000

Mid 19th century
Hosai vase in
earthenware, 9¼in.
high.(Sotheby's
Belgravia)
$998 £520

One of a pair of late
19th century blue
and white vases and
covers, 17¾in. high.
(Sotheby's Belgravia)
$365 £190

First period blue and
white porcelain teapot
and cover, circa 1760,
4½in. high.(Nottingham
Auction Mart)
$137 £70

One of a pair of
Bizan stoneware
19th century
birds, 8½in. high.
(Sotheby's Bel-
gravia)$163 £85

Square Kokuzan dish painted by Masanobu, circa 1900, 7½in. high. (Sotheby's Belgravia)
$538 £280

Mid 17th century Kirman Kalian vase.(Sotheby's)
$6,060 £3,000

Wan Li blue and white saucer dish, 15in. diam. (Christie's)
$2,000 £1,030

One of a pair of late 19th century Oyama vases, 5in. high. (Sotheby's Belgravia)
$115 £60

One of a pair of Chinese export porcelain soup tureens, 16¼in. high. (Sotheby's)
$43,670 £22,000

Late 19th century Unzan Ryosan vase, 12in. high. (Sotheby's Belgravia)
$576 £300

Chinese turquoise glazed double gourd vase. (Phillips)
$1,777 £880

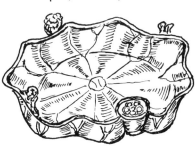

Late 17th century Chinese turquoise glazed lotus leaf dish, 9½in. diameter. (Sotheby's)$3,175 £1,600

Rare Lung Ch'uan fluted baluster jar and cover, 10¼in. high.(Christie's)
$2,860 £1,474

113

Yuan blue and white dish, mid 14th century, 15¾in. diam. (Sotheby's)
$78,127 £40,272

18th century Yi Hsing teapot and cover. (Christie's)$160 £83

Mid 14th century Chinese blue and white porcelain dish of Yuan dynasty, 18¾in. diam. (Sotheby's)
$297,000 £150,000

18th century Lang Yao bottle, 11¼in. high. (Christie's)
$800 £412

One of a pair of late 19th century blue and white jardinieres, 16in. high. (Sotheby's Belgravia)
$768 £400

19th century Chinese sang-de-boeuf vase and cover, 17in. high. (Sotheby's Belgravia)$422 £220

One of a pair of Nauba vases, late 19th century, 10in. high. (Sotheby's Belgravia)$1,248 £650

One of a pair of Yung Ch'eng famille rose dishes, 12½in. diam. (Christie's)$3,300 £1,701

One of a pair of large late 19th century blue and white vases, 39½in. high. (Sotheby's Belgravia) $2,496 £1,300

Late 19th century blue and white jardiniere, 33cm. high. (Sotheby's Belgravia) $264 £135

18th century Yi Hsing teapot and cover, 8in. wide. (Christie's) $180 £92

Yung Cheng monochrome brush pot, 4in. high.(Christie's) $400 £206

One of a pair of transitional style Wu Ts'ai porcelain vases and covers, late 19th century, 35.5cm. high. (King & Chasemore)$1,019 £520

Rare 14th century Yuan dynasty stem cup stand, 7½in. diam. (Christie's) $22,000 £11,340

Early 14th century pale blue wine ewer from the Yuan dynasty, 13¼in. tall. (Christie's N. York) $254,800 £130,000

Early 18th century Lang Yao baluster vase, 14in. high. (Christie's)$880 £453

Late 19th century Toguokuzan vase, 3in. high. (Sotheby's Belgravia) $518 £270

Fine Wu Ts'ai baluster vase and cover, circa 1650-70, 14in. high. (Christie's) $1,100 £567

Early 19th century Yi Hsing teapot and cover. (Christie's) $150 £77

Late 18th century hexagonal jardiniere, one of a pair, in blanc-de-chine, 7¼in. wide. (Christie's) $650 £335

Early 19th century blue and white bidet of pear shape, 61.5cm. long.(Sotheby's Belgravia) $686 £350

18th century blanc-de-chine beaker vase, 7in. high. (Christie's) $700 £360

Tao Kuang blue and white circular sweetmeat dish and cover, 13½in. diam. (Christie's)$1,200 £618

Late Tao Kuang famille rose oviform vase, 12in. high. (Christie's) $935 £481

Late 19th century blue and white jardiniere, 12in. high.(Sotheby's Belgravia) $346 £180

Rare Chinese export Yi Hsing figure, 19th century. (Bonham's) $282 £140

Yuan dynasty celadon incense burner, 3¾in. wide. (Christie's) $700 £360

Clarice Cliff 'bizarre' vase, 20.5cm. high, 1930's. (Sotheby's Belgravia) $68 £35

Attractive Clarice Cliff 'bizarre' teapot and cream jug, 1930's. (Sotheby's Belgravia) $196 £100

Clarice Cliff 'bizarre' vase, 21cm. high, 1930's. (Sotheby's Belgravia)$68 £35

Small Clarice Cliff 'bizarre' vase, 1930's, 18.75cm. high. (Sotheby's Belgravia) $58 £30

Clarice Cliff Toby jug. (King & Chasemore) $121 £60

Clarice Cliff 'bizarre' vase, 1930's, 20.5cm. high. (Sotheby's Belgravia) $68 £35

COALPORT

Coalport gilt and jewelled ewer, 1890's, 10¾in. high.(Sotheby's Belgravia) $588 £300

Coalport slipper, 4¼in. wide, circa 1880. (Sotheby's Belgravia) $235 £120

Coalport jewelled vase, circa 1900, 7½in. high.(Sotheby's Belgravia)$392 £200

Coalport royal blue ground slipper, circa 1890, 5½in. wide. (Sotheby's Belgravia) $627 £320

Rare Coalport scent bottle, 1890's, 5in. high. (Sotheby's Belgravia) $411 £210

Coalport jewelled vase, circa 1905, 5½in. wide. (Sotheby's Belgravia) $392 £200

Pale yellow ground fluted Coalport vase, 9¼in. high, circa 1881-91.(Sotheby's Belgravia)$254 £130

Part of a richly decorated Coalport dinner service. (Russell, Baldwin & Bright) $7,920 £4,000

Rare Coalport 'malachite' vase and cover, circa 1900, 11in. high.(Sotheby's Belgravia) $1,470 £750

Coalport jewelled cabinet cup and saucer, circa 1910. (Sotheby's Belgravia) $254 £130

Fine Coalport vase, 12½in. high, with four scroll feet. (Russell, Baldwin & Bright) $653 £330

Porcelain dessert dish by Coalport, circa 1835. (Gray's Antique Market) $121 £60

Railway mug, circa
1840, 5in. high.
(Sotheby's Belgravia)
$126 £65

Commemorative mug,
1838, made for Vic-
toria's coronation,
3¾in. high.(Sotheby's
Belgravia) $776 £400

Commemorative mug
decorated in sepia
showing 'The Planet'
engine. (Phillips)
$161 £80

Rare commemorative mug
for the coronation of
Queen Victoria, 1838,
3½in. high.(Sotheby's Belgravia) $1,029 £520

Meat paste jar bearing
a print of 'The Landing
of The British Army at
the Crimea'. (Sotheby's
Belgravia) $356 £180

William IV and Queen
Adelaide coronation
mug, circa 1831, 5in.
high.(Sotheby's Bel-
gravia) $336 £170

Railway commem-
orative mug, lilac
printed and show-
ing the 'Novelty'.
(Phillips)$191 £95

Railway plate showing
'The Hero' emerging
from a tunnel.
(Phillips) $60 £30

Commemorative mug
showing the 'Express'
printed in brown, 4in.
high. (Phillips) $70 £35

DELFT

English delft dry drug jar, 7in. high. (Burrows & Day) $232 £120

Rare London delft figure of a cat. (Christie's) $8,080 £4,000

Rare delft mug, mid 18th century, 4½in. high. (Sotheby's) $594 £300

18th century Dutch delft tankard with pewter cover, 25cm. high. (Sotheby's) $901 £460

Dutch delft dish, circa 1700, 35cm. wide. (Sotheby's) $646 £340

Rare Dutch delft pitcher, circa 1691, 34cm. high. (Sotheby's) $3,528 £1,800

Attractive Bristol delft dish, circa 1720-30, 8in. diameter. (Sotheby's) $705 £360

18th century Dutch delft plaque, 39cm. long, repaired. (Sotheby's) $588 £300

Rare dated London delft plate, circa 1705, 8¼in. diam. (Sotheby's) $950 £480

Fulham period De Morgan ruby lustre charger, 11¾in. diam. (Christie's) $232 £120

Large De Morgan ovoid vase, 16¾in. high, circa 1888-97. (Sotheby's Belgravia) $1,470 £750

William De Morgan lustre dish, 14½in. diam., 1888-97. (Sotheby's Belgravia) $829 £420

Large De Morgan vase, circa 1888-97, 14¼in. high. (Sotheby's Belgravia) $1,176 £600

William De Morgan style cream glazed bowl of the late Fulham period, 16in. diam. (Geering & Colyer) $737 £370

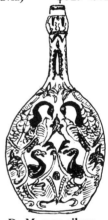

De Morgan silver lustre vase, circa 1888-97, 11¾in. high. (Sotheby's Belgravia) $705 £360

Fulham period De Morgan ochre lustre charger, 11¾in. diam. (Christie's) $814 £420

De Morgan copper lustre charger, 14½in. diam. (Christie's) $426 £220

William De Morgan copper lustre and ochre charger, 12¼in. diam. (Christie's) $465 £240

Commemorative Derby jug, circa 1812, 5½in. high. (Sotheby's) $148 £75

Rare Derby chamberstick, 1760-70, 3in. high. (Sotheby's) $297 £150

One of a pair of chocolate cups and covers. (Neales) $5,975 £3,080

One of a pair of slightly damaged Derby figures. (Burrows & Day) $181 £90

A pair of rare Derby plates, early 19th century, 8¾in. diameter. (Sotheby's) $1,293 £660

Derby figure of a boy under a tree, 6½in. high. (Burrows & Day) $227 £115

Large Derby urn of campana shape, circa 1820, 18½in. high. (Sotheby's) $798 £420

Pair of Derby 'Mansion House' dwarves, circa 1820, 7in. high. (Sotheby's) $901 £460

Royal Crown Derby 'Kedleston' ewer, circa 1905, 10¼in. high. (Sotheby's Belgravia) $205 £105

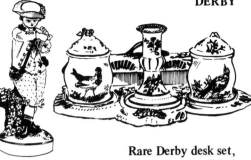

Early 19th century Derby tureen and cover, 14in. wide. (Christie's S. Kensington) $494 £260

Part of a Derby set of the four seasons, late 18th century, 7½in. high. (Sotheby's)
$2,376 £1,200

Rare Derby desk set, 8in. wide, circa 1758-60. (Sotheby's)
$1,306 £660

One of a pair of early 19th century Derby vases with named views. (King & Chasemore) $752 £380

Part of an attractive Bloor Derby dessert service, circa 1830, twenty-five pieces in all. (Sotheby's)
$3,724 £1,900

Derby figure of a boy with a dog at his feet. (Burrows & Day)
$232 £115

Royal Crown Derby Imari pattern watering can, 3in. high, 1911. (Sotheby's Belgravia)
$313 £160

One of a pair of Bloor Derby ice pails, circa 1830, 12in. high. (Sotheby's)
$901 £460

Derby ice pail and cover, late 18th century, 9in. high. (Sotheby's)
$514 £260

Royal Doulton figure
of a cobbler, dated for
1927, 7¾in. high.
(Sotheby's Belgravia)
$313 £160

Doulton Lambeth
stoneware 'rugby'
jug, 1883. (Ridde-
tt's) $272 £135

Royal Doulton jug
of a Regency beau.
(McCartney, Morris
& Barker) $222 £110

One of a pair of Doulton
stoneware vases, 13¼in.
high, 1880-1902.(Sotheby's
Belgravia) $254 £130

One of a pair of Doulton
stoneware vases, 1876,
10½in. high. (Sotheby's
Belgravia) $627 £320

Early 20th century large
Doulton stoneware jar-
diniere and stand, 54½in.
high. (Sotheby's Belgravia)
$1,666 £850

Royal Doulton Sung
vase, circa 1930, 12¾in.
high. (Sotheby's Bel-
gravia) $882 £450

Royal Doulton Sung figure
of Buddha, 6¾in. high,
1926. (Sotheby's Belgravia)
$529 £270

Large Doulton faience
moon flask, 14in. diam.,
circa 1882-91.
(Sotheby's Belgravia)
$529 £270

Royal Doulton Sung vase, circa 1930, 7in. high. (Sotheby's Belgravia) $254 £130

Royal Doulton figure of 'The Parson's Daughter', dated for 1930, 10in. high. (Sotheby's Belgravia) $176 £90

Royal Doulton jug of The Punch And Judy Man. (McCartney, Morris & Barker) $242 £120

Royal Doulton jardiniere and stand, circa 1930, 13½in. high. (Sotheby's Belgravia) $294 £150

One of a pair of Doulton stoneware vases, 9¾in. high, circa 1892. (Sotheby's Belgravia) $470 £240

Doulton stoneware ewer with silver mounts, 12½in. high, circa 1870. (Sotheby's Belgravia) $284 £145

One of a pair of Doulton stoneware vases, circa 1902, 9¾in. high. (Sotheby's Belgravia) $294 £150

Royal Doulton jug 'Hard of Hearing'. (McCartney, Morris & Barker) $484 £240

One of a pair of Doulton faience moon flasks, circa 1888, 9¼in. diameter. (Sotheby's Belgravia) $627 £320

125

One of a pair of Royal Doulton 'London Cry' figures, 6¾in. high, 1927. (Sotheby's Belgravia) $415 £210

Rare Doulton & Watts saltglazed reform flask, circa 1832, 7in. high. (Sotheby's Belgravia) $116 £60

Royal Doulton figure of 'A Victorian Lady', circa 1930, 7¾in. high, hair crack. (Sotheby's Belgravia) $79 £40

Royal Doulton figure of 'Miss 1927'. (McCartney, Morris & Barker) $747 £370

Set of four Royal Doulton graduated jugs, 16.5cm. to 23cm. high. (May, Whetter & Grose) $303 £150

Rare Doulton & Watts stoneware reform flask, circa 1832, 7¼in. high. (Sotheby's Belgravia) $155 £80

Royal Doulton figure of 'Pierette', 1924-38, 7in. high, slightly cracked. (Sotheby's Belgravia) $257 £130

Royal Doulton vase, date code for 1928, 11½in. high. (Sotheby's Belgravia) $217 £110

Royal Doulton 'Pantalettes' lady, impressed 1.10.50. (Phillips) $237 £120

One of a pair of nodding Dresden mandarins, damaged. (Sotheby's Belgravia) $1,513 £780

Late 19th century Dresden gilt metal mounted tankard, 25cm. high. (Sotheby's Belgravia)$316 £160

Dresden inkstand, circa 1860, 9in. wide. (Gray's Antique Market) $222 £110

Late 19th century Dresden gilt metal mounted ewer, 44cm. high.(Sotheby's Belgravia) $470 £240

Pair of early 19th century Dresden figures of a lady and a gallant. (Russell, Baldwin & Bright) $1,782 £900

Late 19th century Dresden plaque, 18cm. wide. (Sotheby's Belgravia) $1,881 £950

19th century hand-painted Dresden charger, 14in. diam. (Alfie's Antique Market) $386 £195

One of a pair of Dresden oviform vases and covers, 25½in. high. (Christie's)$1,746 £900

Dresden plate, circa 1880-90. (Alfie's Antique Market) $191 £95

Pair of Goldschneider book-ends, 1930's, 21cm. high.(Sotheby's Belgravia)$490 £250

Rare Du Paquier 'Hausmaler' teapot and cover, circa 1720-25, 13cm. high. (Sotheby's) $1,520 £800

Nymphenburg model of a parrot, circa 1850-62, 18.7cm. high.(Sotheby's Belgravia) $95 £48

Early 18th century Dutch tin-glazed bird cage, 39cm. high.(Sotheby's) $4,116 £2,100

19th century Continental figure of a nightwatchman.(Russell, Baldwin & Bright) $257 £130

Mid 18th century Zurich plate, 23cm. diameter. (Sotheby's) $1,782 £900

Late 18th century Marcolini part coffee service. (Sotheby's) $2,755 £1,450

Saintonage oval dish, 17th century, 31cm. long.(Sotheby's) $2,850 £1,500

Metal mounted D'Argyl Art Deco decorated earthenware vase, 28cm. high, 1920's. (Sotheby's Belgravia) $426 £220

Swiss tin-glazed chest of drawers, 17.5cm. high. (Sotheby's) $237 £120

Large Nove monteith, circa 1780-90, 49.2cm. wide. (Sotheby's) $988 £520

One of a pair of dated wet drug jars, circa 1616, 11¾in. high. (Neales)$2,626 £1,300

Mettlach vase, circa 1900-1910, 40cm. high.(Sotheby's Belgravia)$574 £290

Crefeld dated plaque, 31cm. high, repaired, 1797.(Sotheby's) $1,140 £600

One of a rare pair of Niderviller covered vases, 15¼in. high, circa 1780. (Warner, Sheppard & Wade) $1,225 £625

Wierner Werkstatte glazed earthenware triple vase, 23cm. high, circa 1910/1920.(Sotheby's Belgravia) $1,125 £580

Zurich spoon tray, circa 1770, 19.5cm. wide. (Sotheby's) $1,029 £520

Jean Dunand egg-shell vase, circa 1925, 23.5cm. high. (Sotheby's Belgravia) $1,980 £1,000

Turn Art Nouveau ceramic dish, Austrian, circa 1900, 44cm. long. (Sotheby's Belgravia) $514 £260

Goss model of 'A Dangerous Encounter', 4¼in. high, circa 1900. (Sotheby's Belgravia) $291 £150

Large Tournai dish decorated at The Hague, circa 1780, 40cm. diam. (Sotheby's) $1,485 £750

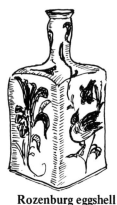

Mid 19th century large majolica urn, stand and pedestal, 150cm. high. (Sotheby's Belgravia) $940 £480

Pair Thuringian candlesticks, circa 1880. (Alfie's Antique Market) $656 £325

Rozenburg eggshell porcelain bottle vase. (Bonham's) $1,980 £1,000

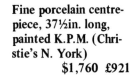

Massive Art Nouveau glazed earthenware jug, circa 1900, 92.1 cm. high. (Sotheby's Belgravia) $388 £200

Fine porcelain centrepiece, 37½in. long, painted K.P.M. (Christie's N. York) $1,760 £921

Rozenburg porcelain vase, circa 1890. (Bonham's) $1,683 £850

Oude Loosdrecht tea-bowl and saucer finely painted in brown, circa 1780.(Sotheby's) $435 £220

Pair of cold-painted plaster busts of Moroccans, circa 1890, signed Kochendorfer, 18¼in. high.(Sotheby's Belgravia) $342 £180

Oude Loosdrecht tea-bowl and saucer, circa 1780, in underglaze blue. (Sotheby's) $158 £80

Burmantofts jardiniere and stand, 50½in. high. (Bonham's) $513 £270

Very rare pair of Tournai figures of gardeners, 17cm. high, circa 1765. (Sotheby's) $5,742 £2,900

Burmantofts jardiniere and stand, 37½in. high, circa 1900. (Sotheby's) $352 £180

Austrian cold-painted plaster figure of a negro banjo player, circa 1900, 27in. high. (Sotheby's Belgravia) $1,691 £850

Mid 19th century painted plaster figure of a boy, 63in. high overall, Austrian. (Sotheby's Belgravia) $752 £380

Very rare Vezzi Venice teapot and cover, 15.3cm. high, circa 1723-27. (Sotheby's) $3,564 £1,800

Early 19th century famille rose jardiniere, 15¼in. high. (Sotheby's Belgravia) $960 £500

Late 19th century compressed famille rose bulb vase, 9in. high. (Sotheby's Belgravia) $250 £130

Late 19th century famille rose celadon garden seat, 18½in. high. (Sotheby's Belgravia) $922 £480

Famille rose figure of a mandarin, 19½in. high. (Neales) $444 £220

Pair of late famille rose ormolu mounted wall vases, 6¼in. high. (Christie's) $500 £257

One of a pair of late 19th century famille rose vases, 12½in. high. (Sotheby's Belgravia) $461 £240

Mid 19th century famille rose oviform vase, 17in. high. (Christie's) $250 £128

Late 19th century famille rose porcelain garden seat. (King & Chasemore) $1,274 £650

Late 19th century famille rose figure, 17in. high. (Sotheby's Belgravia) $192 £100

One of a pair of mid 19th century Chinese famille rose jars and covers. (King & Chasemore) $1,050 £520

Late 19th century famille rose dish, 19in. diam. (Sotheby's Belgravia) $442 £230

One of a pair of famille rose garden seats, 18½in. high.(Sotheby's Belgravia) $3,072 £1,600

Late 19th century famille rose vase, one of a pair, 22in. high.(Sotheby's Belgravia)$1,250 £650

Two late 19th century famille rose figures, 23¾in. high.(Sotheby's Belgravia) $960 £500

Late 19th century famille rose porcelain garden seat. (King & Chasemore) $1,176 £600

One of a pair of famille rose vases, 19th century.(Barber's) $1,045 £550

One of a pair of famille rose fish bowls, Ch'ien Lung.(Christie's) $14,850 £7,500

Large late 19th century famille rose vase, 23in. high. (Sotheby's Belgravia) $518 £270

FAMILLE VERTE

Transitional famille verte oviform jar, circa 1660, 24in. high. (Christie's)$1,000 £515

K'ang Hsi famille verte dish in the Imari style, 21¼in. diam.(Christie's) $4,620 £2,381

One of a pair of famille verte late 19th century vases, 14in. high. (Sotheby's Belgravia) $691 £360

One of a pair of K'ang Hsi famille verte vases and covers, 12¾in. high. (Christie's) $2,860 £1,474

Large late 19th century famille verte porcelain vase and cover. (King & Chasemore)$1,108 £560

One of a pair of famille verte rouleau vases, 17½in. high. (Christie's) $400 £206

Large late 19th century famille verte vase, 20¼in. high.(Sotheby's Belgravia) $960 £500

K'ang Hsi famille verte shallow dish, 13½in. diam. (Christie's) $3,520 £1,814

One of a pair of K'ang Hsi famille verte fruit mounds, 6¾in. high. (Christie's) $1,200 £618

K'ang Hsi famille verte
shallow food box and
cover from a tiered
set, 11in. diam.
(Christie's)$2,640 £1,360

K'ang Hsi famille verte
saucer dish, 13¾in. diam.
(Christie's) $1,000 £515

K'ang Hsi famille verte
porcelain tea caddy,
8.25cm. high. (King &
Chasemore) $845 £440

One of a pair of K'ang
Hsi famille verte wine
ewers and covers,
10¾in. high.(Christie's)
$2,640 £1,360

Massive famille verte
baluster vase, 33in.
high. (Christie's)
$3,000 £1,546

Pair of famille verte
Immortals, 18½in.
high. (Neales)
$1,386 £700

K'ang Hsi famille verte
fluted dish, 15in. diam.
(Christie's)
$2,420 £1,247

Large famille verte
teapot and cover,
10½in. high.
(Christie's)$700 £360

Late 19th century
famille verte dish,
16in. diam.(Sotheby's
Belgravia) $365 £190

135

Late 19th century French faience rhinoceros tureen and cover. (Sotheby's Belgravia) $194 £100

French terracotta bust, 11½in. high, circa 1700.(Sotheby's) $3,230 £1,700

19th century French hard paste porcelain box, 1¾in. long. (Gray's Antique Mews) $109 £54

Boulogne glazed pottery figure, 47.5cm. high, 1925. (Sotheby's Belgravia) $608 £320

Theodore Deck dish, 13¼in. diameter, circa 1880. (Sotheby's Belgravia) $294 £150

Paris porcelain figure of a woman, 31.8cm. high, circa 1920. (Sotheby's Belgravia) $123 £65

Late 19th century pair of French coloured biscuit figures, 40.6cm. high. (Sotheby's Belgravia) $509 £260

Late 19th century French ormolu mounted vase, 92cm. high. (King & Chasemore) $1,777 £880

Pair of French porcelain figures, circa 1870, 8½in. high. (Gray's Antique Mews) $257 £125

One of a pair of Jacob Petit vases, circa 1840, 21.6cm. high.(Sotheby's Belgravia) $490 £250

Mid 17th century Nevers double-handled urn, 33cm. high.   (Sotheby's) $1,411 £720

Late 19th century Theodore Deck duck, 12in. high. (Sotheby's Belgravia) $646 £330

20th century French porcelain tisaniere, 9in. high. (Sotheby's Belgravia) $237 £120

Boulogne crackle glazed pottery figure, 61cm. high, 1920's. (Sotheby's Belgravia) $570 £300

Limoges porcelain vase by L. Bernardaud & Cie., 14.5cm. high, circa 1923. (Sotheby's Belgravia) $228 £120

A pair of French biscuit figures of Spanish dancers, circa 1880, 43.5cm. high.(Sotheby's Belgravia) $891 £450

Small M. Raynaud Limoges jewelled vase and cover, circa 1920, 11.4cm. high. (Sotheby's Belgravia) $254 £130

Rare pair of 19th century French figures of tennis players. (Alfie's Antique Market) $544 £275

Mettlach tankard, circa 1910, 19.8cm. high.(Sotheby's Belgravia) $509 £260

Mid 16th century Cologne stoneware 'Bartmann' krug, 20cm. high. (Sotheby's) $1,482 £780

Frankenthal coffee pot, circa 1760, 10¼in. high. (Graves, Son & Pilcher) $2,079 £1,050

Frankfurt pewter mounted jug, circa 1700, 21cm. high. (Sotheby's) $570 £300

Hertwig & Co. Katzhutte figure of a showgirl, 1930's, 50.1cm. high. (Sotheby's Belgravia) $313 £160

18th century South German tankard with pewter foot, 24.5cm. high. (Sotheby's) $940 £480

Rare Hochst figure of Hearing, circa 1755, 14cm. high. (Sotheby's)$1,881 £950

Late 16th century Hafnerware green-glazed stove tile, 22cm. (Sotheby's) $509 £260

17th century armorial Rhenish bellarmine, 23cm. high. (Sotheby's) $176 £90

Small Rozenburg vase, circa 1900, 11cm. high. (Sotheby's Belgravia) $271 £140

German porcelain dog cream jug, circa 1900. (Alfie's Antique Market) $39 £20

One of a pair of German pot-pourri dishes. (King & Chasemore) $396 £200

South German faience pewter mounted tankard, circa 1744, 20cm. high. (Sotheby's) $1,330 £700

Garniture of three Frankenthal vases, circa 1777. (Christie's) $5,572 £2,800

Rosenthal porcelain group of a young woman and a fawn, 34cm. high, 1930's. (Sotheby's Belgravia) $426 £220

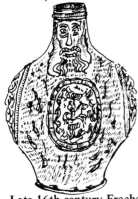

Late 16th century Frechen armorial bellarmine, 19cm. high. (Sotheby's) $3,136 £1,600

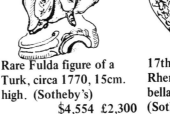

Rare Fulda figure of a Turk, circa 1770, 15cm. high. (Sotheby's) $4,554 £2,300

17th century armorial Rhenish stoneware bellarmine, 8½in. high. (Sotheby's) $431 £220

Early 20th century Goss oven, 3in. high.(Sotheby's Belgravia) $271 £140

Early 20th century Goss model of a Shetland pony, 3½in. high. (Sotheby's Belgravia) $237 £120

Goss model of Dove Cottage, early 20th century, 4in. high. (Sotheby's Belgravia) $232 £120

Early 20th century Carew Ancient Cross, 6in. high.(Sotheby's Belgravia) $232 £120

Early 20th century Goss model of St. Nicholas Chapel, 2in. high. (Sotheby's Belgravia) $122 £62

Early 20th century Goss model of the Iona Ancient Cross, 8½in. high.(Sotheby's Belgravia) $291 £150

20th century Goss model of the Old Market House, Ledbury, 2¾in. high. (Sotheby's Belgravia) $194 £100

Early 20th century Goss model of John Knox's House, 4in. high. (Sotheby's Belgravia) $698 £360

Early 20th century Goss model of the First and Last House in England, 2½in. high.(Sotheby's Belgravia) $62 £32

Han dynasty unglazed
vase, 15½in. high.
(Christie's)
$1,980 £1,020

Unglazed pottery head
from the Han dynasty,
4in. high. (Christie's)
$554 £280

Han dynasty unglazed
pottery triceratops,
10½in. long.
(Christie's)
$2,869 £1,478

HOZAN

One of a pair of Hozan
earthenware vases,
circa 1900, 6¼in. high.
(Sotheby's Belgravia)
$442 £230

Late 19th century Hozan
Satsuma dish with fluted
rim, 10in. diameter.
(Sotheby's Belgravia)
$384 £200

One of a pair of
Hozan vases, circa
1900, 7½in. high.
(Sotheby's Belgravia)
$365 £190

IMARI

18th century Chinese Imari part
dinner service of twenty-one
pieces. (Humberts, King &
Chasemore) $13,965 £7,350

Japanese Imari
vase, circa 1870,
18½in. high.(Gray's
Antique Market)
$565 £280

A fine quality, large
Imari dish. (Christie's
S. Kensington)
$2,673 £1,350

Imari porcelain
goldfish bowl.
(Russell, Baldwin
& Bright)
$1,485 £750

Late 19th century
umbrella stand of
cylindrical form,
24½in. high.
(Sotheby's Belgravia)
$845 £440

Late 17th century Ko-
Imari bottle in Kutani
enamels.(Sotheby's N.
York) $8,500 £4,300

Large late 19th century
Imari dish in under-
glaze blue, 24¼in. diam.
(Sotheby's Belgravia)
$960 £500

Imari dish, circa 1900,
16in. high.(Sotheby's
Belgravia)$230 £120

Late 19th century Imari
bowl decorated in under-
glaze blue, 13¼in. diameter.
(Sotheby's Belgravia)
$653 £340

One of a pair of
Imari vases in blue,
white and gold,
10in. high.(David
Symonds)$111 £57

One of a pair of late
19th century Imari
vases, 18½in. high.
(Sotheby's Belgravia)
$1,190 £620

Late 19th century
Imari jardiniere,
12½in. high.
(Sotheby's Bel-
gravia)$1,037 £540

Late 19th century Imari
porcelain vase, one of a
pair, Japanese, 61.5cm.
high.   (Sotheby's)
$1,425 £720

Fine Japanese Imari
charger, 23½in. diam.
(H. Spencer & Sons)
$1,414 £700

Japanese Imari vase
from the late 19th
century, 62cm. high.
(King & Chasemore)
$1,097 £560

Mid 19th century
Imari covered vase,
32½in. high.
(Sotheby's Belgravia)
$2,688 £1,400

Late 19th century Imari
plate, 14½in. diameter.
(Sotheby's Belgravia)
$288 £150

One of a pair of Imari
Arita porcelain bottles,
circa 1700. (King &
Chasemore)
$3,960 £2,000

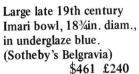

One of a pair of late 19th
century Imari vases and
covers, 12¾in. high.
(Sotheby's Belgravia)
$365 £190

Large late 19th century
Imari bowl, 18¾in. diam.,
in underglaze blue.
(Sotheby's Belgravia)
$461 £240

One of a pair of late
19th century Imari
vases, 11¾in. high.
(Sotheby's Belgravia)
$691 £360

Deruta vase, circa
1520, 27.8cm. high,
with two handles.
(Sotheby's)
$3,366 £1,700

Early 19th century cir-
cular Roman mosaic
plaque, 7.3cm. diam.
(Sotheby's)
$737 £380

Faenza drug jar, circa
1500, 29.3cm. high,
decorated in blue,
green and ochre.
(Sotheby's)
$1,188 £600

Gubbio lustred tondino,
1524, 39.9cm. diameter,
decorated by Maestro
Giorgio Andreoli.
(Sotheby's)$30,690 £15,500

Early 17th century
Palermo allevello,
29.3cm. high.
(Sotheby's)
$1,332 £680

Early 16th century
North Italian 'Sgraf-
fiato' dish, 37cm.
diam. (Sotheby's)
$3,960 £2,000

Late 19th century
Italian faience figure,
39in. high.(Notting-
ham Auction Mart)
$396 £200

Urbino 'Istoriato' dish,
about 1540, 30.3cm.
diam. (Sotheby's)
$1,584 £800

Late 15th/early 16th
century Sicilian albar-
ello, 31cm. high.
(Sotheby's)
$1,782 £900

Large Venice drug jar, second half 16th century, 33cm. high. (Sotheby's) $9,900 £5,000

Urbino majolica dish showing the story of Pluto and Proserpine, circa 1530, 12in. diam. (Sotheby's) $49,000 £25,000

Large late 19th century majolica jardinière with a stand. (Sotheby's Belgravia) $525 £260

Mid 16th century Urbino dish after a design by Battista Franco, 44.3cm. diam. (Sotheby's) $4,116 £2,100

Late 15th century Faenza albarello of cylindrical shape, 19.5cm. high. (Sotheby's) $1,584 £800

Urbino 'Istoriato' dish, 25.5cm. diam., circa 1537, painted by Francesco Xanto Avelli. (Sotheby's) $9,504 £4,800

Early 16th century Faenza albarello, 20.5cm. high. (Sotheby's) $1,584 £800

Interesting early majolica dish, mid 13th century, 19cm. diam. (Sotheby's) $2,970 £1,500

Dated Tuscan albarello, 13.3cm. high, 1600. (Sotheby's) $399 £210

One of a pair of lobed Fukagawa bowls, circa 1900, 10¼in. long. (Sotheby's Belgravia) $442 £230

Early 20th century Japanese incense burner and cover, 12in. high.(Sotheby's Belgravia)$480 £250

Japanese Imari polychrome bowl, circa 1720, 8½in. diam. (Gray's Antique Mews) $707 £350

Late 19th century yellow ground Fukagawa vase, 18in. high. (Sotheby's Belgravia) $1,248 £650

Late 19th century Kinkizan koro and cover, 16¾in. high.(Sotheby's Belgravia) $1,440 £750

One of a pair of late 19th century Fukagawa vases and covers, 16in. high. (Sotheby's Belgravia)$1,382 £720

One of a pair of Hichozan Shinpo bottle vases, late 19th century, 10in. high. (Sotheby's Belgravia) $576 £300

Fukagawa bowl, circa 1900, with incurved rim, 15½in. high. (Sotheby's Belgravia) $849 £440

One of a pair of Hichozan Shinpo vases, circa 1870, 17in. high. (Sotheby's Belgravia) $1,382 £720

K'ang Hsi conical form blue and white porcelain bowl, 21.5cm. diam. (King & Chasemore) $363 £180

K'ang Hsi period famille verte dish, 16in. long. (Gray's Antique Mews) $1,212 £600

One of a pair of K'ang Hsi period blue and white plates, 8in. diam., circa 1700. (Gray's Antique Mews) $505 £250

One of a pair of 19th century famille verte Buddhistic lions. (Christie's S. Kensington) $980 £500

Chinese K'ang Hsi plate, 1662, 9in. diam. (Gray's Antique Mews) $242 £120

One of a pair of blue and white K'ang Hsi vases. (R. L. Lowery & Partners) $1,131 £560

K'ang Hsi period blue and white jar, 17in. high, 17th century. (Gray's Antique Market) $1,300 £650

Late 19th century K'ang Hsi blue and white plate, 37.5cm. diam. (Sotheby's Belgravia) $147 £75

Large blue and white Yen-yen vase of the K'ang Hsi period, 17¼in. high. (Gray's Antique Mews) $848 £420

147

K'ang Hsi blue and
white bowl, 6in.
diameter.(Christie's)
$1,000 £515

K'ang Hsi peach-
bloom glazed brush-
washer, 4½in. diam.
(Christie's)
$1,200 £618

K'ang Hsi mono-
chrome shallow
bowl, 4¾in. diam.
(Christie's)
$300 £154

K'ang Hsi blue and
white saucer dish,
14in. diameter.
(Christie's)
$350 £180

K'ang Hsi blue
and white bottle
vase, 17¾in. high.
(Christie's)
$800 £412

Blue and white
K'ang Hsi saucer
dish, 13½in. diam.
(Christie's)
$450 £231

K'ang Hsi blue
and white beaker
vase, 18in. high.
(Christie's)
$1,000 £515

Late 19th century
K'ang Hsi blue and
white dish, 14½in.
diameter.(Sotheby's
Belgravia)$154 £80

Early K'ang Hsi
baluster vase,
18½in. high.
(Christie's)
$5,280 £2,721

K'ang Hsi egg and spinach bowl, 7¼in. diam. (Christie's) $800 £412

Late 19th century K'ang Hsi blue and white jar and cover, one of a pair, 11in. high.(Sotheby's Belgravia) $576 £300

K'ang Hsi blanc-de-chine small dish. (Smith-Woolley & Perry) $97 £50

One of a pair of K'ang Hsi blue and white dishes, 15in. diameter. (Christie's) $2,200 £1,134

K'ang Hsi blue and white bottle vase, 7½in. high. (Christie's)$160 £82

K'ang Hsi blue and white saucer dish, 13½in. diameter. (Christie's)$450 £231

K'ang Hsi blue and white stem cup, 5½in. high.(Christie's) $400 £206

K'ang Hsi rare under-glaze blue and red jardiniere, 8¾in. diameter.(Christie's) $1,200 £618

K'ang Hsi blue and white beaker vase, 18in. high. (Christie's) $1,000 £515

KINKOZAN

Kinkozan vase of
spheroid form, circa
1900, 4½in. high.
(Sotheby's Belgravia)
$403 £210

Unusual Kinkozan dish,
circa 1900, in three sec-
tions, 12½in. high.
(Sotheby's Belgravia)
$1,248 £650

Good Kinkozan vase,
circa 1900, 12in. high.
(Sotheby's Belgravia)
$1,728 £900

KOREAN

Two Korean pottery
vessels with pierced
bases. (McCartney,
Morris & Barker)
$1,089 £550

16th/17th century Yi
dynasty Korean nona-
gonal pear shaped bottle,
11in. high. (Christie's)
$1,650 £850

12th century Korean
celadon wine ewer,
7in. high. (Christie's)
$356 £180

KUANG HSU

One of a pair of
Kuang Hsu famille
rose shallow bowls,
6in. diameter.
(Christie's)
$1,250 £644

Kuang Hsu fine blue
and white bowl, 8¼in.
diameter. (Christie's)
$1,430 £737

One of a pair of Kuang
Hsu famille rose bowls,
5¾in. diam. (Christie's)
$360 £185

Late 17th century Ko-Kutani bottle.(Sotheby's N. York)
$17,000 £8,550

17th/18th century Ko-Kutani dish, one of a set of six, 16cm. wide. (King & Chasemore)
$269 £140

Late 19th century Kutani drummer boy, 9½in. high. (Sotheby's Belgravia)$250 £130

One of a pair of Kutani vases, circa 1870, 9¾in. high. (Sotheby's Belgravia)
$634 £330

One of a pair of late 19th century blue and white Kutani dishes, 30½in. diameter. (Sotheby's Belgravia)
$1,824 £950

One of a pair of late 19th century Kutani vases, 9¾in. high. (Sotheby's Belgravia)$192 £100

Late 19th century Kutani dish, 13¼in. diam. (Sotheby's Belgravia)$192 £100

Late 19th century Kutani vase with ovoid body, 18in. high. (Sotheby's Belgravia)$461 £240

One of a pair of late 19th century Kutani incense burners, 5in. high. (Sotheby's Belgravia) $557 £290

Rare Lambeth polychrome jar, circa 1700, 4½in. high, with coiled hoop handles. (Sotheby's) $910 £460

Lambeth delft dish, circa 1784. (Christie's) $543 £280

Early Lambeth blue and white apothecary's pill slab, 1687. (Christie's) $9,900 £5,000

LEACH

Bernard Leach stoneware vase, circa 1935, 6¼in. high.(Sotheby's Belgravia)$450 £230

Good Bernard Leach stoneware vase, circa 1960, 11in. high. (Sotheby's Belgravia) $1,920 £980

Bernard Leach incised pot. (W. H. Lane & Sons) $1,117 £570

Bernard Leach stoneware vase, 14¼in. high, circa 1960. (Sotheby's Belgravia) $1,960 £1,000

Bernard Leach stoneware jug, 10½in. high, circa 1965. (Sotheby's Belgravia) $980 £500

Bernard Leach stoneware bottle vase, 11¾in. high, circa 1960. (Sotheby's Belgravia) $352 £180

Late 18th century Leeds
oval creamware plate,
9in. diam. (Nottingham
Auction Mart) $47 £24

Creamware commemorative
ale jug, possibly Leeds,
1776, 8½in. high.
(Sotheby's) $514 £260

One of a pair of unusual
Leeds creamware plates,
circa 1780, 9¾in. diam.
(Sotheby's) $594 £300

LIVERPOOL

Liverpool mug of
cylindrical shape,
circa 1760, 4¾in.
high. (Sotheby's)
      $509 £260

One of a pair of Liver-
pool delft tiles, 1758-
61. (Sotheby's)
      $554 £280

Cylindrical Liver-
pool mug, 4¾in.
high, circa 1760-65.
(Sotheby's)
      $627 £320

One of a pair of Liverpool
delft 'shipping' tiles,
signed Sadler, 5in. square,
circa 1758-61.(Sotheby's)
      $633 £320

Liverpool delft jug,
circa 1760-70, 7¾in.
high. (Sotheby's)
      $836 £440

One of a pair of Liverpool
delft tiles, signed J. Sadler,
5in. square, circa 1758-61.
(Sotheby's) $554 £280

Ludwigsburg group
of dancers, circa
1765, 14.5cm. high.
(Sotheby's)
$792 £400

Ludwigsburg group of a
river god, circa 1770,
20cm. wide. (Sotheby's)
$990 £500

Late 19th century
Ludwigsburg group
of figures, 25.5cm.
high.(Sotheby's
Belgravia)$415 £210

LUSTRE

Sunderland lustre jug,
circa 1840, 7¼in.
high. (Sotheby's Bel-
gravia) $198 £100

Pilkington's Royal Lan-
castrian lustre vase,
1908, 8¾in. high.
(Sotheby's Belgravia)
$274 £140

Iranian lustre jar,
circa 1270, 12½in.
high. (Sotheby's)
$9,950 £5,000

Royal Lancastrian
lustre vase, circa
1910, 9¾in. high.
(Sotheby's Belgravia)
$198 £100

Good Clement lustre
charger, circa 1900,
48cm. diam.
(Sotheby's Belgravia)
$2,574 £1,300

Kashan ewer in
lustre, with con-
temporary design.
(Sotheby's)
$30,300 £15,000

Martin Brothers face jug, 7½in. high, dated 7.1898.(Sotheby's Belgravia) $607 £310

Large Martin Brothers bird, 12¾in. high, dated 4.1884. (Sotheby's Belgravia) $2,352 £1,200

Martin Brothers tyg, 7in. high, dated 9.1911.(Sotheby's Belgravia)$725 £370

Martin Brothers bird, 1905, 23.3cm. high. (King & Chasemore) $1,632 £850

Martin Brothers tankard, 1874, 17cm. high. (King & Chasemore) $691 £360

Martin Brothers bird with blue and brown plumage, 1897, 29.5cm. high.(King & Chasemore) $2,277 £1,150

Martin Brothers vase, dated 7.1890, 9in. high. (Sotheby's Belgravia) $450 £230

Martin Brothers jug, 8½in. high, 1887.(Sotheby's Belgravia) $235 £120

Martin Brothers face jug, 6½in. high, dated 1.1.1903. (Sotheby's Belgravia) $450 £230

Mason's inkstand, circa 1830-40. (Alfie's Antique Market)$376 £190

MENNECY

Impressive Mason's porcelain vase, circa 1810, 25½in. high, small repair. (Sotheby's) $1,019   £520

Large Mason's ironstone blue and white platter, circa 1820. (Alfie's Antique Market)$139 £69

Mid 18th century Mennecy pomade pot and cover, 8.6cm. high. (Sotheby's)$158 £80

Mid 18th century Mennecy mustard pot and cover, 10cm. high. (Sotheby's)$534 £270

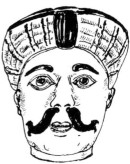

Mid 18th century Mennecy snuff box, 7cm. high, with silver mounts. (Sotheby's) $792 £400

Rare Mennecy snuff box in white, mid 18th century, 4.5cm. high. (Sotheby's)$455 £239

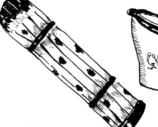

Mid 18th century Mennecy needle case, 9cm. long, with hinged silver mount.(Sotheby's) $633 £320

Mennecy snuff box, circa 1770, 9cm. long. (Sotheby's) $554 £280

Set of three 19th century Meissen figures of the seasons, 5½in. high. (Messenger, May & Baverstock) $453 £220

One of a pair of late 19th century Meissen chamber candlesticks, 12.8cm. long. (Sotheby's Belgravia) $607 £310

Late 19th century Meissen composite condiment set on tray. (Sotheby's Belgravia) $1,215 £620

19th century Meissen group of the Apple Pickers, 10½in. high. (Messenger, May & Baverstock) $741 £360

Nine-piece Meissen porcelain 'Monkey Band' group, circa 1900. (D. M. Nesbit & Co.) $543 £280

19th century Meissen group of the Apple Pickers, 11in. high. (Messenger, May & Baverstock) $762 £370

Late 19th century Meissen group of the Capture of the Tritons, 31.2cm. high. (Sotheby's Belgravia) $588 £300

Late 19th century Meissen figure of a Turkish dignitary, 41.9cm. high. (Sotheby's Belgravia) $1,215 £620

19th century Meissen centrepiece, 8in. high. (Messenger, May & Baverstock) $659 £320

Mid 19th century Meissen bust of a child, 26.1cm. high.(Sotheby's Belgravia) $392 £200

19th century Meissen porcelain figure. (Humberts, King & Chasemore)
$475 £250

Meissen silver gilt mounted tankard and cover, circa 1750.(Christie's)
$1,287 £650

One of a pair of late Meissen two-handled baluster vases, covers and stands, 27½in. high. (Christie's)
$582 £300

Mid 19th century large Meissen figure of The Tailor, 44cm. high. (Sotheby's Belgravia)
$2,871 £1,450

White Meissen porcelain figure of a parrot, 1730's, 26¼in. high. (Sotheby's)
$207,900 £105,000

Meissen swan tureen, circa 1745, 14½in. high.(Christie's)
$7,600 £4,000

Late 19th century Meissen porcelain figures of two children.(Sotheby's Belgravia) $633 £320

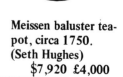

Meissen baluster teapot, circa 1750. (Seth Hughes)
$7,920 £4,000

Meissen tureen and cover. (Sotheby's Belgravia)
$3,564 £1,800

Late Meissen crinoline group of Le Marchands de Coeurs, 12½in. high. (Christie's)
$1,125 £580

A pair of Meissen tea caddies, 19th century. (Gray's Antique Market) $356 £180

Good Meissen swan modelled with white plumage, circa 1870, 31cm. high. (Sotheby's Belgravia)
$1,029 £520

Mid 18th century Meissen figure of a young woman, 19cm. high. (Sotheby's)
$1,026 £540

Meissen group modelled by J. J. Kaendler, 1744, 8½in. high.(Sotheby's)
$12,740 £6,500

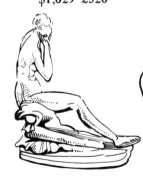

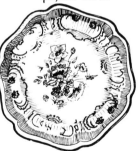

Meissen porcelain figure, 30.5cm. high, circa 1930's. (Sotheby's Belgravia)
$659 £340

One of twelve late Meissen scale-green ground dinner plates, 10½in. diameter. (Christie's)
$1,649 £850

Meissen group of a soldier and companion, 1763-74, 18.5cm. high. (Sotheby's)
$1,140 £600

Meissen pug dog,
circa 1745, 15.3cm.
high. (Sotheby's)
$1,584 £800

Good Bottger/Meissen
teabowl and saucer,
circa 1725.(Sotheby's)
$1,881 £950

One of a pair of Meissen
gros bleu ground vases,
circa 1860, 19.1cm. high.
(Sotheby's Belgravia)
$686 £350

Meissen figure of 'The
Tailor', 8in. high.
(Messenger, May &
Baverstock)$444 £220

Meissen table, 30in.
high. (Christie's S.
Kensington)
$3,880 £2,000

One of a pair of ormolu
mounted Meissen globu-
lar jars, 6½in. high, circa
1725. (Sotheby's)
$990 £500

Late 19th century pair
of Meissen figures,
19.5cm. high.(Sotheby's
Belgravia) $712 £360

Meissen figure of a Tur-
kish woman, mid 18th
century, 13.5cm. high.
(Sotheby's)$1,029 £520

Pair of mid 19th cen-
tury Meissen figures,
19½in. high.(Neales)
$1,187 £625

Meissen chocolate pot, circa 1735, 14cm. high. (Sotheby's) $3,366 £1,700

19th century pair of Meissen 'Bolognese' dogs, 15.5cm. high. (Sotheby's Belgravia) $653 £320

Meissen teapot and cover, Augsburg decorated, 12cm. high, circa 1720. (Sotheby's)$1,980 £1,000

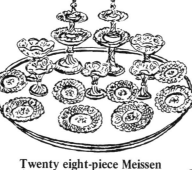

Meissen coffee pot and cover, 27.3cm. high, circa 1763-74. (Sotheby's)$772 £390

Twenty eight-piece Meissen dessert service. (Bonsor Pennington) $3,939 £1,950

Gilt metal mounted Meissen double snuff box of barrel shape, 3½in. high, circa 1750 (Seth Hughes) $3,826 £1,950

Pair of late Meissen figures, 10½in. high. (Christie's) $1,008 £520

Meissen needlecase with silver gilt mounts, circa 1745, 14.7cm. long.(Sotheby's) $633 £320

Pair of late Meissen figures, minor repairs, 12½in. high.(Christie's) $931 £480

14th century Ming celadon deep bowl, 8in. diameter. (Christie's)
$1,320 £680

Blue and white Ming vase, with brass mounts, slightly damaged. (Burrows & Day)
$194 £100

Fine Ming blue and white deep bowl, 6¾in. diameter. (Christie's)
$6,160 £3,175

Rare Ming blue and white Mei P'ing, circa 1500, 12¼in. high. (Christie's)
$9,900 £5,103

Chia Ching Ming blue and white double gourd vase, 11in. high. (Christie's)
$1,800 £927

Ming dynasty pale grey granite head of a Lohan, 10in. high. (Christie's)
$5,280 £2,721

15th century Ming carved red cinnabar lacquer circular box and cover, 3in. diam. (Christie's)
$1,485 £765

Ming dynasty figure of Kuan Ti, God of War. (Sotheby's)
$12,672 £6,400

Rare Ming blue and white deep tripod bulb bowl, 13½in. diam. (Christie's)
$2,420 £1,247

Rare Minton 'Henri Deux' earthenware salt, circa 1870, 7in. wide. (Sotheby's Belgravia) $514 £260

One of a pair of 19th century Minton tiles, 6in. square. (Gray's Antique Mews) $81 £40

Minton majolica 'game' tureen and cover, 14½in. long, dated for 1858. (Sotheby's Belgravia) $475 £240

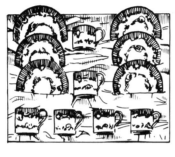

Minton vase, 1901, 19½in. high. (Gray's Antique Mews) $323 £160

Cased Minton coffee set, circa 1916. (Vost's) $146 £76

Minton pate-sur-pate vase, 7¾in. high, circa 1891-1902. (Sotheby's Belgravia) $1,029 £520

Part of a large Minton dinner service, early 20th century, one hundred and fifteen pieces in all. (Sotheby's Belgravia) $495 £250

Minton porcelain plaque, circa 1870, 37cm. high. (King & Chasemore) $365 £190

Minton bowl held up by two cherubs, 9in. high. (Gray's Antique Mews) $171 £85

MOORCROFT

William Moorcroft four-handled vase made for Liberty & Co.(Christie's S. Kensington)$444 £220

Moorcroft vase, 9in. high, circa 1920. (Alfie's Antique Market) $346 £175

Moorcroft 'Tudric' pewter mounted bowl, 8½in. diam., 1920's. (Sotheby's Belgravia) $333 £170

William Moorcroft Burslem pomegranate vase, 12½in. high.(Alfie's Antique Market) $216 £107

ORIENTAL

One of a pair of Moorcroft 'Tudric' pewter mounted vases, 9in. high, 1920's.(Sotheby's Belgravia) $411 £210

One of a pair of Moorcroft vases, circa 1915, 12¼in. high.(Sotheby's Belgravia) $294 £150

Large figure of the god Shou Lao, 28in. high. (Christie's) $3,850 £1,984

17th century Tibetan seated Buddha, 6¾in. high. (Gray's Antique Mews) $1,818 £900

Late 19th century baluster vase, one of a pair, 18in. high. (Sotheby's Belgravia) $576 £300

One of a pair of late orange glazed figures of parrots, 7¾in. high. (Christie's) $400 £206

Porcelain bottle with coral bead stopper. (Christie's)$160 £83

Late 19th century royal blue garden seat, 18¼in. high. (Sotheby's Belgravia) $883 £460

Late 19th century vase with pierced wooden cover and stand, 20in. high. (Sotheby's Belgravia) $576 £300

Two enamelled figures, circa 1900, 14in. high. (Sotheby's Belgravia) $614 £320

One of a pair of late 19th century baluster vases, 18½in. high. (Sotheby's Belgravia) $719 £370

One of three porcelain bottles. (Christie's)$160 £83

One of a pair of late 19th century koros and covers, 4in. high. (Sotheby's Belgravia) $422 £220

One of a pair of Oriental vases and covers on marble plinths, 36in. high. (Worsfolds) $2,828 £1,400

165

One of a pair of late 19th century snarling Shi-Shi, 8in. high. (Sotheby's Belgravia) $346 £180

Earthenware koro and pierced silver cover, 5½in. high.(Sotheby's Belgravia)$1,440 £750

Multi-coloured glazed pottery group, 23in. high. (Phillips) $1,010 £500

Good mid 19th century earthenware vase, 12½in. high. (Sotheby's Belgravia) $2,208 £1,150

One of a 20th century pair of earthenware elephants, 53cm. high. (Sotheby's Belgravia) $646 £330

Unusual earthenware vase, circa 1870, 15¾in. high. (Sotheby's Belgravia) $442 £230

One of a pair of earthenware vases, circa 1870, 12in. high.(Sotheby's Belgravia)$480 £250

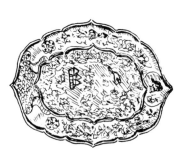

Earthenware dish, circa 1860, 13in. long. (Sotheby's Belgravia) $442 £230

One of a pair of large vases, circa 1870, 21¾in. high. (Sotheby's Belgravia) $1,344 £700

One of a pair of late 19th century Paris pastille burners, 17.8cm. high. (Sotheby's Belgravia) $313 £160

Unusual pair of mid 19th century Paris figures of Victoria and Albert, 31cm. high.(Sotheby's Belgravia) $792 £400

Mid 19th century Paris Rihouet-decorated 'trembleuse' cup and saucer.(Sotheby's Belgravia) $254 £130

Paris porcelain extending lamp stand, 1.26cm. high. (King & Chasemore) $1,616 £800

Pair of 19th century Paris porcelain figures, 24½in. high. (Buckell & Ballard) $1,634 £860

One of a pair of late 19th century Paris 'Schneeballen' vases and covers, 38cm. high. (Sotheby's Belgravia) $415 £210

Paris raspberry ground cache-pot, circa 1870, 18.5cm. high.(Sotheby's Belgravia) $237 £120

Good Delvaux Paris porcelain Art Deco vase, circa 1925, 31.5cm. high. (Sotheby's Belgravia) $594 £300

Late 19th century Paris vase, one of a pair, 51cm. high. (Sotheby's Belgravia) $784 £400

Pot lid 'The Bull Fight' in good condition.(Sotheby's Belgravia) $814 £420

Good small lid 'Little Red Riding Hood'. (Sotheby's Belgravia) $58 £30

Medium pot lid 'Contrast', in good condition.(Sotheby's Belgravia) $54 £28

Medium sized pot lid of 'Our Pets' with registration mark.(Sotheby's Belgravia)$831 £420

Small pot lid, in good condition, showing shells. (Sotheby's Belgravia) $106 £55

Medium pot lid 'The Late Prince Consort'. (Sotheby's Belgravia) $58 £30

English pot lid 'The Net Mender', circa 1860, 4½in. diam. (Gray's Antique Market) $131 £65

Medium small lid depicting bear hunting.(Sotheby's Belgravia)$659 £340

Rare small lid with double line border 'Mother and Daughters', in good condition.(Sotheby's Belgravia) $291 £150

Pot lid showing the
Grand International
Building of 1851.
(Sotheby's Belgravia)
$148 £75

Small pot lid called
'The Bear Pit',
slightly cracked.
(Sotheby's Belgravia)
$95 £48

Pot lid 'Our Home',
one of only two
known examples.
(Phillips)
$5,148 £2,600

Medium pot lid of
'HRH The Prince of
Wales Visiting the
Tomb of Washington'
(Sotheby's Belgravia)
$77 £40

Large pot lid of
Queen Victoria
on balcony.
(Sotheby's Belgravia)
$388 £200

Small lid with scene
of bear shooting, in
good condition.
(Sotheby's Belgravia)
$89 £45

Large pot lid with
fancy border,
showing Wellington.
(Sotheby's Belgravia)
$62 £32

Small pot lid show-
ing bear hunting,
slightly cracked.
(Sotheby's Belgravia)
$118 £60

Medium pot lid,
'England's Pride'.
(Sotheby's Belgravia)
$89 £45

PRATTWARE

Prattware 'serpent' pipe, circa 1780-90, 8¾in. long.(Sotheby's) $336 £170

Attractive Prattware figure of a lion, 9½in. long, circa 1780-'90. (Sotheby's) $792 £400

Prattware malachite ground mug 'The Smokers', circa 1860, 4¼in. high.(Sotheby's Belgravia) $145 £75

Pratt type model of 'The Hearty Good Fellow' jug and cover, 11in. high. (Neales) $352 £180

Part of a Pratt type pottery dessert service. (McCartney, Morris & Barker) $337 £167

Prattware 'Hearty Good Fellow' jug, circa 1775, 11in. high. (Sotheby's) $342 £180

Prattware watch stand, circa 1780, 8½in. high. (Sotheby's) $494 £260

Part of a Prattware dessert service, circa 1860. (Sotheby's Belgravia)$232 £120

Prattware cockerel standing 10in. tall. (Sotheby Bearne) $756 £390

Part of a two hundred and thirteen piece ironstone dinner and dessert service, circa 1820. (Sotheby's) $2,871 £1,450

Large Ridgway parian group of Venus and Cupid, 1858, 18¾in. high. (Sotheby's Belgravia) $333 £170

Part of a Ridgway dessert service, forty pieces, circa 1830. (Sotheby's) $297 £150

Part of a Ridgway tea service of forty pieces, circa 1820-25. (Sotheby's Belgravia) $431 £220

One of a pair of Ridgway ice pails, covers and liners, circa 1815-20. (Sotheby's) $686 £350

ROCKINGHAM

Rare Rockingham dish, circa 1830, 9½in. wide. (Sotheby's) $431 £220

Rockingham claret ground fluted helmet shaped basket, circa 1835. (Christie's) $404 £200

19th century dish from a Rockingham dessert set. (Neales) $1,615 £850

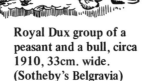

20th century Royal
Dux bust of a young
woman, 48.8cm. high.
(Sotheby's Belgravia)
$1,019 £520

Royal Dux group of a
peasant and a bull, circa
1910, 33cm. wide.
(Sotheby's Belgravia)
$297 £150

Royal Dux Art
Deco lady. (Alfie's
Antique Market)
$297 £150

Royal Dux group of
retour de chasse, circa
1910, 56.4cm. high.
(Sotheby's Belgravia)
$509 £260

Unusual pair of Royal Dux
'clown' figures, 23.4cm.
high, circa 1910.(Sotheby's
Belgravia) $376 £190

Royal Dux group of
Tango dancers, 1930's,
37.5cm. high.
(Sotheby's Belgravia)
$411 £210

Pair of 20th century Royal
Dux figures, 41.5cm. high.
(Sotheby's Belgravia)
$415 £210

Royal Dux camel
group, circa 1910,
45.2cm. high.
(Sotheby's Belgravia)
$509 £260

Pair of Royal Dux fig-
ures of a goatherd and
shepherdess. (King &
Chasemore) $969 £480

Ruskin high-fired vase,
14½in. high, 1926.
(Sotheby's Belgravia)
$392 £200

Ruskin Art vase in
kingfisher glaze, 10in.
high, circa 1913.
(Alfie's Antique Market) $168 £85

Ruskin high-fired vase,
11¾in. high, circa 1904-
20. (Sotheby's Belgravia)
$627 £320

SAMSON

Late 19th century Samson 'Companie des Indes' ewer and basin, 35.6cm. high. (Sotheby's Belgravia)
$272 £140

Late 19th century Samson group of lovers, 19.9cm. high.(Sotheby's Belgravia) $138 £70

Latè 19th century Samson gilt metal mounted tureen and cover, 33.5cm. wide. (Sotheby's Belgravia)
$990 £500

Late 19th century Samson famille rose vase, 45.5cm. high. (Sotheby's Belgravia)
$198 £100

A pair of late 19th century Samson 'Derby' figures of Milton and Shakespeare, 29.3cm. high. (Sotheby's Belgravia) $392 £200

One of four Samson 'Derby' figures, late 19th century, 17cm. high. (Sotheby's Belgravia) $356 £180

Late 19th century Chizau Satsuma koro and cover, 5½in. high. (Sotheby's Belgravia) $442 £230

One of a set of five antique Satsuma buttons, finely gilded. (Gray's Antique Market) $101 £50

Mid 19th century Masanobu Satsuma vase, one of a pair, 4¾in. high. (Sotheby's Belgravia) $518 £270

One of a pair of Tazan Satsuma late 19th century vases, 9in. high. (Sotheby's Belgravia) $384 £200

Two late 19th century Satsuma groups, 6¾in. and 7in. high. (Sotheby's Belgravia) $365 £190

One of a pair of Satsuma vases with twin handles and covers, 15in. high. (Worsfolds) $303 £150

One of a pair of Dozan Satsuma vases, circa 1900, 10in. high. (Sotheby's Belgravia) $614 £320

Enamelled Satsuma bowl, circa 1900, 11¾in. diam. (Sotheby's Belgravia) $691 £360

Late 19th century Satsuma vase, 6¼in. high. (Sotheby's Belgravia) $384 £200 ·

19th century Japanese
Satsuma earthenware
jar, 26.5cm. high.
(King & Chasemore)
$633 £320

19th century Satsuma
bowl. (Christie's)
$2,970 £1,530

Mid 19th century
Satsuma vase, 9½in.
high. (Sotheby's Bel-
gravia) $1,363 £710

Miniature Satsuma
vase, 2in. high, circa
1900. (Gray's Anti-
que Market)
$90 £45

Large 19th century
Satsuma vase.
(Vernon's Chichester)
$300 £150

Mid 19th century Sei-
gade Satsuma vase,
9¾in. high.(Sotheby's
Belgravia) $998 £520

SAVONA

Late 17th century
Savona drug jar and
cover, 34cm. high.
(Sotheby's)
$1,450 £740

Early 17th century
Savona tazza, 25.5cm.
diameter. (Sotheby's)
$509 £260

One of a pair of early
17th century Savona
wet drug jars, 22cm.
high. (Sotheby's)
$1,097 £550

One of a pair of 19th century Sevres porcelain circular shallow dishes, 9½in. diam. (Osmond Tricks) $513 £270

Late 19th century Sevres cup and cover, 9in. high. (Sotheby's Belgravia) $180 £95

Unusual enamelled flask in turquoise glass, circa 1875, 13.8cm. high. (Sotheby's Belgravia) $435 £220

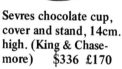

One of a pair of Sevres pattern gilt metal mounted slender oviform vases and covers, 30½in. high. (Christie's) $1,940 £1,000

Sevres chocolate cup, cover and stand, 14cm. high. (King & Chasemore) $336 £170

19th century Sevres two-handled vase, 3ft. high.(Geering & Colyer) $3,960 £2,000

Sevres pattern bleu-celeste vase and cover, 16½in. high.(Christie's) $620 £320

Sevres pattern bleu-celeste two-handled vase and cover, 17¼in. high. (Christie's) $970 £500

Mid 19th century Sevres bleu de roi ground soft paste vase, 40cm. high. (Sotheby's Belgravia) $490 £250

176

Large Sevres pattern trembleuse cup, cover and stand. (Sotheby Bearne) $1,089 £550

19th century Sevres porcelain casket, 12¼in. wide. (Geering & Colyer) $1,203 £620

Sevres soft paste pink ground cache-pot, circa 1860, 18cm. high. (Sotheby's Belgravia) $297 £150

Sevres biscuit figure of Cupid, dated 1906, 31cm. high. (Sotheby's Belgravia) $254 £130

One of a pair of 19th century Sevres double-handled vases, 16cm. high. (King & Chasemore) $653 £330

Mid 19th century ormolu mounted Sevres vase and cover, 23in. high. (Phillips) $848 £420

19th century Sevres porcelain two-handled urn-shaped vase, 33¼in. high. (Geering & Colyer) $3,880 £2,000

One of a pair late 19th century Sevres champleve and gilt metal mounted vases and covers, 39.3cm. high. (Sotheby's Belgravia) $1,019 £520

One of a pair of Sevres pattern ormolu mounted urn-shaped vases and covers, 30in. high. (Christie's) $6,208 £3,200

Spode cup and saucer, pattern 967, circa 1810. (Gray's Antique Mews) $36 £18

Part of a Spode bat-printed tea and coffee service, circa 1800-05. (Sotheby's)$456 £240

Part of a one hundred and twenty piece Spode ironstone 'Japan Pattern' dinner and dessert service, circa 1820. (Sotheby's) $3,366 £1,700

Late 19th century Spode Copeland cabaret. (Manchester Auction Mart) $256 £135

Spode pastille burner and cover, circa 1830, 4in. high.(Sotheby's Belgravia)$426 £220

Part of an attractive Spode dessert service, circa 1810-15. (Sotheby's) $950 £500

Spode commemorative plate of the 1937 Coronation. (Gray's Antique Market)$101 £50

Part of a ninety piece Spode 'New Stone' dinner and dessert service, early 19th century. (Sotheby's) $2,772 £1,400

Plate from a Spode part dinner service. (Spencer's) $3,030 £1,500

18th century Staffordshire saltglaze mug, 4¼in. high. (Sotheby Bearne) $874 £460

Staffordshire figure of Sir Robert Peel, circa 1850, 12¼in. high. (Sotheby's Belgravia) $684 £360

Rare large bust of General Booth, circa 1900, 14in. high. (Sotheby's Belgravia) $950 £480

Staffordshire Toby jug of Father Christmas, 7in. high. (Christopher, Sykes) $164 £85

Rare Staffordshire pottery bust of the Madonna, circa 1810. (Sotheby's N. York) $425 £210

Late 19th century Staffordshire cow group, 7in. long. (Nottingham Auction Mart) $31 £16

Staffordshire flatback group, 1851, 6in. high. (Nottingham Auction Mart) $23 £12

Obadiah Sherratt mantelpiece group, circa 1825-30, 13in. high. (Sotheby's) $435 £220

One of a set of three ormolu mounted Staffordshire tea caddies, sold in ivory casket. (Phillips) $1,980 £1,000

Staffordshire pottery group of Tam O'Shanter and Souter Johnny. (Christopher Sykes) $148 £75

Staffordshire figure of Lord Edward Fitzgerald, circa 1898, 14½in. high. (Sotheby's Belgravia) $178 £90

Staffordshire pottery group of Samuel and Eli. (Christopher Sykes) $128 £65

Staffordshire figure of the King of Prussia, 14in. high, circa 1870. (Sotheby's Belgravia) $237 £120

Staffordshire group of Napoleon and Albert, circa 1854, 14¼in. high. (Sotheby's Belgravia) $148 £75

Staffordshire figure of General Simpson, circa 1854, 13in. high. (Sotheby's Belgravia) $297 £150

Staffordshire group of Alliance, 11in. high, circa 1854.(Sotheby's Belgravia) $79 £40

Staffordshire figure of S. O'Brien, circa 1848, 7in. high. (Sotheby's Belgravia) $435 £220

Slightly chipped group of Miss Nightingale, 10in. high, circa 1855. (Sotheby's Belgravia) $316 £160

Staffordshire pottery group of King John signing the Magna Carta. (Christopher Sykes) $287 £145

Figure of R. Cobden from the Alpha Factory, 7¼in. high, circa 1846.(Sotheby's Belgravia) $128 £65

Late Staffordshire lady riding a goat. (Burrows and Day) $56 £28

Staffordshire figure of the Empress of France, 11¾in. high, circa 1854. (Sotheby's Belgravia) $89 £45

Staffordshire figure of Miss Nightingale, 14¼in. high, circa 1856.(Sotheby's Belgravia) $217 £110

One of a pair of Staffordshire figures. (Christie's S. Kensington) $396 £200

Staffordshire figure of Omer Pacha, circa 1854, 12¾in. high.(Sotheby's Belgravia) $217 £110

Repaired Staffordshire figure of Garibaldi, circa 1861, 14½in. high. (Sotheby's Belgravia) $415 £210

Rare Staffordshire figure of Napoleon, circa 1845, 8½in. high.(Sotheby's Belgravia)$277 £140

181

Rare Staffordshire pitcher, 1817, 8in. high. (Christopher Sykes) $213 £110

Staffordshire lilac-ground pastille burner, 7¼in. high, circa 1840. (Sotheby's Belgravia) $310 £160

One of a pair of Staffordshire lilac-ground pastille burners, circa 1840, 5¾in. high. (Sotheby's Belgravia) $291 £150

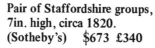

Staffordshire figure of Wellington, 7½in. high, circa 1845. (Sotheby's Belgravia) $213 £110

Pair of Staffordshire groups, 7in. high, circa 1820. (Sotheby's) $673 £340

Staffordshire group of Romeo and Juliet, circa 1852, 10¼in. high. (Sotheby's Belgravia) $426 £220

One of a pair of Staffordshire green transfer-printed plates, 10¼in. diam., circa 1830. (Sotheby's Belgravia) $336 £170

Staffordshire jug with pictorial decoration.(British Antique Exporters) $24 £12

Edwardian Cadbury's Cocoa advertising plate. (Gray's Antique Market) $53 £26

Part of a Swansea pearl-
ware dinner service,
circa 1805. (Sotheby's)
$871 £440

Swansea plate painted
with a view of Pem-
broke Castle. (Russell,
Baldwin & Bright)
$1,148 £580

Rare Dillwyn & Co.
Swansea plate, circa
1814, 9in. high.
(Sotheby's Belgravia)
$79 £40

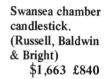

Swansea tea cup and
saucer. (Russell,
Baldwin & Bright)
$831 £420

A pair of Swansea
plates, circa 1825,
8in. diameter.
(Sotheby's)
$415 £210

Swansea chamber
candlestick.
(Russell, Baldwin
& Bright)
$1,663 £840

Swansea plate painted
with two sailing ships
in a rough sea. (Russell,
Baldwin & Bright)
$1,227 £620

Swansea preserve pot
and stand. (Russell,
Baldwin & Bright)
$554 £280

Swansea Mandarin
plate, transfer-printed
and painted in famille
rose. (Bonham's)
$574 £290

183

T'ang dynasty buff
pottery recumbent
ram, 6¼in. long.
(Christie's)
$1,212 £623

T'ang dynasty brown
glazed figure of a
dog, 6in. high.
(Christie's)
$3,080 £1,587

T'ang dynasty buff
pottery figure of a
wild boar, 5½in. long.
(Christie's)
$1,210 £623

T'ang dynasty San Ts'ai
glazed buff pottery fig-
ure of Lokapala, 35¾in.
high. (Christie's)
$8,250 £4,250

T'ang dynasty rare un-
glazed figure of a camel
groom, 16in. high.
(Christie's)
$5,280 £2,721

T'ang dynasty fig-
ure of a groom,
16in. high, in pot-
tery. (Christie's)
$1,760 £907

T'ang dynasty glazed
pottery amphora,
11in. high.(Christie's)
$1,540 £793

T'ang dynasty dark
green globular stor-
age jar, 7¼in. high.
(Christie's)
$8,800 £4,536

Rare glazed T'ang
figure of a lady
shaped to form a
ewer. (Sotheby's)
$64,640 £32,000

Late 19th century Vienna decorated Eaas and Czjzcr Schlaggenwald plaque, 50.3cm. diam. (Sotheby's Belgravia) $5,940 £3,000

Late 19th century Vienna blue ground bowl of boat shape, 25.5cm. wide. (Sotheby's Belgravia) $475 £240

Late Vienna octagonal plate, 13¾in. diam., signed. (Christie's) $582 £300

One of a pair of late Vienna bleu-du-roi ground oval two-handled vases, covers and stands, 14in. high. (Christie's) $1,261 £650

Fine Vienna garniture of three vases. (Osmond Tricks) $1,900 £1,000

One of a pair of Vienna ovoid two-handled vases, covers and stands. (Spencer's) $2,128 £1,120

Late 19th century Vienna plate, 24cm. diam. (Sotheby's Belgravia) $752 £380

Late 19th century Vienna purple lustre ground casket and cover, 31.2cm. wide. (Sotheby's Belgravia) $831 £420

Late Vienna dish, 9¼in. diameter. (Christie's S. Kensington) $151 £75

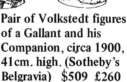

Late 19th century Eckert & Co. Volkstedt group, 22cm. high. (Sotheby's Belgravia) $277 £140

Well modelled Volkstedt group emblematic of song, circa 1910, 28.3cm. high. (Sotheby's Belgravia) $217 £110

Pair of Volkstedt figures of a Gallant and his Companion, circa 1900, 41cm. high. (Sotheby's Belgravia) $509 £260

Volkstedt 'Doccia' tankard and cover, circa 1910, 31.2cm. high. (Sotheby's Belgravia) $196 £100

Volkstedt centrepiece, late 19th century, 37cm. high.(Sotheby's Belgravia) $297 £150

VYSE

Pair of Volkstedt porcelain candlesticks, circa 1800, 14in. high. (Gray's Antique Market) $554 £280

Stoneware model of a leopard by Charles Vyse, Chelsea, 11in. high. (Phillips) $646 £340

Charles Vyse 'Chun Yao' bowl, 5in. high, dated 1938. (Sotheby's Belgravia) $202 £100

Charles Vyse stoneware vase, 1930, 5in. high.(Sotheby's Belgravia)$529 £270

Interesting Wedgwood presentation teapot and cover, 5¼in. high, circa 1875. (Sotheby's Belgravia) $411 £210

Wedgwood Fairyland lustre bowl. (Mawer & Sons) $1,372 £700

Wedgwood jasper chamber candlestick. (Phillips) $698 £360

Wedgwood Fairyland lustre vase. (Sotheby Bearne) $1,603 £810

One of two Wedgwood blue and white jasperware plaques of Apollo and the nine Muses, circa 1780.(Christie's)$15,150 £7,500

19th century Wedgwood blue and white jasperware pot-pourri vase, 14in. high. (Edwards, Bigwood & Bewlay) $494 £260

Late 18th century black basaltes 'encaustic' amphora, probably Wedgwood, 9¾in. high. (Sotheby's) $342 £180

Wedgwood three colour jasper-dip cup and saucer, 1869, 5¾in. diameter, saucer.(Sotheby's Belgravia) $784 £400

Wedgwood Fairyland lustre vase. (Sotheby Bearne) $1,636 £810

Wedgwood Fairyland lustre bowl, 5in. diam., 1920's. (Sotheby's Belgravia) $297 £150

Part of a Wedgwood cream-ware 'shell' service, circa 1790, in Japanese style. (Sotheby's) $871 £440

Wedgwood blue and white jardiniere, circa 1910, 8½in. diam. (Alfie's Antique Market) $78 £38

One of a pair of dark blue jasperware Wedgwood vases, early 19th century, 17in. high. (Jolly's) $836 £440

Late 19th century Wedgwood three colour vase with minor cracks, 5¼in. high. (Sotheby's Belgravia) $435 £220

Wedgwood 'Carrara' bust, 15in. high, circa 1858. (Sotheby's Belgravia) $392 £200

Fine Wedgwood Fairyland lustre bowl, 11in. diam. (Morphets) $1,325 £690

Wedgwood teapot and cover, circa 1763, 4½in. high, slight restoration. (Sotheby's) $990 £500

Wedgwood blue jasper plate, dated for 1887, 8¾in. diam. (Sotheby's Belgravia) $196 £100

Wedgwood Fairyland lustre octagonal bowl, 1920's, 10½in. (Sotheby's Belgravia) $1,188 £600

Rare Wedgwood Fairyland coral and bronze lustre rectangular box and cover, 7¼in. wide, 1920's. (Sotheby's Belgravia) $607 £310

Wedgwood 'Hares, dogs and birds' lustre bowl, 9in. diam., 1920's. (Sotheby's Belgravia) $1,089 £550

Late 19th century Wedgwood three colour gilt metal mounted oil lamp, 16½in. high overall. (Sotheby's Belgravia) $554 £280

19th century Wedgwood blue jasperware circular jardiniere, 9½in. diam. (Manchester Auction Mart) $108 £55

One of a pair of late 18th century Wedgwood blue jasper pot-pourri vases and covers, 16½in. high. (Sotheby's) $1,544 £780

19th century Wedgwood blue jasper plate and nine medallions, 12¾in. diam. (Sotheby's Belgravia) $534 £270

One of a pair of Wedgwood Fairyland lustre trumpet vases, 10in. high, 1920's.(Sotheby's Belgravia) $514 £260

Rare Wedgwood 'ornithological' teacup, coffee cup and saucer, 1812-22.(Sotheby's) $705 £360

Wei dynasty unglazed pottery hound, 6½in. wide. (Christie's)
$990 £510

Early Wei dynasty pottery figures of four tomb attendants, 8in, high. (Christie's)$2,420 £1,247

Wei dynasty grey pottery tomb attendant, 16in. high. (Christie's)
$1,100 £567

WESTERWALD

Late 17th century Westerwald stoneware 'humpen', 13cm. high.(Sotheby's)
$399 £210

18th century Westerwald stoneware tankard, 21.5cm. high.(Sotheby's)
$588 £300

Late 17th century Westerwald saltglaze jug, 23.2cm. high. (Sotheby's)
$901 £460

WOOD

Ralph Wood spill vase, circa 1770, 7½in. high. (Sotheby's)
$297 £150

Ralph Wood type figure jug of The Hearty Good Fellow, 12in. high. (Neales)
$744 £380

Rare and attractive Ralph Wood elephant spill vase, circa 1770-80, 8in. high. (Sotheby's)$1,782 £900

Worcester tankard, printed by Robert Hancock, circa 1765, 3½in. high. (Sotheby's)
$1,097 £560

Fine Worcester Barr, Flight & Barr bowl, 26cm. diam. (King & Chasemore)$659 £320

Royal Worcester vase with pastoral scene. (D. M. Nesbit & Co.)
$545 £270

Fine and rare Worcester 'cabbage-leaf' jug, circa 1756, 8in. high. (Sotheby's)
$6,272 £3,200

Rare Worcester deep plate, circa 1770, 7¾in. diam. (Sotheby's)
$431 £220

Early Worcester coffee pot and cover, 7¼in. high, circa 1753. (Sotheby's)
$10,192 £5,200

Worcester blue and white mug, 6in. high, circa 1765. (Sotheby's)$509 £260

Pair of Worcester green vases, 1870, 10in. high. (Gray's Antique Market)
$1,616 £575

Worcester teapot and cover, circa 1760, 5½in. high.(Sotheby's)
$784 £400

One of a pair of Royal Worcester ivory two-handled octagonal vases, 10½in. high. (Christie's)$970 £500

Royal Worcester vase and cover, 1899. (King & Chasemore) $394 £205

Pair of Royal Worcester candle extinguishers by Jenny Lind, 4¼in. high, 1923.(Sotheby's Belgravia) $411 £210

One of a pair of Worcester two-handled vases, 11in. high. (Christie's)$814 £420

Teabowl and saucer, Worcester, sold with another bowl. (Sotheby's) $1,450 £740

Worcester ivory reticulated oviform vase and cover, 13in. high.(Christie's) $737 £380

Royal Worcester ivory figure of John Bull, 7in. high.(Christie's) $232 £130

One of a pair of Worcester plates.(Christie's S. Kensington) $217 £110

Worcester coffee pot and cover, 23.5cm. high.(King & Chasemore) $1,267 £660

Royal Worcester reticulated two-handled vase, 5¼in. high. (Christie's) $698 £360

Worcester teapot, circa 1758-60, 4in. high, in underglaze blue.(Sotheby's) $509 £260

One of a pair of Royal Worcester shell brackets, 11¼in. long, sold with a vase.(Sotheby's Belgravia) $196 £100

Royal Worcester ivory conical two-handled vase, 18½in. high. (Christie's) $582 £300

Pair of Royal Worcester ivory figures, 6½in. high. (Christie's) $349 £180

Royal Worcester figure of 'Evening Dew', 1912, 15½in. high. (Sotheby's Belgravia) $215 £110

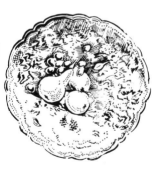

One of a pair of Worcester Flight, Barr & Barr period lidded vases, 11in. high. (Osmond Tricks) $3,040 £1,600

Royal Worcester plate, 9¼in. diameter, 1937. (Sotheby's Belgravia) $450 £230

Worcester straight-sided mug with transfer printed border, circa 1770. (King & Chasemore) $266 £140

Ebonised bracket clock, circa 1890, 16¾in. high. (Sotheby's Belgravia) $712 £360

Dutch walnut wall bracket clock. (Bonham's) $5,940 £3,000

German oak bracket clock, circa 1890, 21½ in. high. (Sotheby's Belgravia) $815 £410

Mahogany bracket clock by F. J. Dent, London, 18in. high, circa 1840. (Sotheby's Belgravia) $411 £210

Ebonised musical bracket clock by Markwick Markham, London, 1ft.9in. high.(Sotheby's) $4,268 £2,200

Unusual George I blue-japanned quarter repeating bracket clock by Wm. Pain, London, 1ft. 9in. high. (Sotheby's) $2,970 £1,500

Good mahogany chiming bracket clock, 23in. high, circa 1910.(Sotheby's Belgravia) $1,568 £800

Walnut bracket clock by Daniel Quare, London, 14in. high. (Sotheby's) $8,910 £4,500

George III mahogany bracket clock by Henry Overall Dover, 1ft.7½in. high. (Sotheby's) $2,970 £1,500

German oak bracket clock, circa 1900, 17¾in. high. (Sotheby's Belgravia) $232 £120

Bracket clock by Joseph Knibb. (Christie's) $11,110 £5,500

Quarter repeating oak bracket clock, circa 1900, 16in. high. (Sotheby's Belgravia) $297 £150

George III mahogany bracket clock by George Peacock, 1ft.3in. high. (Sotheby's) $3,168 £1,600

Victorian bracket clock on bracket. (H. C. Chapman) $1,567 £825

Small ebonised bracket clock by Rimbault, London, 1ft.5in. high. (Sotheby's) $2,178 £1,100

Early 20th century mahogany bracket clock by Vine & Thompson, London, 21¾in. high. (Sotheby's Belgravia) $1,254 £640

Ebonised quarter repeating bracket clock, 1ft. 4in. high.(Sotheby's) $3,465 £1,750

Mahogany cased bracket clock, 30in. high, late 19th century.(Fellow's) $2,376 £1,225

195

BRACKET CLOCKS

Small Regency mahogany striking bracket clock, 11in. high. (Christie's)
$2,134 £1,100

Unusual George III ebonised quarter repeating bracket clock by Thos. Mudge, 14½in. high. (Sotheby's) $6,208 £3,200

George III ebonised striking bracket clock, 17½in. high.(Christie's)
$2,910 £1,500

Mahogany bracket clock by W. Robson, N. Shields, 46cm. high. (King & Chasemore)
$970 £500

Rare ebony and marquetry bracket clock by Daniel Quare, London, 13½in. high. (Sotheby's) $6,596 $3,400

George III ebonised chiming bracket clock, 15½in. high.(Christie's)
$3,298 £1,700

Unusual Japanese striking bracket clock, 170mm. high. (Sotheby's)
$5,432 £2,800

George III mahogany striking bracket clock by John Taylor, London, 19in. high. (Christie's) $3,492 £1,800

George III ebonised striking bracket clock by Jessop, London, 14in. high. (Christie's)
$1,555 £750

George III mahogany bracket clock, 1ft.6in. high.(Sotheby's)
$1,940 £1,000

Dutch ebony gilt mounted bracket clock, 17in. high. (Christie's) $5,820 £3,000

19th century walnut striking bracket clock, 14in. high.(Christie's) $1,455 £750

German walnut alarm bracket timepiece, 12in. high. (Sotheby's)
$1,358 £700

George III mahogany musical bracket clock, 1ft.8in. high.(Sotheby's)
$5,432 £2,800

Mahogany bracket clock by John Taylor, London, 46cm. high. (King & Chasemore) $1,152 £600

Ebony veneered basket top quarter repeating bracket clock, 14in. high. (Sotheby's) $3,686 £1,900

19th century Japanese striking bracket clock, 145mm. high. (Sotheby's)$1,843 £950

George I walnut bracket clock, 17½in. high. (Christie's)$4,850 £2,500

Oak bracket clock, circa 1880, 15¾in. high. (Sotheby's) $333 £170

Unusual George III ebonised bracket clock by Robt. Henderson, London, 1ft.7in. high. (Sotheby's) $4,158 £2,100

George II walnut bracket clock by John Ellicott, London, 1ft.6in. high. (Sotheby's) $6,208 £3,200

Unusual small ebonised Dutch striking bracket clock, 11½in. high. (Sotheby's) $3,880 £2,000

Small and unusual George III mahogany bracket clock. 10½in. high. (Sotheby's) $2,376 £1,200

Rare ebony veneered quarter repeating alarm bracket clock, 1ft.5½in. high. (Sotheby's) $14,440 £7,500

Ebonised bracket clock by P. Hill, Edinburgh, circa 1880, 28in. high. (Sotheby's Belgravia) $666 £340

19th century bracket clock in ebonised and brass mounted case, 26in. high. (Osmond Tricks) $1,900 £1,000

Small mahogany bracket clock by William Allam, London, 1ft. 4in. high. (Sotheby's) $7,128 £3,600

Quarter repeating ebonised bracket clock, circa 1880, 20½in. high. (Sotheby's Belgravia) $1,346 £680

Ornate French bracket clock with ormolu decoration. (Butler & Hatch Waterman) $254 £130

19th century bracket clock, 14in. high, in mahogany and brass case. (David Symonds) $254 £130

George III ebonised quarter repeating bracket clock, 1ft.5in. high. (Sotheby's) $3,564 £1,800

Small Edwardian oak cased bracket clock. (British Antique Exporters) $30 £15

George II quarter repeating bracket clock by Richard Peckover, London, 1ft.7in. high. (Sotheby's) $3,762 £1,900

George III mahogany bracket clock by James Mitchell, London, 1ft. 7in. high. (Sotheby's) $3,762 £1,900

Westminster chime bracket clock, circa 1900, in oak case. (Alfie's Antique Market) $323 £160

Large oak bracket clock, dial signed Clerke 1, London, circa 1900, 25½in. high. (Sotheby's Belgravia) $1,137 £580

199

French brass striking
carriage clock, 6½in.
high. (Christie's)
$1,455 £750

Brass carriage clock
with enamel dial,
5½in. high. (Green
& Co.) $513 £270

Gilt spelter carriage
clock, circa 1890, 6½
in. high. (Sotheby's
Belgravia) $184 £95

Small quarter striking
alarm carriage clock
by Mortecot, Paris,
4¾in. high.(Sotheby's)
$2,134 £1,100

French gilt metal
striking carriage clock,
6¾in. high. (Christie's)
$1,164 £600

Gilt brass repeating
alarm carriage clock,
early 20th century,
7½in. high.(Sotheby's
Belgravia)$485 £250

French gilt metal grande
sonnerie striking carriage
clock, 6in. high.
(Christie's)$1,649 £850

Small oval carriage
clock, 4¼in. high,
in travelling case.
(Sotheby's)$1,425 £720

Late 19th century French
carriage clock by Dro-
court, 5½in. high.(Nottingham Auction Mart)
$1,646 £840

Gilt brass repeating
carriage clock, circa
1900, 7in. high.
(Sotheby's Belgravia)
$554 £280

19th century French
gilded carriage clock,
5½in. high.(Notting-
ham Auction Mart)
$514 £260

Brass and champleve
enamel alarm carriage
clock, early 20th cen-
tury, 5¾in. high.
(Sotheby's Belgravia)
$316 £160

Early 20th century gilt
brass calendar carriage
timepiece, 5¾in. high.
(Sotheby's Belgravia)
$378 £190

Unusual alarm carriage
clock, 6in. high. (Soth-
eby's) $970 £500

Gilt brass alarm repeat-
ing carriage clock, circa
1900, 7in. high.
(Sotheby's Belgravia)
$796 £400

Unusual porcelain moun-
ted alarm carriage clock,
5½in. high.(Sotheby's)
$2,475 £1,250

Enamel mounted carriage
clock in leather case,
6½in. high. (Sotheby's)
$1,584 £800

Late 19th century car-
riage clock, 5½in. high.
(Nottingham Auction
Mart) $1,881 £960

Gilt brass repeating alarm carriage clock, circa 1880, 7in. high. (Sotheby's Belgravia) $990 £500

English gilt metal striking carriage clock, 6½in. high. (Christie's) $2,522 £1,300

Gilt brass repeating carriage clock, circa 1890, 6¾in. high. (Sotheby's Belgravia) $455 £230

French gilt metal carriage clock, 8½in. high. (Christie's) $1,164 £600

Unusual French timepiece carriage clock, 9½in. high. (Christie's) $1,552 £800

French porcelain mounted striking carriage clock, 5¼in. high. (Christie's) $1,843 £950

Early 20th century champleve enamel and gilt metal carriage timepiece, 8½in. high. (Sotheby's Belgravia) $495 £250

French brass cased grande sonnerie carriage clock, 7in. high. (Phillips) $3,737 £1,850

French repeater carriage clock in cloisonne enamel case. (Edmiston's) $1,544 £780

French grande sonnerie alarm carriage clock by Drocourt, 5¾in. high. (Graves, Son & Pilcher) $4,752 £2,400

19th century French brass cased carriage clock, 8in. high. (Geering & Colyer) $1,575 £780

Clock attributed to Mucha, circa 1900, 9in. high. (Gray's Antique Market) $495 £250

Porcelain mounted carriage timepiece, 3in. high. (Sotheby's) $1,287 £650

Multi-piece carriage clock, London 1841, 14cm. high, movement signed Parkinson and Frodsham. (King & Chasemore) $3,084 £1,550

Elaborate gilt metal striking carriage clock, 8¼in. high. (Christie's) $1,358 £700

French gilt metal grande sonnerie carriage clock, 5¾in. high. (Christie's) $2,328 £1,200

Striking carriage clock inset with porcelain panels, 8¼in. high. (Christie's S. Kensington) $1,485 £750

French brass porcelain mounted striking carriage clock, 5in. high. (Christie's) $1,552 £800

203

Early 20th century gilt bronze and Vernis Martin clock garniture. (Sotheby's Belgravia) $633 £320

French clock garniture, circa 1900. (Smith-Woolley & Perry)$594 £300

Gilt spelter 'Sevres' mounted clock garniture, 1880's, clock 16in. high. (Sotheby's Belgravia) $705 £360

Early 20th century ormolu mounted red tortoiseshell clock garniture, clock 15¾in. high.(Sotheby's Belgravia) $607 £310

Gilt spelter clock garniture, circa 1880, clock 14in. high.(Sotheby's Belgravia) $607 £310

Onyx and spelter clock garniture, circa 1910, clock 23in. high.(Sotheby's Belgravia) $277 £140

Gilt bronze and porcelain clock garniture, circa 1890, clock 15¾in. high. (Sotheby's Belgravia) $676 £340

French eight-day striking mantel clock with matching pair of casolettes, 16in. high. (Churchman's) $380 £200

19th century garniture de cheminee, 52cm. high. (King & Chasemore) $1,436 £740

Gilt spelter and porcelain mantel clock garniture, circa 1890.(Sotheby's Belgravia) $895 £450

Art Nouveau patinated metal clock garniture, circa 1900.(Sotheby's Belgravia) $784 £400

Composed gilt spelter and porcelain clock garniture, circa 1880.(Sotheby's) $716 £360

Mid 19th century black marble, onyx and bronze clock garniture.(Sotheby's Belgravia) $411 £210

Gilt bronze and marble clock garniture, circa 1880, clock 15¼in. high. (Sotheby's Belgravia) $450 £230

Gilt bronze clock garniture, circa 1870, 16¾in. high.(Sotheby's Belgravia) $435 £220

Composed porcelain mounted gilt bronze clock garniture, circa 1880. (Sotheby's Belgravia) $490 £250

Gilt brass clock garniture, circa 1890, clock 15in. high.(Sotheby's Belgravia) $666 £340

Gilt bronze and champleve enamel clock garniture, circa 1890, clock 12½in. high.(Sotheby's Belgravia) $736 £370

Mid 19th century black marble and bronze mantel clock and three urns. (Sotheby's Belgravia) $627 £330

Late 19th century gilt metal and alabaster clock garniture.(Sotheby's Belgravia) $768 £400

Gilt spelter and porcelain mounted clock garniture, circa 1870.(Sotheby's Belgravia) $518 £270

Gilt spelter and marble clock garniture, circa 1900, clock 12½in. high. (Sotheby's Belgravia) $417 £210

Mid 19th century Sevres ormolu mounted rose-pompadour clock garniture. (Sotheby's Belgravia) $6,534 £3,300

Late 19th century spelter and onyx clock garniture, signed Detourbet. (Sotheby's Belgravia) $422 £220

Victorian china clock set with transfer decoration. (British Antique Exporters) $170 £85

Gilt bronze and white marble clock garniture, circa 1880, clock 27¾in. high. (Sotheby's Belgravia)$537 £270

Art Deco clock set of unusual design. (Moore, Allen & Innocent)$969 £480

Barbedienne ormolu mounted red marble clock garniture, 1880's. (Sotheby's Belgravia) $5,174 £2,600

Composed white marble and ormolu clock garniture, circa 1870, clock 24½in. high. (Sotheby's Belgravia) $3,582 £1,800

Mid 18th century mahogany long-case clock, 245cm. high. (King & Chasemore)
$3,239 £1,550

18th century maho-gany longcase clock, 75in. tall. (Butler & Hatch Waterman)
$2,121 £1,050

Stained oak long-case clock circa 1880, 85in. high. (Sotheby's Bel-gravia)
$1,858 £920

Mid 18th century longcase clock in mahogany case, 250cm. high. (King & Chasemore)
$3,553 £1,700

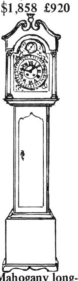

Early 19th century thirty-hour oak cased grandfather clock. (British Anti-que Exporters)
$600 £300

Burr-maplewood month longcase clock, signed Fro-manteel & Clarke, 8ft.8in. high. (Sotheby's)
$9,504 £4,800

Mahogany long-case clock by John Barr, Hous-ton, 80in. tall. (Gray's Antique Market)
$3,232 £1,600

Edwardian maho-gany clock with satinwood cross-banding. (Biddle & Webb)
$1,070 £530

Late 19th century mahogany regulator, 170cm. high. (King & Chasemore)
$3,168 £1,600

George III longcase clock by Walter Turnbull, Caltown. (Alan Fitchett)
$1,881 £950

19th century oak longcase clock by Robert Taylor, 72in. high.(Nottingham Auction Mart)
$470 £240

George III mahogany longcase clock by David Laing, Edinburgh, 7ft.2in.(Sotheby's)
$1,862 £950

Early 19th century longcase musical clock.(Russell, Baldwin & Bright)
$2,970 £1,500

Wickerwork longcase clock. (Sotheby's Belgravia)
$1,372 £700

Edwardian mahogany longcase regulator.(Nottingham Auction Mart)
$588 £300

Figured mahogany longcase clock by James Fenton, London. (Lawrence's)
$4,040 £2,000

Large marquetry
chiming clock,
circa 1900,
105½in. high.
(Sotheby's Bel-
gravia)
$4,554 £2,300

18th century stai-
ned oak longcase
clock, 88in. high.
(Sotheby's Bel-
gravia)
$1,202 £620

18th century Fle-
mish oak longcase
clock, 7ft.9in.
high.(Geering &
Colyer)
$3,939 £1,950

Mid 18th century
lacquerwork clock,
by Zac Mountfort.
(Locke & England)
$1,919 £950

Edwardian long-
case clock.(May,
Whetter & Grose)
$673 £340

Mid 19th century
mahogany long-
case clock, 67in.
high.(Sotheby's
Belgravia)
$1,319 £680

Mahogany longcase
clock by Jn. and Wm.
Mitchell, Glasgow,
mid 19th century,
83in. high.(Sotheby's
Belgravia)
$1,019 £520

Early 19th cen-
tury mahogany
French longcase
regulator time-
piece.(Lawrence's)
$9,292 £4,600

Inlaid longcase clock by James Blaik, Peterhead. (John H. Raby & Son) $673 £340

Ornately carved walnut longcase clock.(Biddle & Webb) $3,960 £2,000

Longcase clock by George Graham in burr-walnut, 7ft.5in. high.(Christie's) $18,810 £9,500

Late 17th century longcase clock by Andrew Brown, Edinburgh. (Edmiston's) $9,306 £4,700

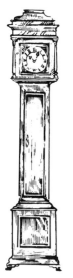

Oak grandmother longcase clock, 5ft.2in. high. (Christie's) $1,261 £650

Georgian mahogany longcase clock by Thomas Burton. (Christie's S. Kensington) $2,828 £1,400

George II mahogany longcase clock, circa 1900, 64in. high. (Sotheby's Belgravia)$776 £400

Marquetry longcase clock by Thos. Farmer, circa 1685.(King & Chasemore) $9,212 £4,700

18th century inlaid mahogany longcase clock by Band & Hine. (Alonzo Dawes & Hoddell) $2,090 £1,100

Large mahogany longcase clock. (Sotheby's Belgravia) $5,940 £3,000

George III regulator longcase clock by Brockbanks, London.(Sotheby's Belgravia) $7,128 £3,600

Carved oak longcased clock by Goodchild of Bradford.(John H. Raby & Son) $792 £400

Thirty hour longcase clock with musical movement.(Lacy Scott & Sons) $2,181 £1,080

Early 19th century oak longcase clock, 80½in. high.(Sotheby's Belgravia) $712 £360

Carved oak chiming longcase clock, circa 1890, 96in. high.(Sotheby's Belgravia) $3,880 £2,000

George III mahogany longcase clock by Henry Fisher, Preston. (Neales) $3,325 £1,750

  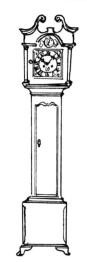 

Small walnut longcase month clock by John Knibb, 6ft.6in. high. (Sotheby's) $17,820 £9,000

Unusual oak longcase clock by John Kay, London, 7ft. 4in. high. (Sotheby's) $2,376 £1,200

George III mahogany longcase clock, 84in. high, by John Turnbull, Hawick. (Sotheby's Belgravia) $2,178 £1,100

Early 19th century mahogany longcase clock, 94in. high.(Sotheby's Belgravia) $656 £330

Large mahogany chiming longcase clock, circa 1910, 101in. high. (Sotheby's Belgravia) $2,871 £1,450

Mid 18th century green ground lacquered longcase clock.(King & Chasemore) $2,016 £1,050

Early 19th century mahogany cased grandfather clock with painted face. (Vernon's Chichester) $900 £450

Walnut and marquetry longcase clock by Thos. Hall, London, 80in. high.(Christie's S. Kensington) $4,158 £2,100

George III lac-
quer musical
longcase clock
by Pridham,
London, 8ft.2in.
high.(Christie's)
$1,261 £650

Mahogany chim-
ing longcase clock
with brass dial,
circa 1910, 93¾in.
high.(Sotheby's
Belgravia)
$2,744 £1,400

George III maho-
gany longcase
clock by Wyke &
Green, Liverpool,
7ft.6in. high.
(Sotheby's)
$2,970 £1,500

Mahogany longcase
clock, circa 1830,
93in. high.(Sothe-
by's Belgravia)
$1,089 £550

Georgian walnut
longcase clock by
Thomas Jenkin-
son, Sandwich.
(Stride's)
$2,871 £1,450

Mid 20th century
small mahogany
and walnut long-
case clock, 65¾in.
high.(Sotheby's
Belgravia)
$796 £400

Dutch walnut mar-
quetry longcase
clock by Andries
Vermeulen, Amster-
dam, 8ft.2in. high.
(Sotheby's)
$10,692 £5,400

Oak longcase
clock, circa
1840, 89in.
high.(Sotheby's
Belgravia)
$835 £420

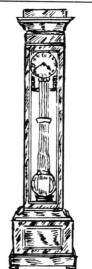

18th century walnut longcase clock. (Buckell & Ballard) $3,332 £1,700

Late 18th century Scottish regulator, signed Thos. Napier, Edinburgh, 82in. high.(Bonham's) $3,230 £1,700

Mahogany and brass mounted longcase regulator by Lepaute, Paris, 6ft.9in. high.(Christie's) $9,700 £5,000

18th century mahogany and satinwood inlaid longcase clock, 8ft.1in. high. (Nottingham Auction Mart) $4,950 £2,500

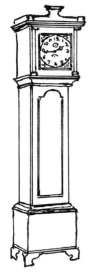

Painted dial thirty-hour oak grandfather clock, 78in. high.(Silvester's) $941 £485

Wrought iron longcase clock, circa 1920, 65½in. high. (Sotheby's Belgravia) $588 £300

George III mahogany longcase clock by Holmes, London, 7ft.7in. high.(Christie's) $4,462 £2,300

Inlaid oak longcase clock by Holroid of Wakefield. (John H. Raby & Son)$1,881 £950

Mahogany miniature longcase clock, 2ft.7in. high.(Sotheby's) $1,067 £550

Jacobean revival oak longcase clock.(Neales) $2,323 £1,150

Marquetry longcase clock by J. Windmills, London, 6ft.10in. high.(Sotheby's) $8,148 £4,200

Carved oak longcased clock by Samuel Whittaker. (John H. Raby & Son) $891 £450

Unusual walnut quarter repeating longcase clock, 7ft.3in. high. (Sotheby's) $8,730 £4,500

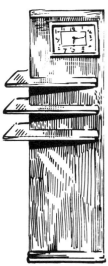

Stylish modernistic clock, 1930's, 112cm. high.(Sotheby's Belgravia) $277 £140

Mid 18th century Louis XV ormolu mounted parquetry longcase clock, 7ft.3in. high. $13,300 £7,000

George III mahogany longcase clock by Vigne, London, 7ft.5in. high.(Christie's) $4,850 £2,500

217

Late 19th century mahogany regulator by Thos. Gammage & Sons, London, 107cm. high. (King & Chasemore) $3,072 £1,600

Mid 18th century banded inlaid mahogany longcase clock by John Ewer, London.(Jordan & Cook's)$2,328 £1,200

Sheraton style mahogany longcase clock by Wm. Stapleton, London, 7ft.1in. high.(Geering & Colyer) $3,104 £1,600

Small olivewood marquetry longcase clock, 6ft. 7in. high. (Sotheby's) $3,686 £1,900

George III carved oak longcase clock, by Jon. Storr, York. (Morphet's) $1,200 £625

Mahogany regulator, dial signed Hone, Hammersmith, 6ft. 9in. high.(Sotheby's) $4,850 £2,500

Late 18th century mahogany longcase clock, 90in. high. (Nottingham Auction Mart) $2,619 £1,350

Early 18th century walnut and marquetry longcase clock, 7ft.11in. high. (Christie's) $4,268 £2,200

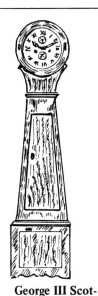

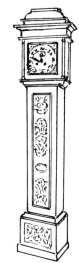

George III mahogany longcase clock, 7ft. 10in. high.(Christie's) $2,522 £1,300

George III Scottish mahogany longcase clock, 6ft.3in. high. (Sotheby's) $1,261 £650

Late 17th century walnut and marquetry longcase clock, 6ft.6in. high. (Christie's) $5,044 £2,600

17th century walnut marquetry longcase clock by Dan Constable. (Wm. H. Brown's) $3,880 £2,000

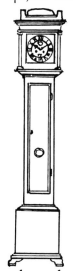

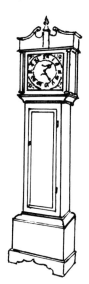

18th century Dutch walnut musical longcase clock, 7ft.7in. high. (Sotheby's) $8,536 £4,400

Burr elmwood longcase clock, signed Markwick, London, 7ft.11in. high. (Sotheby's) $5,432 £2,800

George III mahogany longcase clock, 7ft. 8in. high. (Christie's) $1,358 £700

Oak grandfather clock by Carmalt, Ringwood, 75in. high.(Silvester's) $844 £435

219

18th century longcase clock by Walter Barr of Port Glasgow. (Phillips)
$1,854 £900

Georgian mahogany longcase clock by Thos. Burton, 84in. high. (Christie's S. Kensington)
$2,828 £1,400

Large mahogany month going longcase clock, late 1890's, 112in. high. (Sotheby's Belgravia)
$6,060 £3,000

Georgian clock with oak case and enamel dial.(Biddle & Webb)
$1,282 £635

Walnut longcase clock by Thos. Bolton, Manchester, 1791. (Biddle & Webb)
$2,323 £1,150

Early George III longcase clock by Chas. Smith, London. (Woolley & Wallis)
$2,970 £1,500

19th century mahogany longcase clock, 96in. high.(Nottingham Auction Mart)
$2,626 £1,300 .

Early 19th century oak cased grandfather clock with enamel dial. (Vernon's Chichester)
$640 £320

19th century oak cased grandfather clock with brass face. (Vernon's Chichester) $2,400 £1,200

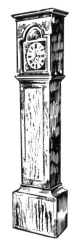

Late 18th century mahogany longcase clock with painted face. (Vernon's Chichester) $800 £400

Georgian longcase clock by Henry Mayhew, Parham. (Stride & Son) $2,121 £1,050

Early 19th century mahogany longcase clock with painted face. (Vernon's Chichester) $850 £425

Scottish longcase clock by David Greig, Perth. (Worsfolds) $1,333 £670

Late 18th century bleached mahogany longcase clock by John Webb, 93in. high. (Sotheby's Belgravia)$4,343 £2,150

Mid 18th century clock by E. Greatrex, Birmingham. (Locke & England) $2,222 £1,100

George III oak longcase clock, circa 1780, 86in. high.(Sotheby's Belgravia) $752 £380

Mid 19th century brass lantern clock, 15½in. high. (Sotheby's Belgravia) $398 £200

English brass quarter striking lantern clock, 12¾in. high.(Christie's) $5,238 £2,700

17th century miniature lantern clock, 7½in. high. (Vost's) $1,800   £1,000

Lantern clock by Thos. Moor, 1ft.3in. high. (Sotheby's) $1,881   £950

English brass striking lantern clock by Peter Closson, London, 11in. high. (Christie's) $2,910 £1,500

Early 18th century brass case lantern clock by Isaac Holmes. (Edwards, Bigwood & Bewlay)$760   £400

Early 18th century lantern clock in brass case, by Wm. Kipling, London, 36cm. high. (King & Chasemore) $1,632 £850

Small brass lantern timepiece with alarm, circa 1700, 170mm. high. (Sotheby's)$2,772 £1,400

English brass quarter striking lantern clock, 16½in. high.(Christie's) $5,044 £2,600

Late 19th century earthenware clock case by J. Vieillard, Bordeaux, 40.5cm. high.(Sotheby's Belgravia) $352 £180

German movement Ting Tang clock in inlaid mahogany case. (Alfie's Antique Market) $343 £170

Late 18th century Meissen oval frame, now converted to a clock, 33.2cm. high. (Sotheby's Belgravia) $940 £480

Solid silver French carriage type clock, 1888, 4½in. high. (Gray's Antique Market) $555 £275

Large gilt brass and painted glass mantel clock, circa 1880, 18¾in. high. (Sotheby's Belgravia) $1,034 £520

Mid 19th century bronze and marble mantel clock, 21½in. high.(Sotheby's Belgravia) $517 £260

Ebonised and ormolu mounted bracket clock by Johnson, London, circa 1800. (Graves, Son & Pilcher) $3,131 £1,550

Red and black perpetual calendar mantel clock, circa 1860, 17½in. high. (Sotheby's Belgravia) $895 £450

Small French balloon shape bracket clock, 12in. high. (Butler & Hatch Waterman) $1,161 £575

Unusual French musical mantel clock, 1ft. 9in. high.(Sotheby's Belgravia)$656 £330

Mid 19th century ormolu mantel clock, 17in. high. (Sotheby's Belgravia)
$634
£330

Mid 19th century gilt bronze mantel clock, 11½in. high. (Sotheby's Belgravia)
$372 £190

Rosewood mantel clock by Arnold Frodsham, London, 11in. high. (Sotheby's)
$7,524 £3,800

Viennese enamelled copper clock, 39cm. high, circa 1910.(Sotheby's Belgravia)
$2,940 £1,500

Late 19th century gilt bronze mantel clock, 18½in. high. (Sotheby's Belgravia)
$338 £170

French Louis XVI style boulle work bracket clock.(Russell, Baldwin & Bright) $990 £500

Mahogany mantel timepiece, dial signed Barraud & Lund, London, 1798, 9½in. high. (Sotheby's Belgravia)
$424 £210

Gilt spelter and porcelain mounted clock sold with a pair of urns, circa 1880.(Sotheby's Belgravia) $294 £150

Late 19th century gilt bronze and alabaster mantel clock, 15½in. high, dial signed Hry. Marc Paris. (Sotheby's Belgravia) $333 £170

Gilt spelter and porcelain mantel clock, circa 1860, 13½in. high. (Sotheby's Belgravia) $298 £150

French ormolu mounted mahogany mantel clock.(Lawrence's) $841 £425

Early 19th century alarm clock by Leblanc a Boulogne, 11½in. high. (Sotheby's) $970 £500

Early Martin Brothers clock case, 10½in. high, dated 10-74.(Sotheby's Belgravia) $470 £240

Gilt brass mantel clock, circa 1900, 12½in. high, signed French Royal Exchange London. (Sotheby's Belgravia) $475 £240

Gilt metal and marble mantel clock, circa 1880, 13in. high. (Sotheby's Belgravia) $568 £290

17th century hexagonal table clock by Plattlico Erhardo, 130mm. diam. (Sotheby's) $5,544 £2,800

Gilt metal table clock, German, late 16th century, 50cm. high. (Sotheby's) $68,600 £35,000

225

Preiss clock with marble base, 1930's, 37cm. high. (Sotheby's Belgravia) $1,176 £600

Restoration bronze and ormolu watch stand, 5¾in. high, circa 1820. (Sotheby's) $2,871 £1,450

Chrome and glass clock, 20th century, by Adnet.(Boisgirard de Heeckeren) $2,781 £1,405

Late George III mahogany bracket clock by Hamley, London, 1ft. 10½in. high.(Sotheby's) $1,425 £720

Louis XVI ormolu mounted white marble mantel clock, 2ft. high, circa 1785.(Sotheby's) $1,330 £700

Brass inlaid ebonised travelling mantel clock, 8in. high. (Sotheby's) $2,673 £1,350

Gilt spelter mantel clock, circa 1880, 13¼in. high. (Sotheby's Belgravia) $323 £170

Gilt bronze mantel clock, circa 1840, 16in. high. (Sotheby's Belgravia) $490 £250

Gilt bronze mantel clock, circa 1880, 14½in. high, dial signed Sykes, Williams & Cullums, London. (Sotheby's Belgravia) $497 £250

Late 19th century four glass and brass mantel clock, 11in. high. (Nottingham Auction Mart) $568 £290

Large gilt bronze and alabaster mantel clock, circa 1870, 23½in. high. (Sotheby's Belgravia) $1,094 £550

Gilt spelter and porcelain mantel clock, 18in. high, with glass dome. (Sotheby's Belgravia) $543 £280

Late 19th century blue enamel and ormolu mounted mantel clock, 14in. high.(Sotheby's Belgravia) $1,830 £920

Black marble and bronze mantel clock, 23½in. high, circa 1870. (Sotheby's Belgravia) $392 £200

Second Empire gilt and bronze mantel clock, circa 1860, 10in. high.(Sotheby's Belgravia)$725 £370

Gilt bronze and porcelain mounted mantel clock, circa 1870, 16in. high.(Sotheby's Belgravia) $725 £370

Lavender jade and black onyx desk clock. (Christie's Geneva) $36,665 £18,518

Gilt spelter and porcelain mantel timepiece, 1870's, 15in. high.(Sotheby's Belgravia) $294 £150

MANTEL CLOCKS

Late 19th century four glass and brass mantel clock, 14in. high. (Nottingham Auction Mart) $999 £510

Art Nouveau inlaid mahogany striking American clock , circa 1900, 15in. high.(Alfie's Antique Market) $121 £60

18th century French bracket clock inscribed 'Mynuel a Paris'. (Phillips)
$1,818 £900

Late 18th century French bracket clock by Roquelon, Paris, 4ft.6in. high. (King & Chasemore)
$4,707 £2,450

Directoire ormolu mounted white marble mantel clock, circa 1795, 15½in. high. (Sotheby's) $1,148 £580

Marble based French clock, circa 1880, with spelter figure.(Alfie's Antique Market)
$232 £115

16th century gilt metal Strasbourg quarter striking astronomical clock. (Sotheby's)
$69,300 £35,000

Louis XV musical clock in ormolu, bronze and Vernis Martin, 29in. high. (Christie's)
$100,880 £52,000

Unusual alabaster rack timepiece with enamel dial, 1ft.5in. high. (Sotheby's)
$633 £320

20th century Italian painted bracket clock and bracket, 24½in. high.(Sotheby's Belgravia) $313 £160

Victorian barometer, clock and thermometer in oak case, 13in. high. (Gray's Antique Mews) $171 £85

Inlaid balloon clock, circa 1890, French movement. (Alfie's Antique Market) $168 £85

Gilt spelter and porcelain mantel clock, circa 1890, 14¾in. high. (Sotheby's Belgravia) $514 £260

Gilt bronze and porcelain mantel clock circa 1880, dial signed Dent a Paris, 11½in. high.(Sotheby's Belgravia) $616 £310

Brass and porcelain mantel clock, circa 1880, 19¼in. high. (Sotheby's Belgravia) $716 £360

Early 19th century French boulle bracket clock, 48cm. high. (King & Chasemore) $1,056 £550

French gilt metal eight-day striking clock, circa 1850, 14in. high. (Gray's Antique Mews) $454 £225

China mantel clock, circa 1880, eight-day French movement. (Alfie's Antique Market) $111 £55

229

Green boulle bracket clock, circa 1880, 13¾in. high.(Sotheby's Belgravia) $676 £340

Louis XV ormolu clock, mid 18th century, signed James McCabe, London, 18in. high.(Sotheby's) $1,584 £800

Gilt brass and porcelain mantel clock, circa 1880, 12½in. high. (Sotheby's Belgravia)$613 £310

Directoire ormolu mounted white marble timepiece, circa 1795, 13½in. high. (Sotheby's) $1,188 £600

19th century mantel clock cased in a bronze urn. (Phillips)$684 £360

Red boulle bracket clock, circa 1880, 16in. high.(Sotheby's Belgravia) $646 £330

Art Nouveau wood clock, circa 1900, 35cm. high.(Sotheby's Belgravia) $455 £230

19th century French ormolu mantel clock. (Nottingham Auction Mart) $274 £140

Rare 18th century French boulle bracket clock by Roquelon, Paris, 108cm. high. (King & Chasemore) $4,851 £2,450

Rare boulle musical calendar bracket clock by John Ellicott. (Sotheby's)
$10,504 £5,200

Victorian black marble mantel clock with brass fittings. (British Antique Exporters)
$30 £15

French ormolu and porcelain mounted portico clock, 20½in. high. (Christie's S. Kensington)
$3,168 £1,600

Spelter mantel clock signed A. Ouver, 15½in. high, circa 1910.(Sotheby's Belgravia) $198 £100

Restoration ormolu mantel clock, circa 1820, 1ft. 7½in. high. (Sotheby's)
$1,292 £680

Gilt spelter and porcelain mantel clock, circa 1880, 14¾in. high. (Sotheby's Belgravia)
$294 £150

19th century French ormolu mantel clock. (Mallam's)$950 £480

Rosewood and parquetry mantel clock, circa 1880, 19¾in. high.(Sotheby's Belgravia) $257 £130

Early 20th century gilt metal and porcelain easel timepiece, 13¼in. high. (Sotheby's Belgravia)
$764 £390

Late 19th century gilt metal and champleve enamelled desk timepiece, 8½in. high. (Sotheby's Belgravia) $250 £130

Small French mantel clock by Paul Garnier, Paris, 6in. high. (Sotheby's) $543 £280

Late 19th century red boulle bracket clock, 14¼in. high.(Sotheby's Belgravia) $518 £270

Vienna gilt metal mounted clockcase.(Humberts King & Chasemore) $1,900 £1,000

Lalique clock, 14¾in. high. (Christie's) $3,104 £1,600

Charles X ormolu mantel clock, 1ft. 3½in. high.(Sotheby's) $543 £280

German tabernacle clock, 9in. high. (Christie's) $6,790 £3,500

Mid 19th century gilt bronze mantel clock, signed Leroy & Fils, Paris, 18½in. high. (Sotheby's Belgravia)$614 £320

Art Nouveau silvered metal clock case, circa 1900, 53cm. high. (Sotheby's Belgravia) $543 £280

Art Deco bronze and marble clock, 26cm. wide, 1920's.(Sotheby's Belgravia) $329 £170

Glass clock case by Lalique, circa 1930, 37.5cm. high. (Sotheby's Belgravia) $1,710 £900

Copper and satinised steel clock 1930's, 31cm. high. (Sotheby's Belgravia) $853 £440

19th century French eight-day aquation clock. (Woolley & Wallis) $4,180 £2,200

Silver and parcel gilt clock by Goldsmiths and Silversmiths Ltd., London, 1929, 13.5cm. high.(Sotheby's Belgravia) $504 £260

French Empire mantel clock in mahogany case, 50cm. high. (King & Chasemore) $749 £390

Gilt bronze and jewelled 'Sevres' mantel clock, 15½in. high, circa 1870.(Sotheby's Belgravia)$722 £380

Lalique glass clock 'Le jour et la nuit', 38.75cm. wide, 1920's.(Sotheby's Belgravia)$8,360 £4,400

Small mahogany mantel clock, dial signed Z. Reid, 9in. high. (Christie's) $873 £450

233

MANTEL CLOCKS

Victorian marble cased mantel clock.(British Antique Exporters) $60 £30

20th century mahogany framed mantel clock. (British Antique Exporters) $14 £7

A fine marquetry cased mantel clock and stand.(British Antique Exporters) $450 £225

Bronze elephant mantel clock, circa 1850, signed Pre. Leurtier, Paris, 18in. high. (Sotheby's Belgravia) $995 £500

Victorian oak cased mantel clock with drawer. (British Antique Exporters) $200 £100

Tortoiseshell and ormolu clock, circa 1870, 19in. high. (Gray's Antique Mews) $1,236 £600

Early 19th century brass and bronzed mantel clock, 15in. high. (Geering & Colyer) $803 £390

20th century walnut cased mantel clock. (British Antique Exporters)$12 £6

20th century oak cased mantel clock. (British Antique Exporters) $30 £15

Brass long duration time-
piece skeleton clock,
12¾in. high. (Christie's)
$1,455 £750

Good quality original
Victorian skeleton time-
piece, circa 1860.(Alfie's
Antique Market)
$564 £285

Brass cathedral skeleton
clock signed C.Fiedemann,
Liverpool. (Christie's Kensington) $4,477 £2,250

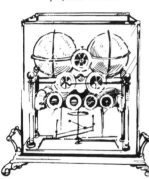

Astronomical skeleton
clock, by James Gorham,
19th century. (Christie's)
$37,810 £19,000

Brass skeleton clock with
enamel dial, circa 1890,
15¼in. high. (Sotheby's
Belgravia) $352 £180

Unusual early 19th century
skeleton clock of 'rafter'
construction. (Russell,
Baldwin & Bright)
$2,574 £1,300

Mid 19th century sil-
vered brass skeleton
timepiece, 12½in. high.
(Sotheby's Belgravia)
$303 £150

Victorian brass skeleton
clock complete with
glass dome. (British Antique Exporters)$440 £220

Skeleton clock with lyre
shaped brass frame in
glass dome. (John H.
Raby & Son)$495 £250

19th century French eight-day striking clock, circa 1880, 31in. high.(Gray's Antique Mews)
$353 £175

Gilt metal wall clock, circa 1850, 20¾in. high. (Sotheby's Belgravia) $174 £90

18th century South German Telleruhr, 1ft.5½in. high. (Sotheby's) $1,707 £880

Small early Louis XVI ormolu cartel timepiece, 1ft.9in. high, circa 1775. (Sotheby's) $4,370 £2,300

19th century American rosewood framed wall clock. (British Antique Exporters) $70 £35

Late 19th century Staartklok, 130cm. high. (King & Chasemore) $1,728 £900

Mid 19th century Viennese regulator clock with ebonised case, 48in. high.(Gray's Antique Market)$656 £325

Dutch walnut hanging wall bracket clock, 31in. high. (Bonham's) $6,060 £3,000

Louis XVI ormolu cartel timepiece, circa 1780, 16½in. high.(Sotheby's) $1,089 £550

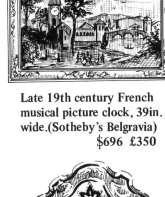

Stained oak wall clock, Austrian, circa 1880, 38in. high.(Sotheby's Belgravia)$574 £290

Late 19th century French musical picture clock, 39in. wide.(Sotheby's Belgravia) $696 £350

Mid 19th century mahogany wall timepiece, dial signed Robt. Mack, Clerkenwell, 16in. high. (Sotheby's Belgravia) $475 £240

Walnut Vienna regulator, circa 1900, 42in. high, with enamel dial (Sotheby's Belgravia) $388 £200

Victorian papier mache wall clock by E. Fixary. (British Antique Exporters) $250 £125

Gilt metal wall clock by Chas. Nicolas de Hemant, Paris, circa 1760.(Moore, Allen & Innocent) $1,131 £560

Vienna regulator in dark walnut, 60in. high, circa 1900. (Sotheby's Belgravia) $495 £250

Early 20th century oak cased wall clock. (British Antique Exporters) $70 £35

Walnut Vienna regulator, circa 1900, 51½in. high. (Sotheby's Belgravia) $613 £310

237

Gold and enamel open-faced lady's lever watch, 33mm. diam.(Sotheby's Belgravia) $297 £150

Small gold and enamel cylinder watch, Swiss, late 19th century. (Sotheby's) $2,231 £1,150

Gold and enamel hunting cased minute repeating clockwatch, 55mm. diam. (Sotheby's)$6,790 £3,500

Silver cased pocket watch, signed Thos. Earnshaw. (King & Chasemore) $1,568 £800

Silver open-faced pocket chronometer, 1854, by Parkinson & Frodsham, 58.5mm. diameter.(Sotheby's) $2,475 £1,250

17th century verge watch by Joseph Chamberlain, Norwich, 52mm. diam. (Phillips) $9,108 £4,600

Gold and enamel hunting cased lever watch, mid 19th century, 47mm. diameter. (Sotheby's) $4,074 £2,100

Gold hunting cased pocket chronometer, 1871, 55mm. diam. (Sotheby's) $2,910 £1,500

Gold hunting cased keyless lever watch, 55mm. diameter. (Sotheby's) $1,261 £650

Gold and enamel cylinder watch by Muller, Geneva, 33mm. diam. (Sotheby's)$990 £500

9-carat gold quarter repeating hunting cased keyless lever watch, 51mm. diam.(Sotheby's Belgravia) $732 £370

Silver quarter repeating verge oignon, early 18th century, 57.5mm. diam. (Sotheby's)
$2,328 £1,200

Fine and rare tourbillon watch by Charles Frodsham, London, 1907.(Bonham's)
$31,680 £16,000

Gold hunter-cased lever watch by Lange & Sohne of Dresden. (Christie's)
$6,868 £3,400

Keyless wind watch by Charles Frodsham, London, 1888.(King & Chasemore)
$15,444 £7,800

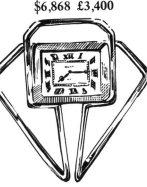

Gold single roller Massey lever watch by Robert Roskell, 53mm. diam. (Sotheby's)
$1,544 £780

Cartier gold breast pocket clip watch, 1930's, 5.3cm. (Sotheby's Belgravia)
$814 £420

Good gold half-quarter repeating duplex watch, 55mm. diam.(Sotheby's)
$2,425 £1,250

Gold and enamel triple cased cylinder watch, 58mm. diam., hallmarked 1812.(Sotheby's) $3,880 £2,000

Gold and enamel verge watch, 49mm. diam., circa 1790. (Sotheby's) $3,298 £1,700

Silver gilt and enamel duplex watch, 56mm. diam. (Christie's) $3,686 £1,900

Gold pair-cased rack lever watch by Robert Roskell, Liverpool, 55mm. diam. (Sotheby's) $1,261 £650

Gold hunting keyless lever chronograph by Samuel Dixon, 50.5mm. diameter. (Sotheby's) $1,397 £720

Gold open faced split seconds keyless chronograph by Tiffany & Co. (Sotheby's) $1,591 £820

Gold pair-cased rack lever watch, by P. Leyland & Co., Liverpool, 54mm. diam. (Sotheby's)$1,397 £720

Early 19th century gold and turquoise set cylinder watch, 47mm. diam. (Sotheby's)$1,397 £720

19th century gold and enamel lever watch, 48mm. diameter. (Sotheby's) $2,037 £1,050

French gold quarter repeating cylinder watch, 52mm. diam. (Christie's)
$3,880 £2,000

Italian gilt metal verge watch by Marc Blondel, Naples, 62mm. diam. (Christie's)$1,843 £950

Swiss gold verge watch, 45mm. diam.(Christie's)
$1,008 £520

Silver cased pocket chronometer, London 1856, 58mm. diam. (Christie's)
$3,492 £1,800

Mid 19th century gold hunting cased pocket chronometer, 52mm. diam. (Sotheby's)
$1,707 £880

Silver cased pocket chronometer, 57mm. diam.(Christie's)
$2,328 £1,200

18th century gilt metal chaise watch, 10.8cm. diam. (Christie's)
$1,940 £1,000

Silver gilt pair-cased centre seconds cylinder watch by Justin Vulliamy, 58mm. diam. (Sotheby's)
$1,455 £750

Gold centre seconds verge watch, circa 1790, 56mm. diam. (Sotheby's)$970 £500

241

Gold and enamel pair-cased verge watch by Edward Prior, London, 41mm. diam.(Sotheby's) $2,910 £1,500

Swiss gold quarter repeating and musical watch, 57mm. diam. (Christie's) $3,492 £1,800

Gold duplex watch by Edward McCreary, London, 49mm. diam. (Sotheby's)$737 £380

Gold hunter cased keywind lever watch, 47mm. diam. (Christie's) $2,716 £1,400

Swiss gold and enamel pendant watch, 32mm. long. (Christie's) $2,328 £1,300

Gold hunting cased minute repeating keyless lever automaton watch, 57mm. diam.(Sotheby's) $4,850 £2,500

  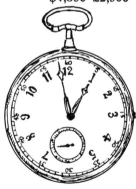

Gold hunting cased keyless lever watch, 56mm. diam. (Sotheby's) $1,397 £720

Gold cased verge watch by Benjamin Webb. London, 1802, 61mm. diam. (Sotheby's) $1,940 £1,000

Gold cylinder watch by James Tregent, London, circa 1800, 54mm. diam. (Sotheby's) $620 £320

Early keyless lever
gold watch, Lon-
don, 49mm. diam.
(Christie's)
  $1,125 £580

Gold and enamel centre
seconds duplex watch,
circa 1810, 57mm. diam.
(Sotheby's)$7,178 £3,700

Gold and enamel pair-
cased verge watch by
George Prior, London,
1815, 51mm. diam.
(Sotheby's)$3,686 £1,900

Heavy gold hunting cased
minute repeating clock-
watch, 59mm. diameter.
(Sotheby's)
  $14,550 £7,500

Early 19th century
gold and enamel
form watch, Swiss,
70mm. long.
(Christie's)
  $1,843 £950

Gold hunter cased
minute repeating key-
less lever watch, 57mm.
diam. (Christie's)
  $4,850 £2,500

Gold and turquoise set
cylinder watch by Grant,
London, 1819, 44m.
diam. (Sotheby's)
  $931 £480

Gold and enamel pair-
cased quarter repeating
ruby cylinder watch,
50mm. diam. (Sotheby's)
  $26,190 £13,500

Repousse gold pair-cased
quarter repeating verge
watch by Isaac Roberts,
London, circa 1770, 47mm.
diam. (Sotheby's)
  $2,425 £1,250

CLOISONNE

One of two different cloisonne vases from the late 19th century, 9¾in. high. (Sotheby's Belgravia) $307 £160

Early 16th century Ming cloisonne enamel incense burner, 11½in. wide. (Christie's) $3,000 £1,546

One of a pair of early 19th century cloisonne vases, 13½in. high. (Sotheby's Belgravia) $921 £480

Late 19th century cloisonne plate, 12in. diam.(Sotheby's Belgravia) $163 £85

One of a pair of cloisonne Buddhist lions, 8in. high. (Sotheby's Belgravia) $806 £420

Late 19th century cloisonne plate, 12in. diam.(Sotheby's Belgravia) $230 £120

One of a pair of Seto porcelain cloisonne vases, circa 1880, 12¼in. high.(Sotheby's Belgravia) $365 £190

One of a pair of cloisonne vases, circa 1900, 9½in. high.(Sotheby's Belgravia) $326 £170

One of a pair of cloisonne vases, circa 1900, 6in. high.(Sotheby's Belgravia) $384 £200

Late 18th century cloisonne enamel bottle.(Christie's) $230 £119

Early 18th century cloisonne enamel incense burner and cover, 5¼in. diam.(Christie's) $1,400 £721

One of a pair of Chinese cloisonne double gourd vases. (Christie's S. Kensington) $1,252 £620

Cloisonne wall plate, circa 1900, 12in. diam. (Sotheby's Belgravia) $326 £170

Early 19th century ewer and cover in cloisonne, 18½in. high.(Sotheby's Belgravia) $998 £520

Cloisonne dish, circa 1900, 18in. diam. (Sotheby's Belgravia) $557 £290

Silver mounted cloisonne vase, circa 1900, 4in. high.(Sotheby's Belgravia)$749 £390

Late 19th century Takasaki Mitsukotsu cloisonne vase, 7½in. high.(Sotheby's Belgravia) $538 £280

One of pair of cloisonne vases, circa 1900, 10¼in. high.(Sotheby's Belgravia) $384 £200

CLOISONNE

One of a pair of Ch'ien Lung cloisonne enamel boxes and covers, 7in. wide. (Christie's) $1,500 £773

19th century cloisonne koro and cover, 11½in. high.(Sotheby's Belgravia) $403 £210

One of a pair of cloisonne enamel shallow bowls, 6in. diam. (Christie's) $160 £82

Ch'ien Lung cloisonne enamel flower vase, 12½in. high. (Christie's) $1,750 £902

One of a pair of cloisonne vases, circa 1900, 9½in. high. (Sotheby's Belgravia) $1,920 £1,000

One of a pair of late 19th century Ku cloisonne vases, 8¾in. high. (Sotheby's Belgravia) $499 £260

One of a pair of early 20th century cloisonne vases from Japan, 11¾in. high. (Sotheby's Belgravia) $326 £170

Cloisonne jardiniere, circa 1900, 12in. high. (Sotheby's Belgravia) $422 £220

One of a pair of cloisonne vases, circa 1900, 7in. high.(Sotheby's Belgravia) $346 £180

One of a pair of Ch'ien Lung cloisonne enamel quail incense burners, 5in. high.(Christie's) $1,500 £773

Large cloisonne vase, 11¾in. high. (Sotheby's Belgravia) $1,766 £920

One of a pair of cloisonne enamel incense burners, circa 1900, 7in. high.(Sotheby's Belgravia)$614 £320

Cloisonne enamel bottle with matching stopper.(Christie's) $180 £93

K'ang Hsi cloisonne enamel Ku, 13in. high.(Christie's) $2,420 £1,247

Hayashi silver mounted cloisonne vase, circa 1900, 8in. high. (Sotheby's Belgravia) $6,144 £3,200

One of a pair of midnight-blue cloisonne vases, circa 1900, 8½in. high. (Sotheby's Belgravia) $269 £140

Ovoid cloisonne jar and cover, circa 1900, one of a pair, 8½in. high. (Sotheby's Belgravia) $403 £210

One of a pair of cloisonne vases, circa 1900, 5in. high. (Sotheby's Belgravia) $538 £280

One of a pair of late 19th century Oriental cloisonne dogs, incense burners, 8in. long. (Gray's Antique Market) $1,212 £600

Chinese cloisonne covered bowl, 14½in. diameter. (Locke & England) $1,171 £580

Japanese cloisonne plate, circa 1870, 18in. diam. (Gray's Antique Mews) $646 £320

19th century cloisonne incense burner, Ch'ien Lung, 27.6cm. high. (Sotheby's Belgravia) $744 £380

Pair of Japanese cloisonne ovoid vases, circa 1870, 14in. high. (Gray's Antique Mews) $1,212 £600

Late 19th century cloisonne ewer and cover, 30cm. high.(Sotheby's Belgravia) $784 £400

One of a pair of large cloisonne altar candle holders, circa 1900. (King & Chasemore) $784 £400

Two-handled cloisonne bowl, early 15th century, 8in. wide. (Christie's) $39,600 £20,000

Chinese cloisonne enamel koro and cover, 11in. high.(Parsons, Welch & Cowell) $950 £480

George III mahogany plate bucket, 14in. high.(Nottingham Auction Mart) $313 £160

18th century Indian exotic bird container, with brass mounts, 12in. high.(Andrew Sharpe & Partners) $760 £400

16th century Nuremberg brass alms dish, 16½in. diam. (Sotheby's) $361 £190

Art Nouveau brass fire tongs 'companion set', circa 1880, 25in. high. (Gray's Antique Market) $131 £65

Good Wiener Werkstatte tea service, circa 1910, 33.5cm. wide.(Sotheby's Belgravia) $3,492 £1,800

Copper warming pan with boxwood handle, 42in. long.(Nottingham Auction Mart) $101 £50

Late 19th century brass fire grate, 38in. wide.(Sotheby's Belgravia) $969 £480

Late 19th century brass candlestick, 18in. high.(Gray's Antique Market) $36 £18

Adam period fire grate in brass and steel. (Vost's) $808 £400

Horse brass, circa 1870. (Christopher Sykes) $35 £18

Georgian copper harvest measure, 34cm. high. (King & Chasemore) $166 £85

Copper and tin pork pie mould, circa 1880. (Gray's Antique Market) $50 £25

Engraved brass and copper warming pan, circa 1850, 40in. long.(Gray's Antique Market) $151 £75

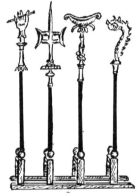

Set of four Chinese ceremonial maces, 65½in. wide. (Sotheby's Belgravia) $595 £310

Copper and brass kettle. (Manchester Auction Mart) $39 £20

Large horse brass on leather with brass buckle.(Christopher Sykes) $75 £38

19th century mahogany and brass cigarette roller. (Gray's Antique Market) $90 £45

Horse brass on a leather strap. (Christopher Sykes) $53 £27

Horse brass on leather. (Christopher Sykes) $55 £28

20th century pressed brass magazine stand. (British Antique Exporters)$24 £12

Horse brass. (Christopher Sykes) $35 £18

Copper and brass jardiniere on stand, Austrian, circa 1910, 53in. high.(Sotheby's Belgravia) $848 £420

One of a pair of patinated and electro-plated copper Christofle vases, 26.5cm. high, 1920's. (Sotheby's Belgravia) $814 £420

Unusual copper and wrought iron illuminated heater, 30in. high, circa 1900. (Sotheby's Belgravia) $444 £220

Late 19th century metal milk container. (Alfie's Antique Market) $89 £45

Small Victorian copper kettle with brass mounted wooden handle. (Alfie's Antique Market)· $76 £38

Horse brass on leather, circa 1870. (Christopher Sykes) $55 £28

COPPER AND BRASS

Mid 19th century gilt brass lion, one of a pair, after Canova, 5in. long.(Sotheby's Belgravia) $589 £310

English brass and copper covered pitcher, circa 1900, 15¼in. high. (Christie's N. York) $264 £138

Antique copper coal-helmet. (Russell, Baldwin & Bright) $138 £70

One of a pair of late 19th century gilt brass candelabra, 21in. high.(Sotheby's Belgravia) $349 £180

Decorative copper gilt frame, 12.7cm. high. (Sotheby's) $1,164 £600

One of a pair of 17th century Flemish brass altar candlesticks, 18¾in. high. (Sotheby's) $776 £400

Early Ch'ien Lung gilt copper wine ewer, one of a pair, 12¾in. high. (Christie's)$1,100 £567

Regency brass and cast iron fireplace and matching fender. (King & Chasemore) $1,176 £600

Rare Louis XV Royal brass mounted copper wall cistern and bowl, late 18th century, 2ft. high.(Sotheby's) $6,930 £3,500

17th century engraved
and embossed brass
alms dish. (Humbert,
King & Chasemore)
$1,858 £920

Brass and lacquer vase
by Jean Dunand, circa
1925.(Sotheby's
Monaco)
$38,047 £19,142

One of a pair of mid
18th century Dutch
brass andirons, 1ft.
5½in. high.(Sotheby's)
$509 £260

Gilt brass and pottery
standard lamp, fitted
for electricity, 1870's,
57in. high.(Sotheby's
Belgravia) $213 £110

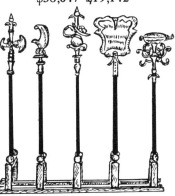

Set of five Chinese cere-
monial maces, 65½in.
wide.(Sotheby's Belgravia)
$595 £310

One of a pair of brass
candelabra, circa 1870,
18¼in. high. (Sotheby's
Belgravia) $192 £100

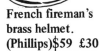

French fireman's
brass helmet.
(Phillips)$59 £30

Late 17th century double
sided brass sandwich box,
5¼in. long. (Phillips)
$570 £300

Copper jar with a sil-
ver cover, surmounted
by a lapis lazuli finial.
(Bonham's)$217 £110

COPPER AND BRASS

19th century brass ritual water ewer from Borneo, 11in. long. (Gray's Antique Market) $303 £150

Victorian brass watering can. (British Antique Exporters) $30 £15

Late 19th century oak framed gong. (British Antique Exporters) $24 £12

Benares embossed brass tray, 23in. diam. (Nottingham Auction Mart) $77 £38

20th century copper washing dolly. (British Antique Exporters) $30 £15

16th century Nuremberg alms dish, 16½in. diam. (Sotheby's) $950 £500

19th century brass fireguard. (British Antique Exporters) $40 £20

Brass and steel fire grate, circa 1900, 39in. wide. (Sotheby's Belgravia) $848 £420

Late 19th century brass coal scuttle. (British Antique Exporters) $40 £20

Coral maiden immortal, 4½in. high, on wood stand. (Christie's)$638 £328

Small German amethystine quartz snuff box, circa 1760, 4.5cm. wide. (Sotheby's) $548 £280

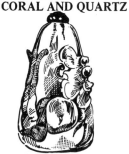

Smokey quartz bottle with tiger's eye stopper. (Christie's) $120 £62

Carved coral group, 6½in. high, on wood stand. (Christie's) $660 £340

Rose quartz group of two maidens, 9½in. high. (Christie's) $900 £463

Coral figure of a goddess, 6½in. high, on wood stand. (Christie's) $682 £351

Carved coral figure of a lady, 7½in. high, on wood stand. (Christie's) $462 £238

Rose quartz figure of two maidens, 6in. high. (Christie's) $400 £206

Coral Kuan Yin, 8in. high, on wood stand. (Christie's)$825 £425

Large chain point collar with scallop edge, circa 1840. (Gray's Antique Mews) $30 £15

Lady's Chinese robe in pure silk, hand embroidered, circa 1860. (Gray's Antique Market)
$376 £190

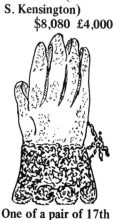

Levee or court coat of the Surrey Yeomanry, circa 1795. (Christie's S. Kensington)
$8,080 £4,000

Mandarin court vest, Hsein Feng period. (Gray's Antique Mews)
$298 £148

A pair of 19th century blonde Chantilly stockings with side lacings, 78cm. long.(Phillips)
$200 £105

One of a pair of 17th century Dutch lady's kid gloves, circa 1635. (Sotheby's)
$1,995 £1,050

First World War fur-lined flying suit, French, circa 1914. (Sotheby's Belgravia)
$148 £75

Pair of Queen Victoria's bloomers. (Bonham's)
$424 £210

19th century lady's Imperial Court dragon robe. (Gray's Antique Mews) $749 £364

Schoneau and Hoff-
meister doll, 21in.
high. (Sotheby's)
$2,156 £1,100

French bisque-headed
doll by Bru, marked
Bebe Bru No. 7.
(Phillips)
$5,684 £2,900

Shoulder bisque-headed
doll, 19in. high, circa
1880, with blonde wig.
(Sotheby's)
$470 £240

Jumeau open mouth
doll with original wig,
1890, 23in. high.
(Gray's Antique Mews)
$1,313
£650

Bisque-headed doll,
'Lucy', 100cm. high,
with ball jointed
limbs. (King & Chase-
more) $1,010 £500

French porcelain headed
doll with jointed limbs
and sleeping eyes.
(Barber's) $616 £305

French Jumeau doll,
1890, 15in. high.
(Gray's Antique Market)
$1,767 £875

Rare brown bisque-
headed bebe Jumeau
doll. (Christie's S. Ken-
sington) $4,356 £2,200

French porcelain headed
doll, with jointed limbs.
(Barber's) $579 £305

German shoulder papier mache doll, 11½in. high, circa 1840.(Sotheby's) $784 £400

Steiner bisque doll, 19in. high, with white broderie anglaise dress. (Sotheby's)$1,607 £820

George III painted wooden doll, legs missing.(Sotheby's) $1,528 £780

German shoulder china doll, 17¼in. high, circa 1860, with a baby. (Sotheby's)$1,058 £540

Heubach mechanical doll which rocks very smoothly.(Sotheby's) $352 £180

Bisque shoulder headed 'googly-eyed' doll with long velvet body. (Christie's S. Kensington) $3,232 £1,600

German porcelain headed talking doll, 60cm. high. (May, Whetter & Grose) $217 £107.50

19th century bisque headed doll by Simon & Halbig, 22in. high.(Sotheby Bearne) $1,590 £840

German porcelain headed baby doll by A.M., 60cm. high. (May, Whetter & Grose) $171 £85

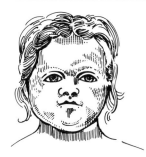

Biedermeier shoulder papier mache doll, 21in. high, circa 1830. (Sotheby's)$1,156 £590

Montanari poured shoulder wax doll, 23in. high, circa 1860.(Sotheby's) $470 £240

Good Pierotti type shoulder wax doll, 10½in. high, circa 1875. (Sotheby's) $352 £180

20th century Jumeau doll with bisque head and body. (Phillips) $6,732 £3,400

Late 19th century wax-faced doll. (Manchester Auction Mart)$233 £118

Rare Biedermeier shoulder papier mache doll, 13in. high, circa 1825. (Sotheby's) $509 £260

Schoenau and Hoffmeister doll, 25in. high, circa 1905. (Bonham's) $247 £130

Carved and painted doll, circa 1710. (Christie's S. Kensington) $3,686 £1,900

One of three wooden peg dolls, 11½in. high, in late Victorian clothes. (Sotheby's) $176 £90

Army doll from the
1914-18 War period.
(Sotheby's)
$282 £140

Simon and Halbig, Kam-
mer and Reinhardt doll,
circa 1905. (Gray's Anti-
que Mews) $353 £175

Army doll of the
1914-18 period.
(Sotheby's)
$282 £140

Bisque-headed German
doll with smiling face,
in original clothes and
box. (Osmond Tricks)
$323 £170

Early 20th century bisque-
headed clockwork walking
doll in original clothes and
box. (Christie's S. Kensington) $3,333 £1,650

German shoulder com-
position doll, circa
1840, 15½in. high.
(Sotheby's Belgravia)
$517 £260

Fine French socketed
bisque fashion doll, circa
1860, 18in. high.
(Sotheby's Belgravia)
$3,582 £1,800

German doll with sleeping
brown eyes, in original
box and clothes. (Osmond
Tricks) $304 £160

Fine Steiner bisque doll,
circa 1880, 21in. high.
(Sotheby's Belgravia)
$1,034 £520

Bilston enamelled
box in dark blue.
(T. Bannister)
$108 £55

French Art Deco enamel
and silver cigarette box,
3½in. long.(Gray's Antique
Mews) $181 £90

Bilston spaniel bon-
bonniere, circa 1770-
75, 5cm. wide.
(Sotheby's)
$653 £320

One of a pair of
Bilston candlesticks,
circa 1770, 31cm.
high. (Sotheby's)
$1,089 £550

One of a pair of champleve
vases, circa 1880, 9¼in.
high. (Sotheby's Belgravia)
$768 £400

Champleve enamel
vase, circa 1870's,
13¾in. high.
(Sotheby's Belgravia)
$285 £150

Russian enamelled egg
with pull-off top by
Pavel Ovtschinnikov,
Moscow, circa 1900.
(Phillips)
$2,375 £1,250

Late 19th century ena-
melled plate, 16¾in.
diam. (Sotheby's Bel-
gravia) $691 £360

Bilston enamelled
box in dark blue.
(T. Bannister)
$69 £35

German enamel snuff
box, circa 1763, 8.5cm.
wide. (Sotheby's)
$548 £280

Small Bilston enamel
box, circa 1760.
(Gray's Antique Mar-
ket) $356 £180

Late 19th century ena-
melled silver box and
cover, 3in. diameter.
(Sotheby's Belgravia)
$346 £180

French enamel bottle
with hinged cover.
(Christie's S. Kensing-
ton) $603 £300

Late 19th century champ-
leve incense burner base,
54½in. high. (Sotheby's
Belgravia) $499 £260

Champleve vase, circa
1880, with ovoid body.
(Sotheby's Belgravia)
$211 £110

Rectangular enamel snuff
box, German, circa 1760,
8cm. wide. (Sotheby's)
$1,568 £800

Gilt metal seal with
enamel handle,
(Christie's S. Kensing-
ton) $424 £210

Mid 18th century German
enamel snuff box, 6.5cm.
wide. (Sotheby's)
$970 £500

English gilt metal chatelaine, circa 1750, hung with an etui.(Sotheby's) $427 £220

Mid 18th century gilt metal chatelaine, hung with thimble box and etui, 23cm. long. (Sotheby's)$427 £220

Unusual English gilt metal etui case on a belt clip. (Sotheby's) $427 £220

Mid 18th century gilt metal and hardstone etui case, 11cm. long. (Sotheby's)$310 £160

English etui, circa 1760, 11cm. long. (Sotheby's) $233 £120

Unusual silver etui, probably English, circa 1770, 10.5cm. long. (Sotheby's) $427 £220

FABERGE

Delicate little carnelian squirrel by Faberge. (Christie's Geneva) $21,387 £10,802

Hardstone figure of a houseboy by Faberge in lapis lazuli, Kalgan jasper and gold. (Sotheby's Zurich) $63,598 £32,448

Faberge circular photograph frame in silver, 2¾in. diam. (Nottingham Auction Mart) $3,332 £1,700

263

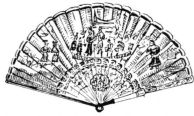

Fan painted with Pierrot's marriage, circa 1740, 10in. wide. (Christie's S. Kensington) $1,050 £520

Woloon, circa 1760, leaf painted fan, 10in. wide.(Christie's S. Kensington) $633 £320

French silk leaf painted fan, circa 1785, with ivory sticks, 10½in. wide. (Christie's S. Kensington)$1,623 £820

Leaf painted fan, circa 1760, with carved mother-of-pearl sticks, 10¾in. wide.(Christie's S. Kensington) $1,485 £750

Edwardian fan painted in the 18th century style with a silk leaf and bone sticks. (Bonham's) $131 £65

Leaf painted fan, circa 1760, with pierced ivory sticks, 10½in. wide. (Christie's S. Kensington)$1,346 £680

Mid 18th century French fan with ivory silk leaf. (Phillips) $376 £190

French painted chicken skin fan, with ivory sticks. (Geering & Colyer) $95 £50

Augsburg leaf painted fan, circa 1760, 11¼in. wide. (Christie's S. Kensington) $1,504 £760

Bone framed hand-painted fan, circa 1860, 18in. wide. (Gray's Antique Mews) $50 £25

English masquerade fan, circa 1740, on ivory sticks, 10½in. wide. (Christie's S. Kensington) $4,158 £2,100

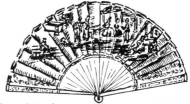

French leaf painted fan, circa 1770, with pressed, pierced ivory sticks, 11in. wide. (Christie's S. Kensington) $792 £400

19th century painted fan, on pierced and gilded mother-of-pearl sticks. (Bonham's) $128 £65

Late 17th century North German leaf painted fan, 12in. wide. (Christie's S. Kensington) $1,584 £800

Late 19th century French ballooning fan, 10¾in. radius. (Sotheby's Belgravia) $396 £200

18th century Flemish fan with carved and pierced ivory sticks, circa 1720's. (Phillips) $124 £65

Salamander Fire Office Society firemark, circa 1822, lead, 6¾in. wide. (Christie's) $446 £230

Sun Fire Office firemark, in lead, circa 1710, 5¾in. wide. (Christie's) $93 £48

Bristol Crown Fire Office mark, circa 1718, lead on wooden mount, 6½in. wide. (Christie's) $329 £170

Hand-in-Hand Fire And Life Insurance Society mark, in lead, 8in. wide. (Christie's) $349 £180

Large engraved brass 'London & Lancashire Fire Insurance Company' wall plaque, 16in. wide. (Christopher Sykes) $166 £85

Bath Fire Office mark in painted lead, 6½in. wide. (Christie's) $465 £240

Rare insurance firemark, 'Bath Sun Fire'. (Christopher Sykes) $186 £95

Firemark of the London Assurance Fire Office, in lead, circa 1720, 7in. wide. (Christie's) $814 £420

Australian copper insurance firemark, 'Victoria'. (Christopher Sykes) $94 £48

Victorian mahogany single bed with panelled ends. (British Antique Exporters) $200 £100

Mid 19th century painted cradle, 38½in. long. (Sotheby's Belgravia) $990 £500

One of a pair of Biedermeier beds in golden burr and straight cut elm, 6ft.5in. long, circa 1840. (Sotheby's) $1,485 £750

Impressive carved oak four poster bed with later additions. (Lawrence's) $6,262 £3,100

Partly 17th century oak four poster bed, 6ft.10in. long. (Sotheby's) $2,985 £1,500

Antique English oak full tester bed, 5ft. 6in. wide. (James Harrison) $7,070 £3,500

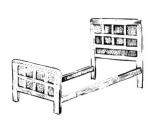

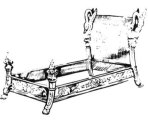

'Mouseman' oak bed by Robert Thompson, circa 1935, 39in. wide. (Sotheby's Belgravia) $404 £200

Early George III carved giltwood and painted four poster bed, 5ft.10in. wide, circa 1765. (Sotheby's) $30,300 £15,000

Unusual giltwood and plaster bed, 19th century, 4ft. wide. (Sotheby's) $1,287 £650

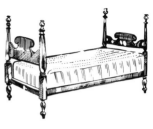

Empire ormolu mounted
mahogany bed, 6ft.6in.
long, circa 1810.
(Sotheby's)
$3,900 £2,100

Late 19th century bed
with cupboards in
frieze, 90in. wide.
(Sotheby's Belgravia)
$1,382 £720

One of a pair of maho-
gany beds, 36in. wide,
1860-80.(Sotheby's
Belgravia) $138 £70

Elizabethan oak tester
bed, 5ft.9in. wide,
posts and backboard,
circa 1600.(Sotheby's)
$19,600 £10,000

19th century carved
oak half-tester bed.
(James Harrison)
$4,085 £2,150

Mid 19th century fruit-
wood and softwood
moon-shaped bed.
(Sotheby's Belgravia)
$4,312 £2,200

Caned mahogany
cradle, circa 1880,
29in. long.
(Sotheby's Belgravia)
$376 £190

Brass half-tester bed, circa
1900, 76in. wide.
(Sotheby's Belgravia)
$464 £230

Walnut half-tester
bed, circa 1900,
83 x 58¼in.
(Sotheby's Belgravia)
$601 £310

Victorian mahogany
bed with quilted
headboard. (Hy.
Duke & Son)
$557 £280

17th century carved
oak four poster bed,
4ft.6in. wide. (But-
ler & Hatch Waterman)
$5,050 £2,500

Victorian painted
metal bed. (Hy.
Duke & Son)
$597 £300

Mid 20th century soft-
wood and simulated
bamboo tester bed,
72¾in. long.
(Sotheby's Belgravia)
$1,176 £600

17th century oak
cradle with pointed
hood, 3ft. long.
(Sotheby's)
$1,465 £740

19th century maho-
gany four poster
bed, 3ft.6in. wide.
(King & Chasemore)
$684 £360

Mahogany and burl
walnut double bed by
Louis Majorelle, circa
1897, 68½in. wide.
(Christie's N. York)
$10,000 £5,050

Giltwood bed, circa
1900, with padded
headboard, 62in.
wide. (Sotheby's Bel-
gravia) $594 £300

Early 17th century
oak four poster bed.
(Phillips)
$2,850 £1,500

Ebonised and gilt bookcase, circa 1870.(Sotheby's Belgravia)$363 £180

One of a pair of early 20th century walnut side cabinets, 29½in. wide.(Sotheby's Belgravia) $1,293 £650

Early Victorian mahogany bookcase, 50in. wide.(Christopher Sykes)$1,115 £575

Carved oak bookcase, 1860's, 31in. wide. (Sotheby's Belgravia) $485 £250

Simulated rosewood bookcase, circa 1840, 104in. wide.(Sotheby's Belgravia) $656 £330

19th century Flemish carved oak bookcase cupboard, 4ft.10in. wide.(Coles, Knapp & Kennedy)$2,880 £1,500

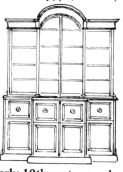

George IV library bookcase, circa 1825, 6ft.2in. wide.(Sotheby's) $3,136 £1,600

Georgian mahogany bookcase on splay feet, 3ft.2¾in. wide. (Geering & Colyer) $1,746 £900

Early 19th century mahogany arch top library breakfront bookcase, 99in. high.(Phillips) $5,130 £2,700

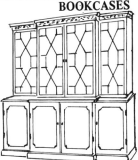

George III mahogany breakfront bookcase, 1890's, 95in. high. (Sotheby's Belgravia) $2,134 £1,100

George III figured and inlaid mahogany breakfront library bookcase. (Edwards, Bigwood & Bewlay)$4,268 £2,200

Georgian style mahogany breakfront bookcase.(Sotheby Bearne)$3,168 £1,600

William IV pedestal bookcase in rosewood, 19½in. high. (Christie's S. Kensington)$4,158 £2,100

One of a pair of Regency rosewood and brass inlaid breakfront dwarf cabinets, 153cm. wide.(King & Chasemore) $3,298 £1,700

George III mahogany bookcase, circa 1800, 3ft.11in. wide. (Sotheby's) $1,580 £820

19th century mahogany bookcase, 5ft.8in. wide. (King & Chasemore) $3,783 £1,950

Victorian glazed bookcase on cupboard base.(Linden Alcock) $1,115 £575

Dutch bookcase with cupboard underneath. (Worsfolds) $1,616 £800

BOOKCASES

Late 19th century walnut secretaire bookcase.(British Antique Exporters) $600 £300

Victorian stripped pine hanging shelves. (British Antique Exporters) $34 £17

20th century oak bookcase, 20in. wide. (British Antique Exporters) $30 £15

Late Victorian carved oak bookcase with cupboard below, 3ft.6in. wide. (Vernon's Chichester) $360 £180

19th century mahogany breakfront library bookcase, 81in. wide. (Parsons, Welch & Cowell) $4,257 £2,150

Oak bookcase with balustraded cornice, 1865-70, 97½in. high. (Sotheby's Belgravia) $1,575 £780

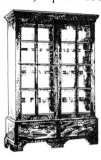

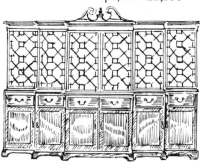

Georgian mahogany bookcase, 5ft.4in. wide. (McCartney, Morris & Barker) $3,366 £1,700

Black-japanned double breakfront library bookcase, 11ft. 4in. wide, circa 1800. (Sotheby's) $6,664 £3,400

Carved oak bookcase, 1920's, 59in. wide, in the manner of Samuel Pepys bookcases. (Sotheby's Belgravia) $1,414 £700

18th century floral marquetry Dutch walnut bureau, 45in. wide.(Messenger, May & Baverstock) $6,060 £3,000

18th century Italian stained wood and mahogany cube parquetry fall front bureau.(Edwards, Bigwood & Bewlay) $3,762 £1,900

Dutch satinwood cylinder bureau, circa 1770, 3ft.6in. wide.(Sotheby's) $2,842 £1,450

Small early 18th century walnut bureau with fall front, 27in. wide.(Butler & Hatch Waterman) $4,646 £2,300

George III satinwood and rosewood cylinder bureau. (Drewatt, Watson & Barton) $12,524 £6,200

20th century oak bureau with oxidised handles. (British Antique Exporters)$130 £65

18th century Dutch walnut and marquetry bureau, 114cm. wide. (King & Chasemore) $5,273 £1,650

19th century rosewood and kingwood bombe bureau de dame with ormolu mounts. (May, Whetter & Grose) $1,212 £600

Antique honey coloured walnut fall front bureau, 3ft. wide. (Worsfolds) $1,818 £900

273

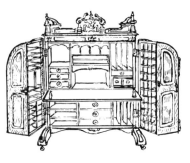

Edwardian inlaid mahogany writing bureau. (D. M. Nesbit & Co.)
$1,010 £500

Wootton Wells Fargo desk. (Christie's S. Kensington)
$5,544 £2,800

18th century oak bureau with fitted interior, 43in. high. (Gray's Antique Mews)
$1,414 £700

Fine Georgian mahogany bureau with square handles.(Bonsor Pennington)
$1,515 £750

Mid 19th century Continental mahogany cylinder bureau. (King & Chasemore) $574 £290

18th century oak bureau on bracket feet, 36in. wide. (Nottingham Auction Mart)$404 £200

Kingwood and tulipwood marquetry bonheur du jour, circa 1900, 62in. wide.(Sotheby's Belgravia)
$4,179 £2,100

Queen Anne walnut kneehole bureau, 3ft. 5in. wide, circa 1710. (Sotheby's)
$7,448 £3,800

Edwardian inlaid rosewood bureau de dame, 76cm. wide. (Pearson's)
$1,368 £720

18th century marquetry bombe bureau, 40in. wide. (Burtenshaw Walker) $5,562 £2,700

Walnut and mahogany Wootton Wells Fargo office desk, late 1870's. (Sotheby's Belgravia) $485 £250

Late 18th century Dutch marquetry cylinder bureau, 50½in. wide. (Christie's) $4,074 £2,100

Late George III mahogany and satinwood small cylinder bureau, 24¼in. wide. (Christie's) $4,116 £2,100

Dutch marquetry bombe bureau. (Edmiston's) $6,534 £3,300

Rare German black-japanned writing cabinet, circa 1700, 3ft. 2in. wide. (Sotheby's) $1,995 £1,050

Late 19th century rosewood and floral marquetry escritoire, 26in. wide. (Neales) $1,178 £620

Queen Anne laburnum bureau, 3ft.2½in. wide. (Parsons, Welch & Cowell) $2,178 £1,100

Late 19th century mahogany and satinwood cross-banded cylinder bureau, 76cm. wide. (King & Chasemore) $1,050 £520

George II walnut
bureau with four
drawers, circa 1740,
41in. wide.(Bonham's)
$1,672 £880

18th century Dutch wal-
nut and floral marquetry
bureau.   (Phillips)
$8,118 £4,100

Queen Anne walnut
bureau, 3ft.4in. wide,
circa 1710.(Sotheby's)
$1,568 £800

Louis XV provincial
walnut bureau, circa
1750, 3ft.7in. wide.
(Sotheby's)
$4,116 £2,100

18th century marquetry
bureau with ball and
claw feet.(W. Brown)
$5,597 £2,900

Mid 19th century Con-
tinental mahogany and
painted cylinder bureau,
97cm. wide.(King &
Chasemore)
$2,112 £1,100

17th century oak arc
bureau, Scottish.
(Coles, Knapp &
Kennedy)$330 £170

Small walnut bureau,
1920's, 26in. wide.
(Sotheby's Belgravia)
$562 £290

Lombard ivory inlaid
walnut bureau, circa
1720.(Sotheby's)
$5,656 £2,800

Edwardian satinwood bonheur du jour with cylinder front, 2ft.6in. wide. (Messenger, May & Baverstock) $1,454 £720

18th century Dutch marquetry double bureau, 4ft.9in. wide. (Woolley & Wallis) $5,510 £2,900

Good walnut bureau, modern, 2ft.7½in. wide. (Sotheby's) $1,649 £850

Queen Anne walnut and crossbanded bureau, 92cm. wide. (King & Chasemore) $2,178 £1,100

18th century Dutch marquetry bureau in walnut.(Woolley & Wallis)$5,771 £2,900

George I walnut bureau in need of repair. (Coles, Knapp & Kennedy) $5,292 £2,700

George III country made oak and mahogany crossbanded bureau, 39in. wide.(Osmond Tricks) $893 £470

Cylinder bureau by C. C. Saunier, 3ft.4in. wide, circa 1780. (Sotheby's) $43,120 £22,000

18th century Dutch mahogany and marquetry bureau. (Watson's) $48,480 £24,000

277

Good early 18th century walnut bureau, 3ft. wide. (Parsons, Welch & Cowell) $2,376 £1,200

Early 18th century cross-banded and figured walnut bureau.(Clifford Dann) $4,550 £2,350

Mid 18th century Dutch marquetry bureau in walnut, 106cm. wide.(King & Chasemore) $6,432 £3,350

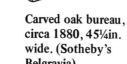

George III mahogany bureau, 40in. wide. (Nottingham Auction Mart) $784 £400

Satinwood and marquetry cylinder bureau, stamped Maple & Co.(Christie's S. Kensington) $4,356 £2,200

Carved oak bureau, circa 1880, 45¼in. wide. (Sotheby's Belgravia) $792 £400

18th century Dutch oak bureau.(King & Chasemore) $2,376 £1,200

Dutch Colonial tulipwood bureau with fall front. (Moore, Allen & Innocent) $2,475 £1,250

18th century Dutch style marquetry bureau. (G. Summersgill) $5,880 £3,000

Louis XV provincial
oak bureau a cylindre,
circa 1770, 3ft.7in.
wide.(Sotheby's)
$3,168 £1,600

18th century Dutch
marquetry bureau.
(Drewery & Wheeldon)
$5,400 £2,700

Early Georgian oak
bureau, 94cm. wide.
(King & Chasemore)
$1,344 £700

Rare Queen Anne
laburnum bureau.
(Parsons, Welch &
Cowell)
$2,178 £1,100

Louis Quinze design
kingwood and cross-
banded bureau a
cylindre, 77cm. wide.
(King & Chasemore)
$1,344 £700

Dutch marquetry cyl-
inder bureau, circa
1810, 3ft.4in. wide.
(Sotheby's)
$2,450 £1,250

Unusual George II small
oak bureau, 2ft.6in.
wide.(Sotheby's)
$1,552 £800

Mid 18th century
mahogany bureau
on bracket feet.
(Fellow's)
$2,134 £1,100

18th century Dutch
floral marquetry bureau.
(Russell, Baldwin &
Bright) $6,138 £3,100

279

Mahogany bureau bookcase, circa 1920, 3ft.6in. wide. (Sotheby's) $1,176 £600

18th century German walnut bureau cabinet. (King & Chasemore) $8,316 £4,200

18th century South German oak and marquetry bureau bookcase, 45in. wide.(Parsons, Welch & Cowell) $3,876 £2,040

Queen Anne period bureau cabinet in oak veneered with walnut, 1.04m. wide. (Christie's) $13,720 £7,000

Rare William and Mary oak bureau bookcase with twin domed top, 42in. wide.(Morphets) $7,878 £3,900

Early 18th century Queen Anne figured walnut bureau bookcase, 75in. high.(Pearson's) $2,422 £1,275

Late 19th century mahogany bureau bookcase, 36in. wide.(Sotheby's Belgravia) $523 £270

Queen Anne walnut double domed bureau bookcase, 3ft.9in. wide. (Sotheby's)$12,152 £6,200

George II mahogany bureau bookcase, 3ft. 4in. wide, circa 1750. (Sotheby's) $5,346 £2,700

Queen Anne oak bureau cabinet, 3ft.8in. wide. (Sotheby's) $3,589 £1,850

George III bureau bookcase in mahogany, 115cm. wide.(King & Chasemore) $5,742 £2,900

Late 19th century oak bureau bookcase, 78in. high.(Sotheby's Belgravia) $691 £360

Fine coloured late Georgian mahogany bureau bookcase, 40in. wide. (Locke & England) $2,323 £1,150

Fine Edwardian walnut secretaire bureau bookcase.(R. J. Garwood) $3,069 £1,550

Italian walnut bureau bookcase, lower part circa 1750, 3ft.8in. wide.(Sotheby's) $3,528 £1,800

Mid 18th century Venetian green lacquer bureau cabinet, 46in. wide.(Christie's) $15,520 £8,000

18th century walnut bureau bookcase. (Stride's)$3,939 £1,950

George III mahogany bureau bookcase, circa 1780, 3ft.6in. wide. (Sotheby's)$2,475 £1,250

281

Georgian mahogany bureau bookcase, 42in. wide, circa 1820. (Silvester's) $1,892 £975

George III oak bureau cabinet, 3ft.2¾in. wide. (Sotheby's) $3,007 £1,550

Inlaid mahogany bureau bookcase with glazed top. (Way, Riddett & Co.) $3,168 £1,600

Venetian scarlet and cream lacquer bureau cabinet, 49¼in. wide. (Christie's) $3,686 £1,900

Red lacquer double domed English bureau cabinet. (H. Spencer & Sons) $5,454 £2,700

Narrow Queen Anne bureau bookcase in burr-walnut.(Clarke Gammon) $25,730 £13,500

Early 19th century Dutch marquetry bureau cabinet, 42in. wide. (Christie's) $5,044 £2,600

Georgian oak bureau bookcase carved in the Abbotsford manner.(Dee & Atkinson) $1,454 £720

Mid 18th century South German walnut bureau cabinet, 56¼in. wide. (Christie's) $48,500 £25,000

George II mahogany bureau with carved cornice, circa 1770. (Langlois)$9,500 £5,000

Oak bureau bookcase. (Swetenham's) $1,114 £560

Queen Anne walnut bureau bookcase, 37in. wide.(Worsfolds) $7,070 £3,500

Walnut veneered Queen Anne style double domed bureau bookcase.(Nottingham Auction Mart) $2,037 £1,050

Queen Anne walnut double domed bureau bookcase, circa 1710, 3ft.5in. wide. (Sotheby's)$7,524 £3,800

George I walnut bureau bookcase. (Christie's N. York) $11,000 £5,800

Mid 18th century Dutch mahogany bureau cabinet, 4ft.1in. wide. (Sotheby's)$4,312 £2,200

George III satinwood cylinder secretaire bookcase, circa 1790, 3ft.2in. wide.(Sotheby's) $3,626 £1,850

Edwardian mahogany bureau bookcase of excellent proportions. (D. M. Nesbit & Co.) $1,919 £950

283

Reproduction Queen Anne figured walnut bureau bookcase, 2ft. 2in. wide. (Lalonde, Bros. & Parham) $1,919 £950

Late 18th century Dutch oak and floral marquetry bookcase, 1.15m. wide. (Phillips) $7,676 £3,800

George III mahogany bureau bookcase, 3ft. 2in. wide, circa 1785. (Sotheby's) $9,504 £4,800

Mahogany bureau bookcase, 1900's, with glazed doors.(Sotheby's Belgravia) $1,979 £980

Small 18th century bureau bookcase in lignum vitae, 34in. wide. (Butler & Hatch Waterman) $3,030 £1,500

18th century mahogany bureau bookcase on bracket feet. (British Antique Exporters) $800 £400

Late 19th century mahogany bureau bookcase on stand, 76cm. wide. (King & Chasemore) $2,828 £1,400

20th century oak bureau bookcase with H stretcher. (British Antique Exporters) $240 £120

George III mahogany bureau cabinet, circa 1770, 3ft.3in. wide. (Sotheby's) $1,980 £1,000

19th century Japanese lacquer cabinet, 19in. high. (Gray's Antique Mews) $969 £480

Mahogany and marquetry side cabinet, circa 1900, 31in. wide. (Sotheby's Belgravia) $594 £300

Early 19th century lacquered cabinet, 3ft.6in. wide. (Weller Eggar) $7,725 £3,750

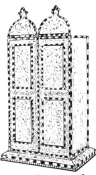

Damascus ivory and brass inlaid hardwood cabinet, circa 1900, 40cm. wide.(Sotheby's Belgravia) $490 £250

Late 19th century lacquer and hardwood shrine. (Sotheby's Belgravia) $11,312 £5,600

Edwardian rosewood, satinwood and ivory inlaid side cabinet, 2ft. wide. (Alfie's Antique Market) $525 £260

17th century carved oak cabinet, 3ft.10in. wide. (Butler & Hatch Waterman) $3,232 £1,600

19th century Italian ebonised and ivory inlaid table cabinet, 28in. high.(Phillips) $2,121 £1,050

One of a pair of 19th century Chinese black lacquered cabinets, inlaid with hardstones (Christie's) $6,464 £3,200

One of a pair of French cabinets with ormolu mounts, circa 1870, 44in. wide.(Silvester's) $1,772 £895

Stylish 1930's cocktail cabinet in pale walnut, 144cm. wide.(Sotheby's Belgravia) $1,176 £600

Rosewood and kingwood parquetry wall cabinet, early 20th century, 1ft. 10in. wide. (Sotheby's) $431 £220

George III mahogany cabinet on stand. (Christie's S. Kensington) $1,980 £1,000

Victorian rosewood miniature collector's cabinet, 22in. high. (Christie's S. Kensington) $633 £320

19th century ornate carved walnut cabinet, 82cm. wide. (King & Chasemore) $1,372 £700

James II red-japanned cabinet on giltwood stand, 41in. wide.(Humberts, King & Chasemore) $12,540 £6,600

Late 17th century scarlet and gold lacquer cabinet on stand, 49in. wide.(Christie's) $7,840 £4,000

16th century North European oak cabinet on stand.(Boardman's) $5,970 £3,000

19th century Chinese
lacquered and carved
cabinet, 63in. high.
(Vincent & Vander-
pump) $1,368 £720

Satinwood bow fronted
side cabinet, 3ft.4in.
wide.(Sotheby's)
$980 £500

Ebonised beechwood
brass inlaid meuble
d'appui, circa 1870,
42¾in. wide.
(Sotheby's Belgravia)
$509 £260

19th century carved
oak cabinet in the
French Gothic style.
(King & Chasemore)
$792 £400

Mahogany and tortoise-
shell boulle cabinet on
stand, 58½in. wide,
1920's.(Sotheby's Bel-
gravia) $1,474 £760

Late 18th century
Dutch mahogany and
marquetry cabinet,
5ft.3in. wide.(Sothe-
by's) $5,684 £2,900

Queen Anne style wal-
nut cabinet on chest,
86cm. wide. (King &
Chasemore)
$1,568 £800

18th century Japanese
lacquer cabinet on stand,
3ft.6in. wide.(Parsons,
Welch & Cowell)
$1,054 £530

19th century carved
oak cabinet in Gothic
style, 82cm. wide.
(King & Chasemore)
$588 £300

Ormolu, ebony and pietra dura cabinet, 1830's, 65¼in. wide.(Christie's) $41,580 £21,000

Amboynawood side cabinet, circa 1870, 41in. wide.(Sotheby's Belgravia)$633 £320

Solid walnut side cabinet, mid 1870's, 73in. wide. (Sotheby's Belgravia) $464 £230

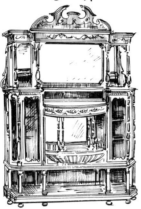

William and Mary walnut cabinet on stand, 3ft.6½in. wide. (Sotheby's) $4,653 £2,250

Satinwood side cabinet with swan neck cresting, circa 1890, 86in. high.(Sotheby's Belgravia) $955 £480

Rare Godwin ebonised mahogany aesthetic cabinet, circa 1869, 96in. high.(Sotheby's Belgravia) $12,120 £6,000

19th century Japanese lacquered spice cabinet, 10½in. high.(Nottingham Auction Mart)$196 £100

Victorian carved oak coal cabinet. (Vernon's, Chichester) $90 £45

Victorian boulle writing cabinet, circa 1880, 14½in. wide.(Sotheby's Belgravia) $633 £320

19th century rosewood music cabinet, 57cm. wide, with glass panelled door. (May, Whetter & Grose) $424 £210

Early 18th century black lacquer cabinet, 3ft.3in. wide. (Sotheby's)
$2,450 £1,250

Early Edwardian rosewood music cabinet, 23in. wide. (May, Whetter & Grose)
$411 £210

19th century buhl writing cabinet with ormolu mounts. (Alonzo, Dawes & Hoddell)
$2,660 £1,400

Mahogany two section cabinet, 5ft.1in. wide. (Woolley & Wallis)
$1,780 £900

Flemish walnut cabinet on stand, circa 1670, 3ft. 8in. wide, with giltwood cresting. (Sotheby's)
$5,880 £3,000

Eugene Printz patin-ated bronze and lac-quered wood cabinet, 1930's, 109cm. high. (Sotheby's Belgravia)
$2,376 £1,200

Elaborate Continental ebonised jewel casket, 14in. high.(Langlois)
$2,970 £1,500

Mid 18th century Anglo-Indian ivory inlaid miniature bureau cabinet, 23in. wide. (Christie's) $3,528 £1,800

CABINETS

Continental ebonised and walnut veneered shrinal cabinet.(Russell, Baldwin & Bright)
$1,584 £800

Mid 19th century mahogany side cabinet, 40in. wide, with hinged top. (Sotheby's Belgravia)
$431 £220

Late 17th century burr-elm cabinet on chest, 3ft.8in. wide.(Sotheby's)
$5,148 £2,600

Walnut dental cabinet, circa 1890, figured in burr-wood, 29¼in. wide.(Sotheby's Belgravia) $776 £400

Early 18th century oak spice cabinet in excellent condition. (William H. Brown)
$505 £250

Chinoiserie cabinet on stand, circa 1920, 39½in. wide. (Sotheby's Belgravia)
$744 £380

George I black and gold lacquer cabinet on stand, 38in. wide. (Christie's)
$1,332 £680

Rare polychrome painted writing cabinet.(Sotheby's Belgravia)
$41,588 £21,000

George II black lacquer and gilt cabinet, 3ft.2in. wide.(Sotheby's)
$2,940 £1,500

290

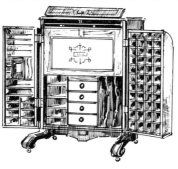

Mahogany secretaire cabinet, French, 1830's, 39in. wide.(Sotheby's Belgravia) $277 £140

Wootton 'Wells Fargo' walnut office desk, circa 1880, 39in. wide.(Sotheby's Belgravia) $5,174 £2,600

Victorian rosewood miniature collector's cabinet, 22in. high. (Christie's S. Kensington) $636 £320

Liberty & Co. tall oak side cabinet, circa 1920, 26in. wide.(Sotheby's Belgravia) $490 £250

Late 17th century Charles II black lacquer cabinet on stand, 43in. wide. (Christie's)$2,548 £1,300

Late 19th century German Dresden mounted side cabinet.(Sotheby's Belgravia) $19,000 £10,000

16th century Flemish oak Renaissance cabinet on stand. (Boardman's) $5,940 £3,000

Antique Dutch oak marquetry cabinet, 3ft.5½in. wide, on stand.(Warner, Sheppard & Wade) $5,390 £2,750

Mahogany collector's cabinet, 1860's, 49¾in. high.(Sotheby's Belgravia) $717 £370

CABINETS

17th century Spanish walnut vargueno, 41½in. wide.(Christie's) $6,596 £3,400

Japanese Edo period lacquer cabinet, 2ft. 1in. wide.(King & Chasemore)$1,202 £620

Late 17th century Spanish walnut cabinet, 73in. wide. (Christie's) $2,425 £1,250

Walnut cabinet of Henry II style, 42in. wide. (Christie's) $2,619 £1,350

One of a pair of mid 19th century ebonised side cabinets, 54½in. wide. (Christie's) $2,716 £1,400

Mahogany cabinet, circa 1895, 68½in. high. (Christie's N. York) $660 £340

17th century Italian walnut cabinet, 63½in. wide. (Christie's) $3,589 £1,850

18th century Spanish vargueno and stand, 3ft. wide. (Messenger, May & Baverstock's) $1,900 £1,000

Partly 17th century Dutch oak cabinet, 64in. wide.(Christie's) $5,238 £2,700

Charles II lacquered and simulated tortoiseshell cabinet on stand. (Christie's)
$7,334 £3,800

17th century Flemish ebony cabinet, 34in. wide. (Christie's)
$5,626 £2,900

Late 17th century Dutch colonial silver mounted cabinet on stand, 47cm. wide. (King & Chasemore)
$3,456 £1,800

Small Art Nouveau breakfront cabinet, circa 1900, 58in. wide. (Christie's N. York) $550 £283

Late 17th century Spanish walnut and tortoiseshell cabinet, 43½in. wide. (Christie's) $4,462 £2,300

Modern rosewood side cabinet, 73in. high. (Sotheby's Belgravia)
$346 £180

17th century North Italian ebony and ivory inlaid table cabinet, 36in. wide.(Christie's)
$1,940 £1,000

Japanese hardwood cabinet with shibayama panels, mid 19th century, 6ft.3in. high. (Gray's Antique Market) $3,232 £1,600

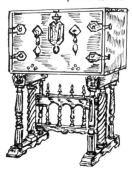

17th century Spanish walnut vargueno, 41½in. wide.(Christie's)
$3,977 £2,050

CABINETS

Mid 19th century Dutch marquetry cabinet, 97cm. wide. (King & Chasemore) $895 £450

Flemish red tortoiseshell and ebony cabinet, 17th century, 34in. high. (Henry Duke & Son) $5,130 £2,700

Victorian pine hanging cabinet with glazed door.(British Antique Exporters) $24 £12

Edwardian satin walnut cabinet with painted decoration. (British Antique Exporters) $600 £300

A pair of ebonised and burr-walnut side cabinets, circa 1880, 36in. wide. (Sotheby's Belgravia) $888 £440

Late 19th century walnut side cabinet. (British Antique Exporters) $170 £75

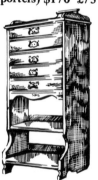

Late 19th century washstand complete with cistern. (British Antique Exporters) $150 £75

Victorian mahogany display cabinet. (British Antique Exporters) $200 £100

Art Nouveau style beechwood music cabinet. (British Antique Exporters) $70 £35

Victorian rosewood canterbury with a drawer below. (Phillips) $323 £160

Regency rosewood canterbury with drawer, 48cm. wide. (King & Chasemore) $675 £350

Edwards and Roberts mahogany canterbury, 1880's, 20in. wide. (Sotheby's Belgravia) $396 £200

Burr-walnut canterbury, 28in. high, circa 1850. (Sotheby's Belgravia) $576 £300

Reproduction mahogany, flat splat canterbury. (British Antique Exporters) $200 £100

Victorian rosewood canterbury/whatnot. (D. M. Nesbit & Co.) $367 £190

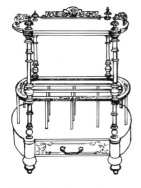

Mid Victorian walnut stand with canterbury below, 2ft.6in. wide. (David Symonds) $646 £330

Walnut canterbury in figured wood, circa 1860, 24in. wide. (Sotheby's Belgravia) $435 £220

Victorian bamboo canterbury with lacquered panels. (British Antique Exporters) $30 £15

DINING CHAIRS

One of a set of seven George III Irish mahogany ladderback dining chairs.(Sotheby's)
$2,871 £1,450

One of two antique oak panelled chairs with solid seats.(Phillips)
$1,232 £610

One of four walnut drawingroom chairs, 1870's.(Sotheby's Belgravia)$422 £220

One of a set of four Regency painted and simulated rosewood chairs, circa 1815. (Sotheby's)$548 £280

One of a set of four mid 18th century German cream painted chairs. (Christie's)$3,686 £1,900

One of a pair of George I oak side chairs, circa 1720. (Sotheby's)
$252 £130

One of a set of six George III mahogany chairs, circa 1780. (Sotheby's)$693 £350

One of a set of six walnut dining chairs. (Christie's)
$3,201 £1,650

One of a set of ten George III mahogany dining chairs, circa 1920.(Sotheby's Belgravia) $1,382 £720

One of a set of six rosewood dining chairs, 1850's.(Sotheby's Belgravia) $659 £340

One of a set of six American rush-seated stained elm and beech chairs, early 18th century.(Sotheby's)$950 £480

One of a set of six Regency mahogany dining chairs.(Hobbs Parker)$2,134 £1,100

One of a pair of 17th century Derbyshire chairs with solid panel seats.(Phillips) $444 £220

Charles II oak chair with shaped toprail, circa 1680. (Sotheby's) $291 £150

One of a set of six George III provincial elm dining chairs, circa 1800. (Sotheby's) $931 £480

One of a set of ten Victorian balloon back chairs in rosewood, circa 1850.(Gray's Antique Mews) $3,118 £1,575

One of a set of six burr-walnut and ebonised wood dining chairs, circa 1860.(Sotheby's Belgravia) $633 £320

One of a set of six walnut dining chairs, 1840's.(Sotheby's Belgravia)$776 £400

DINING CHAIRS

One of a set of six rosewood dining chairs, circa 1840.(Sotheby's Belgravia) $835 £420

One of a set of four mahogany drawingroom chairs, circa 1850. (Sotheby's Belgravia) $495 £250

One of a set of six mid 19th century mahogany dining chairs.(Sotheby's Belgravia)$475 £240

One of a set of six Biedermeier fruitwood chairs, circa 1830. (Sotheby's) $686 £350

One of a set of six Flemish carved oak dining chairs, circa 1880.(Sotheby's Belgravia)$607 £310

One of a set of five Regency simulated rosewood dining chairs, circa 1815. (Sotheby's)$990 £500

One of a set of six early 20th century walnut dining chairs.(Sotheby's Belgravia) $704 £360

One of a set of four mid 19th century stained walnut side chairs.(Sotheby's Belgravia) $313 £160

One of a set of six early 19th century elmwood dining chairs.(Sotheby's) $1,386 £700

One of six ash spindle-back chairs with rush seats.(Russell, Baldwin & Bright) $693 £350

One of a set of six James II oak dining chairs, 1840's.(Sotheby's Belgravia) $523 £270

One of a set of six maho-gany dining chairs, circa 1840.(Sotheby's Belgravia) $588 £300

One of a set of six mahogany chairs, circa 1780.(Sotheby's) $2,134 £1,100

One of a set of ten carved oak Carolean design chairs.(Worsfolds) $1,274 £650

One of a set of six in-laid mahogany chairs, circa 1790. (Sotheby's) $686 £350

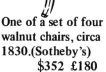

One of a pair of early 20th century Dutch walnut marquetry dining chairs.(Sotheby's Belgravia) $490 £250

One of a set of four walnut chairs, circa 1830.(Sotheby's) $352 £180

Late 19th century German beechwood musical hall chair, 3ft. high. (Sotheby's Belgravia) $497 £250

DINING CHAIRS

One of six late 19th century ebonised beechwood dining chairs.(Sotheby's Belgravia) $346 £175

One of a set of six William IV mahogany dining chairs, 1830's. (Sotheby's Belgravia) $831 £420

One of a set of six George III mahogany dining chairs. (Sotheby's) $4,508 £2,300

William and Mary oak chair, circa 1690. (Sotheby's) $291 £150

One of eight similar fruitwood chairs, late 17th century, possibly Flemish. (Sotheby's)$2,450 £1,250

One of a set of six walnut side chairs, 1860's. (Sotheby's Belgravia) $1,034 £520

One of a set of six walnut drawingroom chairs, 1860's.(Sotheby's Belgravia) $910 £460

One of a set of five painted mahogany dining chairs, 1860's. (Sotheby's Belgravia) $217 £110

One of a set of twelve Carolean design oak dining chairs.(Worsfolds)$2,464 £1,220

One of a pair of Art
Deco giltwood chairs,
94cm. high.
(Sotheby's Belgravia)
$148 £75

One of a set of six
Victorian walnut
framed balloon
back dining chairs.
(May, Whetter &
Grose)$767 £380

William and Mary
oak chair, circa
1690.(Sotheby's)
$291 £150

One of a set of six
Victorian walnut
chairs.(Christie's S.
Kensington)
$980 £500

One of a set of ten Con-
tinental stained frame
chairs with wicker seats.
(May, Whetter & Grose)
$1,030 £510

One of a set of six late
19th century oak din-
ing chairs with drop in
seats. (British Antique
Exporters) $260 £130

One of a set of six
Jacobean stained oak
dining chairs, circa
1880.(Sotheby's Bel-
gravia) $749 £390

One of a set of twelve
17th century style
oak chairs.(May,
Whetter & Grose)
$1,386 £700

One of a set of ten
mahogany chairs in
the Chippendale
manner.(Christie's)
$23,280 £12,000

One of a set of six
mahogany drawing-
room chairs, circa
1850.(Sotheby's)
$929 £460

One of a set of six
William IV rosewood
and mahogany dining
chairs, 1830's.(Sotheby's
Belgravia) $717 £370

One of a set of six
Austrian oak dining
chairs, circa 1900.
(Sotheby's Belgravia)
$235 £120

One of a pair of ebon-
ised and ivory side
chairs, circa 1880.
(Sotheby's Belgravia)
$352 £180

One of a set of six George
III mahogany dining chairs,
circa 1785.(Sotheby's)
$1,764 £900

One of a pair of early
18th century mahogany
framed chairs with cres-
ted pieces.   (Osmond
Tricks) $1,045 £550

One of a set of six wal-
nut side chairs, circa
1860.(Sotheby's Bel-
gravia) $891 £450

One of a pair of 19th
century rosewood
and marquetry chairs.
(Christie's) $504 £260

One of a set of six
walnut side chairs,
circa 1840.(Sotheby's
Belgravia)$814 £420

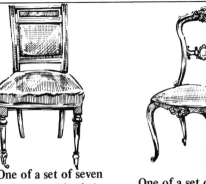

One of a set of seven mahogany side chairs, late 19th century. (Sotheby's Belgravia) $174 £90

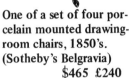

One of a set of four porcelain mounted drawing-room chairs, 1850's. (Sotheby's Belgravia) $465 £240

One of a set of eleven Sheraton period mahogany dining chairs.(Parsons, Welch & Cowell) $5,252 £2,600

Imposing 17th century walnut chair with carved frieze and stretcher. (Butler & Hatch Waterman) $1,010 £500

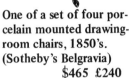

One of a set of six walnut side chairs, 1840's. (Sotheby's Belgravia) $737 £380

One of a set of ten oak dining chairs, circa 1850.(Sotheby's Belgravia) $1,176 £600

One of a pair of 17th century chairs. (Phillips)$464 £230

One of a set of four late 19th century Restoration oak side chairs.(Sotheby's Belgravia) $232 £120

One of a set of six mahogany side chairs, 1840's, with cabriole legs.(Sotheby's Belgravia)$792 £400

Charles II Derbyshire oak chair, circa 1670. (Sotheby's) $504 £260

One of a set of five mahogany dining chairs, 1830's. (Sotheby's Belgravia) $444 £220

One of a pair of ebonised side chairs, 1870's. (Sotheby's Belgravia) $121 £60

One of a set of six late Victorian walnut dining chairs.(Nottingham Auction Mart) $772 £375

One of a pair of Charles II walnut chairs, circa 1680.(Sotheby's) $1,148 £580

Carved cherrywood serpentine fronted musical chair, late 19th century. (Nottingham Auction Mart) $123 £60

One of a set of six Regency beechwood dining chairs.(Humberts, King & Chasemore) $990 £500

One of a pair of George II mahogany chairs, circa 1760. (Sotheby's) $1,215 £620

One of a pair of oak dining chairs by Alfred Waterhouse, 1870's. (Sotheby's Belgravia) $262 £130

One of a set of six 20th century oak dining chairs. (British Antique Exporters) $170 £85

Small strozzi oak spinning chair with pierced carved back and seat. (Butler & Hatch Waterman) $181 £90

One of a pair of George I walnut chairs in very good condition. (Drewatt, Watson & Barton) $3,434 £1,700

One of a set of four Edwardian inlaid mahogany chairs. (British Antique Exporters) $250 £125

Victorian mahogany hall chair on turned legs. (British Antique Exporters) $30 £15

One of a set of six George III mahogany dining chairs, circa 1780. (Sotheby's) $1,862 £950

One of a set of six Victorian mahogany cabriole leg chairs. (British Antique Exporters) $520 £270

One of a set of six 17th century oak standard chairs. (Butler & Hatch Waterman) $2,828 £1,400

One of a set of six late 19th century oak dining chairs. (British Antique Exporters) $50 £25

One of a pair of George
I walnut chairs, circa
1720. (Sotheby's)
$1,411 £720

One of a pair of William
and Mary caned walnut
chairs, circa 1695.
(Sotheby's)$705 £360

19th century reproduction Italian baroque
throne chair in oak, 54in.
high. (Nottingham Auction Mart) $525 £260

Victorian carved oak
hall chair with barley
twist supports.(Vernon's Chichester)$60 £30

One of a set of six Queen
Anne walnut dining chairs.
(Graves, Son & Pilcher)
$5,346 £2,700

One of a set of six 20th
century oak dining
chairs. (British Antique
Exporters) $60 £30

One of a set of six 19th century Hepplewhite style mahogany chairs. (King & Chasemore) $955 £480

One of a pair of 19th
century walnut cabriole chairs from a
set of four. (Gray's
Antique Mews)$646 £320

Fine quality Edwardian
inlaid mahogany salon
chair. (British Antique
Exporters) $70 £35

Two of a set of eight Regency mahogany sabre leg chairs. (King & Chasemore) $4,577 £2,300

Two of a set of ten 19th century mahogany dining chairs in the Chippendale style. (Manchester Auction Mart) $4,242 £2,100

Two of a set of six Regency dining chairs with cane seats. (King & Chasemore) $2,425 £1,250

Two from a set of ten Jacobean style carved oak chairs. (Frank Marshall) $3,282 £1,650

Two of a set of eight dark stained oak frame dining chairs. (May, Whetter & Grose) $484 £240

Two of a set of eight oak framed, leather covered dining chairs. (Vernon's Chichester) $700 £350

Pair of Regency oak armchairs with carved rail-backs.(King & Chasemore)
$2,424 £1,200

Two of eighteen late George III mahogany dining chairs.(Humberts, King & Chasemore) $4,848 £2,400

Two of a set of twelve George III mahogany dining chairs. (Christie's)
$6,664 £3,400

Two of a set of twelve George III black-japanned and gilt chairs.(Spencer's)
$4,560 £2,400

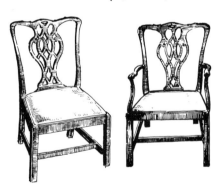

Two of a set of ten George III mahogany dining chairs.(King & Chasemore)
$7,760 £4,000

Two of four 19th century Dutch walnut marquetry chairs.(King & Chasemore) $1,980 £1,000

Two from a set of twelve Gothic style oak dining chairs.(Christie's S. Kensington) $2,525 £1,250

Two of a fine set of six mahogany chairs.(John Milne) $3,333 £1,650

Two of a set of eight rope-back chairs. (Sworder's) $901 £460

Two of a set of six Chippendale style carved mahogany chairs.(King & Chasemore) $970 £500

Two of a set of ten George I oak chairs, circa 1720.(Sotheby's)$1,843 £950

Two of a set of eight walnut dining chairs in William and Mary style. (Christie's) $3,007 £1,550

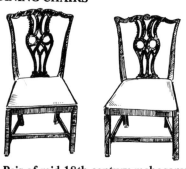

Pair of mid 18th century mahogany chairs of Directoire period. (Gray's Antique Mews) $858 £425

Pair of French mahogany occasional chairs, circa 1890. (Gray's Antique Market) $865 £420

Carved hardwood dining table and six matching chairs, table 81in. wide. (Locke & England) $1,919 £950

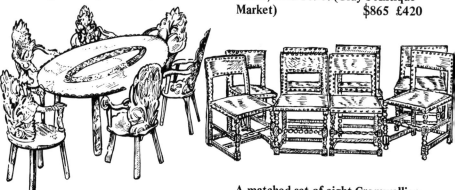

A matched set of eight Cromwellian oak chairs. (King & Chasemore) $3,118 £1,575

Pair from a set of six Regency mahogany dining chairs, early 19th century. (Spear & Sons) $1,140 £600

Two of a set of six 18th century yew and elm Windsor chairs. (Morphets) $1,152 £600

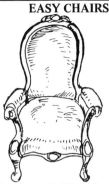

French or Flemish
walnut armchair,
circa 1680. (Soth-
eby's) $1,520 £800

Louis XVI mahogany
fauteuil de bureau,
circa 1785.(Sotheby's)
$3,762 £1,900

Gentleman's Victorian
armchair. (John
Hogbin) $700 £340

One of a pair of late
19th century Louis XV
giltwood fauteuils.
(Sotheby's Belgravia)
$1,352 £680

Dentist's chair upholstered
in leather, circa 1910-15.
(Sotheby's Belgravia)
$222 £110

Part of an early 20th
century suite of gilt-
wood furniture.
(Sotheby's Belgravia)
$1,791 £900

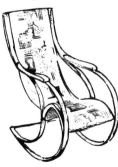

Calvert bent steel 'dig-
estive' rocking chair,
1870's. (Sotheby's
Belgravia) $191 £95

German carved beechwood
fauteuil, circa 1740.
(Sotheby's) $509 £260

Victorian mahogany
framed balloon backed
lady's chair. (Notting-
ham Auction Mart)
$484 £240

One of a pair of George II mahogany armchairs, circa 1750.(Sotheby's) $1,666 £850

One of a set of eight mid 18th century Italian scarlet lacquered and parcel gilt fauteuils.(Christie's) $10,670 £5,500

Charles II walnut armchair, circa 1865.(Sotheby's) $6,860 £3,500

Walnut button back armchair, circa 1860. (Sotheby's Belgravia) $514 £260

Mid 18th century North Italian carved giltwood sleigh seat.(Sotheby's) $1,960 £1,000

Walnut armchair, circa 1920, with seat and back in needlepoint. (Sotheby's Belgravia) $431 £220

Mahogany armchair, 1860's, on cabriole legs with castors. (Sotheby's Belgravia) $415 £210

One of a pair of armchairs by Jacques Rhulmann, circa 1925. (Christie's N. York) $6,380 £3,430

Georgian mahogany framed library chair with reeded legs.(Worsfolds) $1,010 £500

George III mahogany
Gainsborough chair
in lime velour.(Graves,
Son & Pilcher)
$2,772 £1,400

Venetian giltwood arm-
chair, circa 1700, with
stuffed back.(Sotheby's)
$686 £350

Unusual painted beech-
wood throne armchair,
Italian, circa 1880.
(Sotheby's Belgravia)
$485 £250

One of a pair of Anglo-
Indian ebony armchairs,
mid 19th century.
(Sotheby's Belgravia)
$698 £360

Asko fibreglass 'globe'
chair, 1966, 125cm.
diam.(Sotheby's Bel-
gravia) $792 £400

Mid Georgian mahogany
library armchair on cab-
riole legs.(Christie's)
$3,474 £1,800

One of a pair of Louis
XVI style giltwood
fauteuils.(Sotheby's)
$627 £320

One of a pair of Italian
or South German, circa
1850, walnut side chairs.
(Sotheby's Belgravia)
$704 £360

One of a pair of Regency
giltwood caned fauteuils,
circa 1715.(Sotheby's)
$8,360 £4,400

One of a pair of Art
Deco rosewood arm-
chairs, French, circa
1930.(Christie's N.
York)$4,950 £2,551

Walnut button back
armchair, circa 1860.
(Sotheby's Belgravia)
$803 £410

One of a pair of Art
Deco giltwood arm-
chairs, early 1920's.
(Sotheby's Belgravia)
$445 £225

Victorian walnut high
back boudoir chair.
(D. M. Nesbit & Co.)
$407 £210

Mid 18th century Ger-
man blue and pink
painted fauteuil.
(Christie's)
$2,231 £1,150

Rosewood Gothic side
chair, circa 1850.
(Sotheby's Belgravia)
$173 £90

Mid 19th century Victo-
rian mahogany balloon
back chair.(Walker, Bar-
nett & Hill) $437 £230

One of a pair of Art
Deco tub chairs,
early 1920's.
(Sotheby's Belgravia)
$589 £310

George III mahogany
chair, circa 1775.
(Sotheby's)$435 £220

Charles X inlaid pollard-elm bergere, circa 1820. (Sotheby's) $760 £400

Mid 19th century walnut button back armchair.(Sotheby's Belgravia)$980 £500

One of a pair of rosewood armchairs, 1850's.(Sotheby's Belgravia)$291 £150

Victorian walnut high back boudoir chair. (D. M. Nesbit & Co.) $388 £200

Part of an unusual suite of painted wood seat furniture, 1920's. (Sotheby's Belgravia) $1,233 £620

Regency mahogany bergere, circa 1810. (Bonham's) $712 £360

Button upholstered walnut side chair, circa 1860, on cabriole legs. (Sotheby's Belgravia) $392 £200

Large Art Deco giltwood tub chair, early 1920's.(Sotheby's Belgravia) $396 £200

Mid 19th century mahogany button back armchair, one of a pair. (Sotheby's Belgravia) $910 £460

315

One of a pair of early 20th century oak framed tub chairs with leather upholstery. (British Antique Exporters) $100 £50

George II library chair, upholstered in brass studded leather.(Drewatt, Watson & Barton) $1,656 £820

One of a pair of Victorian mahogany tub chairs on cabriole legs. (British Antique Exporters)$130 £65

19th century beechwood bergere chair. (British Antique Exporters) $50 £25

Victorian Abbotsford chair with needlework upholstery. (British Antique Exporters) $150 £75

Victorian rosewood bergere chair on brass castors. (British Antique Exporters) $80 £40

19th century highly carved hardwood easy chair.(British Antique Exporters) $440 £220

Victorian mahogany capstan chair with leather seat. (British Antique Exporters) $50 £25

Late Victorian oak easy chair with padded arms. (British Antique Exporters) $30 £15

One of a pair of late 19th century carved oak armchairs. (Vernon's Chichester) $90 £45

19th century carved mahogany corner chair. (British Antique Exporters) $130 £65

One of a pair of 20th century rush-seated oak elbow chairs. (British Antique Exporters) $120 £60

Highly carved 19th century Oriental hardwood elbow chair. (British Antique Exporters) $250 £125

Early 17th century carved oak wainscot armchair. (Butler & Hatch Waterman) $1,717 £850

Late 18th century elm Windsor stick back chair. (British Antique Exporters) $150 £75

One of a set of eleven George III mahogany dining chairs. (Churchman's) $2,470 £1,300

One of a set of six early 20th century oak framed chairs. (British Antique Exporters) $250 £125

Early 20th century oak rush-seated elbow chair. (British Antique Exporters) $20 £10

317

ELBOW CHAIRS

One of a set of six mid 18th century Venetian rococo giltwood open armchairs. (Christie's) $3,104 £1,600

One of a pair of early 19th century yew wood Windsor armchairs. (King & Chasemore) $1,382 £720

Rosewood and mother-of-pearl inlaid armchair, circa 1880. (Sotheby's Belgravia) $346 £180

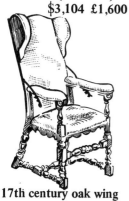

17th century oak wing back armchair. (King & Chasemore) $806 £420

Charles II open armchair, 1662, with curved arms. (Christie's) $1,843 £950

One of a pair of Charles II beechwood armchairs, circa 1685. (Sotheby's)$582 £300

One of a set of seven elmwood Windsor chairs, mid 19th century. (Sotheby's) $1,067 £550

17th century Spanish ebonised open armchair, one of a pair. (Christie's) $1,396 £720

One of a set of ten 19th century Irish chairs in the Chippendale manner. (James Adam's) $3,201 £1,650

One of a pair of rose-
wood armchairs, late
19th century.(Sotheby's
Belgravia) $634 £330

One of four early 19th
century Windsor arm-
chairs. (Sotheby's)
$1,784 £920

One of a set of eight late
19th century rosewood
and marble armchairs.
(Sotheby's Belgravia)
$3,264 £1,700

Gothic walnut arm-
chair, 5ft.11in. high,
circa 1500. (Sotheby's)
$2,134 £1,100

James II oak open arm-
chair, 1680. (Christie's)
$543 £280

Charles II walnut arm-
chair, circa 1680, with
caned back.(Sotheby's)
$349 £180

One of a pair of late 17th
century walnut open arm-
chairs. (Christie's)
$1,552 £800

One of a set of eight North
Country mahogany arm-
chairs. (Christie's)
$2,123 £1,100

Unusual Charles II oak
armchair, circa 1680.
(Sotheby's)$562 £290

One of a pair of mid
18th century Dutch
armchairs.(Sotheby's)
$1,470 £750

One of a set of four
oak armchairs, circa
1895.(Sotheby's Bel-
gravia) $181 £90

One of a set of eight
mahogany dining chairs,
1890's.(Sotheby's Bel-
gravia) $1,584 £800

One of a suite of three
Louis XVI chair frames
by Claude Sene, circa
1787. (Sotheby's)
$9,504 £4,800

Scottish mahogany
armchair, circa 1900.
(Sotheby's Belgravia)
$464 £230

One of a set of six jap-
anned armchairs, mod-
ern, with caned seat
and back.(Sotheby's
Belgravia)$1,194 £600

One of a pair of maho-
gany open armchairs.
(Butler & Hatch Water-
man) $79 £40

One of a pair of Liberty
& Co. oak armchairs,
circa 1900. (Sotheby's
Belgravia) $202 £100

One of a set of eight
mahogany Chippen-
dale dining chairs,
circa 1920.(Sotheby's
Belgravia)$1,393 £700

One of a set of ten beech-wood and oak open arm-chairs. (Christie's)
$6,336 £3,200

Early 20th century walnut Burgomaster chair. (Sotheby's Bel-gravia) $294 £150

Regency ebonised beech-wood open armchair with cane seat.(Geering & Col-yer) $404 £200

One of two provencal rush-seated elmwood fauteuils, late 18th century. (Sotheby's)
$352 £180

Late Elizabethan oak and marquetry armchair, circa 1600. (Sotheby's)
$7,056 £3,600

One of a set of ten late George III mahogany chairs, circa 1800. (Sotheby's)
$5,742 £2,900

Small oak rush-seated armchair by George Walton, circa 1900. (Sotheby's Belgravia)
$1,656 £820

Oriental carved armchair with ivory eyes on arms, circa 1900, 26in. wide. (Gray's Antique Mews)
$454 £225

Part of a stained beech-wood suite, circa 1900, of two armchairs and a settee.(Sotheby's Bel-gravia) $767 £380

One of a pair of William IV caned mahogany bergeres, circa 1835. (Sotheby's)$1,940 £1,000

Good 17th century turned oak chair. (Drewatt, Watson & Barton) $1,656 £820

One of a set of late 19th century oak dining chairs. (Sotheby's Belgravia) $509 £260

Late 17th century Flemish armchair in ebonised wood and veneered ebony. (Sotheby's) $548 £280

Charles I oak armchair, circa 1645, with arched back. (Sotheby's) $1,821 £920

One of a pair of late 18th century Italian caned walnut armchairs.(Sotheby's) $980 £500

A Venetian giltwood throne, circa 1750, upholsted in velvet. (Sotheby's) $1,995 £1,050

One of a pair of late 17th century walnut armchairs, Spanish or Italian.(Sotheby's) $1,019 £520

One of a pair of late Louis XVI mahogany fauteuils, circa 1794, stamped G. Jacob. (Sotheby's) $8,360 £4,400

17th century cock-
fighting chair.
(Russell, Baldwin &
Bright)$1,782 £900

Mid 19th century wal-
nut 'grotto' armchair.
(Sotheby's Belgravia)
$411 £210

Late George II padouk-
wood corner armchair,
circa 1755.(Sotheby's)
$990 £500

One of a pair of Spanish
walnut open armchairs,
basically 17th century.
(Christie's S. Kensington)
$2,352 £1,200

Early 17th century
oak wainscot chair,
with carved back.
(Boardman's)
$1,425 £750

One of eight George
I oak dining chairs,
circa 1720.(Sotheby's)
$1,591 £820

One of a set of eight
late Victorian maho-
gany dining chairs.
(H. Spencer & Sons)
$4,312 £2,200

Part of a stained beech-
wood suite of seat fur-
niture, circa 1910.
(Sotheby's Belgravia)
$713 £360

Empire mahogany fau-
teuil with stuffed back,
circa 1815.(Sotheby's)
$665 £350

ELBOW CHAIRS

One of a set of four
20th century Carine
parquetry armchairs.
(Sotheby's Belgravia)
$803 £410

One of a set of six early
19th century mahogany
dining chairs.(Jackson-
Stops & Staff)
$2,280 £1,200

Early 20th century
Dutch marquetry
corner chair.
(Sotheby's Belgravia)
$431 £220

One of a set of eight
'Chippendale Gothic'
mahogany dining chairs,
circa 1880.(Sotheby's
Belgravia)$3,366 £1,700

One of a set of eight mahogany dining chairs, circa
1900.(Sotheby's Belgravia)
$2,475 £1,250

Early George III maho-
gany armchair, circa
1760. (Sotheby's)
$431 £220

One of a set of five early
19th century Windsor
chairs in elm, sold with
another. (Sotheby's)
$2,134 £1,100

Mid 17th century car-
ved oak armchair.(Rus-
sell, Baldwin & Bright)
$1,683 £850

Late 17th century
North Italian wal-
nut armchair, res-
tored.(Sotheby's)
$274 £140

Mid 17th century carved oak armchair. (Russell, Baldwin & Bright) $1,782 £900

One of a set of ten 'Jacobean' oak dining chairs, 1880's. (Sotheby's Belgravia) $1,784 £920

One of a set of eight late 19th century oak dining chairs.(Sotheby's Belgravia) $883 £460

One of four 18th century Windsor elbow chairs in yew wood and ash.(Russell, Baldwin & Bright) $2,138 £1,080

One of a pair of late 18th century folding campaign chairs. (Sotheby Bearne) $744 £380

Oak armchair with carved back and reeded stretchers.(John H. Raby & Son)$554 £280

One of a set of six stained oak hall chairs, 1880's.(Sotheby's Belgravia) $620 £320

One of a set of six George III mahogany dining chairs.(Christie's) $3,281 £1,700

One of a pair of early 20th century Dutch walnut marquetry armchairs.(Sotheby's Belgravia)$940 £480

Part of a set of seven George III mahogany dining chairs, one arm and six single. (Drewatt, Watson & Barton) $1,102 £580

One of a set of six teak chairs, early 20th century, Indian.(Jackson-Stops & Staff) $798 £420

One of a pair of 17th century oak armchairs.(Spark & Rodgerson) $570 £300

George III mahogany armchair, circa 1785. (Sotheby's)$548 £280

One of a pair of oak open armchairs, circa 1900, 31in. high. (Christie's N. York) $600 £303

One of a pair of late 19th century elm Windsor armchairs. (King & Chasemore) $529 £270

One of a set of eight chairs in mahogany, circa 1860.(Sotheby's) $1,411 £720

One of a pair of Regency oak carved rail-back armchairs.(King & Chasemore) $2,376 £1,200

One of two Colonial carved oak armchairs by Edwards & Roberts.(Jackson-Stops & Staff) $217 £110

Inlaid mahogany
elbow chair.(R. H.
Ellis & Sons)
$133 £66

One of a set of eight
George III mahogany
dining chairs, circa
1880.(Sotheby's Bel-
gravia) $1,784 £920

One of a set of eight
early George III maho-
gany ladderback chairs,
circa 1765.(Sotheby's)
$2,619 £1,350

One of a set of six
George III dining
chairs.(John Francis,
Thomas Jones & Son)
$1,254 £660

Yew wood high back
Windsor elbow chair.
(Neales) $686 £340

One of a set of fourteen
George III mahogany
dining chairs, circa 1810.
(Sotheby's)$3,663 £1,850

One of a pair of
Regency cane seated
lacquer chairs, early
19th century.
(Vost's) $665 £350

One of a set of twelve
early 20th century
stained oak dining
chairs.(Sotheby's Bel-
gravia) $1,287 £650

Part of a set of beech-
wood drawingroom
furniture, 1890's.
(Sotheby's Belgravia)
$504 £260

ELBOW CHAIRS

One of a set of six Charles II beechwood dining chairs, circa 1930. (Sotheby's Belgravia) $929 £460

Early 17th century oak wainscot armchair with carved back. (Butler & Hatch Waterman) $3,232 £1,600

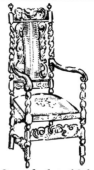

One of a late 19th century set of six rosewood armchairs. (Sotheby's Belgravia) $2,156 £1,100

One of a modern pair of Damascus parquetry armchairs.(Sotheby's Belgravia) $294 £150

Early 20th century stained oak debtor's chair.(Sotheby's Belgravia) $633 £320

One of a set of six 19th century mahogany dining chairs. (British Antique Exporters) $300 £150

One of a set of eighteen early 20th century 'Empire' burr-walnut dining chairs. (Sotheby's Belgravia) $5,572 £2,800

Victorian beechwood smoker's chair with saddle seat.(Vernon's Chichester) $80 £40

One of a set of eight Chippendale mahogany side chairs, circa 1900. (Sotheby's Belgravia) $2,525 £1,250

One of a pair of modern rosewood armchairs with yoke-shaped top-rails. (Sotheby's Belgravia) $666 £340

Victorian carved oak corner chairs. (Vernon's Chichester) $130 £65

Rare Charles II Lancashire oak commode armchair, circa 1685. (Sotheby's) $1,666 £850

One of a pair of Chinese dragon carved rocking chairs, sold with matching table. (Worsfolds) $848 £420

Carlo Bugatti chair of Moorish design. (Phillips N. York) $2,600 £1,287

One of a pair of mid 18th century yew and elmwood armchairs. (Jordan & Cook) $11,330 £5,500

Hepplewhite mahogany armchair. (Woolley & Wallis) $1,153 £560

Part of a giltwood suite, circa 1900, settee, 54in. wide. (Sotheby's Belgravia) $1,990 £1,000

17th century primitive comb-back chair with elmwood seat. (Butler & Hatch Waterman) $606 £300

18th century Italian walnut and ebonised marquetry chest, 145cm. wide.(King & Chasemore)
$2,976 £1,550

Queen Anne walnut chest of drawers, circa 1710, 3ft.1in. wide.(Sotheby's)
$2,425 £1,250

Charles II oak chest, circa 1665, 2ft.4in. wide.(Sotheby's)
$1,504 £760

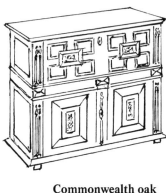

Serpentine fronted Dutch chest of drawers, circa 1800, 38in. high. (Churchman's)
$3,420 £1,800

Mahogany semanier, circa 1900, 23¼in. wide. (Sotheby's Belgravia)
$417 £210

Commonwealth oak chest, 3ft.3in. wide, circa 1660. (Sotheby's)
$1,746 £900

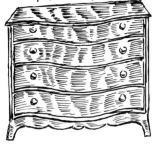

George III mahogany serpentine fronted chest of drawers, 33½in. wide.(Nottingham Auction Mart)$2,231 £1,150

Early Georgian fold-over top gentleman's chest of drawers. (Lalonde Bros. & Parham)
$7,400 £3,700

Early 18th century walnut bachelor's chest. (Pearson's)
$5,415 £2,850

Unusual Jacobean oak chest.(King & Chasemore)
$435 £220

Art Deco burl maple chest of drawers, circa 1925, 51¾in. wide.(Christie's N. York) $440 £226

Mid 17th century inlaid oak chest, circa 1650, 3ft. 8in. wide. (Sotheby's)
$2,772 £1,400

Late 17th century Flemish oak chest, 3ft.4in. wide. (Sotheby's)
$2,134 £1,100

Art Deco burl maple chest of drawers, 63¾in. high.(Christie's N. York) $990 £510

Charles II oak chest, 2ft.11in. wide, circa 1670.(Sotheby's)
$873 £450

Chest of drawers designed by Gordon Russell, circa 1930, 45in. high.(Sotheby's Belgravia)$543 £280

Mahogany Wellington chest of drawers, 1870's, 22¾in. wide. (Sotheby's Belgravia)
$509 £260

Early 18th century English walnut bachelor's chest, 30in. wide. (Christie's)
$8,492 £4,400

331

Fruitwood and oak chest of drawers, circa 1760, 25½in. high. (Gray's Antique Mews) $686 £340

18th century figured mahogany miniature chest of six drawers, 19ins. high. (Nottingham Auction Mart) $504 £260

Commonwealth oak chest, circa 1660, 3ft. 0½in. wide. (Sotheby's) $815 £420

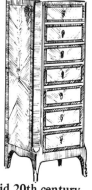

George III mahogany chest, circa 1770, 3ft. wide. (Sotheby's) $1,803 £920

Mid 20th century tulipwood marquetry semanier, 22½in. wide. (Sotheby's Belgravia) $616 £310

18th century Italian walnut and ebonised marquetry chest, 145cm. wide. (King & Chasemore) $2,945 £1,550

William and Mary marquetry chest of drawers. (Christie's) $7,272 £3,600

Mahogany Wellington chest of eight drawers, circa 1880, 53in. high. (Sotheby's Belgravia) $554 £280

William and Mary marquetry chest of four drawers. (Sotheby's) $2,828 £1,400

Charles II oak chest of drawers, 3ft.1½in. wide, circa 1660. (Sotheby's) $4,900 £2,500

19th century Italian carved walnut chest, 5ft. wide. (Sotheby's) $784 £400

George II mahogany chest, circa 1750, 2ft. 6in. wide. (Sotheby's) $1,128 £570

  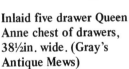

William and Mary oyster-veneered walnut chest, circa 1695, 2ft.10in. wide. (Sotheby's) $4,312 £2,200

Mahogany Wellington chest of seven drawers, circa 1900, 46¾in. high. (Sotheby's Belgravia) $514 £260

Inlaid five drawer Queen Anne chest of drawers, 38½in. wide. (Gray's Antique Mews) $3,333 £1,650

Mid 18th century German walnut chest of drawers, 42in. wide. (Renton & Renton) $3,705 £1,950

Mahogany chest of drawers, circa 1850, 24in. wide. (Silvester's) $392 £198

One of a pair of late 17th century carved oak chests, 33½in. wide. (Sotheby's Belgravia) $484 £240

CHESTS OF DRAWERS

George III oak chest of drawers, circa 1790, 20¼in. wide. (Christopher Sykes) $584 £295

18th century miniature mahogany chest of drawers, 10in. wide. (Sotheby's Belgravia) $257 £130

William and Mary walnut chest of drawers, circa 1690, 3ft. wide. (Sotheby's)$891 £450

Late 17th century oak chest, 100cm. wide.(King & Chasemore) $666 £340

Georgian mahogany chest of drawers, 42in. wide. (Silvester's) $417 £215

Charles II oak chest, 3ft.2in. wide, circa 1670. (Sotheby's) $1,683 £850

Stained oak chest of drawers, circa 1880, 40½in. wide. (Sotheby's Belgravia) $223 £115

Late 16th century Italian walnut chest, 3ft.8in. wide.(Sotheby's)$3,332 £1,700

George III mahogany chest of drawers, circa 1770, 3ft.1¼in. wide. (Sotheby's)$744 £380

Late 17th century oak carved chest, 4ft.3in. wide.(Sotheby's)
$851 £430

Late 19th century floral marquetry inlaid mahogany chest. (Clifford Dann)
$1,386 £700

George III mahogany chest, circa 1785, 4ft. wide. (Sotheby's)
$1,188 £600

Caddy topped mahogany chest of drawers, 42in. wide. (Silvester's) $378 £195

Unusual small Tunbridgeware and walnut Wellington chest, circa 1870, 14½in. wide.(Sotheby's Belgravia) $267 £135

Dutch marquetry chest of drawers, circa 1760, 3ft.1in. wide. (Sotheby's)
$3,234 £1,650

Jacobean oak chest, 98cm. wide.(King & Chasemore)
$1,332 £680

Jacobean walnut and oak chest of drawers. (Boardman's)
$1,373 £680

Walnut and crossbanded miniature chest with star inlay, 30cm. wide. (King & Chasemore)
$1,489 £760

335

Small 17th century oak chest of three drawers, 32in. wide. (Butler & Hatch Waterman) $1,616 £800

20th century Jacobean style oak chest of drawers. (British Antique Exporters)$90 £45

Early 19th century mahogany chest on splay feet. (British Antique Exporters) $150 £75

Queen Anne walnut and crossbanded chest of drawers, 102cm. wide. (King & Chasemore) $824 £400

Small 17th century oak chest of drawers, 31in. wide. (Butler & Hatch Waterman) $2,626 £1,300

Late 18th century oak chest with cockbeaded drawers. (British Antique Exporters) $600 £300

George II walnut chest of drawers with marquetry inlay, 38in. wide. (Locke & England) $2,424 £1,200

Reproduction Georgian style chest on cabriole legs. (British Antique Exporters)$350 £175

Small 17th century oak chest of drawers, 4ft. 6in. wide. (Butler & Hatch Waterman) $2,020 £1,000

18th century walnut chest on stand, 37in. wide. (Nottingham Auction Mart)
$1,940 £1,000

19th century inlaid mahogany chest on tapered legs. (British Antique Exporters)
$180 £90

Early 19th century walnut chest on stand. (British Antique Exporters)
$450 £225

Late 17th century country made chest on stand in oak. (Phillips)
$1,292 £640

Late 17th century Flemish ebonised and decorated chest on stand. (Andrew Grant)
$8,080 £4,000

17th century oak chest on stand, 38in. wide.(Butler & Hatch Waterman)
$1,565 £775

George I oak and walnut chest on stand, 3ft.4¾in. wide, circa 1720. (Sotheby's)
$1,683 £850

19th century marquetry chest in William and Mary style. (West London Auction)
$2,323 £1,150

Late 18th century crossbanded chest on stand.(British Antique Exporters)
$700 £350

CHEST ON CHESTS

George I walnut tall-boy, circa 1720, 3ft. 6in. wide. (Sotheby's) $2,376 £1,200

George II oak chest on chest, mid 18th century, 66in. high. (Spark & Rogerson) $874 £460

19th century figured mahogany tallboy, 42in. high.(Nottingham Auction Mart) $1,649 £850

Mid 18th century mahogany chest on chest. (Nock Deighton) $1,414 £700

George I burr-walnut secretaire chest on chest, 3ft. 8½in. wide, circa 1720. (Sotheby's)$4,116 £2,100

18th century mahogany chest on chest fitted with brushing slide. (McCartney, Morris & Barker) $4,560 £2,400

George I walnut tallboy, circa 1720, 6ft.4in. high, on bracket feet. (Sotheby's)$2,574 £1,300

18th century walnut and crossbanded tallboy, 106cm. wide. (King & Chasemore) $1,812 £880

18th century oak and walnut tallboy, 69½in. high. (Buckell & Ballard) $1,577 £830

19th century mahogany chest on chest with bracket feet. (British Antique Exporters) $500 £250

18th century country made walnut tallboy, 3ft.2in. wide. (King & Chasemore) $3,880 £2,000

George I walnut tallboy, 3ft.7in. wide, circa 1720. (Sotheby's) $8,910 £4,500

Georgian mahogany chest on chest of eight drawers. (Worsfolds) $1,212 £600

George III mahogany secretaire tallboy with brass handles, 44½in. wide. (Graves, Son & Pilcher) $2,475 £1,250

18th century Queen Anne burr walnut cabinet on chest, 109cm. wide.(King & Chasemore) $5,568 £2,900

A fine late 18th century mahogany chest on chest with shaped apron. (British Antique Exporters) $700 £350

Queen Anne walnut crossbanded chest. (Riddett's) $7,070 £3,500

George I walnut secretaire chest on chest, 3ft.7in. wide, sides split. (Sotheby's) $4,508 £2,300

339

CHIFFONIERS

Fine quality rosewood chiffonier, 45in. wide. (Silvester's) $366 £185

Regency chiffonier in rosewood, circa 1820, 36in. wide.(Christopher Sykes) $940 £475

Late 19th century mahogany chiffonier. (British Antique Exporters) $250 £125

Inlaid walnut Victorian chiffonier with brass mounts. (Dickinson, Davy & Markham) $1,038 £530

Late 19th century oak cupboard. (British Antique Exporters)$34 £17

One of a pair of George IV brass inlaid rosewood side cabinets, 3ft.7in. wide, circa 1825. (Sotheby's) $4,158 £2,100

COMMODES AND POT CUPBOARDS

19th century French walnut pot cupboard on shaped legs.(British Antique Exporters) $70 £35

Edwardian inlaid mahogany bedside cupboard. (British Antique Exporters) $40 £20

Victorian bamboo and cane pot cupboard. (British Antique Exporters) $30 £15

George III figured mahogany commode, 24 x 24in. (Nottingham Auction Mart) $970 £500

Victorian mahogany pot cupboard with fluted sides. (British Antique Exporters) $170 £85

French directoire bidet with marble top, 52cm. wide. (Phillips) $4,554 £2,300

Late 18th century George III mahogany tray top bedside table.(Humberts, King & Chasemore) $456 £240

19th century mahogany lift-up commode with shaped apron. (British Antique Exporters) $80 £40

19th century mahogany lift-up commode with ebony inlay. (British Antique Exporters) $130 £65

George III mahogany pot cupboard, circa 1770, 29in. high. (Gray's Antique Mews) $606 £300

Victorian mahogany commode complete with liner. (British Antique Exporters) $40 £20

George III mahogany tray top commode. (British Antique Exporters) $250 £125

341

COMMODE CHESTS

Mid 19th century king-
wood commode, 63in.
wide. (Christie's)
$2,522 £1,300

Scandinavian walnut mar-
quetry chest, circa 1780,
3ft.11½in. high.
(Sotheby's)
$3,135 £1,650

18th century Continen-
tal walnut shaped front
commode, 4ft.2in. wide.
(Messenger, May & Baver-
stock) $3,939 £1,950

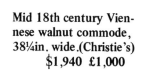

Mid 18th century Liege
green painted and gilded
commode, 37in. wide.
(Christie's)
$2,910 £1,500

One of a pair of late
18th century South
Italian walnut and
marquetry commodes.
(Christie's)
$13,130 £6,500

Mid 18th century Vien-
nese walnut commode,
38¼in. wide.(Christie's)
$1,940 £1,000

Louis XIV marquetry
and ormolu mounted
commode, 122cm.
wide. (Phillips)
$24,812 £12,500

Regency provincial
elm commode, 2ft.
7in. wide, circa 1720.
(Sotheby's)
$2,058 £1,050

Late 18th century Mil-
anese marquetry com-
mode, 4ft.2in. wide.
(Sotheby's)
$2,116 £1,080

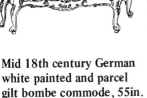

Mid 18th century German white painted and parcel gilt bombe commode, 55in. wide. (Christie's) $10,670 £5,500

Good quality late Georgian mahogany commode with two drawers. (Locke & England) $2,222 £1,100

South German olive-wood commode. (Christie's) $848 £420

Dutch commode with burr-walnut panels, rosewood crossbanding, 39½in. wide. (Graves, Son & Pilcher) $5,148 £2,600

Antique oak dwarf commode, 3ft.10½in. wide. (Warner, Sheppard & Wade) $1,323 £675

Dutch marquetry small serpentine commode, 31½in. wide.(Christie's) $3,298 £1,700

One of a pair of Biedermeier bird's eye maple commodes, 41in. wide. (Christie's) $2,910 £1,500

Late 18th century French commode veneered in tulipwood, 33in. wide. (Riddett's) $3,800 £2,000

French walnut commode, circa 1790, 43½in. wide. (Christopher Sykes) $679 £350

Mid 18th century Dutch painted corner cupboard, 1ft.11½in. wide. (Sotheby's) $980 £500

18th century japanned bow-fronted corner cupboard. (Alfie's Antique Market) $643 £325

Oak corner cupboard, circa 1790, 29½in. high. (Gray's Antique Mews) $252 £125

Walnut veneered early 19th century glazed corner cupboard. (T. Bannister) $921 £475

Georgian mahogany corner display cabinet, 3ft. 6in. wide. (Geering & Colyer) $1,184 £575

George III mahogany corner cabinet, late 19th century, 100in. high. (Sotheby's Belgravia) $620 £320

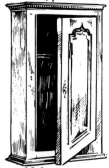

Late 18th century oak corner cupboard, 29in. wide. (Nottingham Auction Mart) $282 £140

One of a pair of South German kingwood and tulipwood standing corner cupboards, mid 18th century. (Christie's) $4,074 £2,100

20th century oak Jacobean style corner cupboard. (Vernon's Chichester) $170 £85

Bow-fronted corner cupboard. (J. M. Welch) $420 £210

Satinwood corner cabinet, circa 1900, with inlaid top and door. (Sotheby's Belgravia) $969 £480

Late 18th century mahogany hanging corner cupboard. (British Antique Exporters) $350 £175

17th century marquetry inlaid bow-fronted double corner cupboard, 4ft.6in. wide. (Worsfolds) $5,252 £2,600

Victorian carved oak corner cupboard with broken arch pediment. (Vernon's Chichester) $330 £165

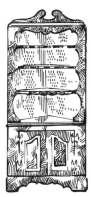

Walnut open corner cupboard, circa 1860, 72 x 29in. (Sotheby's Belgravia) $607 £310

One of a pair of mid 18th century Louis XV ormolu mounted kingwood parquetry encoignures, 3ft. 0½in. high.(Sotheby's) $12,160 £6,400

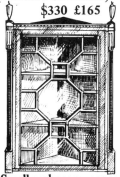

Small mahogany corner cupboard with brass gallery, 1890's, 33½ x 20in. (Sotheby's Belgravia) $465 £240

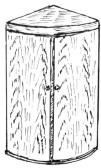

George III bow-fronted corner cupboard. (Nottingham Auction Mart) $504 £260

18th century oak court cupboard, 200cm. wide. (King & Chasemore) $1,730 £840

Court cupboard with panels converted into hinged doors. (May, Whetter & Grose) $1,485 £750

Small 16th century oak court cupboard, 50in. wide.(Butler & Hatch Waterman) $5,757 £2,850

Continental court cupboard with fitted drawer and under tray. (Russell, Baldwin & Bright)$3,762 £1,900

Early Charles II oak cupboard, 5ft.6in. wide. (Sotheby's) $1,358 £700

Late 17th century Welsh oak duodarn, 48in. wide.(Christie's) $1,940 £1,000

Mid 19th century oak court cupboard, 51in. wide. (Sotheby's Belgravia) $607 £310

Stained oak court cupboard, made in the mid 19th century.(Sotheby's Belgravia) $1,148 £580

Bleached oak court cupboard, 57in. wide, circa 1860.(Sotheby's Belgravia) $796 £400

Mid 17th century carved and panelled oak court cupboard. (Russell, Baldwin & Bright) $3,069 £1,550

18th century court cupboard, ornately carved, 56in. high.(Nottingham Auction Mart) $1,656 £820

Elizabethan carved oak court cupboard with open platform base, 124cm. wide. (King & Chasemore) $3,648 £1,900

17th century carved oak court cupboard. (King & Chasemore) $1,188 £600

George II oak and elm court cupboard, 3ft. 7in. wide, circa 1735. (Sotheby's) $5,880 £3,000

20th century Jacobean style oak court cupboard. (Vernon's Chichester) $500 £250

18th century oak court cupboard, 56½in. wide. (Osmond Tricks) $1,900 £1,000

Charles I oak court cupboard, circa 1630, 3ft.8½in. wide. (Sotheby's) $4,312 £2,200

Late 17th century Welsh oak court cupboard. (Russell, Baldwin & Bright) $3,069 £1,550

Gilt metal mounted walnut and burr-chestnut side cabinet, circa 1870, 72in. wide.(Sotheby's Belgravia)
$1,346 £680

Boulle and ormolu credenza, 7ft. wide. (Anderson & Garland) $3,492 £1,800

Walnut side cabinet, circa 1870, 4ft. 9in. wide. (Sotheby's) $1,411 £720

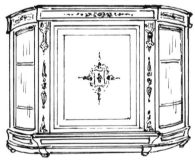

Late 19th century ebonised breakfront credenza, 60in. wide.(Nottingham Auction Mart) $470 £240

Good walnut side cabinet, 1880's, 76in. wide. (Sotheby's Belgravia)
$3,980 £2,000

19th century walnut and floral marquetry side cabinet. (Sotheby Bearne)
$5,970 £3,000

Ebonised mahogany side cabinet, 1870's, 43¾ x 65in.(Sotheby's Belgravia) $333 £170

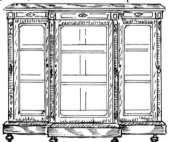

Walnut breakfront side cabinet, 54in. wide, circa 1870.(Sotheby's Belgravia) $960 £500

Victorian walnut and marquetry side cabinet, 82in. wide.(Christie's S. Kensington) $4,462 £2,300

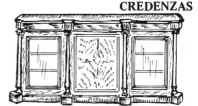

Walnut and burr-walnut side cabinet, circa 1870, 80in. wide.(Sotheby's Belgravia) $1,632 £850

Mid 19th century ebony and boulle dwarf cabinet, 49½in. wide.(Christie's) $1,940 £1,000

Marquetry kingwood porcelain mounted side cabinet, circa 1870, 82in. wide.(Sotheby's Belgravia) $4,074 £2,100

Ebonised and burr-walnut side cabinet, 58in. wide, circa 1860.(Sotheby's Belgravia) $415 £210

Mid 19th century walnut side cabinet, 67in. wide.(Sotheby's Belgravia) $568 £290

Walnut marquetry side cabinet with marble top, circa 1870, 46½in. wide. (Sotheby's Belgravia) $509 £260

Good burr-walnut side cabinet, 1860's, 72in. wide.(Sotheby's Belgravia) $2,885 £1,450

Oak cupboard on stand, circa 1880, 45in. wide. (Sotheby's Belgravia)
$634 £330

Charles I oak cupboard. (Bonham's)
$1,313 £650

Oak buffet, made from 17th century wood, 3ft. 7in. wide.(Sotheby's)
$776 £400

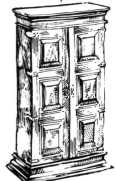

17th century French carved oak cupboard, 65cm. wide.(King & Chasemore)
$285 £150

19th century carved oak cupboard in French Renaissance style. (King & Chasemore)
$1,274 £650

Rare mid 17th century Flemish walnut cupboard, 2ft.10in. wide. (Sotheby's)
$2,156 £1,100

Mid 18th century Louis XV provincial oak cupboard, 4ft.8in. wide. (Sotheby's)
$1,607 £820

Biedermeier fruitwood cupboard, circa 1830, 3ft.8in.(Sotheby's)
$372 £190

George II oak cupboard, 4ft.5in. wide.(Sotheby's)
$659 £340

18th century Dutch walnut and marquetry side cupboard. (Phillips)$8,316 £4,200

Early 18th century oak cupboard, 55in. wide.(Christie's) $873 £450

18th century Continental carved oak bacon cupboard, 200cm. wide. (King & Chasemore) $1,728 £900

Early 18th century Welsh oak tridarn, 51¾in. wide. (Christie's) $1,707 £880

Late 19th century oak side table with cupboard. (British Antique Exporters) $140 £70

Late 19th century hardwood hall cupboard, 49¼in. wide. (Sotheby's Belgravia) $407 £210

19th century Colonial carved teak linen press, 48in. wide.(Alonzo Dawes & Hoddell) $855 £475

Queen Anne oak cupboard or dresser, circa 1705, 4ft.6in. wide. (Sotheby's) $3,395 £1,750

18th century Dutch walnut and marquetry cupboard and stand, 73¼in. wide.(Phillips) $7,980 £4,200

351

Rare mid 16th century
oak dole cupboard.
(Phillips) $2,880 £1,600

Stained oak 'Gothick'
low cupboard, 1860's,
39in. wide. (Sotheby's
Belgravia) $727 £360

Charles I oak ewery
cupboard, circa 1640,
3ft.10½in. wide.
(Sotheby's)
$1,396 £720

Antique Flemish carved
oak cupboard, 5ft.4in.
wide. (Geering & Colyer)
$1,905 £925

Good Charles I oak cup-
board or buffet, 5ft.0½in.
high, circa 1630.
(Sotheby's)$2,619 £1,350

Flemish oak bookcase
cupboard, 19th cen-
tury. (Coles, Knapp &
Kennedy)
$2,910 £1,500

Unusual Charles I oak
hutch cupboard, 3ft.8in.
wide, circa 1640.
(Sotheby's)$1,358 £700

19th century Flemish
tridarn cupboard,
34in. wide.(Notting-
ham Auction Mart)
$686 £340

Early 17th century James
I oak livery cupboard.
(Boardman's)
$3,230 £1,700

Reproduction oak cupboard with panelled doors. (British Antique Exporters) $150 £75

Unique 17th century part open cupboard, 66½in. wide. (Butler & Hatch Waterman) $7,676 £3,800

Mid 18th century Louis XV marquetry coiffeuse, 2ft.4½in. high. (Sotheby's) $9,504 £4,800

Mid 19th century carved oak cupboard, 145cm. wide. (King & Chasemore) $1,372 £700

Good early 18th century Dutch four-door rosewood and ebony cupboard. (Leys Antwerp) $7,972 £3,870

18th century Louis XV provencal walnut garde-manger, 3ft.4in. wide. (Sotheby's) $5,488 £2,800

16th century North European dressoir. (Boardman's) $6,060 £3,000

Edwardian satinwood faced linen press. (D. M. Nesbit & Co.) $1,373 £680

Fine Art Nouveau mahogany sideboard cupboard, French, circa 1900, 59in. wide. (Christie's N. York) $6,000 £3,030

Burr-walnut Davenport, circa 1860, 36in. wide. (Sotheby's Belgravia) $633 £320

Late 19th century walnut Davenport, 24in. wide.(Sotheby's Belgravia) $796 £400

Burr-walnut Davenport, circa 1870, 36 x 21¾in. banded with boxwood and burr-chestnut. (Sotheby's Belgravia) $776 £400

Victorian rosewood Davenport, 53cm. wide.(King & Chasemore) $871 £440

Victorian rosewood piano top Davenport, 25in. wide.(Geering & Colyer) $1,313 £650

Oak Davenport with three quarter gallery, 1880's, 24in. wide. (Sotheby's Belgravia) $475 £240

Mid 19th century rosewood Davenport, 26½in. wide.(Sotheby's Belgravia) $392 £200

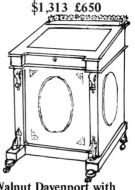

Walnut Davenport with leather writing surface, circa 1860, 33½in. wide. (Sotheby's Belgravia) $653 £330

Walnut Davenport, 1ft.9in. wide, circa 1860.(Sotheby's) $744 £380

Rosewood Davenport,
1870's, with leather-
lined top, 20¾in. wide.
(Sotheby's Belgravia)
$756 £390

Walnut and burr-
walnut Davenport,
1870's.(Sotheby's
Belgravia)
$582 £300

19th century rose-
wood Davenport,
19in. wide.(V. &
V's)$1,108 £560

Rosewood Davenport,
1830's, 19¾in. wide.
(Sotheby's Belgravia)
$1,029 £520

Late 19th century wal-
nut Davenport, 33½in.
high.(Sotheby's Bel-
gravia) $736 £370

Mid 19th century wal-
nut Davenport, 32 x
23½in.(Sotheby's Bel-
gravia) $514 £260

Late 19th century grai-
ned rosewood Daven-
port, 21in. wide.
(Sotheby's Belgravia)
$594 £300

William IV rosewood
Davenport, circa 1830,
1ft.9in. wide.
(Sotheby's)$1,764 £900

Walnut Davenport,
circa 1860, 33 x
21½in. with carved
legs.(Sotheby's Bel-
gravia) $465 £240

Mid Victorian walnut Davenport, 24in. wide. (Christie's S. Kensington) $1,717 £850

Davenport desk in figured walnut and inlaid decoration, circa 1860, 32in. high. (Gray's Antique Mews) $777 £385

Burr-walnut inlaid ebonised Davenport, 22in. wide, circa 1860-80. (Sotheby's Belgravia) $613 £310

Good burr-walnut harlequin Davenport, 22in. wide, 1860's. (Sotheby's Belgravia) $1,190 £620

Good walnut harlequin Davenport, 1860's, 33½in. wide. (Sotheby's Belgravia) $1,267 £640

Walnut harlequin Davenport, 1860's, 23in. wide. (Sotheby's Belgravia) $1,485 £750

Unusual walnut Davenport and canterbury, circa 1870, 24in. wide. (Sotheby's Belgravia) $557 £290

Mid Victorian walnut Davenport with gallery top. (Christie's S. Kensington) $1,616 £800

Victorian burr-walnut piano top Davenport desk. (Boardman's) $1,555 £770

Mid 19th century walnut Davenport, 21¼in. wide. (Sotheby's Belgravia) $495 £250

Victorian rosewood Davenport, 53cm. wide. (King & Chasemore) $862 £440

Unusual walnut Davenport writing table, circa 1870, 20¾in. wide. (Christopher Sykes) $544 £275

Walnut Davenport, circa 1860, 37½in. wide, with central turned balustrade. (Sotheby's Belgravia) $606 £300

Victorian oak Davenport, 21in. wide, circa 1870. (Silvester's) $455 £235

Walnut Davenport, 1870's, 24in. wide, with leather lined writing slope. (Sotheby's Belgravia) $646 £320

Walnut harlequin Davenport, circa 1860, 23in. wide. (Sotheby's Belgravia) $698 £360

Walnut Davenport with satinwood interior, 2ft. 6in. wide. (Worsfolds) $1,212 £600

Victorian inlaid figured walnut piano front Davenport desk, 23in. wide.(Pearson's) $1,710 £900

DISPLAY CABINETS

Small walnut cabinet with gilt mounts, 30in. wide. (Silvester's)
$485 £245

Satinwood display table, circa 1900, 30 x 24in. (Sotheby's Belgravia)
$673 £340

Dutch Colonial hardwood display cabinet, circa 1710, 5ft.8½in. wide.(Sotheby's)
$4,508 £2,300

Burr-walnut display cabinet on stand, 1870's, 79 x 28½in. (Sotheby's Belgravia)
$1,319 £680

Mahogany display cabinet, circa 1910, 48in. wide.(Sotheby's Belgravia) $495 £250

Fine Chinese hardwood display cabinet.(Russell, Baldwin & Bright)
$3,960 £2,000

18th century Dutch figured walnut and marquetry inlaid display cabinet, 37¼in. wide. (Clifford Dann)
$3,135 £1,650

Modern mahogany display table, 32 x 18in. (Sotheby's Belgravia)
$792 £400

Serpentine fronted vitrine in kingwood. (King & Chasemore)
$2,376 £1,200

19th century Japanese Shibayama display cabinet.(Manchester Auction Mart) $7,272 £3,600

Satinwood display table, circa 1900, 24½in. wide. (Sotheby's Belgravia) $480 £250

Good George II red walnut display cabinet, circa 1740, 3ft. 7in. wide.(Sotheby's) $873 £450

Glass fronted oak cabinet, 19in. wide, circa 1840. (Silvester's) $637 £325

Painted satinwood display cabinet, circa 1900, 50in. wide. (Sotheby's Belgravia) $1,764 £900

One of a pair of mahogany display cabinets of light proportions. (Eadon, Lockwood & Riddle) $1,188 £600

19th century Vernis Martin vitrine with ormolu mounts.(Alan Fitchett) $3,705 £1,950

Burr-walnut and marquetry display cabinet, 1860's, 44½ x 48in.(Sotheby's Belgravia) $1,470 £750

19th century mahogany display cabinet on stand. (British Antique Exporters) $500 £250

359

DISPLAY CABINETS

19th century serpentine and bombe French vitrine.(W. H. Lane & Sons) $2,424 £1,200

Mid 18th century Dutch marquetry display cabinet.(Bonham's)
$9,292 £4,600

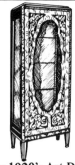

Early 1920's Art Deco walnut and giltwood vitrine, 172cm. high. (Sotheby's Belgravia)
$792 £400

Mahogany and marquetry display cabinet, 1900's, 49in. wide. (Sotheby's Belgravia) $1,029 £520

Mahogany and marquetry display cabinet, circa 1900, 49in. wide. (Sotheby's Belgravia)$636 £320

Mahogany display cabinet, 1890's, 79 x 36in. (Sotheby's Belgravia)
$601 £310

Mid 19th century giltwood display cabinet, 80in. high.(Sotheby's Belgravia)$653 £340

Modern rosewood display cabinet, 72½in. wide. (Sotheby's Belgravia)
$518 £270

Dutch walnut display cabinet, 27in. high. (Hy. Duke) $1,782 £900

Ebonised and Thuya-
wood side cabinet,
circa 1870, 45in.
high.(Sotheby's Bel-
gravia) $518 £270

Satinwood display cabi-
net and bookshelves,
circa 1910, 65in. wide.
(Sotheby's Belgravia)
$1,425 £720

Mahogany vitrine 34
x 17in., 1880-1900.
(Sotheby's Belgravia)
$853 £440

Sheraton mahogany
breakfront display
cabinet.(Russell,
Baldwin & Bright)
$1,584 £800

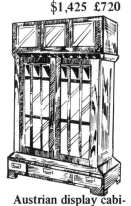

Austrian display cabi-
net, circa 1900-1910,
120.5cm. wide.
(Sotheby's Belgravia)
$1,560 £800

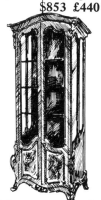

19th century French
kingwood vitrine, door
panels painted in the
Vernis Martin manner.
(Phillips) $7,676 £3,800

Unusual giltwood
display cabinet,
circa 1880, 44in.
wide.(Sotheby's
Belgravia)$704 £360

Mahogany display cabi-
net, circa 1880-1900,
39¼in. wide.(Sotheby's
Belgravia) $548 £280

Dutch floral marquetry
display cabinet with
bombe front.(Russell,
Baldwin & Bright)
$11,400 £6,000

DISPLAY CABINETS

Mahogany vitrine, circa 1895, 68in. high. (Christie's N. York) $660 £340

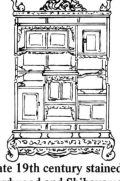

Late 19th century stained hardwood and Shibayama display cabinet, 91in. high. (Sotheby's Belgravia) $2,304 £1,200

Late 19th century display cabinet with ivory mounts, 55½in. high. (Sotheby's Belgravia) $730 £380

Fruitwood marquetry display cabinet by Majorelle, circa 1910, 64cm. wide. (Sotheby's Belgravia) $2,328 £1,200

Satinwood display cabinet, circa 1910, 65in. wide. (Sotheby's Belgravia) $1,382 £720

Marquetry display stand by Emile Galle, 4ft.6in. high. (Bonham's) $4,074 £2,100

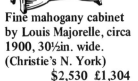

19th century Japanese snuff coloured lacquer cabinet, 44½in. wide.(Christie's) $776 £400

Late 19th century hardwood and ivory display cabinet. (Sotheby's Belgravia) $4,992 £2,600

Fine mahogany cabinet by Louis Majorelle, circa 1900, 30½in. wide. (Christie's N. York) $2,530 £1,304

Mid 19th century gilt metal mounted kingwood vitrine, 45½in. wide.(Christie's) $4,850 £2,500

Late 19th century hardwood etagere, 63in. high. (Sotheby's Belgravia) $710 £370

Late 19th century display cabinet, 84in. high. (Sotheby's Belgravia) $1,920 £1,000

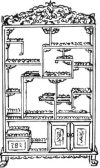

Late 19th century stained rosewood side cabinet, 76in. high.(Sotheby's Belgravia) $960 £500

18th century Dutch marquetry display cabinet, 63in. wide. (Christie's) $13,968 £7,200

Art Nouveau mahogany side cabinet, circa 1900, 53in. wide. (Sotheby's Belgravia) $941 £490

Late 19th century walnut and rosewood display cabinet. (Sotheby's Belgravia) $998 £520

18th century Dutch marquetry display cabinet, 67½in. wide. (Christie's) $9,312 £4,800

Late 19th century small display cabinet, 48in. high.(Sotheby's Belgravia) $4,992 £2,600

DISPLAY CABINETS

19th century burr-walnut display cabinet with brass escutcheons. (British Antique Exporters) $240 £120

19th century mahogany display table with brass embellishments. (British Antique Exporters) $350 £175

Finely carved 18th century Oriental hardwood display cabinet.(British Antique Exporters) $650 £325

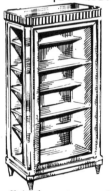

Small 19th century mahogany and satinwood display cabinet, 36cm. wide. (King & Chasemore) $457 £230

Early 18th century Dutch mahogany and marquetry display cabinet, 5ft.6in. wide. (Worsfolds) $7,363 £3,700

William IV rosewood collector's display cabinet, 113cm. wide. (King & Chasemore) $1,515 £750

Early display cabinet by Charles Mackintosh, circa 1895. (Sotheby's Belgravia)$5,050 £2,500

Art Nouveau display cabinet with leaded glazing. (Anderson & Garland) $1,616 £800

Small Edwardian inlaid mahogany display cabinet. (British Antique Exporters) $250 £125

Old English oak dresser with brass loop handles, 84in. wide. (Graves, Son & Pilcher)$3,366 £1,700

17th century oak dresser with original iron handles, 60in. wide. (Butler & Hatch Waterman) $4,242 £2,100

Late 19th century walnut Continental dresser. (Christopher Sykes) $544 £275

Victorian mahogany dresser with brass fittings. (Vernon's Chichester) $800 £400

18th century oak dresser with pierced cornice, 97in. wide. (Osmond Tricks) $1,425 £750

Early 20th century oak dresser with brass handles.(British Antique Exporters)$450 £225

Victorian carved oak dresser with pot board. (Vernon's Chichester) $370 £185

Early 18th century dresser, 50in. wide. (Outhwaite & Litherland) $9,504 £4,800

Louis XV provincial oak buffet, probably Normandy, circa 1760, 4ft. 8in. wide. (Sotheby's) $1,862 £950

Small 18th century oak dresser, 148cm. wide.(King & Chasemore)
$1,729 £880

James I oak buffet with parquetry drawer at top, circa 1610, 4ft.wide. (Sotheby's)
$5,454 £2,700

Unusual 18th century oak dresser, 6ft. wide.(Parsons, Welch & Cowell)
$2,121 £1,050

Late George II oak dresser, 5ft. wide, circa 1760. (Sotheby's)
$2,178 £1,100

Continental cupboard dresser, 47in. wide, circa 1840. (Silvester's)$637 £325

George III oak dresser, circa 1780, 5ft.7in. wide.(Sotheby's)
$1,746 £900

Early 18th century country made oak dresser, 72in. wide. (Osmond Tricks)
$2,185 £1,150

Mahogany buffet, circa 1895, 64in. high.(Christie's N. York)$880 £453

Late 17th century oak dresser with open shelves.(Russell, Baldwin & Bright)
$2,970 £1,500

18th century oak
dresser, 180cm.
wide.(King &
Chasemore)
$2,304 £1,200

18th century Welsh
dresser with cup-
boards and drawers.
(Sotheby Bearne)
$2,400 £1,200

Early 18th century
oak dresser, 107cm.
wide.(King &
Chasemore)
$2,592 £1,350

Victorian 'Dog Kennel'
dresser, circa 1850,
63in. wide.(Silvester's)
$1,029 £525

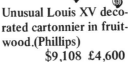

Unusual Louis XV deco-
rated cartonnier in fruitwood.(Phillips)
$9,108 £4,600

Unusual Anglesey
dresser in oak banded
with mahogany. (Rus-
sell, Baldwin & Bright)
$2,772 £1,400

George III oak dresser,
6ft.2in. wide, circa
1800.(Sotheby's)
$2,970 £1,500

Fine Art Nouveau wal-
nut buffet, English,
circa 1900, 68½in. wide.
(Christie's N. York)
$2,200 £1,182

18th century Lancashire
oak and pine dresser.
(Manchester Auction
Mart) $1,584 £800

DRESSERS AND BUFFETS

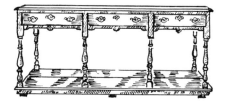

Antique oak dresser, 7ft.9½in. long, with three drawers.(Jackson-Stops & Staff) $2,716 £1,400

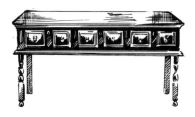

17th century oak dresser base. (Sotheby Bearne) $2,079 £1,050

Late 17th century oak dresser, 6ft.5in. wide, on baluster legs.(Russell, Baldwin & Bright) $2,970 £1,500

17th century oak low dresser, 84in. wide.(Christie's) $3,007 £1,550

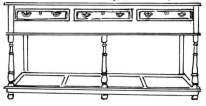

Antique oak small dresser, 4ft.8½in. wide.(Jackson-Stops & Staff)
    $2,328 £1,200

Jacobean dresser base with three drawers.(Boardman's) $4,848 £2,400

Fine Cromwellian oak dresser.(King & Chasemore) $1,485 £750

Charles II oak dresser base, circa 1680, 5ft.9½in. wide.(Sotheby's)
    $2,178 £1,100

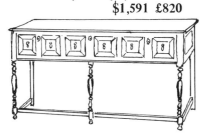

George I oak dresser, circa 1720, 3ft. 11½in. wide.(Sotheby's)
$1,591 £820

Charles II oak dresser, 4ft.11½in. wide. (Sotheby's) $2,037 £1,050

Charles II oak dresser, circa 1680, 5ft. 10in. wide.(Sotheby's) $1,552 £800

Oak dresser base, 80in. wide, circa 1700. (Edwards, Bigwood & Bewlay)
$2,850 £1,500

George III oak dresser base in good condition.(Sotheby Bearne)
$5,050 £2,500

Late 17th century oak dresser, 7ft.1in. long.(Jackson-Stops & Staff)
$3,007 £1,550

Oak dresser with split baluster decoration, circa 1860, 59in. wide. (Silvester's) $882 £455

Early English oak dresser.(Worsfolds)
$2,727 £1,350

369

Late 18th century carved oak lowboy, 3ft. wide. (Charles Taylor & Sons) $202 £100

Queen Anne walnut lowboy with restored top. (Barber's) $1,616 £800

Late 18th century carved lowboy. (British Antique Exporters) $250 £125

Queen Anne walnut side table, circa 1700, 2ft.3in. wide. (Sotheby's) $1,960 £1,000

Georgian oak lowboy. (Russell, Baldwin & Bright) $1,584 £800

Dutch marquetry lowboy, 28in. high, circa 1765. (Gray's Antique Mews) $1,656 £820

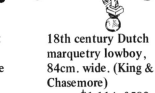

Georgian lowboy in mahogany with brass handles. (John H. Raby & Son) $653 £330

19th century walnut lowboy on cabriole legs. (British Antique Exporters) $450 £225

18th century Dutch marquetry lowboy, 84cm. wide. (King & Chasemore) $1,114 £580

Small oak kneehole desk of nine drawers, 45in. wide. (Butler & Hatch Waterman) $909 £450

Early 20th century oak tambour top desk. (British Antique Exporters) $400 £200

Large mahogany pedestal desk with inset green leather top. (Vost's)$1,212 £600

Oak kneehole desk, circa 1790. (Gray's Antique Mews) $1,060 £525

19th century oak pedestal desk with tooled leather top. (British Antique Exporters) $400 £200

Queen Anne walnut and crossbanded kneehole dressing table, 84cm. wide. (King & Chasemore) $5,150 £2,500

Good George II mahogany kneehole writing table, circa 1745, 2ft. 8½in. wide. (Sotheby's) $4,158 £2,100

Late 19th century mahogany desk with tooled leather top. (British Antique Exporters) $60 £30

Victorian mahogany cylinder top pedestal writing desk. (British Antique Exporters) $600 £300

Mid 19th century mahogany pedestal desk, 36in. wide.(Sotheby's Belgravia) $307 £160

Early 20th century mahogany pedestal display desk with glazed top, 39½in. wide.(Sotheby's Belgravia)$776 £400

Late George II mahogany kneehole writing table, 3ft.3in. wide, circa 1750. (Sotheby's) $1,411 £720

Rosewood and inlaid ivory desk, late 19th century, 46in. wide.(Sotheby's Belgravia) $806 £420

Mid 19th century mahogany partner's desk, 60in. wide.(Sotheby's Belgravia) $1,455 £750

Early 20th century mahogany pedestal desk, 54in. wide.(Sotheby's Belgravia) $288 £150

Carved oak writing desk, circa 1880, 51½in. wide.(Sotheby's Belgravia) $509 £260

Mahogany pedestal desk, circa 1880, 50in. wide.(Sotheby's Belgravia) $497 £250

Unusual rosewood kneehole specimen cabinet, 1840's, 58in. wide.(Sotheby's Belgravia) $853 £440

George I walnut veneered kneehole writing table, 2ft.7in. wide, circa 1720.(Sotheby's) $6,272 £3,200

Queen Anne walnut kneehole desk. (Christie's S. Kensington)
$2,716 £1,400

George II mahogany kneehole writing table, 3ft.3in. wide, circa 1730. (Sotheby's) $1,274 £650

George II mahogany kneehole writing table, circa 1740, 3ft. wide.(Sotheby's)
$1,544 £780

Mahogany pedestal desk with leather top, 4ft.6in. wide, circa 1900. (Sotheby's) $431 £220

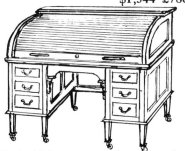

Early 20th century mahogany pedestal cylinder desk, 54½in. wide.(Sotheby's Belgravia) $1,188 £600

Mahogany pedestal desk, circa 1860, 47in. wide.(Sotheby's Belgravia)
$673 £340

Mahogany clerk's desk, circa 1880, gallery missing, 60in. wide. (Sotheby's Belgravia) $633 £320

Walnut partner's desk, circa 1860, 57in. wide, with leather top. (Sotheby's Belgravia) $1,212 £600

Walnut kneehole desk, 1860's, 54in. wide. (Sotheby's Belgravia) $673 £340

Fine George II mahogany kneehole writing desk, circa 1755, 4ft. wide. (Sotheby's) $7,840 £4,000

Late 19th century mahogany pedestal desk, 60in. wide. (Sotheby's Belgravia) $1,212 £600

Georgian mahogany fall flap kneehole bureau. (Phillips & Jolly's) $3,232 £1,600

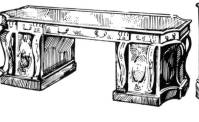

Early 18th century mahogany kneehole desk, 32in. wide. (Chancellor's) $1,235 £650

The Combe Abbey library table in mahogany, by Thomas Chippendale. (Sotheby's) $196,000 £100,000

George II mahogany kneehole desk, 3ft. 2in. wide, circa 1760. (Sotheby's) $10,890 £5,500

Victorian brass firescreen with painted decoration. (British Antique Exporters) $50 £25

Late 19th century hardstone table screen, 46.5cm. high.(Sotheby's Belgravia) $294 £150

Giltwood and stained glass screen, circa 1900, 62in. wide.(Sotheby's Belgravia) $796 £400

Late 19th century Damascus Mishrabaya hardwood three-fold screen, 78in. high. (Sotheby's Belgravia) $490 £250

Late 19th century brass and glass firescreen. (British Antique Exporters) $40 £20

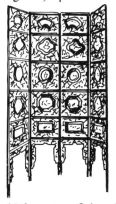

19th century Oriental padouk four-fold screen, 228cm. wide. (King & Chasemore) $3,434 £1,700

20th century Ch'ien Lung six-fold screen, 72½in. high.(Sotheby's Belgravia)$1,920 £1,000

Walnut firescreen, 1860's, 59in. high. (Sotheby's Belgravia) $554 £280

Late 19th century famille rose and blue and white eight-fold screen, 82.2cm. high. (Sotheby's Belgravia) $1,528 £780

375

Large light rosewood woolwork firescreen, 1850's, 53 x 38½in. (Sotheby's Belgravia) $232 £120

20th century Ch'ien Lung six-fold coromandel screen, 72½in. high. (Sotheby's Belgravia) $1,267 £660

American leaded glass firescreen, circa 1900, 45¼in. high.(Christie's N. York) $2,860 £1,537

Louis XVI painted leather screen, 6ft.6in. high, circa 1780.(Sotheby's) $1,140 £600

John Pearson bronze and wrought iron firescreen, circa 1906, 27½in. high.(Sotheby's Belgravia) $363 £180

Three-fold painted screen, circa 1910, panel signed Jules Vernon-Fair. (Sotheby's Belgravia) $744 £380

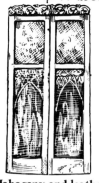

Mahogany pole screen on tripod supports with tapestry in rococo frame. (John H. Raby & Son) $198 £100

Late 19th century Chinese three-fold screen, one of a pair.(Sotheby's Belgravia) $499 £260

Mahogany and leather five-fold screen, circa 1900, 85in. wide overall. (Sotheby's Belgravia) $626 £310

Mid 19th century rose-wood adjustable screen with tapestry, 36in. high.(Gray's Antique Mews) $222 £110

K'ang Hsi period six-fold coromandel wood screen. (King & Chasemore)
$4,224 £2,200

Japanese lacquer fire-screen in carved hard-wood frame.(Christie's S. Kensington)
$1,164 £600

Two-fold lacquer and ivory screen, circa 1900. (Sotheby's Belgravia)
$1,613 £840

Early 19th century six-leaf screen, 70½in. high. (Christie's)$5,500 £2,850

Late 19th century hardwood four-fold screen, 73in. high. (Sotheby's Belgravia)
$634 £330

Late 19th century ivory, mother-of-pearl and Shi-bayama two-fold screen, 64in. high.(Sotheby's Belgravia)$1,920 £1,000

Late 19th century two-fold ivory and mother-of-pearl inlaid fruitwood screen, 73½in. high. (Sotheby's Belgravia)
$614 £320

Late 19th century two-fold red lacquer screen, 71¼in. high.(Sotheby's Belgravia) $384 £200

Dutch marquetry secretaire a abattant, circa 1780, 3ft. wide. (Sotheby's) $2,548 £1,300

Queen Anne walnut secretaire, circa 1700, 63in. high. (Sotheby's) $4,370 £2,300

Regency mahogany secretaire a abattant, 39in. wide.(Christie's) $2,450 £1,250

Charles X mahogany secretaire, circa 1830, 3ft.3in. wide. (Sotheby's) $1,293 £660

George III satinwood veneered secretaire, circa 1790, 3ft.11in. wide. (Sotheby's) $3,920 £2,000

French 19th century floral marquetry escritoire in walnut and kingwood. (Russell, Baldwin & Bright) $1,386 £700

Milanese inlaid mahogany secretaire a abattant, circa 1820, 3ft. 0½in. wide.(Sotheby's) $3,234 £1,650

Victorian rosewood secretaire Wellington chest. (British Antique Exporters) $600 £300

Ormolu mounted kingwood and tulipwood marquetry secretaire a abattant, 3ft.1in. wide. (Sotheby's) $3,168 £1,600

William and Mary walnut secretaire, 66in. high.(Gray's Antique Market)
$3,168 £1,600

South German mahogany secretaire, 1840's, 39in. wide.(Sotheby's Belgravia)
$744 £380

Regency feathered mahogany secretaire a abattant, 56in. high.(Buckell & Ballard) $1,130 £595

Empire ormolu mounted mahogany secretaire a abattant, circa 1810, 3ft.2¼in. wide. (Sotheby's)$7,600 £4,000

Early 19th century Dutch mahogany secretaire. (Woolley & Wallis)
$3,232 £1,600

Biedermeier mahogany secretaire, 3ft. 9in. wide, circa 1820-40.(Sotheby's)
$1,411 £720

Unusual early 19th century rosewood veneered secretaire chest, 22¼in. wide.(Osmond Tricks)
$665 £350

18th century oak escritoire on chest.(Wm. H. Brown) $1,188 £600

Walnut veneered fall front cabinet of William and Mary design, 40in. wide. (Osmond Tricks)
$2,375 £1,250

SECRETAIRE BOOKCASES

Sheraton design satinwood secretaire bookcase, 31in. wide.(Pearson's) $15,840 £8,000

Georgian mahogany secretaire bookcase.(Vidler & Co.) $3,030 £1,500

Satinwood secretaire with scalloped gallery, circa 1900, 27½in. wide. (Sotheby's Belgravia) $744 £380

Late 18th century secretaire bookcase. (Clarke Gammon) $3,230 £1,700

Early 19th century mahogany secretaire bookcase, 4ft. wide. (D. M. Nesbit & Co.) $2,037 £1,050

George III mahogany secretaire bookcase, 3ft. 11in. wide, circa 1790. (Sotheby's) $3,724 £1,900

Narrow mahogany secretaire bookcase, 1840-60, 32in. wide.(Sotheby's Belgravia) $693 £350

George III mahogany secretaire bookcase, 44in. wide. (Brooks) $3,230 £1,700

Unusual American mahogany secretaire, 40in. wide, circa 1860-80.(Sotheby's Belgravia) $336 £170

Mahogany secretaire bookcase with fall front. (Stooke, Hill & Co.)$1,089 £550

Early Victorian figured mahogany breakfront secretaire bookcase, 230cm. wide. (King & Chasemore) $3,072 £1,600

Late George III mahogany secretaire bookcase, 3ft.8in. wide, circa 1800. (Sotheby's)$2,277 £1,150

Early Victorian mahogany and floral marquetry secretaire bookcase, 121cm. wide. (King & Chasemore) $2,929 £1,450

Regency mahogany breakfront secretaire bookcase, 84in. wide. (Christie's) $6,664 £3,400

Sheraton period secretaire bookcase. (G. Knight & Sons)$20,295 £10,250

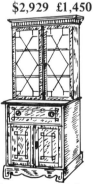

Mahogany secretaire bookcase, circa 1900, 29¼in. wide.(Sotheby's Belgravia) $691 £360

Satinwood inlaid and painted secretaire bookcase, circa 1790, 4ft. 4½in. wide. (Sotheby's) $35,890 £18,500

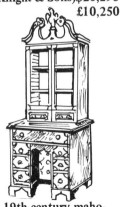

Mid 19th century mahogany kneehole secretaire display cabinet, 105cm. wide.(King & Chasemore) $4,242 £2,100

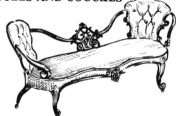

Victorian walnut framed serpentine shaped settee, 183cm. wide. (King & Chasemore) $922 £480

Late 19th century rosewood and mother-of-pearl inlaid settee. (Sotheby's Belgravia) $1,229 £640

Charles II walnut day bed, circa 1660, 5ft. long with caned back.(Sotheby's) $4,312 £2,200

Ornately carved Victorian walnut settee. (King & Chasemore) $855 £450

Venetian rococo green painted and parcel gilt settee, circa 1760, 3ft.2in. wide.(Sotheby's) $2,940 £1,500

19th century ornate carved oak settle in French Renaissance style, 195cm. wide. (King & Chasemore) $1,960 £1,000

Chippendale mahogany chair-back settee, circa 1880-1900, 72in. wide. (Sotheby's Belgravia) $776 £400

Early George III three chair-back settee, 5ft.5in. wide. (Sotheby's) $990 £500

Louis XVI carved boxwood canape, circa 1780, 5ft. wide, stamped Delaisement. (Sotheby's)
$11,484 £5,800

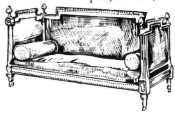

Louis XVI oak lit d'alcove, 6ft.7in. long, circa 1785.(Sotheby's)
$1,805 £950

Edwards and Roberts walnut hall settee, circa 1893, 43½ x 54in. (Sotheby's) $1,114 £580

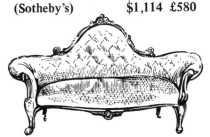

Walnut settee, 75in. long, circa 1860, with carved toprail.(Sotheby's Belgravia) $792 £400

Regency simulated rosewood chaise longue with scroll ends. (King & Chasemore) $589 £310

One of a pair of mid 19th century Louis XV beechwood small settees, 4ft.10in. wide. (Sotheby's)
$3,040 £1,600

Mahogany and marquetry settee, circa 1900, 51½in. wide.(Sotheby's Belgravia) $407 £210

Italian parcel gilt mahogany chaise longue, circa 1815, 5ft.9in. long. (Sotheby's) $1,710 £900

SETTEES AND COUCHES

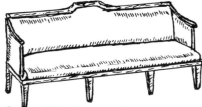

George III mahogany three-seater sofa, 71½in. long.(Nottingham Auction Mart) $2,522 £1,300

Fine quality Regency couch in mahogany inlaid with ormolu.(Worsfolds) $545 £270

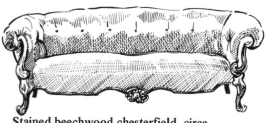

Stained beechwood chesterfield, circa 1870, 84in. wide.(Sotheby's Belgravia) $313 £160

17th century box seat settle in oak, 150cm. (King & Chasemore) $970 £500

Part of a stained mahogany marquetry and ivory inlaid suite, circa 1900. (Sotheby's Belgravia) $230 £120

George II giltwood centre couch, 81in. wide, circa 1880.(Sotheby's Belgravia) $892 £460

Edwardian carved oak settle with hinged lid, 46in. wide.(Nottingham Auction Mart) $568 £290

Late 19th century oak settle, 49¾in. wide.(Sotheby's Belgravia)$232 £120

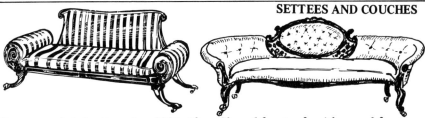

Regency painted settee, circa 1805, 6ft. 11in. wide. (Sotheby's) $646 £330

Shaped front sofa with carved frame. (May, Whetter & Grose) $627 £320

Regency black painted and parcel gilt chaise longue, 6ft.3in. long, circa 1810. (Sotheby's) $465 £240

German bleached mahogany settee, 90½in. wide, circa 1840.(Sotheby's Belgravia) $352 £180

Early 19th century Indian hardwood palanquin, 4ft.4in. wide.(Sotheby's) $392 £200

Mid 19th century grained rosewood chaise longue.(Sotheby's Belgravia) $333 £170

19th century carved walnut twin chair-back settee.(King & Chasemore) $396 £200

19th century oak settle with lift-up seat, 51in. wide.(Nottingham Auction Mart) $588 £300

385

SETTEES AND COUCHES

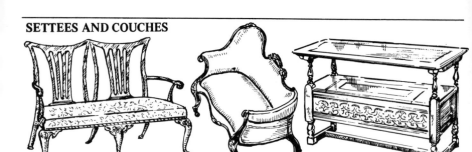

George II mahogany two-chairback settee, 4ft.10in. wide. (Sotheby's)
$1,666 £850

Ornately carved early Victorian settee.(Butler & Hatch Waterman)
$594 £300

20th century oak monk's bench.(British Antique Exporters) $120 £60

Victorian cabriole leg rosewood settee. (British Antique Exporters) $550 £275

Oak hall settle, circa 1900, 57in. wide, with needlework back panel.(Sotheby's Belgravia) $796 £400

Victorian mahogany scroll end settee on turned legs.(British Antique Exporters) $400 £200

Oak and beaten copper inlaid settle, 1900-1910. (Sotheby's Belgravia) $363 £180

Victorian carved oak monk's bench. (Vernon's Chichester) $330 £165

Dralon covered four-seater conversation piece. (Edwards, Bigwood & Bewlay) $407 £210

Mirror glazed and super-structured sideboard, 6ft. wide, in bird's-eye maple. (May, Whetter & Grose) $784 £400

Victorian mahogany sideboard with cellarette drawer. (British Antique Exporters) $200 £100

19th century painted satinwood sideboard. (British Antique Exporters) $850 £425

George III bow-front sideboard. (King & Chasemore) $3,366 £1,700

German walnut sideboard, 1870's, 113½in. high.(Sotheby's Belgravia) $627 £320

19th century inlaid mahogany sideboard with brass gallery. (British Antique Exporters) $300 £150

Mid 19th century rosewood sideboard, 68 x 66in. (Sotheby's Belgravia) $310 £160

Late 19th century carved oak sideboard with brass fittings. (Vernon's Chichester) $370 £185

Small 20th century Jacobean style oak sideboard.(British Antique Exporters) $80 £40

SIDEBOARDS

Small sideboard in pale walnut, 1930's, 136.5cm. wide.(Sotheby's Belgravia) $343 £175

George III mahogany sideboard, circa 1785, 5ft.3in. wide. (Sotheby's) $1,940 £980

Stained oak sideboard, circa 1880, 56in. wide.(Sotheby's Belgravia)$407 £210

George III mahogany serpentine fronted sideboard, 6ft.9in. wide. (Sotheby's) $1,683 £850

Late Georgian mahogany bow-fronted small sideboard.(Russell, Baldwin & Bright) $2,019 £1,020

Oak and parquetry sideboard, circa 1870, 94in. wide.(Sotheby's Belgravia) $614 £320

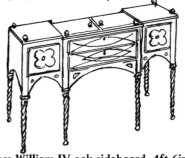

Rare William IV oak sideboard, 4ft.6in. wide, circa 1830.(Sotheby's) $931 £480

George III satinwood bow-front sideboard or dressing table, 4ft.1in. wide. (Sotheby's) $1,764 £900

Large sideboard in pale walnut, 1930's, 175cm. wide.(Sotheby's Belgravia) $343 £175

George III Scottish mahogany serpentine fronted sideboard, circa 1790, 7ft. 3in. wide.(Sotheby's) $1,164 £600

George III mahogany bow-front sideboard.(Lawrence's) $1,520 £800

George III mahogany sideboard, circa 1780, 5ft.4in. wide.(Sotheby's) $1,346 £680

Late 19th century painted satinwood sideboard, 53in. wide.(Sotheby's Belgravia) $883 £460

18th century mahogany chest sideboard inlaid in the Sheraton manner. (Abbotts) $554 £280

Mid 19th century oak sideboard, heavily carved, 90in. wide.(Osmond Tricks) $1,520 £800

Small English ebonised mahogany sideboard.(Sotheby's Belgravia) $565 £280

George III mahogany toilet stand, circa 1790, 16in. square.(Christopher Sykes) $247 £125

Porcelain mounted parquetry jardiniere, circa 1870, 9¼in. wide. (Sotheby's Belgravia) $398 £200

Late 19th century hardwood urn stand, 33½in. high. (Sotheby's Belgravia) $614 £320

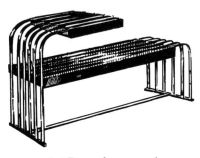

One of a pair of oak Solomonic torcheres, 75in. high.(Christie's S. Kensington) $1,330 £700

Art Deco chrome and mirror coatrack with umbrella stand, circa 1925.(Christie's N. York) $1,870 £963

Rosewood quatrelobed etagere by Emile Galle, circa 1895, 24in. wide. (Christie's N. York) $1,500 £757

Unusual kingwood circular cupboard, circa 1900, 35¼in. high. (Sotheby's Belgravia)$235 £120

Marquetry jardiniere, circa 1890, 31 x 27in. (Sotheby's Belgravia) $356 £180

Two-tiered rosewood jardiniere stand, circa 1895, 16in. square. (Christie's N. York) $1,500 £757

Late 19th century urn stand in rosewood, 32in. high. (Sotheby's Belgravia) $442 £230

Mahogany folio rack, 1840's, 46 x 32in. (Sotheby's Belgravia) $792 £400

20th century hardwood urn stand, 34in. high.(Sotheby's Belgravia) $422 £220

Regency William IV double music stand in rosewood. (Cubitt & West) $691 £360

Red tortoiseshell and gilt metal stationery rack, circa 1900, 15in. long.(Sotheby's Belgravia) $589 £310

One of a pair of hardwood pedestals, circa 1900, 51½in. high. (Sotheby's Belgravia) $403 £210

One of a pair of marquetry etageres, circa 1870, 30¼in. high.(Sotheby's Belgravia)$548 £280

Early 20th century kingwood etagere with gilt metal supports, 35in. wide.(Sotheby's Belgravia) $411 £210

Ebonised wood and kingwood parquetry occasional table, circa 1880, 31½in. high.(Sotheby's Belgravia) $333 £170

Late 19th century walnut washstand with tiled splashback.(British Antique Exporters) $80 £40

Oriental hardwood marble topped stand. (British Antique Exporters) $200 £100

Victorian mahogany towel rail on twist supports. (British Antique Exporters) $30 £15

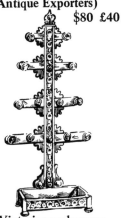

Victorian mahogany hatstand in the Gothic manner.(British Antique Exporters) $130 £65

Late 19th century oak hall stand with brass fittings. (British Antique Exporters) $80 £40

One of a pair of Italian ebony and majolica plant stands. (Worsfolds) $424 £210

Late 19th century mahogany shaving stand. (British Antique Exporters) $170 £85

20th century oak hall stand. (British Antique Exporters) $50 £25

20th century mahogany folding cake stand. (British Antique Exporters) $40 £20

20th century oak umbrella stand. (British Antique Exporters)$24 £12

Victorian marble topped walnut washstand. (British Antique Exporters) $80 £40

20th century oak hall stand with barley twist supports. (British Antique Exporters) $50 £25

One of a pair of pottery mounted ebonised torcheres, circa 1850, 51½in. high. (Sotheby's Belgravia) $376 £190

Edwardian oak hall stand. (British Antique Exporters)$30 £15

Carved oak 'Gothick' torchere, 77in. high, 1840's. (Sotheby's Belgravia)$294 £150

Late 19th century walnut urn stand, 22½in. high. (Sotheby's Belgravia) $616 £310

Victorian marble topped mahogany washstand. (British Antique Exporters) $70 £35

Early 1920's wrought iron and marble gueridon, 86.5cm. high. (Sotheby's Belgravia) $297 £150

Early 1920's wrought iron and marble gueridon, 109.5cm high. (Sotheby's Belgravia) $297 £150

Late 19th century Italian neo-classical jardiniere, 29in. wide. (Christie's) $2,910 £1,500

Early 18th century walnut linen press, 5ft. high. (Gray's Antique Mews) $555 £275

Victorian mahogany hat and stick stand. (British Antique Exporters) $90 £45

Edwardian oak towel rail with spiral supports. (British Antique Exporters) $20 £10

19th century mahogany easel. (British Antique Exporters) $70 £35

One of a pair of red and green tortoiseshell boulle centre pedestals, circa 1830. (Sotheby's Belgravia) $835 £420

Edwardian oak shaving stand. (British Antique Exporters) $100 £50

Late Victorian mahogany marble topped stand. (British Antique Exporters) $30 £15

One of a pair of Carolean oak coffin stools. (Russell, Baldwin & Bright) $1,069 £540

Rosewood combined canterbury and music stool, 21 x 21½in., 1870's. (Sotheby's Belgravia) $326 £170

One of a pair of Carolean oak coffin stools, 1ft.6in. high.(Russell, Baldwin & Bright) $1,069 £540

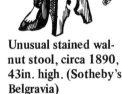

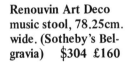

Charles II walnut stool, 3ft.3in. wide, circa 1680. (Sotheby's) $1,803 £920

Unusual stained walnut stool, circa 1890, 43in. high. (Sotheby's Belgravia) $1,803 £920

Renouvin Art Deco music stool, 78.25cm. wide. (Sotheby's Belgravia) $304 £160

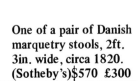

Late 19th century oak piano stool with cane-work seat. (British Antique Exporters) $40 £20

Charles I oak joint stool, 1ft.6in. wide, circa 1635, with moulded top. (Sotheby's) $1,666 £850

One of a pair of Danish marquetry stools, 2ft. 3in. wide, circa 1820. (Sotheby's)$570 £300

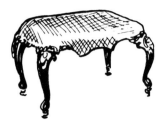

Mid 18th century rect-
angular gilt gesso stool,
23in. wide. (Phillips)
$909 £450

19th century maho-
gany framed stool.
(British Antique
Exporters)$30 £15

Georgian style maho-
gany stool on shaped
legs. (British Antique
Exporters) $40 £20

James I oak joint
stool, circa 1610,
1ft.6in. wide.
(Sotheby's)
$1,227 £620

20th century beech framed
piano stool. (British Antique
Exporters) $30 £15

Rare Henry VIII
oak joint stool, 1ft.
6in. wide, circa
1540, top restored.
(Sotheby's)
$3,822 £1,950

One of a pair of French
oak high stools, 1ft.1in.
wide. (Sotheby's)
$1,274 £650

Late 19th century oak
joint stool. (Vernon's
Chichester) $40 £20

Late 19th century
elm stool. (British
Antique Exporters)
$20 £10

Part of a set of eight walnut chairs, circa 1890. (Sotheby's Belgravia)
$1,194 £600

Part of a suite of Louis XVI giltwood seat furniture of five pieces, circa
1880. (Sotheby's Belgravia) $6,567 £3,300

Part of a seven-piece Edwardian suite. (Gray's Antique Mews)
£1,656 £820

Part of an Art Deco drawingroom suite, late 1930's, upholstered in velvet.
(Sotheby's Belgravia) $707 £350

Suite of tubular chromed metal cantilever seat furniture, 1930's, 80cm. high.(Sotheby's Belgravia) $349 £180

Part of a nine-piece suite, settee 54½in. wide. (Christie's)$8,148 £4,200

Part of a Victorian nine-piece suite in walnut.(Parsons, Welch & Cowell)
$4,312 £2,200

Suite of Art Nouveau walnut seat furniture, circa 1900, 48in. wide.
(Christie's N. York) $3,080 £1,587

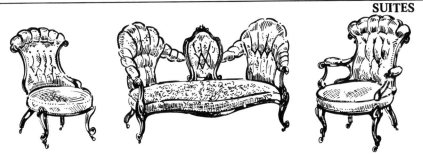

Button-upholstered walnut drawingroom suite, 1860's. (Sotheby's Belgravia) $1,513 £780

Very fine mid Victorian walnut salon suite.(Locke & England) $3,939 £1,950

Part of an Edwardian inlaid mahogany drawingroom suite.(Edmiston's) $3,366 £1,700

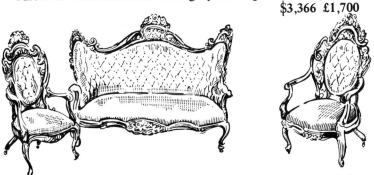

Victorian suite of sofa and two chairs in rosewood with velvet upholstery. (Morton's, New Orleans) $42,000 £21,000

Late George II mahogany card table, circa 1755, 3ft. wide. (Sotheby's) $1,078 £550

Regency mahogany card table, circa 1810, 2ft.11¾in. wide. (Sotheby's)$737 £380

Georgian mahogany tea table with drawer, 35in. wide. (Silvester's)$306 £155

George II red walnut tea or games table, circa 1740, 2ft.8in. wide.(Sotheby's) $588 £300

Regency brass inlaid rosewood card table, 2ft.11½in. wide, circa 1810.(Sotheby's) $1,089 £550

One of a pair of mid 19th century English folding card tables. (Phillips) $10,100 £5,000

One of a pair of late George III mahogany card tables, 2ft.10in. wide.(Sotheby's) $3,267 £1,650

Small George III satinwood semi-circular card table, 2ft.6in. wide, circa 1780.(Sotheby's) $823 £420

18th century mahogany tea table of Chippendale design.(Worsfolds) $1,019 £520

19th century inlaid mahogany and flap-over card table.(R. H. Ellis & Son)
$292 £145

Mahogany pedestal tea table, circa 1840, 36in. wide. (Silvester's)
$485 £245

Late 18th century country Chippendale mahogany tea table, 72cm. wide. (May, Whetter & Grose) $383 £190

Rare George IV satinwood card table, circa 1825, 3ft. wide. (Sotheby's)
$1,188 £600

Early George II red walnut triple top card table, circa 1730, 2ft.9in. wide. (Sotheby's)
$1,742 £880

Rosewood card table, 1840's, 36½in. wide. (Sotheby's Belgravia)
$232 £120

19th century marquetry and kingwood swivel top card table.(Jordan & Cook) $1,940 £1,000

One of a pair of French Empire rosewood and walnut folding top card tables, 2ft.9½in. wide.(Walker, Barrett & Hill) $3,325 £1,750

Regency brass inlaid burr-elm card table, circa 1820, 3ft.2in. wide.(Sotheby's)
$737 £380

Mahogany envelope card table, 23½in. square. (Hexton & Cheney) $237 £120

Serpentine fronted mahogany card table on carved pedestal, 37in. high.(Nottingham Auction Mart) $535 £260

19th century mahogany serpentine fronted folding card table, 34in. wide. (Nottingham Auction Mart) $744 £380

Rosewood card table, 1840's, 36in. wide. (Sotheby's Belgravia) $444 £220

One of a pair of Regency rosewood tea tables. (Christie's) $5,148 £2,600

Early Victorian serpentine front burr-walnut folding top card table. (British Antique Exporters) $550 £275

One of a pair of late George III mahogany card tables, circa 1805, 2ft.10in. wide. (Sotheby's)$1,803 £920

Late 18th century satinwood fold-over top card table, 36in. wide. (Riddett's) $1,900 £1,000

Burr-walnut card table, 1860's, 35in. wide. (Sotheby's Belgravia) $565 £280

Regency mahogany card table. (Alfie's Antique Market) $524 £265

George III flame mahogany folding top card table. (British Antique Exporters) $370 £185

Charles II oak gateleg games table, circa 1670, 2ft.9in. diam. (Sotheby's) $4,116 £2,100

George III bleached mahogany fold-over card table, 36in. wide. (Nottingham Auction Mart) $1,552 £800

Good Victorian walnut folding top card table. (British Antique Exporters) $600 £300

George II walnut card or games table, circa 1930. (Sotheby's Belgravia) $614 £320

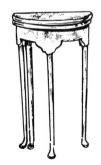

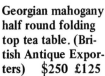

Georgian mahogany half round folding top tea table. (British Antique Exporters) $250 £125

Early 19th century rosewood card table, 36in. long. (Gray's Antique Mews) $659 £320

George I walnut card table, 2ft.7½in. wide, circa 1720. (Sotheby's) $3,234 £1,650

Fine lacquered wood and chrome consol by Donald Desky, circa 1927, 72in. wide. (Christie's N. York) $4,620 £2,483

Mid 18th century Genoese painted consol table, 4ft. 1in. wide.(Sotheby's) $4,356 £2,200

Early 19th century parcel gilt consol table, 5ft.8in. wide. (Sotheby's) $509 £260

Giltwood consol table, circa 1765, by Robert Adam. (Christie's) $23,880 £12,000

Mid 18th century German white painted and parcel gilt consol table, 27½in. wide.(Christie's) $2,134 £1,100

William IV consol table in rosewood, 3ft.2in. wide. (Sotheby's) $784 £400

 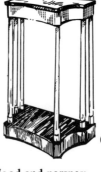 

Charles X mahogany consol table, circa 1825, 4ft.4in. wide. (Sotheby's) $823 £420

Wood and perspex consol table, 1930's, 91.25cm. high. (Sotheby's Belgravia) $323 £170

Mid 19th century rosewood consol table, one of a pair, 48in. wide. (Sotheby's Belgravia) $910 £460

Regency mahogany breakfast table. (Sotheby's)
$6,984 £3,600

Tripod table, circa 1780, 29½in. diam. (Gray's Antique Mews) $353 £175

William IV mahogany dining table, 1830's, 48in. wide.(Sotheby's Belgravia) $1,373 £680

Victorian rosewood oval loo table, 42in. wide. (Nottingham Auction Mart) $404 £200

20th century oak draw-leaf table on twist supports. (British Antique Exporters) $30 £15

Walnut breakfast table, circa 1860, 53½in. wide. (Sotheby's Belgravia) $525 £260

Victorian mahogany centre table on quadruple base. (British Antique Exporters) $600 £300

19th century mahogany snap-top table on tripod base. (British Antique Exporters) $150 £75

A good early Victorian inlaid burr-walnut centre table. (British Antique Exporters) $550 £275

DINING TABLES

Walnut centre table, circa 1870, 48½in. wide.(Sotheby's Belgravia) $349 £180

Sheraton style satinwood oval top centre table, 3ft.10¼in. wide. (Geering & Colyer) $784 £400

Rosewood circular breakfast table, 64in. diameter, 1830's. (Sotheby's Belgravia) $911 £470

 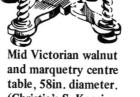 

Rosewood circular breakfast table, 4ft. 4in. diameter, 1860's. (Sotheby's)$627 £320

Mid Victorian walnut and marquetry centre table, 58in. diameter. (Christie's S. Kensington) $1,862 £950

Satinwood library table, circa 1900, 3ft. diameter. (Sotheby's) $940 £480

Fine mahogany breakfast table, 4ft.6in. x 3ft.6in.(Worsfolds) $646 £320

19th century snaptop breakfast table in mahogany, 66in. long.(Woolley & Wallis)$2,280 £1,200

Mahogany drum table, circa 1840, 3ft.10in. diameter.(Sotheby's) $1,274 £650

Early Victorian marquetry centre table, 64in. diameter, circa 1840. (Christie's)
$6,664 £3,400

Large George II mahogany breakfast table, 5ft. diameter, circa 1800.(Sotheby's)
$7,372 £3,800

Late George III mahogany octagonal rent table, circa 1805, 3ft. 10in. diameter. (Sotheby's)
$4,554 £2,300

Late George III mahogany breakfast table, circa 1810, 3ft.10in. wide.(Sotheby's)
$1,117 £570

Part of a set of padouk-wood extending dining table and eight chairs. (Brooks)$4,040 £2,000

Mahogany oval dining table, circa 1840, 53½in. wide.(Sotheby's Belgravia) $509 £260

Walnut breakfast table, 1860's, 51in. wide. (Sotheby's Belgravia)
$475 £240

Strahan burr-walnut breakfast table, circa 1860, 55in. wide. (Sotheby's Belgravia)
$455 £230

Mid 19th century Batavian ebony centre table, 47in. diameter. (Christie's)$1,062 £550

DINING TABLES

Early 1920's oval mahogany table, 85cm. wide. (Sotheby's Belgravia) $198 £100

Regency mahogany centre table, circa 1815, 4ft.1in. diameter. (Sotheby's) $1,881 £950

Early 17th century Italian walnut table, 41¾in. diameter. (Christie's S. Kensington) $4,356 £2,200

Georgian mahogany circular top drum table, 3ft. 3in. diameter. (Messenger, May & Baverstock) $1,777 £880

Mid Victorian walnut and marquetry tilt-top table, circa 1860, 35in. diam. (Gray's Antique Market) $404 £200

German walnut centre table, 1860's, 49in. wide. (Sotheby's Belgravia) $594 £300

Rosewood circular breakfast table, 64in. diam., 1830's. (Sotheby's Belgravia) $893 £470

Louis VI gilt bronze and porcelain centre table, circa 1860, 32½in. diam. (Sotheby's Belgravia) $5,970 £3,000

George III fiddleback mahogany breakfast table, 67½in. wide. (Christie's) $5,140 £2,600

Ebonised centre table, circa 1870, 51in. wide. (Sotheby's Belgravia) $450 £230

17th century German walnut centre table. (Boardman's) $2,178 £1,100

Victorian mahogany centre table, 3ft. wide, on cabriole legs. (Alfie's Antique Market) $297 £150

Walnut circular breakfast table, circa 1870, 45¾in. diameter. (Sotheby's Belgravia) $752 £380

Burr-walnut circular breakfast table, 1860's, 48in. diameter. (Sotheby's Belgravia) $892 £460

Mahogany and marquetry centre table, circa 1900, 40½in. wide. (Sotheby's Belgravia) $1,683 £850

Burr-walnut and ebonised loo table, circa 1870, 48in. wide. (Sotheby's) $349 £180

Regency mahogany breakfast table, 5ft. 6in. long, circa 1810. (Sotheby's) $7,128 £3,600

Mahogany octagonal breakfast table, circa 1880, with inlaid top. (Sotheby's Belgravia) $215 £110

DRESSING TABLES

Part of a suite of Betty Joell satinwood bedroom furniture, circa 1930. (Sotheby's Belgravia) $565 £280

Liberty & Co. oak toilet table, 38½in. wide, circa 1900. (Sotheby's Belgravia) $323 £160

Louis XV style ormolu mounted dressing table. (Bonham's) $1,212 £600

Part of a three-piece Arts and Crafts bedroom suite. (Biddle & Webb) $1,455 £750

A fine quality Victorian mahogany dressing table. (British Antique Exporters) $250 £125

Louis XV kingwood and tulipwood parquetry coiffeuse, 3ft.1in. wide, circa 1760. (Sotheby's) $6,270 £3,300

Mirror glass dressing table, 1930's, 97cm. wide, with triple mirror. (Sotheby's Belgravia) $392 £200

A kidney-shaped dressing table, sold with two chairs. (Christie's N. York) $4,000 £2,020

High Kitsch dressing table, 161cm. high, 1930's. (Sotheby's Belgravia) $504 £260

Italian walnut drop-leaf
table, circa 1610, 3ft.
11½in. long. (Sotheby's)
$1,960 £1,000

17th century Italian
walnut centre table.
(Boardman's)
$1,454 £720

Regency mahogany ex-
tending dining table,
circa 1815, 8ft.4in.
long. (Sotheby's)
$2,574 £1,300

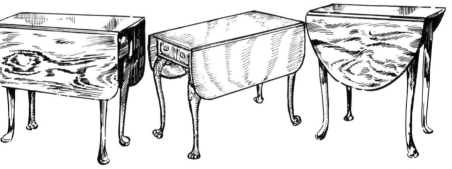

19th century Cuban
mahogany drop-leaf
table. (British Anti-
que Exporters)
$240 £120

Mahogany drop-leaf table,
circa 1740, 3ft.1in. wide.
(Sotheby's) $392 £200

19th century maho-
gany drop-flap table
on pad feet.(British
Antique Exporters)
$250 £125

Dutch marquetry gate-
leg dining table, 51in.
wide. (Christie's)
$3,104 £1,600

George III rectangular
mahogany and cross-
banded drop-leaf spider
gateleg table. (Phillips)
$1,414 £700

George II period red
walnut drop-leaf table,
30in. wide. (Christo-
pher Sykes)$564 £285

GATELEG TABLES

William and Mary oak gateleg table, 3ft.6in. long. (Sotheby's)
$970 £500

Charles II oak oval gateleg table, circa 1680, 4ft.10in. wide. (Sotheby's)
$4,018 £2,050

Charles II oak gateleg table, circa 1670, 3ft. 2in. wide. (Sotheby's)
$3,136 £1,600

Charles I oak gateleg table, circa 1640, 4ft. 9in. wide, open. (Sotheby's)
$1,683 £850

Small 17th century oak gateleg table of oval form, 42in. wide, open. (Butler & Hatch Waterman)
$1,717 £850

Charles II oak gateleg table, 4ft. wide, circa 1665. (Sotheby's)
$1,450 £740

Jacobean oak gateleg table. (Jordan & Cook) $873 £450

Charles I oak gateleg table, circa 1640, 3ft. open. (Sotheby's)
$543 £280

Mid 17th century carved oak gateleg table, 72in. wide, open. (Sotheby's)$646 £320

20th century oak reproduction refectory table. (Vernon's Chichester) $330 £165

George III mahogany d-end dining table. (Phillips) $10,100 £5,000

Mahogany dining table, circa 1920's, 96in. wide extended. (Sotheby's Belgravia) $646 £320

Large oak refectory table, 1880's, 108in. long. (Sotheby's Belgravia) $1,050 £520

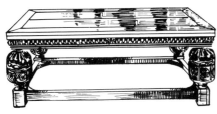

Elizabethan oak draw-leaf refectory table, 2ft.10in. wide. (Russell, Baldwin & Bright) $20,790 £10,500

Small 17th century oak refectory dining table, 54in. long. (Butler & Hatch Waterman) $6,060 £3,000

Double pedestal telescopic action dining table. (P. F. Windibank) $5,454 £2,700

19th century mahogany extending dining table on claw and ball feet. (British Antique Exporters) $400 £200

One of a pair of Italian oval tables.
(Christie's S. Kensington)
$8,148 £4,200

Mid 19th century mahogany centre
table, 51½in. wide.(Sotheby's Belgravia)
$1,154 £580

Walnut centre table, circa 1860, 48in.
wide.(Sotheby's Belgravia) $426 £220

Burr-walnut centre table, 42in. wide,
circa 1870.(Sotheby's Belgravia)
$431 £220

Oak refectory table, 6ft. x 2ft.8in.
(Worsfolds) $245 £125

Mid 19th century mahogany expanding
dining table, on ten turned legs.
(Sotheby's Belgravia) $814 £420

Unusual Regency mahogany extending
dining table, circa 1810, 3ft.10in. wide.
(Sotheby's) $3,007 £1,550

20th century mahogany dining table
with marble top, 58in. wide.(Sotheby's
Belgravia) $646 £330

19th century mahogany Wake's table. (British Antique Exporters)$600 £300

American mahogany dining table and set of chairs, circa 1900.(Christie's N. York) $1,430 £737

Mid 19th century walnut centre table, 72in. long.(Sotheby's Belgravia)
                              $1,280 £660

Early 19th century mahogany three pedestal dining table, extending to 12ft. with extra pedestal. (Sotheby's)
                            $2,871 £1,450

Early 17th century Dutch oak drawleaf table, 7ft.7in. wide, open.(Sotheby's)
                            $3,528 £1,800

Rosewood library or centre table, circa 1840, 52½in. wide.(Sotheby's Belgravia)
                              $349 £180

William IV rosewood library table, 1830's, 54in. wide.(Sotheby's Belgravia)
                              $407 £210

Oak refectory table. (Stride's)
                            $3,939 £1,950

Early 17th century oak drawleaf
dining table, 133in. wide.(Christie's)
$3,880 £2,000

17th century Flemish pale oak draw-
leaf dining table, 90in. wide.(Christie's)
$5,820 £3,000

17th century oak and beechwood centre table, 83in. long.(Christie's)
$1,746 £900

Fine Charles I oak drawleaf refectory
table, 198cm. long.(King & Chasemore)
$6,930 £3,500

Irish mahogany Wake or Hunt table.
(Sotheby's) $4,848 £2,400

James II oak refectory table. (King &
Chasemore) $1,861 £940

Mid·19th century American pitch pine
refectory table, 96½in. long.(Sotheby's
Belgravia) $594 £300

Early 17th century Italian walnut
centre table, 65in. wide.(Christie's)
$3,589 £1,850

Early 17th century oak dining table, 73½in. wide.(Christie's)$2,910 £1,500

Old oak refectory table, 7ft.2in. long, with carved frieze. (Green & Co.)
$893 £470

James II oak refectory table, 82cm. wide.(King & Chasemore)$1,782 £900

17th century oak and elm serving table, inscribed M.G. (King & Chasemore)
$6,766 £3,400

19th century Chinese hardwood low table. (British Antique Exporters)
$200 £100

Early 17th century pale oak refectory table, 96in. wide.(Christie's)
$2,425 £1,250

Charles I oak drawleaf table, 5ft.1in. wide.(Sotheby's) $3,201 £1,650

Charles I oak table, circa 1640, 6ft. 11in. long.(Sotheby's) $2,231 £1,150

417

Fine 18th century mahogany tea table, with tray top, circa 1750. (Christopher Sykes) $2,425 £1,250

Regency mahogany wine table, 72in. wide. (Christie's)$1,372 £700

Late 19th century Singalese table, 36in. high. (Gray's Antique Mews) $60 £30

Early Georgian mahogany turnover tea table, 32in. wide. (Locke & England) $1,616 £800

Mahogany display table, circa 1890, 33in. high.(Sotheby's Belgravia)$597 £300

George II mahogany small table with cabriole legs, 27in. high. (Gray's Antique Market) $272 £135

Late 19th century carved oak triangular top table with flaps. (Vernon's Chichester) $90 £45

Thuyawood and sycamore centre table, circa 1880, 51½in. wide. (Sotheby's Belgravia) $1,171 £580

Victorian carved oak occasional table. (Vernon's Chichester)$40 £20

Liberty & Co. oak
and beaten copper
occasional table,
circa 1920, 24in. wide.
(Sotheby's Belgravia)
$222 £110

Marquetry centre table,
circa 1870, 62in. wide,
by H. Goodall, Newcastle.
(Sotheby's Belgravia)
$2,121 £1,050

Oval marquetry and
mahogany centre
table, 1900's, 40½in.
wide. (Sotheby's Bel-
gravia) $1,030 £510

Fine quality Chinese
Chippendale mahogany
table. (Gray's Antique
Market) $494 £245

William and Mary
yew wood and
crossbanded bow
front corner table.
(King & Chasemore)
$2,716 £1,400

19th century Burmese
teak occasional table,
legs in the form of
elephants' heads.
(Vernon's Chichester)
$110 £55

Edwardian inlaid pede-
stal table, 29½in. high.
(Gray's Antique Mews)
$191 £95

Nest of four tables by
Galle with inlaid tops.
(Sotheby's N. York)
$3,737 £1,850

Late 18th century
elm dishtop table,
19in. diameter.
(Gray's Antique Mews)
$238 £118

419

One of a pair of North Italian kingwood d-shaped bedside cupboards, 1ft.10in. wide. (Sotheby's)
$2,090 £1,100

Marquetry specimen wood circular table, circa 1880, 30½ x 28½in.(Sotheby's Belgravia)$620 £320

Rosewood coffee table by Jacques Rhulmann, circa 1925, 26½in. diam. (Christie's N. York)
$2,860 £1,537

Queen Anne elm and fruitwood cricket table, 2ft.1in. diam., circa 1705.(Sotheby's)
$1,411 £720

Set of four marquetry tables with glass tops, circa 1900, by Galle. (Sotheby's Belgravia)
$2,328 £1,200

Edwards and Roberts mahogany occasional table, 29½in. wide, circa 1900.(Sotheby's Belgravia)$422 £220

Walnut and parquetry tip-top table, 28½in. diameter, 1842. (Sotheby's Belgravia)
$310 £160

Syrie Maugham painted wood table or jardiniere, circa 1936, 93.75cm. wide.(Sotheby's Belgravia)
$532 £280

Octagonal walnut inlaid table, circa 1840, 28in. high. (Gray's Antique Mews)$594 £300

Mid 20th century
rosewood occasional
table with marble
top, 27½in. wide.
(Sotheby's Belgravia)
$509 £260

Louis XV walnut toilet
table, 35¾in. wide.
(Christie's)
$4,268 £2,200

Mid 19th century
nest of rosewood
occasional tables.
(Sotheby's Belgravia)
$403 £210

Rosewood and marquetry
occasional table, late 19th
century, 18¼in. wide.
(Sotheby's Belgravia)
$333 £170

James I oak hutch
table, circa 1620, 2ft.
8in. wide.(Sotheby's)
$2,842 £1,450

Rosewood and maho-
gany bedside table,
by Louis Majorelle,
37½in. high.
(Christie's N. York)
$1,200 £606

Syrie Maugham painted
wood occasional table,
circa 1936, 66.5cm.
high.(Sotheby's Bel-
gravia) $247 £130

Ebonised and marquetry
occasional table, 1880's,
44in. wide.(Sotheby's
Belgravia) $698 £360

Late 19th century
mahogany vide poche,
1ft.6in. wide.
(Sotheby's)$392 £200

OCCASIONAL TABLES

19th century table in rosewood and marquetry, 45½in. wide.(Christie's)
$776 £400

Hardwood camel, 28in. high, which supports a carved coffee table. (Bradley & Vaughan)
$435 £220

Three-tier coffee table in pale walnut, 1930's, 91.5cm. wide.(Sotheby's Belgravia)$196 £100

Late 19th century centre table in rosewood, 28½in. high. (Sotheby's Belgravia)
$979 £510

Brass mirror-topped table, 1900, 73cm. high.(Sotheby's Belgravia) $156 £80

Galle fruitwood marquetry occasional table, circa 1900, 78cm. wide. (Sotheby's Belgravia)
$1,782 £900

Mid 18th century Portuguese jacaranda tripod table, 32in. wide.(Christie's)
$1,649 £850

Late 18th century mahogany architect's table, with ormolu handle.(Hobbs Parker) $1,513 £780

Emile Jacques Rhulmann table, 74.5cm. wide, circa 1925. (Sotheby's Belgravia)
$3,465 £1,750

Rosewood and kingwood marquetry occasional table, circa 1900, 30½ x 41¼in.(Sotheby's Belgravia) $538 £280

One of three late 19th century rosewood and mother-of-pearl occasional tables, 31½in. high.(Sotheby's Belgravia) $1,306 £680

Mahogany silver table of Chippendale period. (Neales)$3,267 £1,650

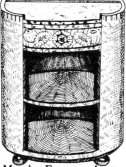

Marquetry two-tier table by Emile Galle, circa 1890, 26in. square.(Christie's N. York)$1,500 £757

Mercier Freres walnut and ivory bedside table, early 1920's, 63cm. high.(Sotheby's Belgravia) $297 £150

Early 1920's marble topped Art Deco occasional table, 54.5cm. square.(Sotheby's Belgravia) $198 £100

French mahogany centre table, circa 1900, 36in. wide. (Christie's N. York) $600 £303

Kingwood table de milieu of Louis XVI design, 20¾in. wide. (Christie's) $1,164 £600

Dainty mahogany single drawer table, 22in. wide, circa 1840.(Silvester's) $190 £98

423

19th century mahogany occasional table on tripod base. (British Antique Exporters) $60 £30

Late 19th century low table, mounted in hardstone. (Sotheby's Belgravia) $365 £190

Victorian burr-walnut occasional table on tripod base. (British Antique Exporters) $70 £35

20th century parquetry occasional table, 37in. wide. (Sotheby's Belgravia) $384 £200

Victorian bamboo occasional table with lacquered top. (British Antique Exporters) $30 £15

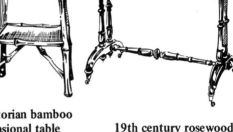

19th century rosewood centre table. (British Antique Exporters) $240 £120

18th century elm cricket table. (British Antique Exporters) $60 £30

19th century walnut, kingwood and tulipwood serpentined top centre table, 3ft.3½in. wide. (Geering & Colyer) $947 £460

19th century lacquered nest of tables. (British Antique Exporters) $170 £85

Small George III speckled, lacquered Pembroke table. (Phillips)
$4,950 £2,500

Sheraton period satinwood and mahogany Pembroke table, 37¾in. wide open. (Geering & Colyer)
$388 £200

Fine late 18th century figured mahogany Pembroke table, 32in. wide.(Nottingham Auction Mart)
$1,436 £740

George III satinwood Pembroke table, circa 1780, 2ft.10in. wide. (Sotheby's)
$1,881 £950

Mahogany Pembroke table of Hepplewhite design, 29in. wide. (V. & V. Auctions)
$1,292 £640

Rare matching George III fiddle-back mahogany and satinwood crossbanded Pembroke table and tray.(Phillips)
$9,090 £4,500

Regency rosewood Pembroke table, 44½in. wide open. (Christie's)
$1,158 £600

George III mahogany 'butterfly' shaped Pembroke table, 2ft.6in. wide, circa 1780. (Sotheby's) $1,010 £500

George III mahogany Pembroke table, circa 1790, 2ft.4in. high. (Sotheby's)
$2,871 £1,450

425

One of a pair of late 19th century mother-of-pearl and rosewood side tables.(Sotheby's Belgravia)$1,536 £800

Oak side table, 1880's, 28 x 43in.(Sotheby's Belgravia) $252 £130

One of a pair of George II giltwood side tables. (Christie's) $17,640 £9,000

William and Mary oak side table, 2ft.6in. wide. (Sotheby's) $504 £260

Dutch marquetry side table, circa 1750, 2ft. 8in. wide. (Sotheby's) $1,332 £680

16th century oak side table with deep drawer and shaped plank supports.(Phillips & Garrod Turner) $1,980 £1,000

William and Mary oak side table, 2ft.6in. wide. (Sotheby's) $543 £280

18th century black lacquer side table with tray top, 2ft.6in. wide. (King & Chasemore) $1,843 £950

Late 17th century oak side table. (Drewatt, Watson & Barton) $2,400 £1,250

Charles II walnut side table, 2ft.10in. wide, circa 1680, possibly Flemish. (Sotheby's)
$2,156 £1,100

Stained oak side table, circa 1880, 38in. wide. (Sotheby's Belgravia)
$446 £230

Serpentine front walnut side table, 2ft.10in. wide. (David Symonds)
$392 £200

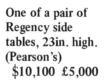

George III satinwood side table, 51¾in. wide. (Christie's)
$1,139 £580

One of a pair of Regency side tables, 23in. high. (Pearson's)
$10,100 £5,000

20th century mahogany side table, 57in. wide.(Sotheby's Belgravia)$455 £230

One of a pair of George III white painted and parcel gilt side tables, 25in. wide.(Christie's)
$784 £400

Antique walnut side table with three drawers, 3ft.6in. wide. (Warner, Sheppard & Wade) $548 £280

James I oak side table, circa 1620, 3ft.0½in. wide. (Sotheby's)
$3,136 £1,600

Dutch marquetry serpentine side table, 35in. wide. (Christie's) $3,104 £1,600

George III mahogany d-shaped side table, 5ft. 11½in. wide.(Sotheby's) $1,724 £880

Mid 19th century rosewood side table, 66in. wide. (Sotheby's Belgravia) $396 £200

George III satinwood marquetry side table, 2ft. wide, circa 1790. (Sotheby's) $2,548 £1,300

Late George III mahogany bow-fronted side table, 2ft.11in. wide, circa 1805. (Sotheby's) $1,862 £950

Unusual William IV rosewood side table, circa 1835, 3ft. wide. (Sotheby's) $582 £300

A fine 19th century carved rosewood side table. (British Antique Exporters) $600 £300

Rare 18th century Portuguese colonial side table, 29¼in. high. (Locke & England) $1,616 £800

Late 19th century rosewood side table, 34 x 50in. (Sotheby's Belgravia) $1,037 £540

17th century Spanish
walnut side table,
46in. wide. (Christie's)
$3,007 £1,550

Late 18th century oak
side table. (British
Antique Exporters)
$70 £35

William and Mary wal-
nut side table, circa
1690, 2ft.10in. wide.
(Sotheby's)
$4,116 £2,100

Unusual William
and Mary oak side
table, 26in. high.
(Sotheby's)
$3,131 £1,550

Mid 18th century Louis XV
walnut and elm provencal
side table, 6ft.4in. long.
(Sotheby's) $2,450 £1,250

Late 17th century
oak side table, 33in.
wide. (Christie's)
$892 £460

George II oak side table,
2ft.6in. x 1ft.9in. (Alfie's
Antique Market)
$565 £280

20th century oak
side table.(British
Antique Exporters)
$40 £20

Late 19th century rose-
wood side table, 34 x
50in. (Sotheby's Bel-
gravia) $1,037 £540

429

William IV rosewood
sofa table, 88cm. wide.
(King & Chasemore)
$601 £310

Dutch marquetry and
mahogany sofa table,
circa 1820, 4ft.2in.
wide. (Sotheby's)
$2,548 £1,300

Unusually good example
of a Regency brass in-
laid sofa table in rose-
wood. (Burtenshaw
Walker)$3,626 £1,850

One of a pair of Regency
rosewood sofa tables by
John McLean, 2ft. deep.
(Sotheby's)
$19,800 £10,000

Mahogany and mar-
quetry sofa table,
circa 1890, 44in.
wide. (Sotheby's
Belgravia)
$970 £490

Mahogany sofa table,
circa 1840, 54in. wide.
(Sotheby's Belgravia)
$329 £170

Regency rosewood
sofa table. (Lawrence
Fine Art)
$1,901 £980

Regency mahogany
sofa table, circa 1815,
5ft.10in. wide.
(Sotheby's)
$792 £400

Regency mahogany
sofa table, 5ft. wide
open. circa 1810.
(Sotheby's)
$2,871 £1,450

Regency mahogany
sofa table, 59½in.
wide open.
(Christie's)
$2,509 £1,300

Regency brass inlaid
rosewood sofa table,
circa 1815, 3ft.7in.
wide. (Sotheby's)
$2,475 £1,250

19th century rosewood
sofa table. (Edwards,
Bigwood & Bewlay)
$2,323 £1,150

George III mahogany
sofa table, circa 1800,
2ft.2in. wide. (Sotheby's)
$4,554 £2,300

Regency rosewood
sofa table, 4ft.3in.
long. (Phillips)
$2,678 £1,300

Regency calaman-
derwood sofa table,
58¾in. wide, open.
(Christie's)
$1,700 £850

Regency rosewood
sofa table with satin-
wood inlaid top, 26in.
wide. (Morphets)
$909 £450

Small late George II
mahogany sofa
table, 1ft.9in. wide,
circa 1800.
(Sotheby's)
$1,227 £620

Regency rosewood
sofa table, 59½in.
wide, open.
(Christie's)
$2,050 £1,200

Victorian rosewood work table.(Russell, Baldwin & Bright) $950 £480

Mid 19th century walnut games table, 23 x 23¼in. (Sotheby's Belgravia)$455 £230

Regency needlework table in inlaid rosewood.(Geering & Colyer)$990 £500

Rosewood work table, circa 1850, 30 x 22½in. (Sotheby's Belgravia) $336 £170

George IV boulle games table, circa 1830, 1ft.6in. wide. (Sotheby's) $1,058 £540

Chinese export black and gilt lacquer games table, circa 1850, 35in. wide.(Sotheby's Belgravia) $975 £490

Walnut work table, circa 1860, 28½in. wide. (Sotheby's Belgravia)$554 £280

William IV brass inlaid rosewood chess table, 1ft.9in. wide, circa 1830. (Sotheby's)$495 £250

Walnut combined work and games table, 1860's, 33¼in. wide.(Sotheby's Belgravia) $795 £410

French Empire work
table in mahogany.
(James & Lister Lea)
$336 £170

Rosewood and maho-
gany sewing table,
1840's, 1ft.8in. wide.
(Sotheby's)$431 £220

Walnut games or
work table, circa
1860, 22in. wide.
(Sotheby's Belgravia)
$736 £370

19th century burr-
walnut work or games
table. (J. M. Welch)
$853 £440

Victorian fitted burr-
walnut work table.
(J. M. Welch)
$594 £300

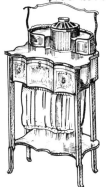

A lady's small mahogany
combined writing desk
and work table, circa
1900, 10½in. high.
(Sotheby's Belgravia)
$504 £260

Anglo-Indian ebony
games table, 30 x
22in. (Sotheby's Bel-
gravia) $422 £220

Regency mahogany games
table, circa 1810, 3ft.3in.
wide open. (Sotheby's)
$1,822 £930

20th century Carine par-
quetry games table, 37in.
wide.(Sotheby's Belgravia)
$830 £410

433

Small 19th century French kingwood sewing table, 2ft. high, inset with Sevres plaques. (Messenger, May & Baverstock) $909 £450

19th century mahogany workbox on platform base. (British Antique Exporters)$200 £100

Victorian chinoiserie lacquer work table, 28in. high. (Gray's Antique Mews)
$575 £285

Walnut combined games and work table, circa 1870, 21¾in. wide. (Sotheby's Belgravia) $686 £340

Victorian rosewood work table with sliding bag. (British Antique Exporters) $250 £125

Modern Damascus parquetry games table, 30¼in. wide.(Sotheby's Belgravia) $509 £260

Victorian rosewood teapoy on tripod base.(British Antique Exporters) $350 £175

Louis XVI kingwood and tulipwood tric-trac table with reversible top. (Bonham's) $6,868 £3,400

Mid 19th century ebony sewing table, 25in. high.(Churchman's) $646 £340

434

Late 19th century oak folding desk. (British Antique Exporters)$90 £45

Late George III mahogany library writing table, 6ft. wide, circa 1800. (Sotheby's) $4,158 £2,100

Early Victorian child's desk in mahogany, circa 1840, 32½in. high. (Gray's Antique Mews) $373 £185

Good bamboo writing desk.(Sotheby's Belgravia)$282 £140

Walnut marquetry writing table, 1860's, 38¼in. wide. (Sotheby's Belgravia) $888 £440

Queen Anne oak writing table, 31½in. wide. (Butler & Hatch Waterman) $3,838 £1,900

Art Nouveau mahogany writing table with drawer. (Garrod Turner) $2,424 £1,200

Late 18th century French carved oak bonheur du jour, 40in. wide.(Nottingham Auction Mart) $545 £270

Victorian pine and cast iron school desk and chair. (British Antique Exporters) $30 £15

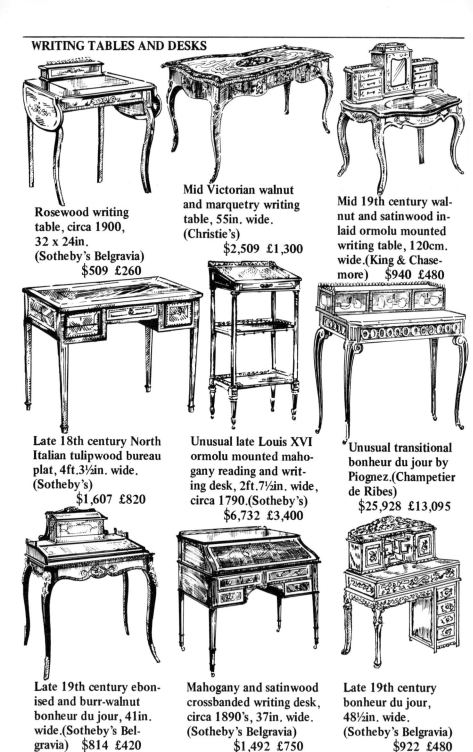

Rosewood writing table, circa 1900, 32 x 24in. (Sotheby's Belgravia) $509 £260

Mid Victorian walnut and marquetry writing table, 55in. wide. (Christie's) $2,509 £1,300

Mid 19th century walnut and satinwood inlaid ormolu mounted writing table, 120cm. wide.(King & Chasemore) $940 £480

Late 18th century North Italian tulipwood bureau plat, 4ft.3½in. wide. (Sotheby's) $1,607 £820

Unusual late Louis XVI ormolu mounted mahogany reading and writing desk, 2ft.7½in. wide, circa 1790.(Sotheby's) $6,732 £3,400

Unusual transitional bonheur du jour by Piognez.(Champetier de Ribes) $25,928 £13,095

Late 19th century ebonised and burr-walnut bonheur du jour, 41in. wide.(Sotheby's Belgravia) $814 £420

Mahogany and satinwood crossbanded writing desk, circa 1890's, 37in. wide. (Sotheby's Belgravia) $1,492 £750

Late 19th century bonheur du jour, 48½in. wide. (Sotheby's Belgravia) $922 £480

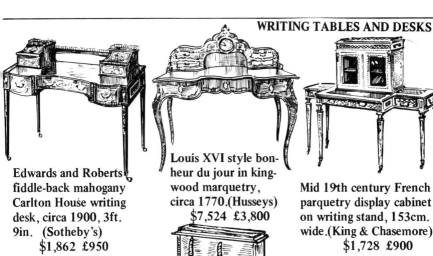

Edwards and Roberts fiddle-back mahogany Carlton House writing desk, circa 1900, 3ft. 9in. (Sotheby's) $1,862 £950

Louis XVI style bonheur du jour in kingwood marquetry, circa 1770.(Husseys) $7,524 £3,800

Mid 19th century French parquetry display cabinet on writing stand, 153cm. wide.(King & Chasemore) $1,728 £900

Mid 19th century figured walnut veneered bonheur du jour, 48in. high.(H. C. Chapman) $2,327 £1,225

Mahogany and walnut portable writing desk, 22in. wide, circa 1860. (Silvester's)$320 £165

Louis XIV boulle bureau mazarin, circa 1680, 3ft.2½in. wide. (Sotheby's) $14,060 £7,400

Sheraton design satinwood and tulipwood crossbanded reading table, 22in. wide. (Mallam's)$1,414 £700

'Regence' contra partie boulle writing table, circa 1850, 32½in. wide. (Sotheby's Belgravia) $1,411 £720

Rosewood bonheur du jour, circa 1900, 44¼ x 24in. (Sotheby's Belgravia) $653 £330

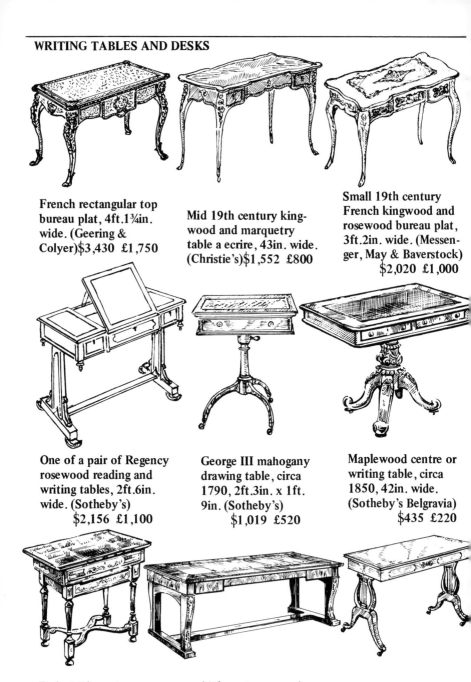

French rectangular top bureau plat, 4ft.1¾in. wide. (Geering & Colyer)$3,430 £1,750

Mid 19th century kingwood and marquetry table a ecrire, 43in. wide. (Christie's)$1,552 £800

Small 19th century French kingwood and rosewood bureau plat, 3ft.2in. wide. (Messenger, May & Baverstock) $2,020 £1,000

One of a pair of Regency rosewood reading and writing tables, 2ft.6in. wide. (Sotheby's) $2,156 £1,100

George III mahogany drawing table, circa 1790, 2ft.3in. x 1ft. 9in. (Sotheby's) $1,019 £520

Maplewood centre or writing table, circa 1850, 42in. wide. (Sotheby's Belgravia) $435 £220

Early 17th century South German walnut marquetry writing table, 2ft.7in. high.(Sotheby's) $4,116 £2,100

19th century ormolu mounted mahogany writing table, 5ft.11in. wide. (Sotheby's) $2,945 £1,550

Unusual rosewood centre table, 3ft. x 1ft.8in., early 19th century. (Sotheby's)$1,646 £840

Victorian carved oak library table on bulbous legs.(Vernon's Chichester)
$500 £250

William IV rosewood writing table, 47in. wide, circa 1835.(Silvester's)$727 £375

French ormolu mounted parquetry bureau plat, 44½in. wide. (Christie's)
$3,880 £2,000

George III mahogany writing table with leather top. (Sotheby Bearne)
$26,190 £13,500

One of a pair of painted satinwood bonheur du jours, 1880, 29in. wide. (Sotheby's Belgravia)
$2,450 £1,250

Walnut marquetry bureau plat, 55in. wide, circa 1860.(Sotheby's Belgravia)
$1,261 £650

George III Chippendale style writing table, 46in. wide.(Nottingham Auction Mart)
$2,716 £1,400

William IV carved mahogany bonheur du jour, 42in. wide. (Nottingham Auction Mart)$352 £180

Late 18th century library table in mahogany and oak, 146cm. long. (Phillips)
$25,740 £13,000

Late 15th century Piedmontese walnut cassone, 4ft.8in. wide.(Sotheby's) $5,220 £2,800

Early 17th century oak chest, 3ft.9in. wide.(Sotheby's) $718 £370

17th century Italian walnut cassone. (Parsons, Welch & Cowell) $1,710 £900

Dutch Colonial nadun wood chest, 40in. wide.(Geering & Colyer) $1,131 £560

Early 17th century large oak chest, 8ft.6in. wide.(Sotheby's) $737 £380

Unusual panel front oak chest, 50in. wide, circa 1750.(Silvester's) $519 £265

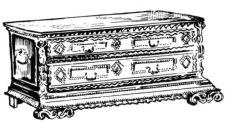

Early 17th century Italian cassone in walnut, 2ft.7in. high x 5ft.8in. wide. (Sotheby's) $1,274 £650

Oak linen chest, circa 1660, 5ft. wide. (Sotheby's) $732 £370

Late 15th century Italian giltwood cassone, 74½in. long.(Christie's)
$6,080 £3,200

Late 16th century Italian walnut cassone, 73in. wide. (Christie's)
$5,820 £3,000

Jacobean oak panelled coffer.(J. M. Welch & Sons) $705 £360

Charles II oak chest, 4ft.9in. wide, circa 1680.(Sotheby's)$495 £250

Rare early 17th century oak coffer, 3ft.3½in. wide.(Sotheby's)
$582 £300

17th century carved oak coffer, 120cm. wide.(King & Chasemore) $509 £260

George I oak mule chest, 56½in. long. (Christopher Sykes) $555 £275

Late Gothic oak chest, circa 1500, 4ft. 3½in. wide. (Sotheby's)$4,268 £2,200

James I oak chest, 4ft.10in. wide, circa 1610. (Sotheby's)
$1,504 £760

Small 15th century plank built oak coffer with original lock plate, 40in. wide. (Butler & Hatch Waterman)
$1,262 £625

Late 19th century walnut coffer. (Vernon's Chichester) $100 £50

Late 17th century oak coffer, 48in. long. (Gray's Antique Mews)
$585 £290

16th century oak dower chest, 44in. wide, with carved front panels. (Graves, Son & Pilcher)
$2,277 £1,150

Early 17th century carved oak coffer with iron lock, 48in. wide. (Butler & Hatch Waterman) $2,727 £1,350

Late Gothic chest in oak, circa 1530, 2ft.8in. wide. (Sotheby's)
$5,044 £2,600

James I period oak coffer. (R. L. Lowery & Partners) $909 £450

Charles II oak chest, circa 1685, 4ft. 4½in. wide. (Sotheby's) $891 £450

16th century carved oak coffer with triple front, 40in. wide. (Butler & Hatch Waterman) $1,717 £850

Carved and stained pine chest, 17th century, 4ft.6½in. wide. (Sotheby's) $435 £220

Late 18th century pine coffer on bracket feet. (British Antique Exporters) $80 £40

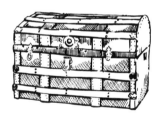

Edwardian oak and metal banded trunk. (British Antique Exporters) $20 £10

18th century carved oak coffer with inset panel top, 41in. wide. (Nottingham Auction Mart) $404 £200

Henry VIII painted oak chest, 3ft. 1¾in. wide, mid 16th century. (Sotheby's) $970 £500

18th century painted leather travelling trunk. (Geering & Colyer) $970 £500

Wardrobe designed by Gordon Russell, circa 1930, 72in. high.(Sotheby's Belgravia)$718 £370

Late 18th century Dutch faded mahogany wardrobe, 70in. wide. (H. Spencer & Sons) $2,842 £1,450

Late George III mahogany wardrobe, 4ft. 4in. wide. (Sotheby's) $1,346 £680

Good French 18th century walnut wardrobe, 7ft.6in. high. (Sotheby's) $1,089 £550

Rare painted wardrobe by Wm. Burges, 1870's, 53in. wide.(Sotheby's Belgravia) $1,717 £850

Mid 18th century Louis XV walnut provincial armoire, 4ft.9in. wide. (Sotheby's) $1,078 £550

George III country made mahogany wardrobe, 6ft. 3½in. high. (Sotheby's) $1,940 £1,000

Art Nouveau style oak wardrobe with mirror door. (British Antique Exporters) $50 £25

Early Louis XVI provincial armoire in chestnut, 5ft. wide. (Humberts, King & Chasemore) $3,283 £1,650

17th century Dutch
oak armoire, 220cm.
wide. (King & Chase-
more) $2,475 £1,250

Solid walnut breakfront
wardrobe by Peter
Waals. (Woolley & Wallis)
$4,200 £2,100

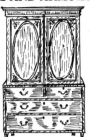

George III maho-
gany wardrobe.
(Humberts, King
& Chasemore)
$1,069 £540

Rosewood armoire by
Louis Majorelle, 103in.
high. (Christie's N.
York) $9,000 £4,545

Early 1920's walnut
and ivory wardrobe,
designed by Leon
Jallot, 193cm. high.
(Sotheby's Belgravia)
$594 £300

Late 16th century
Flemish walnut
armoire, 5ft.6in.
wide. (Sotheby's)
$4,508 £2,300

18th century Flemish
oak armoire.
(Worsfolds)
$4,848 £2,400

Heal's wardrobe
of 1898. (V. & V's.)
$2,231 £1,150

Early 18th century
French walnut pro-
vincial armoire,
150cm. wide. (King
& Chasemore)
$1,248 £650

445

Papier mache and mother-of-pearl whatnot, 1840's, 52½in. high. (Sotheby's Belgravia) $2,673 £1,350

Victorian carved oak serving trolley.(British Antique Exporters) $350 £175

Rosewood whatnot, circa 1850, 28in. high. (Gray's Antique Market) $444 £220

Large walnut canterbury, 37in. high, circa 1860. (Sotheby's Belgravia) $673 £340

Victorian walnut whatnot of serpentine form. (Gray's Antique Market) $594 £300

20th century oak serving trolley. (British Antique Exporters) $26 £13

19th century ebonised etagere with brass embellishments.(British Antique Exporters) $250 £125

Victorian walnut rectangular three tier whatnot, 107cm. wide. (King & Chasemore) $836 £400

Victorian inlaid walnut three-tier whatnot, 42in. high. (Gray's Antique Mews) $424 £210

446

Fine Georgian oval brass bound wine cooler. (C.T. & G. H. Smith)
$3,838 £1,900

Large solid rosewood Anglo-Indian wine cooler, circa 1840, 30in. wide. (Sotheby's Belgravia) $356 £180

Georgian mahogany wine cooler, 18in. wide, circa 1820. (Silvester's)
$921 £475

George III sarcophagus top cellarette, 14in. high. (Nottingham Auction Mart) $737 £380

George III mahogany and brass bound wine cooler, 60cm. wide. (King & Chasemore)
$1,631 £820

Brass bound mahogany wine cooler. (Allen & May)
$1,656 £820

Early George III octagonal mahogany wine cooler with brass bands. (Heathcote, Ball & Co.)
$2,020 £1,000

George IV mahogany wine cooler, circa 1820, 2ft.5in. wide.(Sotheby's)
$470 £240

George III oval brass bound wine cooler, 22in. high. (Nottingham Auction Mart)
$2,910 £1,500

Bohemian gilt beaker, circa 1840, 10.5cm. high. (Sotheby's Belgravia) $548 £280

18th century enamelled Bohemian beaker, 4in. high. (Sotheby's) $1,470 £750

Rare St. Louis millefiori beaker, 10cm. high. (Sotheby's) $848 £420

Rare German beaker, 16th/17th century, 4½in. high. (Sotheby's) $1,784 £920

Late 19th century enamelled humpen, 21.4cm. high. (Sotheby's Belgravia) $574 £290

German engraved armorial beaker, circa 1740, 12cm. high. (Sotheby's) $1,171 £580

17th/18th century 'Ochsenkopf' humpen with enamelled body, 6in. high. (Sotheby's) $9,800 £5,000

Dated Elizabethan engraved inscription beaker. (Christie's) $151,500 £75,000

Early 19th century transparent beaker, 10.5cm. high. (Phillips) $6,270 £3,300

Good Bohemain engraved beaker, circa 1830, 13.8cm. high. (Sotheby's Belgravia) $862 £440

One of a pair of egg-yolk yellow Pekin glass beakers, 9½in. high. (Christie's) $8,250 £4,304

Venetian enamelled beaker, circa 1520, 8¾in. high.(Sotheby's) $43,120 £22,000

Unusual 18th century Spanish tumbler, 12cm. high. (Sotheby's)$888 £440

17th/18th century Franconian drinking glass, 15cm. high, with enamelled decoration. (Sotheby's)$9,900 £5,000

One of a pair of Silesian engraved fluted beakers with minor chips, 4¼in. high, circa 1755.(Christie's) $342 £180

Facon-de-Venise flared beaker, 16th/17th century, 6in. high. (Christie's) $950 £500

Unusual amber-flashed beaker of thistle form, circa 1850, 16.2cm. high. (Sotheby's Belgravia) $316 £160

Venetian enamelled tumbler, 18th century, 4½in. high. (Sotheby's) $1,008 £520

Sealed wine bottle,
circa 1780, 10in.
high. (Sotheby's)
$254 £130

German enamelled
pharmacy bottle,
circa 1740, 9.5cm.
high. (Sotheby's)
$484 £240

Early sealed wine
bottle, circa 1710,
6½in. high.
(Sotheby's)$784 £400

Rare set of enamelled 'mock china' cruet bottles, circa 1760, 4¾in. to
7¼in. high. (Sotheby's) $1,784 £920

Early 19th century Zara
Seal liqueur bottle with
ring-postil base.(Gray's
Antique Market)$76 £38

Early sealed wine
bottle, circa 1683,
6in. high.(Sotheby's)
$1,515 £750

19th century Zara
Seal liqueur bottle.
(Alfie's Antique
Market) $50 £25

Sealed wine bottle of onion shape, 1705, 6¾in. high.(Sotheby's) $1,202 £620

Good enamelled bottle, circa 1870, 11.8cm. high, with gilt rim.(Sotheby's Belgravia) $257 £130

Unusually large early sealed wine bottle, 10in. high, circa 1728.. (Sotheby's) $1,148 £580

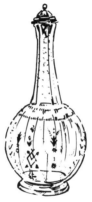

Tiffany green ground bottle, circa 1905. (Gray's Antique Market) $4,950 £2,500

One of a set of four gilt toilet bottles, 20cm. high, circa 1830, with matching stoppers. (Sotheby's) $646 £320

Sealed wine bottle, 1742, 9¼in. high. (Sotheby's) $329 £170

One of three spirit bottles and stoppers, possibly Cork glass, 16.5cm. high.(Sotheby's Belgravia) $166 £85

Early sealed wine bottle, seal inscribed 'Robt. Tanner 1725', 8¾in. high. (Sotheby's) $485 £250

Rare early wine bottle, circa 1660, 8in. high. (Sotheby's) $329 £170

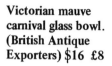

German 'Maigerlein',
16th century, 4¼in.
diameter. (Sotheby's)
$1,513 £780

Victorian mauve
carnival glass bowl.
(British Antique
Exporters) $16 £8

Rare mounted cameo
glass wall flowerbowl,
13in. diam. (Christie's
N. York) $1,650 £863

Very rare double-walled
bowl attributed to Thos.
Hawkes, 4¼in. diameter,
circa 1830-37.
(Sotheby's)
$1,008 £520

Large flared bowl stipple
engraved by Laurence
Whistler, 9¾in. diam.
(Christie's)
$1,615 £850

Early 18th century
glass bowl, 11¼in.
diameter.
(Phillips)
$7,600 £4,000

Green glass bowl, cover
and stand, circa 1850,
31cm. high. (Sotheby's
Belgravia)$1,274 £650

Signed glass bowl by
Sabena, France.
(Alfie's Antique
Market) $141 £70

Miniature cameo
glass bowl, circa
1880, 3.8cm. high.
(Sotheby's Belgravia)
$514 £260

Large cut glass column with faceted stem, circa 1900, 54.5cm. high. (Sotheby's Belgravia) $415 £210

Large cut glass column, circa 1900, 56.5cm. high to top.(Sotheby's Belgravia) $431 £220

Bronze and Favrile glass candlestick, by Tiffany, 8in. high.(Christie's N. York) $462 £248

CASKETS

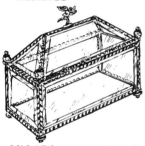

Mid 17th century French rock crystal miniature casket, 4½in. long. (Sotheby's) $5,320 £2,800

Blue glass casket with six perfume bottles, circa 1850, 15.2cm. wide. (Sotheby's Belgravia) $396 £200

Late 19th century ruby glass casket, 9cm. wide. (Sotheby's Belgravia) $215 £110

CUPS AND MUGS

One of a pair of unusual Punch or Custard Cups, circa 1790, 8cm. high. (Sotheby's Ireland) $215 £110

Engraved coin ale mug of bell shape, 6¾in. high. (Christie's) $190 £100

One of a set of four Tiffany iridescent glass mugs, circa 1900, 6.5cm. high.(Sotheby's Belgravia) $368 £190

One of a pair of George III Waterford glass decanters, 19in. high, circa 1780. (Sotheby's)$6,060 £3,000

19th century cut glass decanter.(British Antique Exporters)$24 £12

St. Louis decanter, 21.5cm. high, with dark blue and opaque white bands. (Sotheby's) $444 £220

Jacobite decanter, circa 1760, 10in. high. (Sotheby's) $1,008 £520

Late 19th century Persian glass decanter with portraits.(Sotheby's Belgravia) $1,520 £800

Large Bohemian enamelled decanter and stopper, circa 1850, 54cm. high.(Sotheby's Belgravia) $1,485 £750

Large green glass decanter and spire stopper, circa 1850, 52cm. high. (Sotheby's Belgravia) $392 £200

One of a pair of cut glass decanters and stoppers, circa 1810, 10½in. high. (Sotheby's)$235 £120

One of a pair of panel cut decanters, 33.5cm. high. (May, Whetter & Grose) $85 £42.50

George III Waterford glass decanter, 20in. high, circa 1780. (Sotheby's) $4,444 £2,200

Pair of Victorian glass gilded decanters, circa 1860, 12in. high. (Gray's Antique Mews) $363 £180

One of a pair of Sunderland Bridge decanters and stoppers, circa 1820, 9½in. high. (Sotheby's) $871 £440

Signed and dated decanter and stopper by L. Whistler, 1973, 28.8cm. high.(Sotheby's Belgravia) $1,227 £620

Small Cork decanter, circa 1800, 19.5cm. high. (Sotheby's) $484 £240

19th/20th century enamelled decanter of Persian interest, 26.8cm. high. (Sotheby's Belgravia) $396 £200

Bohemian or Spanish enamelled milchglas decanter and stopper, circa 1780, 11¼in. high.(Sotheby's) $372 £190

Set of three blue glass decanters and stand, 19th century, 9½in. high. (Sotheby's) $465 £240

Large glass decanter and stopper, circa 1850, 56cm. high. (Sotheby's Belgravia) $1,764 £900

Victorian orange
carnival glass dish.
(British Antique
Exporters)$20 £10

Lalique frosted glass dish,
45.25cm. wide, 1920's.
(Sotheby's Belgravia)
$435 £220

Victorian mauve
carnival glass dish.
(British Antique
Exporters)$20 £10

Silesian stemmed
sweetmeat glass,
6¼in. high.
(Christie's)
$152 £80

Late 19th century gilt
and enamelled glass
dish. (Sotheby's Bel-
gravia) $190 £100

Mid 16th century
Facon de Venise
enamelled tazza,
6in. high.(Christie's)
$7,220 £3,800

Unusual sweetmeat
dish, with cup shaped
bowl, 3¾in. high, circa
1720. (Sotheby's)
$505 £250

Galle glass dish carved
as a shell, 1890's, 34cm.
long. (Sotheby's Belgravia)
$588 £300

Balustroid sweet-
meat glass, 3¾in.
high. (Christie's)
$104 £55

Antique silveria dish
by Royal Brierley
Crystal, 1901.
(Christie's)
$770 £388

Opaque twist small
sweetmeat glass,
3½in. high.
(Christie's)
$104 £55

Mid 16th century Vene-
tian gilt and enamelled
dish, 5¾in. diameter.
(Sotheby's)
$2,328 £1,200

One of a rare pair of
18th century enamelled
opaque white tureens,
4½in. high. (Sotheby's)
$620 £320

Cut glass sweetmeat
glass with double
ogee bowl, 6in. high.
(Christie's) $85 £45

Webb cameo shallow
circular dish, 8½in.
diameter.
(Christie's)
$1,330 £700

Silesian stemmed
small tazza, 3½in.
high. (Christie's)
$76 £40

Unusual 18th century
set of five graduated
tazzas. (Sotheby's)
$814 £420

Fine Anglo-Venetian
sweetmeat dish, circa
1700, 3¼in. high.
(Sotheby's)
$282 £140

Early 18th century miniature European enamelled flask, 3in. high. (Sotheby's) $627 £320

Cut glass flask, possibly Waterford, circa 1800, 19cm. long. (Sotheby's Ireland) $69 £35

One of a pair of enamelled moon flasks, circa 1870, 21cm. high. (Sotheby's Belgravia) $313 £160

Early 18th century bottle shaped flask of dark blue, 7½in. high, Netherlandish. (Christie's) $1,102 £580

Central European enamelled flask, circa 1750, 21.5cm. high. (Sotheby's)$424 £210

Early flattened oviform flask, circa 1690, 5½in. high. (Christie's) $456 £240

Central European milchglas flask, circa 1750, 5in. high. (Sotheby's) $388 £200

Central European enamelled flask, 18cm. high, circa 1750.(Sotheby's) $1,050 £520

Central European enamelled flask, circa 1750, 5in. high. (Sotheby's)$407 £210

One of a set of four
engraved goblets, circa
1870, 18.5cm. high.
(Sotheby's Belgravia)
$257 £130

Portrait overlay goblet
with round funnel
bowl, circa 1850,
14.5cm. high.
(Sotheby's Belgravia)
$294 £150

One of a set of four
finely engraved goblets,
circa 1870, 16.4cm.
high. (Sotheby's Bel-
gravia) $415 £210

Bohemian pink stained
goblet and cover, circa
1850, 31cm. high.
(Sotheby's Belgravia)
$352 £180

Rare Bohemian engraved
goblet, circa 1810, 11cm.
high. (Sotheby's Belgravia)
$415 £210

Tall engraved goblet,
47.5cm. high, circa
1880, with funnel
bowl.(Sotheby's
Belgravia)$254 £130

Amber flashed goblet,
circa 1850, 14.5cm.
high. (Sotheby's Bel-
gravia) $168 £85

Rare engraved Presen-
tation goblet, 1824,
24.5cm. high.
(Sotheby's Belgravia)
$1,485 £750

Good ruby stained gob-
let and cover, circa
1850, 32cm. high.
(Sotheby's Belgravia)
$316 £160

Rare electioneering
goblet, 6¾in., circa
1760. (Sotheby's)
$659 £340

Giant engraved goblet,
circa 1800, 11½in. high.
(Sotheby's)$465 £240

Fine baluster goblet,
circa 1700, 8½in.
high. (Sotheby's)
$1,373 £680

Dutch engraved and
cut goblet, 9¼in. high.
(Christie's)$2,090 £1,100

One of a pair of red glass
Bohemian goblets and
covers, circa 1814, 16½in.
high. (King & Chasemore)
$108 £56

Baluster goblet with
slender bell bowl,
7¾in. high.(Christie's)
$684 £360

Engraved composite stem-
med goblet of Jacobite
significance, 7½in. high.
(Christie's) $665 £350

Presentation goblet by Gia-
como Verzelini, 1584, 6¼in.
high. (Christie's)
$148,500 £75,000

Saxon gilt goblet and
cover, circa 1740, 12in.
high, engraved with a
hunting scene.(Sothe-
by's) $1,319 £680

German goblet by Hermann Benkert, circa 1680, 20.5cm. high. (Christie's) $23,760 £12,000

Rare two-handled coin goblet, circa 1710, 6in. high. (Sotheby's) $767 £380

Large engraved goblet, 9½in. high, circa 1700, with replaced foot. (Sotheby's) $484 £240

Bohemian engraved goblet and cover, circa 1700, 13½in. high. (Christie's) $570 £300

Fine Royal Potsdam portrait goblet and cover, circa 1710, 13¼in. high. (Sotheby's) $5,820 £3,000

Bohemian engraved goblet with funnel bowl, circa 1720, 9½in. high. (Christie's) $247 £130

Engraved Potsdam/Zechlin goblet, 6¾in. high, circa 1735. (Sotheby's) $4,656 £2,400

Early 17th century Facon de Venise glass goblet, 6¾in. high. (Phillips) $3,582 £1,800

Late 16th century Facon de Venise goblet, 10¼in. high, possibly Venetian. (Christie's) $6,080 £3,200

461

Glass lemonade jug with electroplated mounts, 1880's, 22.25cm. high. (Sotheby's Belgravia) $257 £130

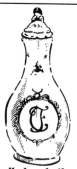

Enamelled and gilt milch-glas jug and cover, 25.5cm. high, circa 1770. (Sotheby's) $415 £210

William IV frosted glass ewer with silver gilt mounts by Paul Storr, London, 1836, 8¾in. high. (Sotheby's) $6,400 £3,200

Unusual glass jug of urn shape, circa 1820, 29cm. high.(Sotheby's Ireland) $588 £300

Mid 16th century Venetian gilt and enamelled jug, 8¾in. high. (Sotheby's) $1,590 £820

Late 16th century Venetian amethyst baluster ewer, 9½in. high. (Christie's) $3,800 £2,000

Victorian cut glass ewer. (British Antique Exporters) $24 £12

18th century Venetian cruet jug, 4¾in. high. (Sotheby's)$176 £90

Victorian claret jug with tall panel cut neck, 34.5 cm. high. (May, Whetter & Grose) $68 £34

Decanter and six
glasses in stand,
circa 1840. (Alfie's
Antique Market)
$222 £110

Good Moser glass set, circa
1900, in clear glass.
(Sotheby's Belgravia)
$980 £500

Glass decanter and six
glasses with silver
mounts and silver over-
lay, circa 1920.(Alfie's
Antique Market)
$168 £85

Victorian cut glass claret
jug and goblets. (Smith-
Woolley & Perry)
$126 £65

Etched liqueur service
in glass, 1930's.
(Sotheby's Belgravia)
$380 £200

19th century Bohemian
gilt drinking set, jug
33.5cm. high.(Sotheby's
Belgravia) $313 £160

Modernist glass liqueur
set with tray, 1930's.
(Sotheby's Belgravia)
$237 £120

Rare silver gilt and
red lacquer water set,
jug 28cm. high.
(Christie's)
$8,415 £4,166

Unusual liqueur set of
oak, glass and silver,
57oz., London, 1881-2.
(Woolley & Wallis)
$3,492 £1,800

MISCELLANEOUS GLASS

Early 19th century Swiss gold and enamel zarf, 2¼in. high. (Bonham's) $505 £250

Electroplated mounted frosted and cut glass whisky barrel and tot, 1863. (Sotheby's Belgravia) $368 £190

One of a pair of gilt green glass lustres, circa 1850, 31cm. high. (Sotheby's Belgravia) $411 £210

Lalique glass hand mirror, 1920's, 29.75 cm. high. (Sotheby's Belgravia) $1,176 £600

Lalique glass bracket shelf, 1930's, 26.25cm. wide. (Sotheby's Belgravia) $2,376 £1,200

Rare 18th century Venetian figurine, 6in. high, in opaque white glass.(Sotheby's) $1,047 £540

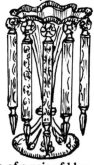

One of a pair of blue overlay lustre vases, circa 1850, 10½in. high. (Gray's Antique Mews) $575 £285

Bohemian rose water sprinkler, circa 1850, 30.5cm. high. (Sotheby's Belgravia) $792 £400

20th century Lalique glass figure of a kneeling woman, 21cm. high. (Sotheby's Belgravia) $1,782 £900

Dated St. Louis pen-holder, 1973, 13.6cm. high, set on a paper-weight base. (Sotheby's Belgravia) $222 £110

Pair of Walter pate-de-verre bookends, 1920's, 17cm. high. (Sotheby's Belgravia) $2,940 £1,500

One of a pair of large covered urns, circa 1850, 46cm. high. (Sotheby's Belgravia) $509 £260

Large late 19th century enamelled humpen and cover, dated 1899, 49cm. high. (Sotheby's Belgravia) $316 £160

Late Victorian stained glass panel, one of a pair, 56in. high. (Gray's Antique Mews) $1,151 £570

Lalique glass figure of a cockerel, 1930's, 19.5cm. high. (Sotheby's Belgravia) $2,376 £1,200

Late 19th century glass biscuit barrel with plated mounts. (British Antique Exporters) $20 £10

Lalique glass car mascot, 1920's, 14cm. wide. (Sotheby's Belgravia) $1,980 £1,000

18th century German stangenglas, 8in. high. (Phillips) $209 £110

465

Walter pate-de-verre figure of a pike, 1920's, 53.25cm. long. (Sotheby's Belgravia) $1,330 £700

Mid 19th century overlay lustre, one of a pair, 29.8cm. high.(Sotheby's Belgravia)$411 £210

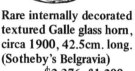

Rare internally decorated textured Galle glass horn, circa 1900, 42.5cm. long. (Sotheby's Belgravia) $2,376 £1,200

Gilt and enamelled German armorial Standenglas, circa 1598, 15½in. high. (Sotheby's) $43,670 £22,000

Fine bronze mounted pate-de-verre plaque of Isadora Duncan, 17½in. high. (Christie's N. York) $8,250 £4,435

German puzzle glass, 11in. high. (Sotheby's) $1,881 £950

A triptych stained glass thistle window by Tiffany, circa 1904, 36in. wide. (Christie's N. York) $2,020 £1,000

Lalique frosted glass mascot, circa 1920, 17.5cm. high. (Sotheby's Belgravia) $990 £500

A triptych stained glass landscape window, circa 1905. (Christie's N. York) $3,030 £1,500

St. Louis dated dahlia
weight, 1970, with
certificate and box.
(Sotheby's Belgravia)
$138 £70

One of a set of twelve 20th
century Baccarat sulphide
zodiac weights, 7cm. wide.
(Sotheby's Belgravia)
$396 £200

Unusual Lalique glass
paperweight, 1920's,
12cm. wide.
(Sotheby's Belgravia)
$237 £120

Baccarat double clem-
atis and garland weight,
7.5cm. diameter.
(Sotheby's)
$808 £400

Rare St. Louis marbrie
salamander weight,
8.5cm. high, damaged.
(Sotheby's)$222 £110

Baccarat anemone
weight, 7.1cm. diam.,
with star cut base.
(Sotheby's)
$505 £250

St. Louis dated car-
pet ground weight,
1972.(Sotheby's
Belgravia)
$151 £75

St. Louis double clem-
atis weight, 7.5cm.
diam. (Sotheby's)
$929 £460

St. Louis amber flash
posy weight, 6.6cm.
diam. (Sotheby's)
$363 £180

SCENT BOTTLES

Guerlain 'Mitsouko' glass bottle and stopper. (Sotheby's Belgravia) $40 £20

Moulded glass perfume bottle and stopper of triangular form, 1920's. (Sotheby's Belgravia) $161 £85

Blue glass scent bottle, late 19th century, with gilt metal mounts, 3½in. high. (Gray's Antique Mews)$96 £48

Moulded glass perfume bottle and stopper, 1920's, 13cm. high. (Sotheby's Belgravia) $53 £28

Decorated clear glass perfume bottle and stopper, 13.75cm. high. (Sotheby's Belgravia) $152 £80

French or Italian double scent bottle, circa 1770, 4¾in. long. (Sotheby's) $1,319 £680

Rare sulphide scent bottle of flattened circular form, 7cm. diam. (Sotheby's) $303 £150

Moulded glass perfume bottle and stopper, 12cm. high, 1920's. (Sotheby's Belgravia) $190 £100

Art Nouveau silver and blue enamel perfume bottle, 2¼in. wide. (Gray's Antique Mews) $59 £30

Webb double overlay globular scent bottle and silver screw cover, 4in. high. (Christie's) $361 £190

Black glass perfume bottle with atomiser, 9.8cm. high. (Sotheby's Belgravia) $57 £30

George III silver cut glass scent bottle, 2¼in. high. (Bonham's) $848 £420

One of two glass perfume bottles, 1920's. (Sotheby's Belgravia) $71 £35

Modernist glass bottle and stopper, circa 1930, 26cm. high. (Sotheby's Belgravia) $247 £130

Delvaux enamelled scent bottle and stopper, 1920's, 11.25cm. high. (Sotheby's Belgravia) $123 £65

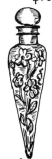

Cameo glass scent bottle with silver stopper, 1885, 13cm. high. (Sotheby's Belgravia) $333 £170

Decorated glass atomiser, 10.5cm. high, circa 1920. (Sotheby's Belgravia) $190 £100

Overlay ruby glass scent bottle and stopper, circa 1850, 27.5cm. high. (Sotheby's Belgravia) $274 £140

TANKARDS

Central European enamelled tankard, circa 1750, 5¾in. high. (Sotheby's)
$372 £190

Unusual hunting overlay tankard, circa 1850, 16.5cm. high.(Sotheby's Belgravia) $792 £400

Enamelled milchglas tankard, Bohemian, circa 1770, 12cm. high. (Sotheby's)
$514 £260

Central European enamelled tankard and cover, circa 1750, 24cm. high. (Sotheby's)
$1,089 £550

Ruby glass tankard with silver hinged cover, 8in. high. (McCartney, Morris & Barker)
$747 £370

Fine Central European enamelled milchglas tankard, circa 1750, 6½in. high.(Sotheby's)
$407 £210

TAZZAS

Good Irish canoe fruit bowl, 14in. wide, circa 1810. (Sotheby's)$509 £260

17th century Venetian tazza, 8in. diameter. (Sotheby's)$705 £360

Late 16th century Facon-de-Venise enamelled glass tazza, 5.9in. high. (Christie's)
$7,524 £3,800

Unusual enamelled flask in turquoise glass, circa 1875, 13.8cm. high. (Sotheby's Belgravia) $435 £220

One of an unusual pair of glass vases, circa 1880, 24.5cm. high. (Sotheby's Belgravia) $990 £500

Good Lobmeyr 'Islamic' enamelled vase, 13.6cm. high, 1870's. (Sotheby's Belgravia) $455 £230

Victorian opaque glass epergne. (British Antique Exporters) $150 £75

Green tinted vase with gilt metal mounts, 17th century, 6½in. high. (Sotheby's) $1,215 £620

One of a pair of portrait overlay green glass vases, circa 1850, 33.8 cm. high. (Sotheby's Belgravia)$435 £220

One of a pair of Venetian 'bleu de roi' glass vases, early 20th century. (Sotheby's Belgravia) $396 £200

One of a pair of ruby overlay vases, circa 1850, 25.2cm. high. (Sotheby's Belgravia) $376 £190

One of a pair of mid 19th century enamelled vases, 37.8cm. high. (Sotheby's Belgravia) $376 £190

Late 19th century Webb cameo glass vase, 9.5cm. high. (Sotheby's Belgravia) $1,019 £520

Square section blue floral cameo glass vase by Galle, 7½in. high. (Gray's Mews) $1,383 £685

Rare cameo vase with white relief on a green ground, 16cm. high. (King & Chasemore) $525 £260

One of a pair of ruby glass portrait overlay vases, circa 1850, 29.9 cm. high. (Sotheby's Belgravia) $297 £150

Champleve enamel vase, circa 1870's, 13¾in. high. (Sotheby's Belgravia) $285 £150

One of a pair of Bohemian gilt and enamelled overlay vases, 17¼in. high. (Messenger, May & Baverstock) $808 £400

German blue overlay vase by F. Zach, circa 1857, 22cm. high. (Sotheby's Belgravia) $627 £320

One of a pair of gilt and enamelled overlay vases and covers, circa 1850, 38.8cm. (Sotheby's Belgravia) $744 £380

One of a pair of pink ground enamelled opaline vases, circa 1850, 36cm. high.(Sotheby's Belgravia) $294 £150

Late 19th century cameo glass vase, 23cm. high. (Sotheby's Belgravia) $1.764 £900

Red overlay glass vase of 18th century origin. (Phillips) $808 £400

Cameo glass vase by Thomas Webb & Sons, 10.8cm. high. (King & Chasemore)$747 £370

One of a pair of blue overlay glass vases, circa 1850, 38.5cm. high. (Sotheby's Belgravia) $237 £120

Webb three colour cameo glass vase. (Sotheby's N. York) $10,605 £5,250

One of a pair of Bohemian overlay trumpet shaped vases. (Humbert, King & Chasemore) $396 £200

Tall French enamelled vase, circa 1900, 48cm. high. (Sotheby's Belgravia) $274 £140

Signed Daum Nancy vase in orange, cream and green, 6½in. high. (Alfie's Antique Market) $198 £100

Facon de Venise 'verre a serpents' of 17th century Netherlandish origin. (Sotheby's) $3,636 £1,800

Galle cameo glass vase, circa 1904, signed.(Gray's Antique Market) $1,138 £575

Stevens & Williams cameo oviform vase, 7½in. high.(Christie's) $532 £280

18th century royal blue bottle vase, 9in. high. (Christie's) $450 £231

Le verre Francais-Charder cameo glass vase, 1920's, 35cm. high. (Sotheby's Belgravia) $418 £220

Legras etched and internally decorated glass vase, 1920's, 31.5cm. high. (Sotheby's Belgravia) $114 £60

Legras etched and internally decorated glass vase, 39cm. high, 1920's. (Sotheby's Belgravia) $142 £75

Late 19th century cameo glass vase, 22.5cm. high. (Sotheby's Belgravia) $455 £230

18th century blue glazed baluster vase, 21½in. high. (Christie's) $2,000 £1,030

Finely engraved Webb's glass vase, 12in. high. (Phillips) $199 £105

18th century pale
blue ground bottle
vase, 8¾in. high.
(Christie's)
$500 £257

Small 18th century Sang-
de-Boeuf bottle, 4¾in.
high.(Christie's)
$350 £180

18th century powder
blue vase, 9½in. high.
(Christie's)
$500 £257

Degue overlaid and
etched glass vase,
1920's, 40.5cm. high.
(Sotheby's)
$532 £280

Le verre Francais cameo
glass vase, 1920's, 47.5cm.
high.(Sotheby's Belgravia)
$380 £200

Late 16th century
Venetian mould-
blown oviform vase,
9in. high. (Christie's)
$3,800 £2,000

One of a pair of flower
encrusted bottle vases.
(Christie's S. Kensing-
ton) $910 £460

One of a pair of English
white overlay glass vases,
circa 1870, 12½in. high.
(King & Chasemore)
$806 £420

One of a pair of mid 19th
century enamelled 'moon-
stone' vases, 29.5cm. high.
(Sotheby's Belgravia)
$356 £180

Scottish Jacobite opaque twist firing glass, 3½in. high. (Christie's)$475 £250

Masonic firing glass of drawn trumpet shape, 3¾in. high. (Christie's)$114 £60

18th century Newcastle wine glass. (Graves, Son & Pilcher) $4,850 £2,500

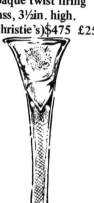

Jacobite wine glass with air twist stem, circa 1750, 5¾in. high.(Sotheby's) $523 £270

Double-flint wine glass, 7in. high, circa 1700.(Sotheby's) $659 £340

Tartan twist wine glass, circa 1760, 6½in. high. (Sotheby's) $1,202 £620

Rare deceptive baluster glass, circa 1700, 5in. high.(Sotheby's) $582 £300

Battle of the Boyne commemorative rummer, 1690, 6in. high.(Christie's) $266 £140

Composite stemmed wine glass in four parts, circa 1750, 6½in. high.(Sotheby's) $310 £160

German Royal com-
memorative glass,
engraved with a horse-
man. (Phillips)$41 £20

Rare mead glass,
4¾in. high, circa
1700.(Sotheby's)
$1,513 £780

Wine glass with round
funnel bowl, circa
1740, 6in. high.
(Sotheby's) $176 £90

Kit-Kat wine glass,
circa 1720, 6in.
high. (Sotheby's)
$329 £170

George III commem-
orative rummer, 1809,
8in. high. (Christie's)
$494 £260

Unusual wine glass,
6in. high, circa
1720.(Sotheby's)
$184 £95

Fine, large gilt wine
glass, circa 1760,
7½in. high.(Sotheby's)
$291 £150

Baluster champagne glass,
circa 1720, 5½in. high.
(Sotheby's) $310 £160

Sunderland engraved
rummer with bucket
bowl, 8¾in. high.
(Christie's)$570 £300

18th century wine
glass with trumpet
stem, 6½in. high.
(Geering & Colyer)
$126 £65

Large engraved rummer,
circa 1800, 7in. high.
(Sotheby's) $121 £60

Baluster wine glass,
circa 1700, 7¼in.
high, with bell bowl.
(Sotheby's)
$868 £430

Cut and engraved
wine glass, circa
1780, 6in. high.
(Sotheby's)$808 £400

17th/18th century
Rhenish green tin-
ted roemer, 15.5cm.
high.(Sotheby's)
$565 £280

Knopped wine glass,
circa 1700, 5½in.
high. (Sotheby's)
$666 £340

Gilt wine glass, circa
1770, 5¾in. high.
(Sotheby's)
$323 £160

Multi-knopped air twist
wine glass, circa 1750,
6¼in. high. (Sotheby's)
$795 £410

One of a set of six
George III cordial
glasses.(Woolley &
Wallis) $514 £260

Beilby enamelled glass, circa 1770, 6in. high, with ogee bowl. (Sotheby's)$1,070 £530

Wine glass, circa 1725, with four sided shouldered tapering stem. (Sotheby's) $383 £190

Composite stemmed wine glass, circa 1750, 6½in. high.(Sotheby's) $329 £170

Rare Jacobite colour twist wine glass, 7in. high, circa 1760. (Sotheby's)$853 £440

Very rare wine glass, circa 1740, 7½in. high. (Sotheby's) $776 £400

Engraved light baluster wine glass, 6½in. high. (Christie's)$209 £110

Rare pink twist cordial glass, circa 1760, 5½in. high.(Sotheby's) $698 £360

Engraved light baluster wine glass with funnel bowl, 6½in. high. (Christie's)$304 £160

Balustroid coin goblet with bell bowl, 7in. high.(Christie's) $722 £380

Colour twist wine glass, circa 1760, 6in. high.(Sotheby's) $744 £380

Anglo-Venetian wine glass, circa 1700, 5½in. high, with conical bowl. (Sotheby's) $509 £260

Cordial glass with cylindrical bowl, circa 1730, 6½in. high. (Sotheby's) $274 £140

Wine glass with conical bowl, circa 1740, 6in. high. (Sotheby's)$78 £40

Engraved colour twist wine glass, 7in. high, circa 1760.(Sotheby's) $1,513 £780

Baluster wine goblet with round funnel bowl, circa 1710, 6½in. high. (Sotheby's) $352 £180

Jacobite wine glass, 6in. high, with drawn trumpet bowl. (Sotheby's) $509 £260

Finely engraved armorial rummer, circa 1798, 6¾in. high. (Sotheby's) $1,411 £720

Rare gilt and enamelled armorial wine glass, circa 1730, 6in. high. (Sotheby's) $1,666 £850

Air twist wine glass, circa 1740, 6in. high, with ogee bowl. (Sotheby's) $176 £90

Wine glass with bell bowl set on a bladed knop, circa 1720, 6in. high. (Sotheby's) $215 £110

Wine glass with conical bowl, circa 1700, 5in. high. (Sotheby's) $627 £320

Dutch stipple engraved Newcastle wine glass. (Graves, Son & Pilcher) $2,716 £1,400

Wine glass with bucket bowl, circa 1750, 6in. high. (Sotheby's) $215 £110

Engraved wine glass, circa 1740, 6in. high. (Sotheby's) $107 £55

Bohemian enamelled wine glass, circa 1745, 6½in. high.(Sotheby's) $431 £220

Pink twist wine glass, circa 1760, 6½in. high. (Sotheby's) $137 £70

Newcastle wine glass, circa 1750, 8½in. high, with bell bowl. (Sotheby's)$411 £210

GOLD

George II gold five guineas young head, 1729, uncirculated. (Phillips) $6,666 £3,300

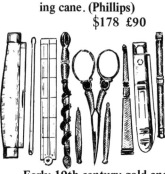

Mid 18th century gentleman's gold topped walking cane. (Phillips) $178 £90

Mid 18th century gold box by Francois Marteau, France.(Sotheby's Zurich)$60,709 £30,970

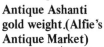

Antique Ashanti gold weight.(Alfie's Antique Market) $50 £25

Early 19th century gold and mother-of-pearl necessaire, probably French, 15.5cm. wide. (Sotheby's)$582 £300

Antique gold oval seal, circa 1800, spirally fluted. (Neales)$242 £120

George III Scottish gold oval medallion, 2in. long, Edinburgh, 1817. (Sotheby's) $548 £280

Circular gold mounted Vernis Martin box, 7.6cm. wide, 1768-75. (Sotheby's) $272 £140

Late 17th century German gold and enamel scent flask, 5.5cm. high. (Sotheby's) $330 £170

Early 19th century gold and lapis lazuli vinaigrette, 3.7cm. long. (Sotheby's) $272 £140

Gold mounted oval shell cameo brooch, 2½in. high. (Burrows & Day) $142 £72

Yellow gold carte de bal set with blue enamel and rose cut diamond monogram. (King & Chasemore) $3,553 £1,700

Gold and enamel snuff box, circa 1781-89, French. (Christie's Geneva) $33,271 £16,975

Irish bronze age gold pennanular dress fastener, circa 180BC. (Sotheby's) $8,232 £4,200

Gold snuff box inset with a miniature of Queen Maria Christina of Spain.(Christie's) $40,400 £20,000

Mixtec gold lip-plug, circa 1200-1521. (Sotheby's N. York) $101,518 £51,795

Gold mounted shell cameo hair ornament, circa 1810, 10cm. wide. (Sotheby's) $427 £220

Heavy gold oblong seal, carved with flowers and shells, circa 1830.(Neales) $145 £72

Two gold seals on split ring, circa 1840. (Neales) $444 £220

Gold and tortoiseshell snuff box, Paris, 1740. (Bonham's) $2,940 £1,500

Mid 18th century Swedish gold and mother-of-pearl snuff box, 8.2cm. wide. (Sotheby's)$1,125 £580

18ct. gold cup and cover in 18th century style, Birmingham, 1923, 61oz. (Sotheby's Belgravia) $8,740 £4,600

Gold and enamel pair-cased watch and matching chatelaine, watch 51mm. diam. (Sotheby's) $4,950 £2,500

George III 18ct. gold Freedom box, by Edward Murray, Dublin, 1817, 3in. diam. (Sotheby's Ireland) $5,454 £2,700

Early 18th century rhinoceros horn libation cup, 3½in. high. (Christie's) $500 £257

K'ang Hsi rhinoceros libation cup, 4¼in. high. (Christie's) $1,200 £618

One of a rare pair of hornbill skulls, 7½in. long. (Christie's) $1,200 £618

Bohemian carved staghorn powder flask. (Wallis & Wallis) $1,252 £620

Victorian brass and horn gong complete with hammer. (British Antique Exporters) $40 £20

Good brass mounted cowhorn powder flask, 10¼in. long. (Wallis & Wallis) $317 £160

Tiny Ozaki Kokusai study of an owl in staghorn.(Sotheby's) $21,210 £10,500

One of a fine pair of buffalo horn armchairs. (Christie's) $3,900 £1,900

Early 19th century horn snuff mull, 5in. long. (Sotheby's) $333 £170

18th century gold lacquer four case inro, signed Toyo. (Christie's) $495 £255

19th century three case red lacquer inro. (Christie's)$528 £272

19th century four case lacquer inro.(Christie's) $1,012 £521

19th century three case red lacquer inro, inlaid with pewter. (Christie's) $550 £283

19th century four case inro, inlaid with pewter and aogai.(Christie's) $605 £311

Two case wood inro. (Phillips)$712 £360

19th century four case lacquer inro, 7cm. high.(King & Chasemore) $787 £410

19th century four case lacquer and ivory inro by Shomosai, 8.25cm. high.(King & Chasemore)$653 £340

19th century lacquered ivory inro, 9cm. high. (King & Chasemore) $653 £340

485

INSTRUMENTS

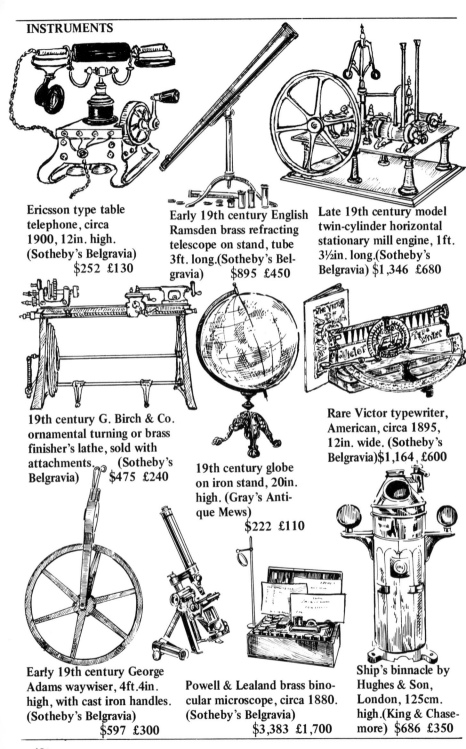

Ericsson type table telephone, circa 1900, 12in. high. (Sotheby's Belgravia) $252 £130

Early 19th century English Ramsden brass refracting telescope on stand, tube 3ft. long.(Sotheby's Belgravia) $895 £450

Late 19th century model twin-cylinder horizontal stationary mill engine, 1ft. 3½in. long.(Sotheby's Belgravia) $1,346 £680

19th century G. Birch & Co. ornamental turning or brass finisher's lathe, sold with attachments. (Sotheby's Belgravia) $475 £240

19th century globe on iron stand, 20in. high. (Gray's Antique Mews) $222 £110

Rare Victor typewriter, American, circa 1895, 12in. wide. (Sotheby's Belgravia)$1,164 £600

Early 19th century George Adams waywiser, 4ft.4in. high, with cast iron handles. (Sotheby's Belgravia) $597 £300

Powell & Lealand brass binocular microscope, circa 1880. (Sotheby's Belgravia) $3,383 £1,700

Ship's binnacle by Hughes & Son, London, 125cm. high.(King & Chasemore) $686 £350

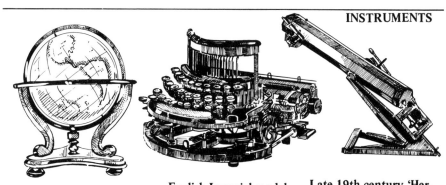

Manning & Wells terrestrial globe, 20in. diam., circa 1854.(Sotheby's Belgravia)$349 £180

English Imperial model 'B' typewriter, circa 1915, 1ft. wide. (Sotheby's Belgravia) $139 £70

Late 19th century 'Herschel type' Newtonian refracting telescope, tube 4ft.4in. long. (Sotheby's Belgravia) $995 £500

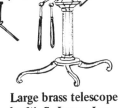

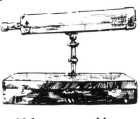

Mid 19th century Edwin Ponting multiple writing machine, 17in. wide. (Sotheby's Belgravia) $136 £65

Large brass telescope by W. S. Jones, London, circa 1800. (Sotheby's) $1,818 £900

Mahogany cased brass reflecting telescope, circa 1760, 19½in. long. (Christopher Sykes) $1,313 £650

Mid 19th century Culpeper type monocular microscope, 11in. high. (Sotheby's Belgravia) $696 £350

Late 19th century English brass sextant, 7½in. radius. (Sotheby's Belgravia) $415 £210

George III Cary's celestial globe, 1799, 2ft. 4in. diam.(Sotheby's) $3,168 £1,600

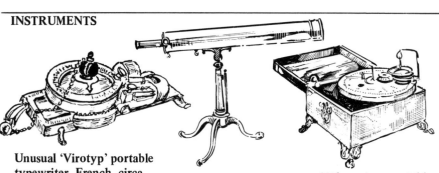

Unusual 'Virotyp' portable typewriter, French, circa 1914, 6¼in. long. (Sotheby's Belgravia) $523 £270

Brass astronomical telescope by Harris. (Stride's)$673 £340

19th century portable orrery by W. Jones, 195mm. diameter. (Sotheby's) $2,871 £1,450

Mid 19th century Johnston 30in. terrestrial globe, 47 x 40in. (Sotheby's Belgravia) $2,673 £1,350

Two day marine chronometer by Breguet & Cie, dial 8cm. diam. (Christie's)$6,208 £3,200

Mid 19th century English zeotype, 14in. high.(Sotheby's Belgravia)$659 £340

Late 19th century Troughton & Simms brass transit theodolite, 1ft.2in. high. (Sotheby's Belgravia) $835 £420

Late 19th century English brass refracting telescope on stand, tube 2ft.9in. long.(Sotheby's Belgravia) $378 £190

Vernier sextant by Cary, London, in fitted case.(Phillips) $349 £180

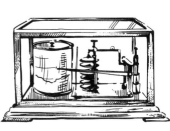

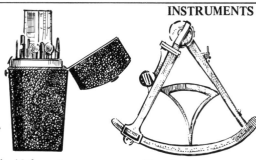

Barograph by Short
and Mason. (May,
Whetter & Grose)
$232 £115

Early 19th century
set of drawing instru-
ments, 5in. long.
(Sotheby's Belgravia)
$199 £100

Rare brass sextant
by George Adams,
circa 1760, 152mm.
radius.(Sotheby's)
$2,574 £1,300

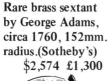

Late 19th century Swift
& Sons brass binocular
microscope, 1ft.5in.
high. (Sotheby's Bel-
gravia) $477 £240

Clocking-in machine
by Time Records
(Leeds) Ltd., circa
1930, 35½in. high.
(Sotheby's Belgravia)
$213 £110

Newton, Son & Berry
celestial globe, circa
1840, 10in. diam.
(Sotheby's Belgravia)
$238 £120

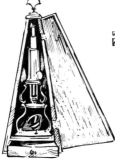

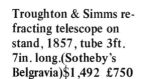

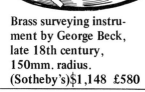

Early 19th century
brass Culpeper type
microscope, box
441mm. high.
(Sotheby's)$871 £440

Troughton & Simms re-
fracting telescope on
stand, 1857, tube 3ft.
7in. long.(Sotheby's
Belgravia)$1,492 £750

Brass surveying instru-
ment by George Beck,
late 18th century,
150mm. radius.
(Sotheby's)$1,148 £580

Small French sewing machine, 8in. high. (Gray's Antique Market) $95 £48

English lacquered brass circular slide rule, 4in. diam., by Parsons, London. (Christie's) $164 £85

Early 20th century Heath & Co. brass sextant, 7in. radius. (Sotheby's Belgravia) $378 £190

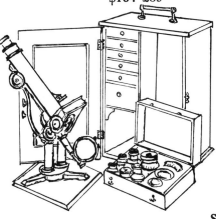

Late 19th century Elliott brass level, 1ft.6in. long, on wooden tripod. (Sotheby's Belgravia) $258 £130

Mid 19th century English Smith & Beck brass monocular microscope, 18in. high. (Sotheby's Belgravia) $737 £380

Ship's Bridge Telegraph in brass, signed 'Bloctube Controls', 105cm. high. (King & Chasemore) $509 £260

Early 19th century Cary pocket microscope, 6½in. wide.(Sotheby's Belgravia) $457 £230

Danish magneto desk telephone, circa 1920, 1ft.1in. high.(Sotheby's Belgravia) $218 £110

Rare early 19th century Edward Massey brass ship's log and spinner. (Sotheby's Belgravia) $237 £120

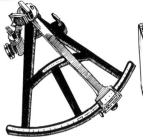

Early 19th century Cary octant with ebony frame, 11½in. radius. (Sotheby's Belgravia) $835 £420

Unusual Odell typewriter No. 4, circa 1890, 10in. square. (Sotheby's Belgravia) $437 £220

Rare mahogany cased brass gravity sextant, circa 1865.(Christopher Sykes)$959 £475

Early mariner's instrument made in boxwood. (Christie's S. Kensington)
$3,838 £1,900

Late 19th century English double projection lantern, 26in. high. (Sotheby's Belgravia)$349 £180

Ship's Bridge Telegraph in brass, 105cm. high, signed 'Bloctube Controls'. (King & Chasemore)
$490 £250

Regency mahogany terrestrial globe, 2ft.2in. diam., by Cary's, London, 1815.(Sotheby's)
$3,038 £1,550

Mid 19th century Negretti and Zambra brass binocular microscope, 1ft.2in. high. (Sotheby's Belgravia)
$537 £270

Brass pantograph by 'Silberrad, London', circa 1810.(Christopher Sykes)$505 £250

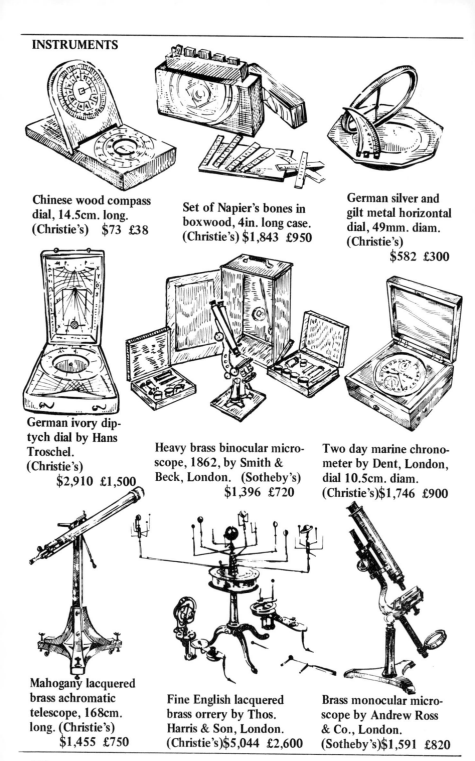

Chinese wood compass dial, 14.5cm. long. (Christie's) $73 £38

Set of Napier's bones in boxwood, 4in. long case. (Christie's) $1,843 £950

German silver and gilt metal horizontal dial, 49mm. diam. (Christie's)
$582 £300

German ivory diptych dial by Hans Troschel. (Christie's)
$2,910 £1,500

Heavy brass binocular microscope, 1862, by Smith & Beck, London. (Sotheby's)
$1,396 £720

Two day marine chronometer by Dent, London, dial 10.5cm. diam. (Christie's)$1,746 £900

Mahogany lacquered brass achromatic telescope, 168cm. long. (Christie's)
$1,455 £750

Fine English lacquered brass orrery by Thos. Harris & Son, London. (Christie's)$5,044 £2,600

Brass monocular microscope by Andrew Ross & Co., London. (Sotheby's)$1,591 £820

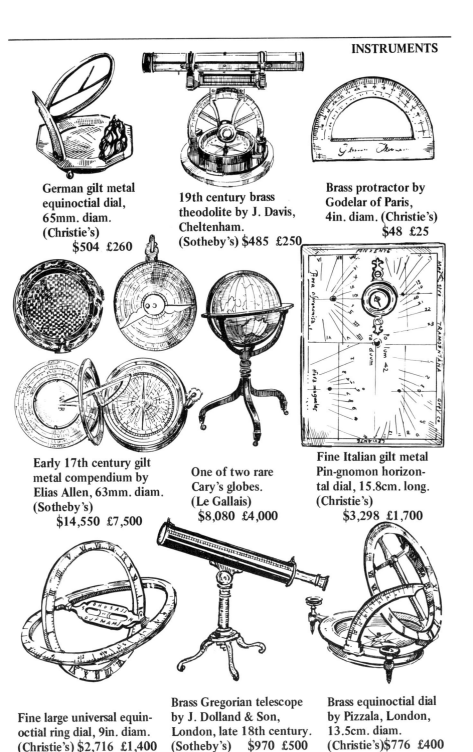

German gilt metal
equinoctial dial,
65mm. diam.
(Christie's)
$504 £260

19th century brass
theodolite by J. Davis,
Cheltenham.
(Sotheby's) $485 £250

Brass protractor by
Godelar of Paris,
4in. diam. (Christie's)
$48 £25

Early 17th century gilt
metal compendium by
Elias Allen, 63mm. diam.
(Sotheby's)
$14,550 £7,500

One of two rare
Cary's globes.
(Le Gallais)
$8,080 £4,000

Fine Italian gilt metal
Pin-gnomon horizon-
tal dial, 15.8cm. long.
(Christie's)
$3,298 £1,700

Fine large universal equinoctial ring dial, 9in. diam.
(Christie's) $2,716 £1,400

Brass Gregorian telescope
by J. Dolland & Son,
London, late 18th century.
(Sotheby's) $970 £500

Brass equinoctial dial
by Pizzala, London,
13.5cm. diam.
(Christie's)$776 £400

Brass universal equinoctial dial by Troughton & Simms, London, 13.5cm. diameter. (Christie's) $873 £450

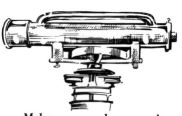

Mahogany cased surveyor's sighting level by Troughton & Simms, London, circa 1860, 14½in. long. (Christopher Sykes)
$575 £285

Model of a ship's binnacle, circa 1920. (Gray's Antique Market)
$346 £175

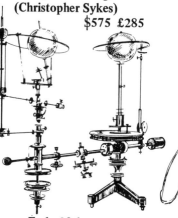

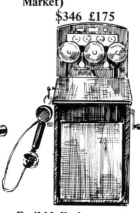

L.M. Ericsson magneto wall telephone, circa 1900, 2ft. 4in. high. (Sotheby's Belgravia) $437 £220

Early 20th century orrery, 3ft 5in. wide, with sectioned diagram. (Sotheby's Belgravia)
$1,194 £600

Emil Moller's magneto wall telephone, circa 1905, 2ft.3in. high. (Sotheby's Belgravia)
$218 £110

Early 20th century J. B. Winter brass transit theodolite, 1ft.1½in. high. (Sotheby's Belgravia) $597 £300

Brass watchmaker's topping tool, 12in. long.(Sotheby's Belgravia) $329 £170

Johnston terrestrial globe, 30in. diam. (Sotheby's Belgravia) $2,673 £1,350

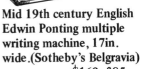

Pair of 19th century walnut nutcrackers. (McCartney, Morris & Barker) $285 £150

Early 19th century simple microscope with racked column, 4¼in. wide. (Sotheby's Belgravia) $169 £85

Mid 19th century English Edwin Ponting multiple writing machine, 17in. wide.(Sotheby's Belgravia) $169 £85

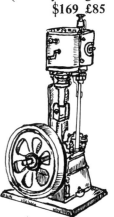

Rare mid 19th century transit telescope, 16in. high, by Troughton & Simms. (Wingett's) $1,539 £810

Large terrestrial globe by Smith of London, in a mahogany stand. (Boardman's) $3,636 £1,800

Small vertical single cylinder stationary steam engine, circa 1920, 9¼in. high. (Sotheby's Belgravia) $89 £45

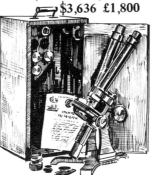

18th century oak coffee mill, 7¼in. high, with brass mounted grinder handle. (Sotheby's)$485 £250

A. Abrahams & Co. brass binocular microscope, 1ft. 6in. high, 1873.(Sotheby's Belgravia) $696 £350

Powell & Lealand brass binocular microscope, 1ft.5in. high.(Sotheby's Belgravia)$2,587 £1,300

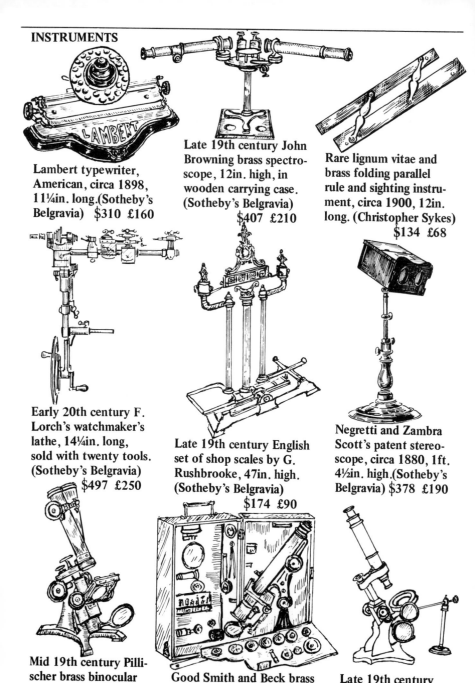

Lambert typewriter, American, circa 1898, 11¼in. long.(Sotheby's Belgravia) $310 £160

Late 19th century John Browning brass spectro-scope, 12in. high, in wooden carrying case. (Sotheby's Belgravia) $407 £210

Rare lignum vitae and brass folding parallel rule and sighting instru-ment, circa 1900, 12in. long. (Christopher Sykes) $134 £68

Early 20th century F. Lorch's watchmaker's lathe, 14¼in. long, sold with twenty tools. (Sotheby's Belgravia) $497 £250

Late 19th century English set of shop scales by G. Rushbrooke, 47in. high. (Sotheby's Belgravia) $174 £90

Negretti and Zambra Scott's patent stereo-scope, circa 1880, 1ft. 4½in. high.(Sotheby's Belgravia) $378 £190

Mid 19th century Pilli-scher brass binocular microscope, 13in. high, sold with accessories. (Sotheby's Belgravia) $349 £180

Good Smith and Beck brass monocular microscope, mid 19th century, 17in. high, with accessories.(Sotheby's Belgravia) $737 £380

Late 19th century Baker brass monocu-lar microscope, 15in. high.(Sotheby's Bel-gravia) $407 £210

Fuller's rule and calculator with a brass attachment. (Phillips) $108 £55

Fine pyramid walnut cased metronome, 9in. high.(Christopher Sykes) $95 £48

W. Watson & Sons stereoscopic 'detective' binocular camera, circa 1900, 8in. high.(Sotheby's Belgravia) $2,189 £1,100

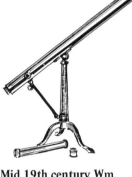

Mid 19th century Wm. Harris brass refracting telescope on stand, tube 2ft.6in. high.(Sotheby's Belgravia) $756 £380

Unusual London Stereoscopic Co. double stereoscopic viewer, circa 1880, 1ft.8in. high.(Sotheby's Belgravia) $318 £160

Candle lit cine projector complete with films.(Christopher Sykes) $93 £48

Good Baker brass binocular microscope, circa 1860, 19in. high. (Sotheby's Belgravia) $562 £290

Late 19th century Dolland brass refracting telescope on stand, tube 3ft.5in. long. (Sotheby's Belgravia) $696 £350

Rare James Smith brass monocular microscope, circa 1840, 17in. high, with accessories. (Sotheby's Belgravia) $1,125 £580

Eastman Studio scale by Kodak, New York, 9in. wide. (Alfie's Antique Market)
$80 £40

Early 19th century Wm. Struthers gregorian reflecting telescope on stand, tube 2ft.0½in. long.(Sotheby's Belgravia)
$1,094 £550

Single valve radio, circa 1925, with original valve and tuning coil. (Gray's Antique Market)
$133 £65

Brass celestial telescope on mahogany tripod stand, 45in. long. (Christopher Sykes)
$960 £485

19th century globe on metal and brass stand. (Gray's Antique Market)
$381 £185

19th century brass astronomical telescope on a steel stand by Jas. Parker & Son. (Phillips)
$1,292 £640

Silver letter balance, Birmingham, 1949, 3¼in. high. (Alfie's Antique Market)
$113 £55

Unusual sundial cannon. (Weller & Dufty)
$495 £250

Late 19th century galvanometer. (Gray's Antique Market)$141 £70

Late 17th century German door lock with brass finials. (Sotheby's) $342 £180

Early 17th century French steel key, 5½in. long. (Sotheby's) $1,140 £600

Late 17th century German door lock in iron, 13in. long, with original key. (Sotheby's) $950 £500

Oxidised metal coal container. (British Antique Exporters) $24 £12

Early 19th century oak and iron Suffolk cart jack, 36in. long.(Gray's Antique Mews) $140 £68

Victorian cast iron stove in working order. (Alfie's Antique Market) $98 £49

Flemish iron strong box, circa 1680, 2ft. 2in. wide. (Sotheby's) $1,782 £900

19th century pair of Persian gold damascened steel scissors, 10½in. long. (Sotheby's) $356 £180

German iron casket, circa 1600, 8½in. wide. (Sotheby's) $2,755 £1,450

Cast iron fronted painted wooden Mail Box, circa 1910, with brass lock, 29in. high.(Christopher Sykes)$584 £295

A pair of German iron candlesticks, circa 1910, 21cm. high. (Sotheby's Belgravia) $217 £110

19th century Iranian steel cat with silver and gold harness. (Sotheby's) $24,240 £12,000

Old Islamic bottle shaped vase in steel, 8¾in. high. (Parsons, Welch & Cowell) $55 £28

George III style cast iron fire grate and ash tray, 37in. wide.(Sotheby's Belgravia) $464 £230

Wrought iron gate, 1860's, 78 x 40in. (Sotheby's Belgravia) $823 £420

Iron and wood coffee grinder, circa 1870. (Alfie's Antique Market) $80 £40

Wrought iron fire basket. (Spear & Sons) $178 £90

Early 19th century painted metal Dutch oven, 27¼in. high. (Sotheby's Belgravia) $277 £140

Early 20th century inlaid Komei iron dish showing a warrior, 8¾in. diameter. (Sotheby's Belgravia) $442 £230

Mid 19th century cast iron jewellery casket, 18½in. wide.(Sotheby's Belgravia) $1,188 £600

Pair of Japanese damascened metal stirrups. (Buckell & Ballard) $1,683 £850

Mid 19th century cast iron firescreen, 47in. high. (Sotheby's Belgravia) $384 £200

Oak and wrought iron jardiniere, 37in. wide, circa 1870.(Sotheby's Belgravia) $361 £190

Unusual 18th or 19th century iron Buddhist travelling shrine. (Christie's)$858 £442

Early wrought iron rushlight holder in wood base, 8¾in. high.(Christopher Sykes) $112 £58

Wrought iron fire basket. (Spear & Sons) $376 £190

Late 19th century articulated iron crayfish, 9in. long. (Sotheby's Belgravia) $518 £270

IVORY

Late 19th century Okimono style figure of a hunter. (Christie's) $286 £147

One of two ivory bottles on wooden stands. (Christie's) $170 £87

17th century ivory Ming figure, 5in. high. (Christie's) $1,430 £752

19th century mid European ivory tankard with silver mounts, 12½in. high. (Gribble, Booth & Taylor) $4,920 £2,400

Indian painted ivory chess set, Madras, circa 1800. (Christie's) $3,080 £1,563

18th century Italian carved ivory jug, 48cm. high. (King & Chasemore)
$4,416 £2,300

Early 19th century bone watchstand, prisoner-of-war. (King & Chasemore)
$297 £150

Chinese Keiwo ivory box and cover carved with sparrows. (Sotheby's Belgravia)
$744 £380

Louis XVI ivory carnet de bal. (Bonham's)
$217 £110

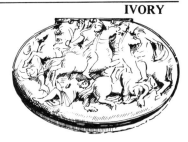

19th century Rajasthani in ivory, 3½in. high. (Gray's Antique Mews) $1,584 £800

One of a pair of Ch'ien Lung ivory lanterns and stands, 15¼in. high. (Christie's)$2,500 £1,288

Oval ivory snuff box, 9cm. wide. (Sotheby's)$970 £500

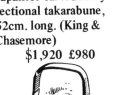

Carved ivory figure of 'Idaten', the Buddhist deity of peace, 27.5cm. high, circa 1900.(King & Chasemore) $372 £190

Japanese carved ivory sectional takarabune, 52cm. long. (King & Chasemore) $1,920 £980

Carved ivory figure of Hsi Wang Mu, 34cm. high, Chinese, circa 1900. (King & Chasemore) $588 £300

Large whale's tooth scrimshaw, mid 19th century, 7in. high. (Sotheby's Belgravia) $237 £120

19th century French ivory and ormolu card case and purse. (Gray's Antique Market) $693 £350

Late 19th century ivory tusk vase, 25.5cm. high.(King & Chasemore) $1,036 £540

One of a pair of ivory bottles with heads as stoppers. (Christie's) $160 £83

One of a pair of Ch'ien Lung ivory fan carvings, 8½in. wide. (Christie's) $700 £360

One of seven 19th century Persian miniatures painted on ivory. (Sotheby's Belgravia) $230 £120

Japanese Aikuchi in carved ivory, circa 1900, 31.5cm. long. (King & Chasemore) $490 £250

Indian ivory chess set with polychrome decoration, kings 10.8cm. high.(Christie's) $5,544 £2,800

Late 17th century Dutch ivory handled fork, 22.5cm. long.(Sotheby's) $427 £220

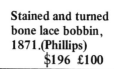

Japanese ivory group, circa 1870, 10in. high. (Gray's Antique Mews) $949 £470

Late 19th century pair of carved rhinoceros horns, 25½in. high.(Sotheby's Belgravia) $2,688 £1,400

Stained and turned bone lace bobbin, 1871.(Phillips) $196 £100

17th century ivory French equestrian figure of Alexander the Great.(Christie's Geneva) $9,165 £4,629

Japanese carved ivory group, 13½in. long. (Sotheby Bearne) $1,881 £940

Early 18th century ivory portrait plaque.(Humberts, King & Chasemore) $712 £360

A pair of ivory bottles with heads forming stoppers. (Christie's) $160 £83

Mid 17th century Dutch ivory handled presentoir.(Sotheby's) $252 £130

Japanese carved ivory figure of 'Shou Lao', 26cm. high, circa 1900. (King & Chasemore) $352 £180

19th century Japanese carved ivory figure. (Lacy Scott & Sons) $1,616 £800

'Boat of Plenty', carrying eight figures, 9in. long, on wooden base. (Phillips) $404 £200

Mid 19th century whale's tooth scrimshaw, 7in. high. (Sotheby's Belgravia) $237 £120

IVORY

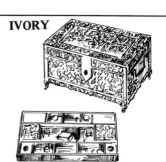

Chinese carved ivory sewing box with brass handles, circa 1870, 4¾in. high. (Gray's Antique Mews) $969 £480

Japanese carved ivory figure of Hotei with a boy on his shoulders, 17.5cm. high. (King & Chasemore)$525 £260

One of a pair of carved ivory sphinx candlesticks, 11½in. high, early 19th century. (Sotheby's Belgravia) $9,696 £4,800

Large Japanese carved ivory figure of a man, inlaid green seal, 23.5cm. high. (King & Chasemore)$444 £220

Lacquer and ivory panel, circa 1900, 32½in. long. (Sotheby's Belgravia) $509 £260

Japanese carved ivory figure of 'Fukorokuju', 38.5cm. high, circa 1900. (King & Chasemore) $431 £220

19th century ivory tamper, 2½in. long. (Gray's Antique Mews) $131 £65

Japanese ivory Okimono sectional group, signed Kyokumei, late 19th century, 7in. high. (Manchester Auction Mart) $1,818 £900

One of a pair of 19th century carved Japanese tusk vases. (Christie's S. Kensington) $2,929 £1,450

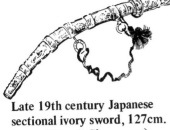

Rare ivory bottle carved in the shape of a reclining lady. (Christie's) $150 £77

Late 19th century Japanese sectional ivory sword, 127cm. long. (King & Chasemore) $3,234 £1,650

Japanese ivory carving. (Phillips) $727 £360

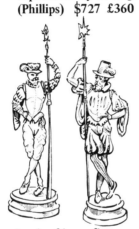

Late 19th century Japanese ivory Okimono, 9¾in. high. (Manchester Auction Mart) $323 £160

A pair of ivory figures, circa 1865, French, 29½in. high. (Sotheby's Belgravia) $30,300 £15,000

Japanese carved ivory figure of a Buddhist deity, 34cm. high, circa 1900. (King & Chasemore) $490 £250

Japanese carved ivory figure of a man, 16cm. high, inlaid red seal. (King & Chasemore) $404 £200

Carved ivory table centrepiece, mid 19th century, 49in. long. (Sotheby's Belgravia) $56,560 £28,000

Japanese ivory Okimono, late 19th century, 8½in. high. (Manchester Auction Mart) $282 £140

Ch'ien Lung white jade brushwasher, 5¾in. wide.(Christie's) $2,200 £1,134

Ch'ien Lung white pierced jade bowl and cover, 5in. diameter.(Christie's) $1,760 £907

Ch'ien Lung carved and pierced white jade brushwasher, 5½in. wide. (Christie's) $2,750 £1,417

White jade bottle with emerald and white jade stopper. (Christie's) $240 £123

19th century jadeite Jui sceptre, 19¼in. long, with silk tassels. (Bonham's) $34,650 £17,500

One of a pair of jade Phoenixes. (Sotheby's) $11,484 £5,800

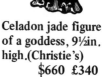

Pale green jade figure of a lady, 12½in. high. (Christie's) $1,400 £721

Large celadon jade bowl, Ch'ien Lung, 11½in. wide. (Christie's) $6,600 $3,473

Celadon jade figure of a goddess, 9½in. high.(Christie's) $660 £340

Ch'ien Lung pale grey jade brush-washer.(Christie's) $350 £180

Chrysanthemum dish in dark green jade, 10in. wide.   (Christie's) $3,850 £1,984

Leys jar in white jade, 2in. high. (Christie's) $660 £340

Ch'ien Lung greyish white jade globular jar and cover. (Christie's) $4,180 £2,154

One of a pair of early 18th century joss stick burners, in celadon jade, 9¾in. high. (Christie's)$4,950 £2,551

Pale grey foliate dish in jade, 7¾in. diam. (Christie's) $1,000 £515

Early 18th century koro and cover, in pale green jade, 5½in. high.   (Christie's) $24,200 £12,474

Mottled Ch'ien Lung grey and russet jade brush-washer, 6¾in. wide. (Christie's) $2,300 £1,185

Late Ch'ien Lung greyish white jade bowl, 5¾in. diam. (Christie's) $1,210 £623

Mottled white and brown jade bottle. (Christie's)$200 £103

Mottled spinach jade tripod incense burner, 7in. wide. (Christie's) $1,540 £793

Mottled spinach green jade bottle with inlaid metal stopper. (Christie's)$420 £218

Greenish white jade hanging vase and cover, 10in. high. (Christie's) $1,650 £868

Mottled grey and russet jade bottle with matching stopper. (Christie's) $180 £93

Celadon jade Ting, 8¾in. high. (Christie's) $5,000 £2,577

Mottled grey and russet jade bottle with matching stopper.(Christie's) $200 £103

Pale celadon jade brush-washer, 4¾in. wide. (Christie's) $1,045 £538

Leys jar in white jade, 2in. high. (Christie's) $660 £340

Mottled white, brown and green jade bottle. (Christie's)$180 £93

Ch'ien Lung mottled white jade koro and cover, 6¾in. wide. (Christie's) $2,530 £1,331

Mottled green and brown jade bottle with grey jade bead stopper. (Christie's) $120 £61

Ch'ien Lung fine white jade vase and cover, 9½in. high. (Christie's) $8,000 £4,123

Mottled white and russet jade bottle with green glass bead stopper. (Christie's)$200 £103

18th century pale celadon jade vase and cover, 8½in. high. (Christie's) $3,300 £1,736

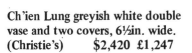

Pale grey jade hexagonal vase, 4¼in. high. (Christie's) $400 £206

Ch'ien Lung greyish white double vase and two covers, 6½in. wide. (Christie's) $2,420 £1,247

White jade bottle with emerald and white jade stopper. (Christie's) $240 £123

Cornflower blue sapphire surrounded by diamonds. (Alfie's Antique Market) $475 £240

Pair of antique diamond earrings. (Phillips) $1,858 £920

Platinum set single stone diamond ring, main diamond weighs 1.70 carats.(King & Chasemore) $5,940 £3,000

Corsage ornament by Georges Fouquet. (Sotheby's Monaco) $46,116 £23,529

Pearl and enamel brooch. (Smith-Woolley & Perry) $87 £44

Diamond and ruby brooch in Art Nouveau style. (King & Chasemore) $1,980 £1,000

Attractive Art Deco enamelled bracelet, 19cm. long, 1920's. (Sotheby's Belgravia) $435 £220

Victorian miniature brooch. (Christie's S. Kensington)$247 £130

Victorian hardstone, gold and pearl demi parure.(King & Chasemore)$787 £410

Late 19th century diamond star brooch. (Neales) $514 £260

Lady's diamond set dress ring, centre stone 1.49carat. (King & Chasemore) $5,184 £2,700

Pair of 18th century gold mounted diamond and pearl shaped earrings. (Phillips) $848 £420

Victorian unmarked gold bangle, set with split pearls, circa 1870.(King & Chasemore) $422 £220

Victorian gold and black enamel mourning brooch set with half pearls and diamonds.(Sotheby Bearne)$532 £280

Hair brooch with pearl border. (Smith-Woolley & Perry) $75 £38

Art Nouveau necklace, by Murrle Bennet & Company, of gold set with amethysts. (Phillips) $1,050 £520

Diamond bracelet. (Neales) $693 £350

Diamond and emerald set brooch. (King & Chasemore) $8,712 £4,400

Matched set of earrings and pendant necklace in gold. (King & Chasemore) $285 £150

One of a pair of pearl ear clips belonging to Eleanora Duse. (Christie's Geneva) $22,128 £11,176

Victorian mourning ring.(Smith-Woolley & Perry) $95 £48

Attractive antique gold and diamond fern leaf shaped brooch. (Phillips)$2,525 £1,250

18ct. gold diamond cluster ring.(Smith-Woolley & Perry) $3,049 £1,540

Mid Victorian diamond and emerald brooch. (D. M. Nesbit & Co.) $4,656 £2,400

Platinum set diamond pendant on a fine chain. (King & Chasemore) $1,386 £700

Mirror locket in Art Nouveau style in yellow gold set with turquoise matrix. (King & Chasemore) $411 £210

Fine antique diamond pendant surmounted by a ribbon bow on chain. (Phillips) $1,818 £900

Oval hardstone cameo, signed Verge, circa 1800, 7cm. high. (Sotheby's Zurich) $2,928 £1,478

Liberty & Co. plique-a-jour enamel pendant, circa 1905, 4.5cm. long.(Sotheby's Belgravia) $435 £220

Bracelet with a cabo-
chan sapphire centre-
ing a ten-diamond
cluster. (King & Chase-
more) $2,277 £1,150

Victorian diamond, gold
and enamel necklace.
(Lawrence's)
$7,600 £4,000

Diamond, ruby and
pearl ring. (Smith-
Woolley & Perry)
$277 £140

Matching brooch and
earrings of gold and
amethyst, circa 1845.
(Neales) $627 £330

Dunand eggshell lac-
quer pendant panel,
13.8cm. long.
(Sotheby's Belgravia)
$543 £280

Gold and enamel
diamond set watch
and chatelaine, 1790,
43.5cm. diameter.
(Sotheby's)
$5,940 £3,000

Diamond three row
crescent brooch,
late 19th century.
(Neales)
$2,178 £1,100

Hexagonal silver brooch,
2.5cm. high, circa 1900.
(Sotheby's Belgravia)
$54 £28

Victorian diamond
and pearl brooch-
pendant.(King &
Chasemore)
$6,336 £3,300

Heart shaped pendant, with a locket to the back. (King & Chasemore)
$2,592 £1,230

Art Deco sapphire, emerald and diamond brooch, mounted in platinum.(Christie's N. York) $17,170 £8,500

18 carat gold and platinum navette shaped diamond ring.(King & Chasemore) $950 £480

Pair of antique pear shaped diamond pendant earrings. (Phillips)
$2,020 £1,000

Elegant bow brooch of circular cut diamonds. (King & Chasemore)
$2,686 £1,350

Pair of Victorian earrings in ruby, sapphire and pearl.(Alfie's Antique Market)
$381 £185

Oval shaped gold backed silver set diamond brooch, diamonds 6ct. weight. (King & Chasemore)
$5,434 £2,600

15 carat gold shaped pendant brooch-necklace set with sapphires and pearls. (Geering & Colyer)
$2,352 £1,200

Emerald and diamond cluster ring in yellow and white gold mount. (King & Chasemore)
$3,553 £1,700

Bronze and ivory lamp
by Ferdinand Ligerth,
circa 1910, 17¾in. high.
(Sotheby's Belgravia)
$570 £300

Spider web leaded glass,
mosaic and bronze table
lamp by Tiffany.(Christie's
N. York)$150,000 £74,257

Bronze table lamp with
pierced bowl.(Phillips &
Jolly) $495 £250

Silvered metal Art
Nouveau lamp, 40cm.
high, circa 1900.
(Sotheby's Belgravia)
$2,352 £1,200

Galle cameo glass lamp,
circa 1900, 34.25cm.
high.(Sotheby's Belgravia)
$9,800 £5,000

Art Deco lady lamp, 15in.
high.(Alfie's Antique Market) $103 £50

Art Deco clown table
lamp. (Alfie's Antique
Market) $111 £55

Tiffany spider web lamp
with bronze baluster
base. (Christie's N. York)
$151,500 £75,000

Royal Worcester oil
lamp. (Drewatt, Wat-
son & Barton)
$332 £175

517

LAMPS

Favrile glass and gilt bronze desk lamp by Tiffany, 9¼in. high. (Christie's N. York) $770 £413

Wild rose leaded glass and gilt bronze lamp by Tiffany, 22½in. high. (Christie's N. York) $7,700 £4,139

Art Deco bronze table lamp, French, circa 1925, 38cm. high. (Sotheby's Belgravia) $310 £160

Bronze and Favrile glass linen fold floor lamp by Tiffany, 55in. high. (Christie's N. York) $1,210 £650

Leaded glass and bronze bridge floor lamp by Tiffany, 54½in. high. (Christie's N. York) $880 £473

Gilt bronze and Favrile glass twelve light lily floor lamp by Tiffany, 55¾in. high.(Christie's N. York)$8,800 £4,731

Leaded glass and bronze miniature apple blossom lamp by Tiffany, 18½in. high. (Christie's N. York) $3,520 £1,892

Early Favrile glass and silvered bronze kerosene student lamp by Tiffany, 24in. high. (Christie's N. York) $5,500 £2,956

Glass and wrought iron table lamp, circa 1920, 20¼in. high.(Christie's N. York)$2,420 £1,247

Art Nouveau leaded glass and bronze table lamp, circa 1910, 64.5cm. high. (Sotheby's Belgravia) $3,880 £2,000

Turtle back leaded glass table lamp by Tiffany, 23½in. high.(Christie's N. York) $4,950 £2,661

Poppy leaded glass and gilt bronze table lamp by Tiffany, 25½in. high. (Christie's N. York) $10,450 £5,618

Wrought iron and glass floor lamp, circa 1945, 64½in. high.(Christie's N. York) $2,420 £1,247

One of a pair of Tiffany studios gilt bronze candle holders, circa 1900, 47.5cm. high.(Sotheby's Belgravia) $1,164 £600

Favrile glass and bronze bridge floor lamp by Tiffany, 55½in. high. (Christie's N. York) $2,640 £1,419

Poppy leaded glass and bronze table lamp by Tiffany, 27¼in. high. (Christie's N. York) $19,800 £10,206

Lalique glass lamp, 1920's, 31.25cm. high. (Sotheby's Belgravia) $1,940 £1,000

Gilt bronze and glass linen fold table lamp by Tiffany, 24in. high. (Christie's N. York) $6,050 £3,118

519

Ship's anchor riding
light in copper with
brass attachments,
50cm. high.(King &
Chasemore) $127 £65

Gilt bronze and Favrile glass
three-light lily table lamp by
Tiffany, 13in. high.(Christie's
N. York) $1,320 £709

One of a pair of iri-
descent Favrile glass
candle lamps, by
Tiffany, 14in. high.
(Christie's N. York)
$1,265 £680

Spelter lamp, 16in.
high, 1920's, fitted
for electricity.
(Sotheby's Belgravia)
$784 £400

Novelty bedside lamp,
circa 1920, 20in. high.
(Sotheby's Belgravia)
$418 £220

Good Tiffany glass
table lamp. (Philips)
$6,860 £3,500

Attractive Boilot bronze
table lamp, circa 1900,
39.5cm. high.(Sotheby's
Belgravia) $776 £400

Table oil lamp by Hawks-
worth, Eyre & Co., Shef-
field, 1912.(Sotheby's)
$627 £320

Art Deco bronze lamp,
1930's, 52.75cm. high.
(Sotheby's Belgravia)
$514 £260

Daum glass lamp carved with marine motifs.(Sotheby's Monaco)
$32,144 £16,400

Opaque glass lamp-shade, 22in. wide, circa 1910. (Sotheby's Belgravia)
$271 £140

Ship's masthead riding light in copper, 55cm. high.(King & Chasemore)$146 £75

Tiffany studios bronze table lamp with leaded glass shade, circa 1900. (Sotheby's Belgravia)
$2,772 £1,400

Bronze and ivory two-light table lamp by Preiss, 26in. high. (Christie's)
$2,134 £1,100

20th century mille-fiori lamp, 41cm. high. (Sotheby's Belgravia) $198 £100

Early 20th century silver plated table lamp in the Art Nouveau style, 38in. high. (Locke & England)
$2,121 £1,050

Rare Webb's Burmese glass nightlight stand, circa 1887, 28cm. high.(Sotheby's)
$1,029 £520

Early 20th century cut glass lamp with detachable shade. (Sotheby's Belgravia)
$554 £280

Art Nouveau lamp in full working order. (Gray's Antique Market)
$199 £99

One of a very fine pair of Portuguese silver mounted carriage lamps, 2ft.6in. high, mid 19th century. (Sotheby's)
$3,528 £1,800

Tiffany studios bronze lamp base, circa 1910, 57.5cm. high. (Sotheby's Belgravia)
$1,227 £620

Facon de Venise bird lamp, 9in. high. (Sotheby's)
$155 £80

One of a pair of stylised chromed metal standard lamps, 1930's, 179.5cm. high. (Sotheby's Belgravia)
$235 £120

1930's standard lamp, with white glass shade, 188cm. high. (Sotheby's Belgravia)
$196 £100

20th century French Art Deco wrought iron standard lamp, 77¾in. high. (Peter Wilson)
$855 £450

Royal Worcester oil lamp, circa 1890, 64in. high. (Sotheby's Belgravia)
$940 £480

One of a set of four mid 19th century lead garden figures, 25in. high. (Sotheby's Belgravia) $633 £320

Britain's Royal Army Service wagon. (Phillips N. York) $250 £123

19th century lead figure of Pan, 49in. high. (King & Chasemore) $3,610 £1,900

Part of a lot of twenty-eight mounted lead figures of the South Australian Lancers and First Lifeguards. (Sotheby's Belgravia) $179 £90

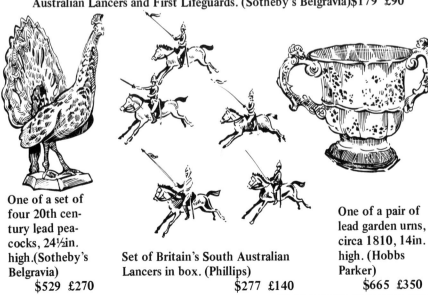

One of a set of four 20th century lead peacocks, 24½in. high.(Sotheby's Belgravia) $529 £270

Set of Britain's South Australian Lancers in box. (Phillips) $277 £140

One of a pair of lead garden urns, circa 1810, 14in. high. (Hobbs Parker) $665 £350

French marble bust
of a young girl, 1890's,
26in. high.(Sotheby's
Belgravia) $457 £230

Mid 17th century Italian
marble portrait relief,
9¾in. high. (Sotheby's)
$2,090 £1,100

Mid 18th century
French white marble
of a putto, 24in.
high. (Sotheby's) $855
£450

White marble bust by
J. Lombardi, circa
1877, 72in. high over-
all. (Sotheby's Belgravia)
$895 £450

White marble and ivory
figure, signed E. Seger,
circa 1920, 16½in. high.
(Sotheby's Belgravia)
$969 £510

One of a pair of veined
yellow marble columns,
circa 1900, 40in. high.
(Sotheby's Belgravia)
$1,069 £540

Black conglomerate mar-
ble head from the T'ang
dynasty, 9½in. high.
(Christie's) $3,080 £1,620

One of a large pair of
white marble seated
Buddhistic lions, 44in.
high. (Christie's)
$3,850 £1,984

Mid 19th century Italian
marble figure, 43½in.
high.(Sotheby's Belgravia)
$3,781 £1,900

Italian white marble bust of Winter, circa 1700, 29½in. high. (Sotheby's) $912 £480

Marble bust of a lady by Sir John Steell, 23in. high. (Sotheby's) $509 £260

Marble and bronze figure of a woman, 1900-1910, signed P. Aichele. (Sotheby's Belgravia) $772 £390

One of a pair of 19th century French white marble and ormolu casseolettes, 11in. high. (Messenger, May & Baverstock) $727 £360

Two marble figures by Kitson of Rebecca and Abel. (Spencer's) $2,812 £1,480

Marble figure of a boy by G. Buffoni, Milan, circa 1877. (Sotheby's Belgravia) $1,592 £800

Marble bust of Pharaoh's daughter, circa 1904, 26½in. high.(Sotheby's Belgravia) $222 £110

Mid 19th century Second Empire verde antico marble and gilt bronze column, 39¼in. high.(Sotheby's Belgravia) $756 £380

Mid 16th century Italian white marble bust of a boy, 17in. high. (Sotheby's) $3,325 £1,750

525

Early 18th century Venetian giltwood mirror, one of a pair, 4ft.5in. high. (Sotheby's) $8,316 £4,200

Late 18th century neoclassical gilt frame hanging mirror, 4ft.8½in. wide. (Geering & Colyer) $490 £250

Late George II oval giltwood mirror, 1880's, 45in. high. (Sotheby's Belgravia) $349 £180

Large Art Deco mirror frame, early 1920's. (Sotheby's Belgravia) $118 £60

Sue and Mare Art Deco gilt bronze mirror frame, 1923, 25.6cm. high. (Sotheby's Belgravia) $396 £200

One of a pair of Thuringian mirror frames, circa 1880, 99cm. high. (Sotheby's Belgravia) $2,475 £1,250

One of a pair of mid 18th century Italian giltwood girandoles, 20½in. wide.(Christie's) $1,940 £1,000

George III giltwood mirror, 45½ x 31in. (Christie's) $2,123 £1,100

Good hardwood mirror, circa 1880, 70in. high.(Sotheby's Belgravia) $1,766 £920

George II gilt gesso mirror, circa 1900, 42¼ x 25½in. (Sotheby's Belgravia) $403 £210

George III mahogany oval toilet mirror, 16in. wide. (Nottingham Auction Mart)$407 £210

One of a pair of silver, copper and wood Art Deco mirror frames, circa 1925, 62cm. high. (Sotheby's Belgravia) $198 £100

Rosewood and mahogany mirror by Louis Majorelle, 67in. high.(Christie's N. York) $3,000 £1,515

Italian Art Nouveau mirror with carved pearwood frame, 92½in. high.(Christie's N. York)$2,530 £1,304

Late 18th century mahogany and parcel gilt wall mirror, 38in. high.(King & Chasemore) $1,710 £900

Late 17th century Grinling Gibbons school gilt wall mirror of carved limewood, 50in. high. (Bonham's)$1,748 £920

Mid 19th century giltwood wall mirror, 50 x 38in.(Sotheby's Belgravia) $970 £500

One of a pair of giltwood and gilt plaster girandole mirrors, 1880's, 41½in. high.(Sotheby's Belgravia) $446 £230

527

MIRRORS

Giltwood mirror, circa 1900, 67in. high.(Sotheby's Belgravia)$396 £200

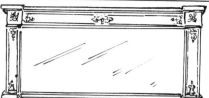

19th century gilt and ebony pier mirror, 51in. wide. (Nottingham Auction Mart) $291 £150

Black lacquer toilet mirror with chinoiserie decoration. (Christie's S. Kensington)$303 £150

Silver and enamel frame by William Hutton & Sons Ltd., London, 1903, 19.75cm. high. (Sotheby's Belgravia) $659 £340

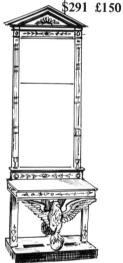

Rare Swedish giltwood pier glass and consol table, circa 1800, 2ft. 11½in. wide. (Sotheby's)$1,235 £650

19th century pier glass with giltwood frame. (J. M. Welch) $1,313 £650

George III walnut veneered mirror, 46in. high.(Nottingham Auction Mart) $1,746 £900

19th century French silver toilet mirror, by H. Boucheron, Paris, 32½in. high.(Christie's) $3,298 £1,700

George II giltwood mirror, circa 1735, 2ft. 9½in. wide. (Sotheby's) $2,352 £1,200

528

Queen Anne walnut
dressing table mirror,
with fall front.
(Worsfolds) $784 £400

Mid 18th century gilt-
wood overmantel, 4ft.
3in. wide. (Sotheby's)
$1,623 £820

Giltwood overmantel
mirror, circa 1900,
35in. wide. (Sotheby's
Belgravia) $188 £95

Late 19th century hard-
wood and ivory inlaid
mirror. (Sotheby's
Belgravia) $403 £210

One of a pair of mid
18th century German
giltwood pier glasses
and matching consols.
(Sotheby's) $5,700 £3,000

Rare North Italian pain-
ted and giltwood mirror,
2ft.1in. wide, circa 1700.
(Sotheby's) $940 £480

Flemish gilt metal
and ebonised wood
mirror, 45in. high.
(Sotheby's Belgravia)
$435 £220

Large giltwood overmantel
mirror, circa 1840, 90 x
70in. (Sotheby's Belgravia)
$756 £380

Flemish tortoiseshell
and ebony mirror,
circa 1690, 3ft.2½in.
high. (Sotheby's)
$980 £500

Sheraton mahogany swing mirror, 20in. wide, circa 1810. (Christopher Sykes) $134 £68

William and Mary style wall mirror, late 19th century, 2ft.3in. wide. (Sotheby's)$784 £400

Mahogany Sheraton toilet mirror, circa 1880.(Christopher Sykes) $112 £58

One of a pair of painted wood chinoiserie wall mirrors, 1920's, 44½ x 18in. (Sotheby's Belgravia) $548 £280

Giltwood overmantel, circa 1860, 71 x 69in. (Sotheby's Belgravia) $684 £360

One of a pair of gilt-plaster girandoles, circa 1890, Italian, 38in. high.(Sotheby's Belgravia)$237 £120

Late 17th century Florentine giltwood mirror, 3ft.7in. high.(Sotheby's) $470 £240

Satinwood cheval mirror, 57½in. high, circa 1900.(Sotheby's Belgravia) $543 £280

19th century Indian carved teak mirror. (Jolly's)$2,716 £1,400

Sheraton mahogany box toilet mirror, 1ft. 10½in. wide.(David Symonds)$196 £100

One of a pair of mid 19th century giltwood wall mirrors, 35½ x 40in. (Sotheby's Belgravia) $372 £190

Toilet mirror by Gordon Russell, circa 1930, 26½in. high. (Sotheby's Belgravia)$272 £140

Heavily carved early 20th century wall mirror, 78¾in. high. (Sotheby's Belgravia) $883 £460

19th century carved mahogany wall mirror. (Andrew Grant) $752 £380

George III gilt mirror, circa 1780, 2ft. 1in. wide.(Sotheby's) $1,019 £520

Late 18th century carved giltwood wall mirror, 71in. high. (Sotheby Bearne) $1,520 £800

Walnut cheval mirror, 1850's, 78in. high. (Sotheby's Belgravia) $455 £230

George II giltwood mirror, circa 1735, 2ft.6in. wide. (Sotheby's) $1,528 £780

MIRRORS

Queen Anne black-japanned toilet mirror, 1ft.5in. wide, circa 1710. (Sotheby's)$1,666 £850

William and Mary oyster veneered walnut wall mirror, 2ft. high, circa 1685. (Sotheby's) $633 £320

Good Regency giltwood mirror, circa 1810, 3ft. 2in. high. (Sotheby's)
$594 £300

Early George III giltwood looking glass. (Robert Dowie)
$5,454 £2,700

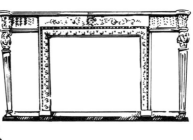

Fine 19th century carved pier mirror, 50in. wide. (Nottingham Auction Mart) $98 £50

Regency giltwood convex mirror, circa 1805, 2ft.4in. high.(Sotheby's)
$396 £200

Regency wall mirror. (Neales) $824 £400

Mid 19th century giltwood overmantel, 59in. wide. (Sotheby's Belgravia)
$323 £160

Stylish Hagenauer chromed metal hand mirror, 1920's, 21.5cm. high. (Sotheby's Belgravia) $257 £130

George II walnut and parcel gilt mirror, circa 1740, 2ft.7in. wide. (Sotheby's) $2,772 £1,400

Victorian mahogany dressing table mirror. (British Antique Exporters) $50 £25

William and Mary marquetry cushion frame mirror, circa 1690, 2ft.9in. wide. (Sotheby's) $1,470 £750

Sienese giltwood wall mirror, circa 1850, 46in. wide. (Sotheby's Belgravia) $23,482 £11,800

18th century wall mirror in walnut frame, 58in. high. (Graves, Son & Pilcher) $3,960 £2,000

Early George I silver gilt toilet mirror by Paul Crespin, London, 1728, 19in. high, 34oz.6dwt. (Sotheby's)$3,000 £1,500

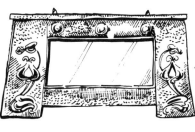

Fine early Victorian rosewood framed cheval mirror. (British Antique Exporters) $240 £120

Copper and enamel mirror, circa 1900, 40in. wide. (Sotheby's Belgravia) $303 £150

Regency circular gilt framed wall mirror, 44in. wide.(Osmond Tricks) $950 £500

MISCELLANEOUS

Early 18th century elm wheelbarrow, 22in. long. (Gray's Antique Market)
$151 £75

Viennese Meerschaum pipe, circa 1870. (Alfie's Antique Market) $164 £80

Rare early Victorian cricketer's belt in beadwork. (Geering & Colyer)$370 £180

Very fine Sand Bell, Victorian, 9½in. high. (Alfie's Antique Market)
$195 £95

1811 edition of 'Sense and Sensibility' in original publisher's boards. (Christie's S. Kensington)
$9,120 £4,800

Bottle of first growth 1858 Chateau Lafite claret. (Bonham's)
$1,212 £600

Rock crystal picture frame, 3½in. diam. (Christie's)
$14,744 £7,600

One of a pair of Rowley Gallery silvered wood doors, 1920's, 216cm. high. (Sotheby's Belgravia)
$396 £200

Late Victorian scallop edge collar, 12in. deep. (Gray's Antique Mews)
$36 £18

Victorian carved oak adjustable bookstand. (British Antique Exporters) $24 £12

Mid 19th century red boulle clock bracket, 14½in. high. (Sotheby's Belgravia) $446 £230

Tunbridgeware clothes brush. (Parsons, Welch & Cowell) $4 £2

Tunbridgeware obelisk with mercury filled thermometer, 7½in. high. (Parsons, Welch & Cowell) $21 £11

17th century English needlework picture. (Peter Wilson) $1,191 £590

Rare Solomon Islands shield. (Lawrence's) $16,464 £8,400

Late 18th century silk embroidered floral group. (May, Whetter & Grose) $51 £26

Victorian sporran, dirk and companion Skein Dhu, Glasgow, 1859. (Sotheby's) $1,274 £650

Victorian heart shaped pin cushion, 7in. long. (Gray's Antique Mews) $28 £14

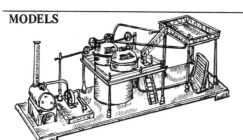

Unusual early Bing tinplate model brewery, circa 1905, 1ft.7¾in. long. (Sotheby's Belgravia) $1,683 £850

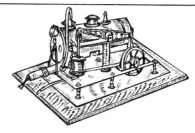

Model of a steam Beam engine in glass case. (Phillips) $484 £240

Early 19th century saddler's model of a dapple grey stallion, 15.2 hands high. (Christie's S. Kensington) $2,090 £1,100

Working model of a hand weaving loom, circa 1900, English, 2ft.1½in. high. (Sotheby's Belgravia) $1,094 £550

Rare Bing 'Spider' steam-driven carriage, circa 1900, German. (Sotheby's Belgravia) $6,138 £3,100

Unusual 19th century model of a steam horseless carriage compound, 11½in. long. (Sotheby's Belgravia) $1,881 £950

Model steam fairground traction engine. (Thomas Miller) $2,716 £1,400

19th century working model of a muzzle loading bombardment mortar, 24in. long. (Phillips) $500 £253

Early 20th century bone and wood model of a French man-of-war, 12 x 10in. (Sotheby's Belgravia)
$2,574 £1,300

Modern English model of HMS Victory, 2ft.5in. long. (Sotheby's Belgravia)
$297 £150

English man-of-war model ship, circa 1815, in excellent condition, 58in. long. (Bradley & Vaughan)
$3,636 £1,800

Boxwood, ebony and copper sheathed model of a frigate. (Christie's)
$5,544 £2,800

19th century model of the clipper 'Nordic', 24in. long. (Gray's Antique Market) $757 £375

Modern English 1/40 scale model of the Baltimore schooner 'Albatross', 20 x 26in. (Sotheby's Belgravia)
$534 £270

Rare tinplate French carpet toy train, 15in. long, circa 1870.
(Sotheby's Belgravia) $188 £95

Good German clockwork locomotive
'Mercury', 1ft.4½in. long.(Sotheby's
Belgravia) $316 £160

19th century 4½in. gauge
brass and copper live steam
coal-fired engine, 1ft.5½in.
long. (Sotheby's Belgravia)
                    $514 £260

'Heilan Lassie', 3½in. gauge model locomotive.
(Christie's) $1,764 £900

Early spirit-fired brass 'Piddler'
engine, mid 19th century, 9in.
long.(Sotheby's Belgravia)
                    $237 £120

The Super Claud model locomotive, 5in.
gauge. (Christie's) $5,880 £3,000

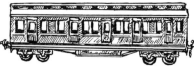

Two gauge 'One' bogie passenger coaches by Carette for Basset-Lowke, 1ft.4¼in.
long. (Sotheby's Belgravia) $198 £100

Early Marklin gauge 'One' clockwork locomotive, 12in. long.(Sotheby's Belgravia) $891 £450

Marklin gauge 'One' clockwork tank locomotive, circa 1915, 1ft.5in. long. (Sotheby's Belgravia) $1,227 £620

German 2½ gauge 'Three' live steam spirit-fired locomotive, 1ft.6in. long. (Sotheby's Belgravia) $613 £310

Rare and early tinplate carpet toy train and carriages, French, circa 1880, 1ft.7in. long. (Sotheby's Belgravia) $495 £250

Early Bing gauge 'One' GNR bogie passenger coach, 1ft.1½in. long, circa 1915.(Sotheby's Belgravia) $396 £200

Marklin gauge 'One' live steam-fired locomotive 'The Great Bear', 2ft.5in. long, circa 1910. (Sotheby's Belgravia) $4,950 £2,500

Issmayer gauge 'O' clockwork train set, late 1920's. (Sotheby's Belgravia) $198 £100

Bassett-Lowke gauge 'O' L.M.S. 12-wheeled dining car. (King & Chasemore) $101 £50

A good German gauge 'One' live steam spirit-fired reversing locomotive, 1ft.6½in. long. (Sotheby's Belgravia) $594 £300

Bing gauge 'O' clockwork train set. (Sotheby's Belgravia) $148 £75

Live steam coal-fired 3½in. gauge 0-4-0 'Tich' tank engine, 15½in. long. (Sotheby's Belgravia) $594 £300

Early gauge 'Three' Ernst Plank live steam boxed train set, circa 1905. (Sotheby's Belgravia) $514 £260

Part of a Lionel gauge 'O' model railway collection. (Sotheby's Belgravia) $574 £290

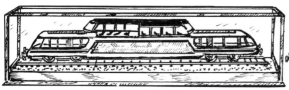

Unusual 2½in. gauge static model of a SNCF diesel-electric panoramic railcar, 4ft.7in. long. (Sotheby's Belgravia) $495 £250

Gauge 'O' Bassett-Lowke 'Flying Scotsman' locomotive and tender. (King & Chasemore) $969 £480

Marklin gauge 'One' bogie CIWR sleeping car, circa 1919, 1ft.8¾in. long. (Sotheby's Belgravia) $792 £400

Mint condition Hornby gauge 'O' electric locomotive, 1ft.3in. long. (Sotheby's Belgravia)$554 £280

Carl Bub electric model railway in original box. (Sotheby's Belgravia)
$257 £130

Attractive Bassett-Lowke gauge 'O' electric locomotive 'Arsenal', 17in. long. (Sotheby's Belgravia)
$613 £310

Fully operational 15in. gauge live steam coal-fired locomotive built by A. Barnes & Co., Rhyl, circa 1920, 17ft.5¼in. long.(Sotheby's Belgravia) $17,820 £9,000

Early German gauge 'O' model railway collection. (Sotheby's Belgravia)
$237 £120

Tinplate reversing engine 'London' by Mathias Hess, circa 1885, in original box. (Bonham's)
$792 £400

Gauge 'O' Bassett-Lowke 'Royal Scot' electric locomotive and tender. (King & Chasemore)
$606 £300

Late 19th century 'Trick Pony' cast iron money bank, 7½in. wide. (Sotheby's Belgravia) $238 £120

Late 19th century American 'Leap-Frog Bank', 7½in. wide. (Sotheby's Belgravia) $437 £220

Unusual musical tinplate money bank, 4¾in. high, sold with another. (Sotheby's Belgravia) $55 £28

Tinplate 'Chocolat Menier' dispenser money box, circa 1920, 10½in. high. (Sotheby's Belgravia) $59 £30

Unusual German 'Royal Trick' elephant tinplate mechanical money bank, 6in. long. (Sotheby's Belgravia) $895 £450

Late 19th century American owl cast iron money bank, 7¾in. high. (Sotheby's Belgravia) $318 £160

Late 19th century American monkey and barrel-organ cast iron money bank, 6½in. high. (Sotheby's Belgravia) $437 £220

Late 19th century American 'Uncle Sam' cast iron money box, 11½in. high. (Sotheby's Belgravia) $338 £170

Late 19th century jockey and mule money box, 9¾in. long, by James H. Bowen. (Sotheby's Belgravia) $238 £120

Late 19th century Swiss musical box, 24in. long. (Lalonde, Bros. & Parham) $1,575 £780

'The Speaking Picture Book', circa 1880. (Gray's Antique Market) $454 £225

Interesting phonograph mechanism, 1ft.2in. long, in need of attention. (Sotheby's Belgravia) $258 £130

Musical praxinoscope with eight-air movement. (Christie's S. Kensington) $3,434 £1,700

Edison standard phonograph, American, circa 1906-1908.(Sotheby's Belgravia) $407 £210

American 'AM J' juke box case, circa 1945-50, 70in. high. (Sotheby's Belgravia) $213 £110

David Lecoultre keywound cylinder musical box, 1ft. 4in. wide. (Sotheby's Belgravia) $796 £400

Mini record player with case, circa 1910, 8in. high. (Gray's Antique Market)$262 £130

Nicole Freres keywound cylinder musical box, circa 1860, 14½in. wide. (Sotheby's Belgravia) $1,067 £550

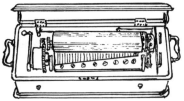

Swiss overture cylinder musical box, circa 1880, 26in. wide.(Sotheby's Belgravia) $1,261 £659

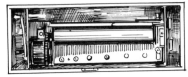

Nicole Freres cylinder musical box, circa 1881, 1ft.5in. wide.(Sotheby's Belgravia) $358 £180

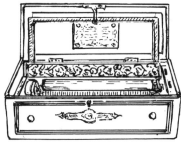

Du Commun-Girod 'hidden bells, drums and castanets' cylinder musical box, 24in. wide, circa 1860. (Sotheby's Belgravia) $1,008 £520

Francois Nicole keywound cylinder musical box, circa 1835.(Sotheby's Belgravia) $1,094 £550

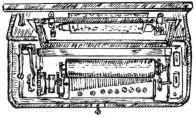

Good Nicole Freres cylinder musical box, 24in. wide, circa 1890. (Sotheby's Belgravia) $970 £500

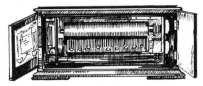

Swiss Langdorf sublime harmonie cylinder musical box, 1ft.10½in. wide. (Sotheby's Belgravia) $1,492 £750

Swiss A. Riverni orchestral musical box, 1880-1890, 38in. wide. (Sotheby's Belgravia) $2,619 £1,350

Late 19th century German Mignon paper roll organette, 1ft.8in. wide. (Sotheby's Belgravia) $895 £450

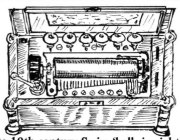

Late 19th century Swiss 'bells in sight' musical box, 23in. wide.(Sotheby's Belgravia) $776 £400

'Hidden bells and drum' cylinder musical box, 1870-1880, 1ft.8in. wide. (Sotheby's Belgravia) $696 £350

Paillard, Vaucher Fils 'Voix-Celeste' cylinder musical box, 35in. wide, circa 1880.(Sotheby's Belgravia) $2,328 £1,200

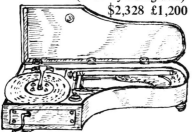

Rare German orpheus mechanical zither by Ehrlichs, 34in. wide, circa 1904, together with seventy-six cardboard discs. (Sotheby's Belgravia) $1,552 £800

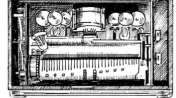

Swiss Paillard, Vaucher Fils 'bells and drums in sight' cylinder musical box, circa 1880, 2ft. wide. (Sotheby's Belgravia) $2,189 £1,100

Improved Berliner gramophone, American, circa 1900.(Sotheby's Belgravia) $756 £380

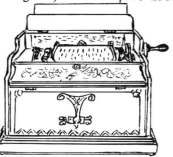

American Celstina paper roll organette, circa 1880, 15in. wide. (Sotheby's Belgravia) $698 £360

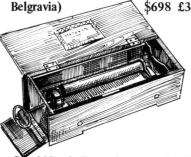

Good Nicole Freres keywound cylinder musical box, 1ft.6in. wide, circa 1848. (Sotheby's Belgravia) $1,393 £700

Ebonised musical box which plays ten tunes. (King & Chasemore)
$1,086 £560

Early 20th century German symphonion disc musical box, 11in. wide, sold with nine discs. (Sotheby's Belgravia)
$318 £160

Edison fireside phonograph, circa 1910. (Sotheby's Belgravia)
$796 £400

Late 19th century Portuguese Carlos Arigotti Dulcimer, 3ft.7in. high. (Sotheby's Belgravia)
$756 £380

Fine Gramophone and Typewriter Ltd. senior monarch gramophone, circa 1908.(Sotheby's Belgravia) $1,393 £700

Silver model of Marconi's disc discharger, 3½in. high, 1912. (Sotheby's Belgravia)
$99 £50

HMV model 460 table gramophone, circa 1925, 12in. turntable. (Sotheby's Belgravia)
$349 £180

Mid 19th century Hicks Dulcimer, 2ft.10in. high. (Sotheby's Belgravia)
$1,791 £900

Fine Swiss 'bells in sight' interchangeable cylinder musical box on stand, 3ft.10in. wide.(Sotheby's Belgravia) $3,781 £1,900

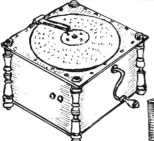

Ariston organette, 16in. wide, circa 1900, sold with sixty-five cardboard discs.(Sotheby's Belgravia) $271 £140

Early 20th century German symphonion disc musical box, 1ft.1in. wide, sold with ten metal discs. (Sotheby's Belgravia) $696 £350

Edison gem phonograph, circa 1910. (Sotheby's Belgravia) $477 £240

Gramophone in the form of a miniature grand piano, circa 1930, English, 3ft. 1½in. high.(Sotheby's Belgravia) $437 £220

Late 19th century Swiss 'bells in sight' interchangeable cylinder musical box on stand, 2ft.5in. wide. (Sotheby's Belgravia) $3,383 £1,700

Early 20th century polyphone disc musical box, 3ft.8in. high, with nineteen metal discs. (Sotheby's Belgravia) $1,094 £550

Late 19th century German 9¾in. monopol disc musical box, 13in. wide, with one metal disc.(Sotheby's Belgravia) $291 £150

Early 20th century German 8¼in. symphonion disc musical box, 10½in. wide. (Sotheby's Belgravia) $310 £160

Late 19th century German polyphon disc musical box, 2ft.9in. high, with twenty-four discs.(Sotheby's Belgravia) $1,791 £900

Good Bing 'Bingola I' child's tinplate gramophone, German, circa 1920.(Sotheby's Belgravia) $194 £100

Late 19th century Swiss 'bells in sight' cylinder musical box, 25in. wide. (Sotheby's Belgravia) $426 £220

Mid 19th century Swiss key wound cylinder musical box, 1ft.3in. wide.(Sotheby's Belgravia) $517 £260

Edison spring motor phonograph, American, circa 1898-1901. (Sotheby's Belgravia) $426 £220

Early 20th century German, 7¾in. symphonion 'musik spar bank' disc musical box, 15in. high. (Sotheby's Belgravia) $3,104 £1,600

Late 19th century Austrian musical clock picture, by A. Olbrich.(Sotheby's Belgravia) $892 £460

Columbia AA graphophone, American, circa 1906.(Sotheby's Belgravia) $179 £90

Late 19th century, Swiss, 17¼in. Stella disc musical box, 27in. wide, with eighteen discs.(Sotheby's Belgravia) $1,358 £700

Good Puck type phonograph, probably German, circa 1903, with tin horn. (Sotheby's Belgravia) $298 £150

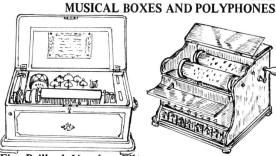

Swiss Nicole Freres key-wound cylinder musical box, 18in. wide, circa 1860.(Sotheby's Belgravia) $1,008 £520

Fine Paillard, Vaucher Fils orchestral musical box, circa 1888, 29in. wide.(Sotheby's Belgravia) $3,104 £1,600

Late 19th century Melodia paper roll organette, 12in. wide, sold with nine paper rolls. (Sotheby's Belgravia) $698 £360

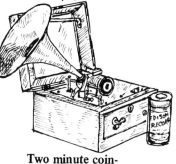

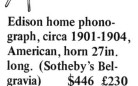

Two minute coin-operated phonograph, probably Continental, circa 1905. (Sotheby's Belgravia) $698 £360

Rare German 25in. Kalliope panorama automat disc musical box on stand, circa 1903, 7ft.10in. high.(Sotheby's Belgravia)$5,174 £2,600

Edison home phonograph, circa 1901-1904, American, horn 27in. long. (Sotheby's Belgravia) $446 £230

Good Edison home phonograph, circa 1902, with 2ft.5½in. brass horn.(Sotheby's Belgravia) $477 £240

Rare Swiss key-wound musical box, 13in. wide, circa 1820-30. (Sotheby's Belgravia) $1,086 £560

Early 20th century, 8¾in. chalet disc organette, 12in. wide, together with eighteen discs.(Sotheby's Belgravia) $446 £230

Violin by Nicola Amati, 1651, length of back 13¾in. (Christie's) $3,492 £1,800

Italian violin by Joseph Guadagnini, length of back 14in. (Sotheby's) $11,760 £6,000

French violin by Chas. Collin-Mezin, Paris, 1893, length of back 14in. (Sotheby's) $1,411 £720

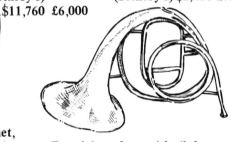

Mahogany cased silver plated cornet, 12½in. long, circa 1860. (Christopher Sykes) $555 £275

French brass horn with gilt lacquer interior. (V. & V's.) $727 £360

Violin by Charles Francois Gand. (Phillips) $9,900 £5,000

Set of Brain Boru Irish war pipes, circa 1910, by Henry Starck. (Gray's Antique Market) $633 £320

Violin by David Tecchler, Rome, 1702, length of back 14in. (Christie's) $15,520 £8,000

Important violin by
Antonius Stradivarius,
1726, length of back 14in.
(Christie's) $8,730 £4,500

Italian violin by Antonio
Gragnani, Leghorn, 1776,
length of back 14in.
(Sotheby's)
$10,192 £5,200

Violin by Jacobus
Stainer.(Phillips)
$31,310 £15,500

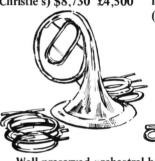

Well-preserved orchestral horn by Rudall
Carte & Co., London, circa 1880.
(Christie's) $1,008 £520

Silver plated cornet by
Boosey & Co., London,
15½in. long. (Christopher
Sykes) $151 £75

Violoncello by Antonius
Stradivarius, Cremona,
1710, with original label.
(Sotheby's)
$275,500 £145,000

Late 19th century
round mandolin,
15in. long. (Gray's
Antique Market.
$222 £110

German violin, circa
1770, sold by Charles
and Samuel Thompson.
(Gray's Antique Market)
$297 £150

Fine violin by George
Wulme-Hudson, Lon-
don, circa 1910,
length of back 14in.
(Sotheby's)$3,038 £1,550

Fine violin by Thomas
Kennedy, London, circa
1830, length of back 14in.
(Sotheby's) $1,764 £900

English viola by Duke,
length of back 15in., in
shaped case. (Sotheby's)
$1,528 £780

Composite violin, pro-
bably Italian, 1674.
(Sotheby's)
$2,744 £1,400

English Serpent by Thos.
Key, London, mid 19th
century, 7ft.8¾in. long.
(Sotheby's)$2,121 £1,050

Rosewood and nickel
silver flute by Butler,
London and Dublin, 15in.
long.(Christopher Sykes)
$76 £38

Violin by Gustave Meinel,
London, 1902, length of
back 14in. (Sotheby's)
$1,862 £950

French violin by Charles
Collin-Mezin, Paris, 1910,
length of back 14¼in.
(Sotheby's)$1,215 £620

Italian violoncello by
Joseph Nadotti, length of
back 29¼in.(Sotheby's)
$6,664 £3,400

Interesting violin by
Wm. Wilkinson, Lon-
don, length of back
14in.
(Sotheby's)
$1,019£520

Fine Italian violin by
Eugenio Degani, Venice,
1895, length of back
14¼in. (Sotheby's) $5,684
£2,900

Fine French violin by
Justin Derazey, circa
1870, length of back
14in.   (Sotheby's)
$1,666£850

Five-string banjo inlaid
with mother-of-pearl,
circa 1890, 42in. long.
(Gray's Antique Mews)
$252 £125

Seven-key flute in rosewood
and ivory with silver keys,
circa 1815. (Gray's Antique
Market) $333 £165

Spruce guitar lute with
pearwood inlay, circa
1890. (Gray's Antique
Mews) $454£225

Fine French violin by
Dominique Didelot,
circa 1830, length of
back 14¼in.(Sotheby's)
$1,332 £680

Violin by Bernardus
Calanius, Genoa, 1736,
length of back 13¾in.
(Christie's)$9,700 £5,000

English violin by Alfred
Vincent, London, 1929,
length of back 13¾in.
(Sotheby's)
$1,411 £720

Ivory Okimono style netsuke of two Oni, carved with a head of Shohi, signed Gyoku. (Christie's) $418 £220

Ivory netsuke by Kaigyokusai Masatsugu. (Christie's) $38,380 £19,000

18th century netsuke, signed Okakoto. (Gray's Antique Market) $1,287 £650

Ivory netsuke of a man and boy resting against a tree trunk. (Bonham's) $310 £160

18th century Japanese ivory netsuke of Sennin. (King & Chasemore) $356 £180

18th century unsigned wood netsuke of Okame, 6.5cm. high. (King & Chasemore) $288 £150

19th century carved ivory netsuke, 4cm. wide. (King & Chasemore) $230 £120

19th century ivory netsuke of Ashinaga and Tenaga. (Christie's) $440 £226

Late 19th century carved ivory netsuke, signed, 4.5cm. high. (King & Chasemore) $346 £180

Carved ivory netsuke by Masayuki, early 19th century, 3.5cm. high. (King & Chasemore) $182 £95

Mid 19th century wood netsuke by Masakazu, 3.5cm. wide. (King & Chasemore) $691 £360

Early 19th century ivory netsuke. (Christie's) $418 £215

19th century ivory netsuke of the three heroes of Han. (Christie's) $330 £170

Mid 19th century ivory netsuke, signed Mitsusada. (Christie's) $2,640 £1,360

19th century ivory netsuke of a rat-catcher, signed Hansaku.(Christie's) $352 £181

18th century Japanese ivory netsuke of a Shoki. (King & Chasemore) $435 £220

Unsigned 19th century wood netsuke. (Christie's) $462 £238

18th century unsigned carved ivory netsuke, 7cm. high. (King & Chasemore) $288 £150

One of a pair of Liberty & Co. 'Tudric' pewter and enamel candlesticks, circa 1905, 16cm. high. (Sotheby's Belgravia) $343 £175

Liberty & Co. 'Tudric' pewter and enamel biscuit box and cover, 14cm. high, after 1903. (Sotheby's Belgravia) $294 £150

Large WMF pewter jardiniere, 32.5cm. wide, circa 1900. (Sotheby's Belgravia) $594 £300

Pewter Art Nouveau mirror frame, 49.5cm. high, German, circa 1900.(Sotheby's Belgravia) $1,188 £600

18th century German pewter alms dish, 15½in. diameter. (Christie's) $465 £240

WMF pewter mounted green glass decanter, circa 1900, 38.5cm. high.(Sotheby's Belgravia) $712 £360

18th century pewter lidded tankard. (Manchester Auction Mart) $196 £100

Attractive WMF pewter mirror, circa 1900, 50.5cm. high. (Sotheby's Belgravia) $520 £260

Late 18th century Scottish uncrested tappit-hen pewter measure, 12¼in. high. (Christie's)$213 £110

Liberty & Co. 'Tudric' pewter stand with glass liner, circa 1905, 16.5cm. high. (Sotheby's Belgravia) $297 £150

Liberty & Co. 'Tudric' pewter bowl with glass liner, circa 1905, 10.25cm. high. (Sotheby's Belgravia) $343 £175

Large Maurel Art Nouveau patinated metal jardiniere, circa 1900, 29cm. high.(Sotheby's Belgravia) $633 £320

WMF pewter candlestick, 26.25cm. high, circa 1900.(Sotheby's Belgravia) $673 £340

18th century pewter charger, 18in. diam. (Phillips) $237 £120

One of a pair of pewter mounted green glass decanters, circa 1900, 42.45cm. high. (Sotheby's Belgravia) $196 £100

Large WMF Art Nouveau pewter tureen and cover, circa 1900, 48cm. high.(Sotheby's Belgravia) $392 £200

Kayserzinn pewter jug, circa 1905, 26.75cm. high. (Sotheby's Belgravia) $245 £125

18th century French pewter pitchet, 11¼in. high. (Phillips) $1,656 £820

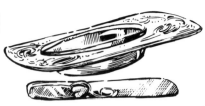

Early 19th century baluster pewter tankard, 6in. high. (Nottingham Auction Mart) $20 £10

Liberty & Co. pewter butter dish and knife in 'Tudric' style, after 1903, 17.75cm. long.(Sotheby's Belgravia) $156 £80

Early 18th century Swiss pewter Glockenkanne. (Sotheby's) $1,071 £520

Early 18th century Swiss pewter Stegkanne, 12¼in. high. (Sotheby's) $2,472 £1,200

Pewter cornucopia chariot with Cupid, circa 1880, 10in. high. (Gray's Antique Market) $96 £48

Irish gallon 'haystack' measure in pewter, circa 1860, 12in. high overall. (Sotheby's) $1,040 £520

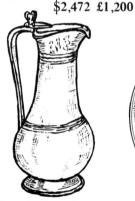

Late 18th century Normandy pichet by L. D. Gueroult, 31cm. high. (Sotheby's) $1,040 £520

Plain pewter olive dish, 20¾in. diam. (Edmiston's) $543 £280

Good Dutch pewter flagon, circa 1700, 22.5cm. high. (Sotheby's) $2,300 £1,150

Pewter coffee pot with domed cover, 10in. high.(Nottingham Auction Mart)
$44 £22

One of a pair of North German guild tankards, circa 1680, 15.2cm. high. (Sotheby's)
$1,600 £800

One of a pair of Victorian pewter egg cups, circa 1884. (Gray's Antique Market)
$44 £22

Very fine Charles I pewter flagon, circa 1630, 13¼in. high. (Sotheby's)
$3,000 £1,500

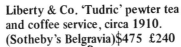

Liberty & Co. 'Tudric' pewter tea and coffee service, circa 1910. (Sotheby's Belgravia) $475 £240

Late 18th century Scottish crested tappit-hen pewter measure, 12½in. high. (Christie's)
$620 £320

Dutch pewter pear shaped flagon, circa 1721. (Sotheby's)
$1,400 £680

Late 18th century Scottish crested tappit-hen measure in pewter, 11¾in. high. (Sotheby's)
$860 £430

Silesian pewter pear shaped flagon, circa 1720. (Sotheby's)
$1,133 £550

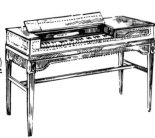

Square piano by John Broadwood, London, 1785, 5ft.2½in. long. (Sotheby's) $1,069 £540

Upright iron framed piano by John Brinsmead, London. (British Antique Exporters)$120 £60

Square piano by Frederick Beck, London, 1784, 4ft.10¼in. long. (Sotheby's) $1,386 £700

Steinway grand piano with full marquetry inlays. (Phillips) $12,928 £6,400

Upright oak Broadwood 'Manxman' piano, circa 1900, 56½in. wide. (Sotheby's Belgravia) $1,010 £500

Pleyel painted boudoir grand piano, circa 1890-95, 76in. x 53in. (Sotheby's Belgravia) $1,990 £1,000

Square piano by John Broadwood, London, 1795, 5ft.2½in. long. (Sotheby's) $1,980 £1,000

Miniature harmonium by George Jeffreys, circa 1870. (Christie's S. Kensington) $450 £230

Square piano by Goulding, Phipps, D'Almaine & Co., London, circa 1804, 5ft.5½in. long. (Sotheby's)$831 £420

Louis Phillipe piano by Pape & Co., Paris. (Phillips)
$7,920 £4,000

Street barrel piano, circa 1900, 3ft.4in. wide. (Sotheby's Belgravia)$1,584 £800

Important spinet by James Scoular, London circa 1765, length of back 73in. (Christie's)
$6,984 £3,600

Early 20th century Bechstein piano in mahogany case. (H. C. Chapman)
$6,080 £3,200

Grand pianoforte by Sebastian Erard, London and Paris, circa 1840, 94in. long. (Christie's)
$5,820 £3,000

Strohmenger painted satinwood baby grand piano and duet stool. (Sotheby's Belgravia)
$1,782 £900

Walnut cased half concert grand piano by Bosendorfer, Vienna, 84in. long. (Christie's)
$114,000 £60,000

Square piano by John Broadwood, London, 1799, 63½in. long. (Christie's)$970 £500

20th century red lacquer chinoiserie baby grand piano by Bluthner. (Sotheby's Belgravia)$2,522 £1,300

Small ivory ground
Shirvan prayer rug, 4ft.
x 3ft.2in. (King &
Chasemore) $1,036 £540

Kashan pictorial rug,
circa 1900.(Sotheby's)
$34,340 £17,000

Patou rug, circa
1900, 8ft.10in. x
5ft.9in. (Sotheby's)
$194 £100

Talish rug, circa
1900, 7ft.3in. x
3ft.7in. (Sotheby's)
$815 £420

Rare Kashan silk 'Art Deco'
pictorial rug, circa 1925, 5ft.
10in. x 5ft. (Sotheby's)
$25,560 £13,500

Dark blue ground
Shirvan palace strip,
10ft. x 4ft. (King &
Chasemore)
$2,688 £1,400

Ghom rug in good con-
dition, circa 1950, 7ft.
x 4ft.8in. (Sotheby's)
$1,396 £720

Erivan prayer rug, circa
1930, 5ft.3in. x 3ft.
(Sotheby's) $698 £360

Ghashghai carpet, in good
condition, 9ft.10in. x 6ft.
9in. (Sotheby's)
$2,231 £1,150

Fine quality Chond-
zorek antique rug.
(King & Chasemore)
$2,496 £1,300

Tekke Engsi rug
with fringe. (E. J.
Brook)
$2,328 £1,200

Kerman rug, circa
1900, 7ft. x 4ft.7in.
(Sotheby's)
$1,164 £600

Good Kashmir rug,
modern, 7ft.7in. x
4ft.6in. (Sotheby's)
$1,008 £520

Fine pictorial Kashan
rug, 4ft.2in. x 3ft.5in.
(King & Chasemore)
$2,880 £1,500

One of a pair of Kashan
rugs in superb condition,
7ft. x 4ft. (King & Chasemore) $4,608 £2,400

One of a pair of Kashan
rugs, 7ft. x 4ft.5in.
(King & Chasemore)
$4,224 £2,200

Tabriz rug, circa 1930,
6ft.3in. x 4ft.7in.
(Sotheby's $1,319 £680

One of a pair of fine
Kirman Lauer rugs,
7ft. x 4ft. (King &
Chasemore)
$8,832 £4,600

563

Turkestan rug, 6ft.3in. x 4ft.3in. (Worsfolds) $303 £150

Caucasian rug with dark blue field. (Drewatt, Watson & Barton) $3,069 £1,550

Fine quality Anatolian prayer rug, 6ft. x 4ft.2in. (King & Chasemore) $1,019 £520

Cabristan corridor carpet, 8ft.6in. x 4ft. 4in. (King & Chasemore) $901 £460

Fine late 16th century Feuilles-de-Chaux Audenarde tapestry. (King & Chasemore) $29,760 £15,500

Finely woven Nain rug, 4ft.8in. x 3ft.6in. (Messenger, May & Baverstock)$1,939 £960

Pinde Bokhara rug, 6ft.11½in. x 4ft.7in. (Geering & Colyer) $764 £390

Hereke silk and metal-thread prayer rug, 3ft.3in. x 2ft. 2in. (Sotheby's) $980 £500

Karabagh rug with red field and ivory border, 96in. long. (Sotheby's N. York) $2,100 £1,105

Fine Tabriz rug slightly worn, 7ft.2in. x 4ft. 7in. (Messenger, May & Baverstock)$1,757 £870

Kazak prayer rug, 71in. x 38in. (Humberts, King & Chasemore) $3,325 £1,750

Fringed and bordered off-white ground Shirvan rug, 6ft.5in. x 4ft. 5in. (Lalonde Bros. & Parham) $606 £300

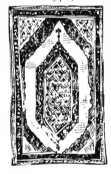

Tabriz carpet, circa 1900, 17ft.7in. x 12ft.6in.(Sotheby's) $5,880 £3,000

Extremely rare rug, a Tekke Khalyk. (Phillips) $8,820 £4,500

Kazak rug with tile red field, 6ft.6in. x 4ft.2in. (King & Chasemore) $904 £480

Persian silk rug, 1.8m. x 1.24m. (Christie's) $29,700 £15,000

Sarough rug, circa 1900, 5ft. x 3ft.4in. (Sotheby's) $1,067 £550

Unusual Kashan prayer rug, circa 1940, 4ft.10in. x 3ft.4in. (Sotheby's) $1,313 £650

Japanese carved Shibayama and ivory figure, circa 1900, 15.5cm. high. (King & Chasemore) $585 £290

Japanese Shibayama and silver filigree tray, circa 1900, 30cm. wide. (King & Chasemore) $2,424 £1,200

One of a pair of Shibayama and enamelled silver vases, circa 1900, Japanese, 27cm. high. (King & Chasemore) $2,376 £1,200

Shibayama and lacquer tsuba, signed, 4½in. high. (Burrows & Day) $3,131 £1,550

Fine quality Japanese Shibayama incense burner. (Christie's S. Kensington) $2,592 £1,350

Shibayama box and cover, signed Masasada, 3¼in. wide.(Burrows & Day) $3,131 £1,550

Lacquer vase, with Shibayama panels, 14¼in. high.(Sotheby's Belgravia) $864 £450

Late 19th century silver filigree and Shibayama tray. (King & Chasemore) $1,766 £920

Shibayama, gold lacquer and silver vase, signed Masayuki, 10in. high. (Burrows & Day) $3,030 £1,500

Trumans enamelled pub sign 'The Flying Eagle', circa 1945, 3ft.6in. high. (Sotheby's Belgravia) $13 £7

Good 'JRDC' enamel car radiator shield, circa 1930, 3in. long. (Sotheby's Belgravia) $118 £60

Rare incised grey slate Bass Ale advertisement, circa 1890, 30in. high. (Christopher Sykes) $172 £87

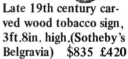

Good glass sign for Stower's Lime Juice, circa 1915, 39in. long. (Sotheby's Belgravia) $316 £160

Carved wood tobacconist's sign, circa 1750, 2ft.5½in. high.(Sotheby's Belgravia) $527 £265

Late 19th century carved wood tobacco sign, 3ft.8in. high.(Sotheby's Belgravia) $835 £420

Copper fire insurance wall plaque 'Sun Fire Office 1710', mounted on oak panel. (Christopher Sykes) $113 £58

Brass heraldic plaque on oak shield. (Christopher Sykes) $94 £48

'Motor Cycling Club' enamel badge, circa 1920, 3¼in. diam. (Sotheby's Belgravia) $108 £55

BASKETS

George III octagonal silver footed sweetmeat basket, London, 1794, by Robert Hennell. (Parsons, Welch & Cowell)
$514 £260

Victorian silver dessert basket, London, 1894, 26½oz. (Parsons, Welch & Cowell) $534 £270

George III boat shaped cake basket by Paul Storr, London, 1802, 30oz.12dwt.(Sotheby's) $2,910 £1,500

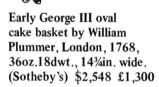

George III oval cake basket, 12½in. wide, by Richard Morton & Co., Sheffield, 1777, 23oz.8dwt.(Sotheby's) $1,212 £600

George III pierced silver basket by Robert Hennell, 1786, 6oz. (Phillips)$626 £310

Early George III oval cake basket by William Plummer, London, 1768, 36oz.18dwt., 14¾in. wide. (Sotheby's) $2,548 £1,300

German WMF silvered metal oval basket in Art Nouveau manner, 10in. wide.(Burrows & Day) $178 £90

George III swing-handled sugar basket, circa 1765, 10cm. high. (Phillips) $161 £85

Victorian silver fruit bowl by Joseph Angell, London, 1835, 13½in. diameter, 37oz. (Nottingham Auction Mart) $1,028 £530

George IV shaped oval cake basket by James Fray, Dublin, 1824, 50oz., 13¾in. wide. (Sotheby's Ireland) $1,136 £580

Victorian dessert basket, embossed and chased, 14in. long, London, 1894, 26½oz. (Parsons, Welch & Cowell) $534 £270

Early 19th century German oval sugar vase on foot, 7oz. 10dwt.(Phillips) $252 £125

George IV oval cake basket by James Fray, Dublin, 1821, 13¾in. wide. (Sotheby's) $2,525 £1,250

Small George III pierced silver basket by Robert Hennell, 1787, 4oz. (Phillips) $585 £290

George IV shaped oval cake basket, 13½in. wide, by Kirkby Waterhouse & Co., Sheffield, 1821, 38oz. 12dwt. (Sotheby's) $1,050 £520

George III boat shaped sweetmeat basket by Hester Bateman, London, 1784, 5½in. wide, 5oz. (Sotheby's) $1,332 £680

Silver basket, 1901, 16in. high. (Gray's Antique Market) $515 £255

Unusual George III hexagonal fruit basket, London, 1809, 10¾in. wide, 23oz.10dwt.(Sotheby's) $540 £270

George III cylindrical
beaker by Joseph
Creswell, London,
1773, 4in. high, 7oz.
2dwt. (Sotheby's)
$606 £300

Silver Groningen
beaker, circa 1650.
(Phillips)
$3,839 £1,900

Dutch beaker, 4½in.
high, circa 1636, 3oz.
17dwt. (Christie's)
$5,404 £2,800

18th century Swedish
parcel gilt beaker by
Erik Lemon, Uppsale,
7¾in. high, 8oz.14dwt.
(Sotheby's)$873 £450

Early 18th century parcel
gilt beaker and cover,
11.8cm. high, 155gm.
(Sotheby's Zurich)
$3,045 £1,538

18th century Swedish
parcel gilt beaker, 9in.
high, 16oz.6dwt.
(Sotheby's)
$1,360 £680

George III tapered cylin-
drical beaker by Thomas
Chawner, London, 3in.
high, 4oz.8dwt.
(Sotheby's) $594 £300

Silver gilt beaker by
Johann Mittnach,
Augsburg, 1736, 6½in.
high. (Sotheby's)
$2,871 £1,450

Inscribed parcel gilt
silver beaker, circa
1560. (Sotheby's
Zurich)
$112,743 £57,522

George I brandy saucepan by Erasmus Cope, Dublin, 1717, 1¾in. high, 4oz. (Sotheby's Ireland) $772   £390

Large George IV brandy saucepan and cover by James Scott, Dublin, 1824, 5½in. high, 21oz. 10dwt. (Sotheby's Ireland) $1,148   £580

George II large saucepan by William Kidney, London, 1737, 4¾in. high, 37oz.12dwt. (Sotheby's) $1,386   £700

BOTTLES

Four silver medicine bottles sold with another bottle. (Christie's) $120   £61

Five silver medicine bottles with matching stoppers. (Christie's) $150   £77

BUCKLES

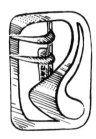

Rectangular Art Nouveau silver buckle, London, 1902, 5.5cm. wide. (Sotheby's Belgravia) $59   £30

Silver belt buckle, 1892, 3¼in. long. (Gray's Antique Mews) $58   £29

Oval silver Art Nouveau buckle, London, 1901. (Sotheby's Belgravia) $63   £32

Chinese export silver
bowl, circa 1880.
(Gray's Antique Market) $277 £140

Silver fruit bowl and four
smaller bowls by John
Dixon & Sons, 1893,
180oz. (May, Whetter &
Grose) $2,475 £1,250

Early 20th century
silver bowl, 9¾in.
high, 34oz.12dwt.
(Sotheby's Belgravia)
              $787 £410

William III monteith
bowl by Robert Peake,
London, 1700, 50oz.
10dwt., 11in. diameter.
(Sotheby's)
         $8,400 £4,200

Large Victorian silver
punch bowl, 68oz.
(Russell, Baldwin &
Bright) $990 £500

Early 18th century
Italian circular basin,
13½in. diameter,
39oz.4dwt.(Sotheby's)
         $1,200 £600

William IV Scottish punch
bowl by Robert Gray,
Glasgow, 1832, 10in. diam.,
36oz.14dwt. (Sotheby's)
              $823 £420

Victorian two-handled oval
bowl, 15in. long, Glasgow,
1901, 78oz. (Christie's)
              $2,134 £1,100

George III Scottish
bowl, 6½in. diam.,
by Alexander Gaird-
ner, Edinburgh, 1767,
12oz.15dwt.(Sotheby's)
              $980 £500

George III Scottish circular bowl, by R. Gray & Son, Edinburgh, 1811, 8oz.8dwt., 5in. diam. (Sotheby's)
$1,078 £550

Silver gilt and shaded cloisonne enamel kovsh. (Christie's Geneva)
$17,773 £8,950

George II Scottish bowl by Harry Beathune, Edinburgh, 1731, 6in. diameter, 7oz.8dwt.(Sotheby's)
$823 £420

Indian silver rose-bowl on stand. (May, Whetter & Grose)
$99 £50

William Hutton & Sons Ltd. silver bowl, London, 1909, 20.5cm. diam. (Sotheby's Belgravia) $291 £150

Silver gilt bowl by Edward Farrell, 1820, 17in. wide. (Sotheby's)
$6,336 £3,200

James II bleeding bowl by T. G., London, 1688, 7in. wide, 5oz. 11dwt. (Sotheby's)
$2,156 £1,100

Squat silver sugar bowl by Abraham Pootholt and Jan van Giffen, 1779, 4in. high. (Sotheby's)
$2,871 £1,450

Large Chinese silver bowl, circa 1910, 96oz.14dwt. (Sotheby's Belgravia)
$768 £400

George II provincial
bowl by Jonathan Buck,
Limerick, circa 1740,
9oz., 5in. diam.
(Sotheby's Belgravia)
$1,980 £1,000

A set of three jardinieres,
one 19in., two 13¼in. wide,
131oz.10dwt. (Sotheby's)
$2,254 £1,150

18th century Dutch
brandy bowl, 9¾in.
wide, 7oz.15dwt.
(Sotheby's)
$2,020 £1,000

George III circular sugar
bowl by Matthew West,
Dublin, circa 1780,
5½in. diam., 5oz.10dwt.
(Sotheby's Ireland)
$509 £260

William IV sweetmeat
bowl, London, 1831,
16oz.13dwt., 4½in.
high. (Sotheby's)
$808 £400

George II circular sugar
bowl by Richard Williams,
Dublin, circa 1752, 5in.
diam., 6oz.10dwt.
(Sotheby's Ireland)
$490 £250

George III circular bowl
by John Laughlin, Dublin,
circa 1750, 18oz., 7in.
diam. (Sotheby's Ireland)
$1,881 £950

Gilt metal Art Nouveau
jardiniere, German, circa
1900, 72cm. wide.
(Sotheby's Belgravia)
$698 £360

20th century silver
metal bowl, 11in.
high, 44oz.16dwt.
(Sotheby's Belgravia)
$691 £360

Early 18th century
German shaped oval
sugar box and cover,
3¾in. wide, 5oz.1dwt.
(Sotheby's)
    $1,358 £700

Burmese silver coloured
metal box, circa 1900,
18in. long. (Sotheby's
Belgravia) $576 £300

Dutch silver tobacco
box by H. Kuilenburg,
1849, 5oz.17dwt., 5in.
wide. (Sotheby's)
    $940 £470

Charles II circular
box, 2in. diam.,
London, 1684.
(Sotheby's)
    $1,227 £620

Goldsmiths and Silversmiths
silver box, 1903, 2¾in.
long. (Gray's Antique Mews)
    $125 £62

Late 17th century oval
tobacco box, 4in. wide,
5oz.13dwt. (Sotheby's)
    $1,136 £580

South African oval
sugar box and cover,
circa 1800, 8oz.13dwt.
(Christie's)
    $1,448 £750

Rare Elizabethan silver spice
casket by T. B., 23oz.
(Christie's)
    $79,200 £40,000

18th century Dutch
oval tobacco box,
1779, 15oz.12dwt.,
5¾in. high.(Sotheby's)
    $3,686 £1,900

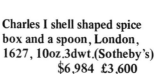

18th century German oval sugar box, 5½in. wide, 5oz.13dwt. (Sotheby's)$1,900 £950

Charles I shell shaped spice box and a spoon, London, 1627, 10oz.3dwt.(Sotheby's) $6,984 £3,600

George I spherical soap box, by Edward Feline, London, 1721, 5oz.3dwt.(Sotheby's) $2,522 £1,300

Queen Anne oval tobacco box by Edward Cornock, London, 1709, 3¾in. wide, 3oz.16dwt. (Sotheby's) $1,568 £800

20th century chest of drawers in silver coloured metal, 4½in. high.(Sotheby's Belgravia) $730 £380

Small silver counter box, circa 1650, with pull-off cover. (Bonham's) $1,545 £750

Early 18th century circular covered box, 2¼in. diameter. (Sotheby's)$543 £280

William IV silver gilt casket, by Edward Farrell, London, 1835, 6in. wide.(Sotheby's) $4,312 £2,200

17th century Dutch silver and enamel spice box, 3.5cm. high. (Sotheby's) $233 £120

One of a pair of George III silver gilt three-light candelabra by John Schofield, London, 1795, 17½in. high, 125oz. (Sotheby's) $13,968 £7,200

Unusual Regency five-light candelabrum by Edward Farrell, London, 1819, 30in. high, 463oz. (Christie's) $10,450 £5,304

Old Sheffield plate candelabrum, 1825, 27in. high. (Gray's Antique Mews) $1,414 £700

One of a pair of Sheffield plated three-light candelabra. (Russell, Baldwin & Bright) $297 £150

Silver centrepiece by Barnard & Sons, 1838, 61oz. (Sotheby's Belgravia) $1,575 £780

One of a pair of candelabra, 2ft.4in. high. (Messenger, May & Baverstock) $927 £450

One of a pair of two-branch three-light silver candelabra, Sheffield, 1901, 52cm. high.(King & Chasemore) $2,189 £1,100

Stylish German six-light candelabrum, circa 1910, 57cm. high, in silver coloured metal.(Sotheby's Belgravia) $5,148 £2,600

William IV candelabrum by E., J. & W. Barnard, London, 1834, 26¾in. high, 174oz. 7dwt. (Sotheby's) $4,312 £2,200

One of a pair of Continental 19th century table candlesticks, 9in. high, 20½oz. (Parsons, Welch & Cowell) $653 £330

One of a pair of George II cast table candlesticks by John Cafe, 1758, 40oz., 10in. high. (Neales) $1,373 £680

One of a pair of George III table candlesticks by Elizabeth Cooke, London, 1767, 13¾in. high. (Sotheby's) $1,552 £800

One of two early George III table candlesticks by William Cafe, London 1765, 46oz. 11dwt. (Sotheby's) $1,764 £900

A pair of silver gilt caryatid candlesticks with matching candelabrum, by John Parker and William Pitts, 151oz. (Nottingham Auction Mart) $9,504 £4,800

One of a pair of George II cast rococo candlesticks. (Parsons, Welch & Cowell) $3,030 £1,500

One of a set of four small table candlesticks by William Gould, 1732, 44oz. (Christie's) $11,716 £5,800

One of a pair of James Dixon & Sons large silver candlesticks, Sheffield, 1918, 30.5cm. high. (Sotheby's Belgravia) $693 £350

One of a pair of George II table candlesticks by Thomas Parr, London, 1741, 33oz.17dwt. (Sotheby's) $2,813 £1,450

One of a set of four table candlesticks, 12in. high, London, 1913, 69oz. (Parsons, Welch & Cowell)
$1,702 £860

One of a pair of William and Mary candlesticks by F.S.S., London, 1690, 4½in. high, 16oz.8dwt. (Sotheby's)
$7,448 £3,800

One of a pair of WMF electroplated candlesticks, circa 1900, 27cm. high.(Sotheby's Belgravia) $336 £170

One of a pair of George IV beaded candlesticks. (King & Chasemore)
$1,034 £520

Set of four table candlesticks and matching candelabrum, London, 1881-1883. (Messenger, May & Baverstock) $2,424 £1,200

One of two Cooper Bros. & Sons Ltd. silver candlesticks, 19cm. high, 1903. (Sotheby's Belgravia)
$504 £260

One of a set of four William IV rococo style silver candlesticks by John Watson, Sheffield, 1835. (King & Chasemore) $2,985 £1,500

One of a pair of William III wall sconces by Martin Stockar, 1701, 30oz. (Christie's)
$83,160 £42,000

One of a pair of George III telescopic pillar candlesticks by J. Rowbotham & Co., Sheffield, 1808. (Burrows & Day)
$633 £320

One of a pair of George II table candlesticks by J. Hyatt and C. Semore, London, 1759, 60oz.8dwt., 11½in. high. (Sotheby's) $3,298 £1,700

One of a pair of George II table candlesticks by John Cafe, London, 1751, 10¾in. high, 45oz. 17dwt. (Sotheby's) $2,037 £1,050

One of a pair of George II table candlesticks by John Quantock, London, 8in. high, 25oz.8dwt. (Sotheby's) $1,591 £820

One of a pair of George II table candlesticks by Thos. England, London, 8in. high, 34oz.2dwt. (Sotheby's Belgravia) $2,716 £1,400

One of a pair of George III table candlesticks by John Roberts & Co., Sheffield, 1808, 22in. high.(Sotheby's) $1,411 £720

One of a pair of George III candlesticks, by John Carter, 1769, 12in. high. (Phillips) $707 £350

One of a set of four candlesticks in the 17th century style, London, 1913, 12in. high, 69oz. (Parsons, Welch & Cowell) $1,702 £860

One of a pair of 18th century Austrian table candlesticks, 19oz. 6¾in. high.(Sotheby's) $1,500 £750

George II silver taperstick.(Parsons, Welch & Cowell) $504 £260

One of four telescopic table candlesticks, Sheffield, 1811-23, 11in. high.(Sotheby's) $2,300 £1,150

George II silver taperstick by William Shaw and William Priest, 4½in. high. (Parsons, Welch & Cowell) $485 £250

George II taperstick by Wm. Paradise, London, 1730, 3oz. 3dwt., 4in. high. (Sotheby's) $728 £375

One of a pair of 19th century Continental candlesticks, 9in. high, 20½oz.(Parsons, Welch & Cowell) $653 £330

A pair of table candlesticks by L. A. Crichton, London, 10¼in. high, 1921. (Sotheby's) $627 £320

George II silver taperstick. (Parsons, Welch & Cowell)$504 £260

One of a pair of George II cast table candlesticks by John Cafe, 1756, 41oz., 10in. high. (Neales) $1,616 £800

One of a pair of silver candlesticks, London, 1894.(Christie's S. Kensington)$455 £230

One of a set of four William IV table candlesticks.(Russell, Baldwin & Bright) $2,079 £1,050

Early 18th century octagonal caster by Charles Adam, London, 8¼in. high, 12oz. 14dwt. (Sotheby's) $1,000 £500

Set of three George III casters by John Delmester, London, 1762, 18oz.8dwt.(Sotheby's) $1,500 £750

Dutch vase shaped fluted caster by Reynier de Haan, 1756, 16oz.4dwt. (Christie's) $5,238 £2,700

George III baluster caster by James Warner, Cork, circa 1790, 5¾in. high, 3oz. (Sotheby's Ireland) $1,069 £540

A pair of George III Scottish casters, 4in. high, by Robert Keay, Perth, 1807, 8oz. (Sotheby's) $1,019 £520

George I vase shaped caster, Dublin, 1717, 9oz., 7¼in. high. (Sotheby's Ireland) $1,148 £580

George I octagonal caster by Glover Johnson, London, 1717, 6oz.13dwt. (Sotheby's) $1,313 £650

Set of Edwardian pepper casters, 1906, Birmingham. (Alfie's Antique Market) $161 £80

One of a set of three George III silver casters by Wm. Davie, Edinburgh, 1770, 14oz.(Sotheby's) $892 £460

Victorian silver centre-
piece, 19in. high, circa
1860. (Nottingham
Auction Mart)
$1,715 £875

George III epergne by Thomas
Pitts, London, 1788, 16in.
high, 124oz. (Sotheby's)
$4,656 £2,400

George IV centrepiece
by Philip Rundell, Lon-
don, 14¼in. high, 110oz.
14dwt. (Sotheby's)
$2,352 £1,200

Unusual Victorian cran-
berry glass vase with
plated mounts, 11¾in.
high. (Gray's Antique
Mews) $78 £38

Silver plated epergne,
circa 1825, 15½in.
high. (Sotheby's)
$594 £300

WMF Art Nouveau Ger-
man silver centrepiece,
1925, 30in. high.(Gray's
Antique Mews)
$1,386 £700

WMF Art Nouveau centre-
piece, 14½in. high, circa
1900. (Gray's Antique
Mews) $707 £350

One of a pair of silver
fruit stands by John
Hunt, London, 1858,
10½in. high.(Bonham's)
$1,980 £1,100

George III silver epergne.
(Parsons, Welch &
Cowell) $2,272 £1,125

George III chamber candlestick by R. & S. Hennell, London, 1802, 10oz., 5¼in. diameter. (Sotheby's) $363 £180

One of a pair of George III chamber candlesticks, London, 1814, 40oz. 14dwt., sold with snuffers. (Sotheby's) $3,200 £1,600

One of a pair of chambersticks and snuffers by Henry Chawner and John Emes. (H. C. Chapman) $1,008 £520

George IV taperstick in the form of a chamber candlestick. (Sotheby Bearne) $646 £320

A pair of unusual Hukin & Heath chamber candlesticks, 17oz. (Sotheby's Belgravia) $505 £250

George IV silver chamber candlestick, Sheffield, 1823, 8oz.15dwt. (Geering & Colyer) $464 £230

Small George III chamber candlestick by Wm. Sharp, London, 1819, 5oz.7dwt., 4¼in. diam. (Sotheby's) $752 £380

One of a pair of George II chamber candlesticks by Phillips Garden, London, 1742, 5¾in. diam. 24oz. 12dwt. (Sotheby's) $1,980 £1,000

Unusual George IV chamber candlestick, London, 1829, 6oz.12dwt., 4in. high. (Sotheby's) $1,100 £550

Eggshell lacquer modernist cigarette case, 11.6cm. wide, late 1920's. (Sotheby's Belgravia) $990 £500

Silver and enamel cigarette case, 1925, 8.4cm. wide. (Sotheby's Belgravia) $396 £200

Eggshell lacquer cigarette case, 1920's, 8.5cm. high. (Sotheby's Belgravia) $346 £175

Small Liberty & Co. silver and enamel vesta case, Birmingham, 1902, 4.75cm. high.(Sotheby's Belgravia) $79 £40

German cigarette case, circa 1910, 10.5cm. long. (Sotheby's Belgravia) $100 £52

Silver Art Nouveau cigarette case, Birmingham, 1905, 9cm. high.(Sotheby's Belgravia) $196 £100

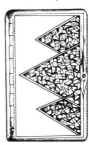

Silver and eggshell lacquer cigarette case, 8.2cm. wide, 1926.(Sotheby's Belgravia)$396 £200

Silver and enamel cigarette case, 8cm. wide, Glasgow, 1926. (Sotheby's Belgravia) $198 £100

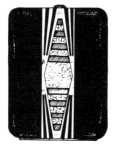

Eggshell lacquer modernist cigarette case, late 1920's, 11.6cm. wide. (Sotheby's Belgravia) $396 £200

CHOCOLATE POTS

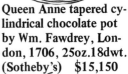

George III baluster chocolate pot, London, 11in. high, 30oz.6dwt. (Sotheby's)
$2,940 £1,500

Rare George III baluster chocolate pot by Richard Williams, Dublin, circa 1770, 10in. high, 36oz. (Sotheby's Ireland)
$5,148 £2,600

Queen Anne tapered cylindrical chocolate pot by Wm. Fawdrey, London, 1706, 25oz.18dwt. (Sotheby's) $15,150 £7,500

CLARET JUGS

Victorian cut glass claret jug with silver mount, Sheffield, 1871, 28cm. high. (King & Chasemore) $815 £410

Claret jug, Sheffield, 1919, 9in. high. (Burrows & Day)
$326 £165

Walker and Hall silver mounted claret jug, London, 1883, 25cm. high. (Sotheby's Belgravia)
$396 £200

Cut glass and silver claret jug, 1902. (Alfie's Antique Market)$292 £145

John Foligno claret jug, London, 1806. (Bonham's)$969 £480

One of a pair of silver mounted cut glass wine jugs, German, circa 1860, sold with another. (Sotheby's Zurich)
$1,287 £650

One of a pair of George IV wine coasters by S. C. Younge & Co., Sheffield, 7in. diam. (Sotheby's)
$1,274
£650

One of a pair of George IV silver gilt wine coasters, London, 1826. (Humberts, King & Chasemore)
$1,978 £1,020

One of a set of four George III silver gilt wine coasters, 5½in. diam., by D. Scott and B. Smith. (Sotheby's)
$10,000 £5,000

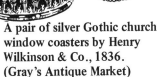

One of a set of three George III silver coasters, by R. Hennell, London, 1780.(King & Chasemore)
$1,254 £640

A pair of silver Gothic church window coasters by Henry Wilkinson & Co., 1836. (Gray's Antique Market)
$1,515 £750

One of a pair of George III wine coasters by Wm. Eaton, London, 1813, 6¾in. diam.(Sotheby's)
$1,100 £550

One of a pair of George III wine coasters by R. Hennell, London, 1793, 4½in. diam. (Sotheby's)
$1,411 £720

One of a pair of William IV wine coasters, 5½in. diam., by Edward Farrell, London, 1835. (Sotheby's)$1,212 £600

One of a set of four George III circular pierced coasters by R. Hennell, 12.5cm. diam. (Phillips)
$2,060 £1,020

One of a pair of George IV silver coasters by John and Thomas Settle, London, 1825, 6½in. diam. (Nottingham Auction Mart) $485 £250

Silver wine wagon, by R. Hennell, 1838, 14½in. wide. (Christie's)
$2,481 £1,250

One of a pair of George III coasters by Wm. Bateman, London, 1820. (Drewatt, Watson & Barton)$900 £500

Italian fluted pear shaped coffee pot, 10½in. high, circa 1775, 24oz.(Christie's) $2,522 £1,300

Coffee pot by Thomas Wirgman, London, 1751, 26oz. (Drewatt, Watson & Barton) $2,277 £1,150

George II baluster coffee pot by Fuller White, London, 1758, 10½in. high, 27oz.8dwt. (Sotheby's) $2,000 £1,000

George II baluster coffee pot by Shaw & Priest, London, 1757, 9¾in. high, 26oz. 4dwt. (Sotheby's) $1,785 £920

Mid 18th century Old Sheffield plate coffee pot, 11in. high. (Parsons, Welch & Cowell) $361 £190

George III coffee pot, London, 1768, 38oz., 13in. high.(Messenger, May & Baverstock) $828 £410

George III silver coffee pot, London, 1776, 27oz. (Butler, Hatch & Waterman) $1,649 £850

Part of a Victorian four-piece tea and coffee set, Exeter, 1850, 71oz.2dwt. (Sotheby's) $1,552 £800

George III silver coffee pot by Young and Jackson, London, 1774, 11¼in. high. (Woolley & Wallis) $2,673 £1,350

George III silver coffee pot. (Vidler & Co.) $1,568 £800

George III hot water jug by Charles Wright, London, 1775, 15oz., 9½in. high.(Nottingham Auction Mart) $388 £200

George III baluster coffee pot by James Stamp, London, 1772, 30oz.16dwt., 10½in. high. (Sotheby's) $1,843 £950

William III coffee pot by Isaac Dighton, London, 1700, 19oz., 9¼in. high. (Sotheby's) $4,400 £2,200

George II tapering cylindrical coffee pot, 13in. high, by John Swift, London, 1751, 55oz.19dwt. (Sotheby's) $5,684 £2,900

Fine late Georgian hot water jug, London, 1831, 27½oz., 10½in. high. (Locke & England) $848 £420

George II tapering cylindrical coffee pot by Charles Sprage, London, 1736, 9½in. high, 26oz. 19dwt. (Sotheby's) $1,862 £950

Turkish silver coloured metal coffee pot, circa 1900, 23oz.14dwt., 27cm. high.(Sotheby's) $254 £130

French Empire vase shaped coffee pot, Paris, circa 1800, 26.3cm. high, 840gm. (Sotheby's Zurich) $1,639 £828

George II silver coffee pot by Richard Beale, London, 1731, 15½oz., 20.5cm. high.(King & Chasemore)$1,358 £700

George IV small coffee pot by Charles Price, London, 1815, 7in. high, 23oz.16dwt. (Sotheby's)$712 £360

Mid 19th century Sheffield plate coffee pot. (Parsons, Welch & Cowell) $349 £180

William IV Scottish baluster coffee pot, 11½in. high, by J. McKay, 31oz.4dwt. (Sotheby's)$980 £500

George III coffee pot by R. & D. Hennell, 1795, 12¾in. high, 25oz.4dwt.(Sotheby's) $1,784 £900

Sheffield plate coffee pot, circa 1760.(Parsons, Welch & Cowell) $361 £190

George III baluster coffee pot by John Laughlin, Dublin, 12½in. high, 31oz. 10dwt. (Sotheby's Ireland) $2,058 £1,050

George III Scottish coffee pot by Ker & Dempster, Edinburgh, 1763. (Sotheby's) $1,136 £580

George I silver coffee pot by Thomas Farrer, London, 1722.(Humberts, King & Chasemore) $7,920 £4,000

Victorian pear shaped coffee pot.(Russell, Baldwin & Bright) $712 £360

George III baluster coffee pot, London, 1770, 11¼in. high, 28oz.12dwt. (Sotheby's) $1,623 £820

George II embossed silver coffee pot.(Russell, Baldwin & Bright) $950 £480

Swedish coffee pot, circa 1832, 25oz. (McCartney, Morris & Barker) $874 £460

Liberty & Co. silver coffee pot, 24.5cm. high, circa 1900. (Sotheby's) $329 £170

Victorian coffee pot by W. & J. Barnard, London, 1855, 30¼oz. (Drewatt, Watson & Barton) $1,584 £800

Vase shaped fluted coffee jug by Ambrose Boxwell, Dublin, circa 1775, 27½oz. (Drewatt, Watson & Barton) $1,306 £660

George III vase shaped coffee pot, London, 1780, 30oz.9dwt., 13½in. high.(Sotheby's) $1,372 £700

George II coffee pot by John Pero, 15oz., 18.5cm. high.(King & Chasemore) $1,048 £540

George III baluster coffee pot by C. Wright, London, 1772, 11½in. high, 29oz.16dwt. (Sotheby's)$1,919 £950

George III baluster coffee pot, 11in. high, 1765, 33oz. 2dwt. (Sotheby's) $3,333 £1,650

George II tapered cylindrical coffee pot by Gabriel Sleath, circa 1745, 9in. high, 22oz. 5dwt.(Sotheby's) $1,313 £650

George II tapering cylindrical coffee pot by T. Farren, London, 1738, 22oz.3dwt., 9¼in. high. (Sotheby's)$1,485 £750

George III coffee jug on lampstand by R. Garrard, London, 1818-19, 11½in. high, 38oz.11dwt. (Sotheby's)$1,500 £750

George II tapering cylindrical coffee pot by R. Gurney & Co., London, 8¾in. high, 27oz.1dwt. (Sotheby's)$2,156 £1,100

George III coffee jug by Paul Storr, London, 1792, 10in. high, 16oz. 16dwt. (Sotheby's) $2,450 £1,250

George III vase shaped coffee jug by G. Smith, 1790, 12¼in. high, 28oz. 3dwt. (Sotheby's) $2,058 £1,050

George III baluster coffee pot by J. Robins, London, 1788, 23oz. 9dwt., 11½in. high. (Sotheby's)$1,515 £750

Early 19th century Russian milk jug, 6in. high, circa 1825, 12oz. 8dwt. (Sotheby's)
$529 £270

George II helmet shaped milk jug, Dublin, circa 1748, 8oz., 4½in. high. (Sotheby's Ireland)
$1,069 £540

George I pitcher cream jug by Mungo Yorstoun, 1714, 7oz.17dwt., 4½in. high. (Sotheby's Belgravia) $2,970 £1,500

George III helmet shaped cream jug, 5¾in. high, London, 1793, 3oz.13dwt. (Sotheby's)$376 £190

Sugar bowl and cream jug by Thomas Wright, London, 1811, 13¼oz. (Parsons, Welch & Cowell)
$475 £240

18th century German milk jug, 5in. high, Hamburg, 1750, 6oz. 3dwt. (Sotheby's)
$504 £260

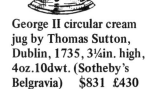

George II oval cream boat, 6in. wide, Newcastle, 1740, 6oz. (Sotheby's)
$1,148 £580

George III helmet shaped milk jug by Peter and Jonathan Bateman, 1790, 6in. high, 3oz.17dwt. (Sotheby's) $792 £400

George II circular cream jug by Thomas Sutton, Dublin, 1735, 3¼in. high, 4oz.10dwt. (Sotheby's Belgravia) $831 £430

CRUETS

Victorian silver cruet frame with eight cut glass bottles. (D. M. Nesbit & Co.
$989 £490

George III eggstand by William Elliott, London, 1814. (Drewatt, Watson & Barton) $798 £420

Jensen silver cruet, circa 1950-55. (Sotheby's Belgravia) $237 £120

George III four bottle decanter stand by Wm. Allen III, 10½in. high, sold with four wine labels. (Sotheby's)
$2,156 £1,100

Silver decanter stand by John Schofield, circa 1790. (Hy. Duke)
$621 £320

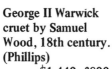

George II Warwick cruet by Samuel Wood, 18th century. (Phillips)
$1,440 £800

George II Warwick cruet frame by Samuel Wood, 1738, 33oz. (Christie's)
$1,728 £900

George III cruet frame by Paul Storr, 11½in. high, 31oz.1dwt., with six cut glass bottles. (Sotheby's)
$1,919 £950

George III pierced silver cruet stand, London, 1804, 16oz. (King & Chasemore)
$909 £450

594

18th century Channel Islands christening cup, 2¾in. high. (Parsons, Welch & Cowell)
$514 £260

A pair of silver gilt fox mask stirrup cups, Sheffield, 1786, 4¾in. long. (Lacy Scott)
$3,880 £2,000

Queen Anne provincial tumbler cup by John Langwith, York, 1708, 1¾in. high, 1oz. 18dwt. (Sotheby's)
$1,136 £580

Charles I wine cup, 7in. high, London, 1628, 10oz.13dwt. (Sotheby's)
$2,646 £1,350

George I Britannia silver cup and cover by Wm. Gamble, London, 1717, 29½oz., 24.5cm. high. (King & Chasemore)
$1,045 £500

One of a pair of George III wine cups by John Denziloe, London, 1783, 5½in. high, 13oz. 2dwt. (Sotheby's)
$1,078 £550

Silver gilt two-handled cup and cover by R. Garrard, 1812, 98oz. (Christie's)
$1,113 £580

William IV campana shaped cup and cover by C. Fox, London, 35oz.15dwt., 13¼in. high. (Sotheby's)
$548 £280

George III cup and cover by Roberts, Cadman & Co., Sheffield, 1805, 56oz.2dwt., 13¼in. high. (Sotheby's)$1,010 £500

18th century Norwegian parcel gilt tumbler cup, 1oz. 9dwt., 1¾in. high. (Sotheby's)$718 £370

17th century English silver caudle cup, 7½in. high.(Sotheby's) $7,760 £4,000

Late 19th century Russian cup shaped goblet, 4¼in. high, 5oz. 9dwt. (Geering & Colyer) $621 £320

George IV two-handled cup by John Bridge, London, 1825, 33oz. 13dwt., 8½in. high. (Sotheby's)$560 £280

W. C. Connell silver gilt two-handled cup, 1907, 21.5cm. high.(Sotheby's Belgravia) $504 £260

Large silver gilt two-handled presentation cup and cover, London, 1912, 129oz.(Messenger, May & Baverstock) $1,090 £540

George II two-handled cup by Wm. Atkinson, London, 1725, 4½in. high, 9oz.(Nottingham Auction Mart)$292 £150

One of a pair of George II wine cups by Solomon Hougham, London, 1800, 25oz.15dwt., 8½in. high. (Sotheby's) $960 £480

Silver loving cup by Hester Bateman, circa 1789. (Gray's Antique Mews) $653 £330

One of a pair of George III wine cups, by Walter Brind, London, 1781, 5½in. high, 12oz.19dwt. (Sotheby's)$1,100 £550

Rare 17th century German parcel gilt horn shaped cup, 13cm. high, 375gm. (Sotheby's Zurich) $15,230 £7,692

One of a pair of silver stemmed cups, Chester, 1905, 17.5cm. high.(Sotheby's Belgravia) $435 £220

George III two-handled cup and cover, 18½in. high, by John Robins, London, 1786, 117oz. 3dwt.(Sotheby's) $1,552 £800

Early 18th century German wager cup, 16.8cm. high, 190gm. (Sotheby's Zurich) $4,391 £2,218

George III silver gilt vase shaped two-handled cup and cover, by P. & W. Bateman, 1811, 107oz.(Christie's) $2,200 £1,150

T'ang dynasty silver gilt stem cup. (Sotheby's)$122,760 £62,000

Victorian silver two handled cup and cover by Eames & Barnard, London 1834, 30oz., 11in. high. (Nottingham Auction Mart) $627 £320

George III silver gilt cup, by John Emes, London, 1805, 8½in. high, 29oz.10dwt. (Sotheby's)$862 £440

One of a set of four George III oval entree dishes and covers by Paul Storr, 12½in. wide, 141oz.18dwt. (Sotheby's) $5,050 £2,500

Victorian silver gilt sweetmeat stand by Charles Fox, London, 1840, 19oz. (King & Chasemore) $808 £400

One of a set of six George III boat shaped dishes by Daniel Pontifex, London, 5¾in. wide, 18oz. 3dwt. (Sotheby's) $1,666 £850

One of two Victorian silver dishes, London, circa 1890, 28oz., 10in. diam. (Parsons, Welch & Cowell) $663 £353

Charles I two-handled oval sweetmeat dish, 6¾in. long, 2oz.15dwt. (Christie's) $1,746 £900

17th century German silver gilt circular dish, 10½in. diam., 7oz. 5dwt. (Sotheby's) $1,372 £700

Victorian silver muffin dish by J. McKay, Edinburgh, 1853, 21.5cm. diam., 19oz. (King & Chasemore) $267 £135

Good Kayserzinn meat dish and cover, 55cm. long, circa 1900. (Sotheby's Belgravia) $232 £120

Victorian Irish potato dish, Dublin, 1896, 10in. diam., 24oz. (Parsons, Welch & Cowell) $693 £350

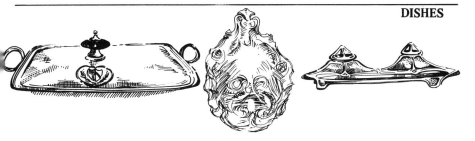

George III bacon dish
by Michael Plummer,
London, 1791, 14oz.,
11in. wide. (Sotheby's)
$1,575 £780

One of pair of Vic-
torian silver bon-bon
dishes by Garrard,
London, 1870, 27½oz.
(D. M. Nesbit & Co.)
$787 £390

Art Nouveau electro-
plated dish, circa 1900,
33.75cm. wide.
(Sotheby's Belgravia)
$118 £60

18th century East Euro-
pean parcel gilt dish and
cover, 10¾in. diameter,
22oz.5dwt. (Sotheby's)
$909 £450

German silver filigree
dish. (Alfie's Antique
Market) $76 £38

One of a pair of silver
gilt dishes, circa 1825.
(Humberts, King &
Chasemore)
$1,938 £1,020

One of two late 18th
century oval butter
dishes, 7½in. wide,
17oz.9dwt.
(Sotheby's)
$2,000 £1,000

One of a pair of George
III entree dishes with
plated covers by Henry
Nutting, London, 61oz.
12dwt., 12½in. wide.
(Sotheby's)
$1,485 £750

George III oval entree
dish and cover by
Thomas Daniel, Lon-
don, 1787, 49oz.18dwt.
(Sotheby's)
$1,287 £650

George III circular
vegetable dish and
cover by Paul Storr,
London, 1796, 107oz.
1dwt., 12¾in. diam.
(Sotheby's)$3,200 £1,600

Guild of Handicrafts
Ltd. single loop-han-
dle dish, London,
1905, 18cm. wide.
(Sotheby's Belgravia)
$792 £400

WMF silvered metal Art
Nouveau dish, 47cm.
wide, circa 1900.
(Sotheby's Belgravia)
$336 £170

One of a pair of Louis XV
oval shaped meat dishes by
Alexis Loir, Paris, 1744,
103oz. (Sotheby's)
$41,200 £20,000

WMF silvered metal
dish, circa 1900,
17.5cm. high.
(Sotheby's Belgravia)
$316 £160

One of a pair of Vic-
torian embossed and
chased dishes, Lon-
don, 1890, 10in.
diam., 28oz.(Parsons,
Welch & Cowell)
$663 £335

One of four George III
shaped oblong entree
dishes and covers, 12¼in.
wide, 270oz.(Sotheby's)
$3,686 £1,900

Austrian electroplated
dish, 17.5cm. high,
circa 1910-20.
(Sotheby's Belgravia)
$297 £150

One of a pair of entree
dishes and covers, circa
1810, 11¾in. wide.
(Sotheby's)$404 £200

One of four George IV shaped circular entree dishes and covers, 10in. diam., by Joseph Cradock, London, 1825, 177oz. (Sotheby's)
$3,686 £1,900

One of a pair of Victorian silver vegetable dishes on warming stands.(Christie's S. Kensington)
$1,386 £700

One of a pair of 18th century silver scallop shell butter dishes, Dublin, 9¾oz.(King & Chasemore)
$557 £290

George III oblong toasted cheese dish by Paul Storr, London, 1797, 9¼in. wide, 34oz.11dwt. (Sotheby's)$2,910 £1,500

WMF silvered metal dish, 26.25cm. wide, circa 1900. (Sotheby's Belgravia)
$396 £200

Silver gilt kovsh given by Empress Catherine II to a merchant. (Sotheby's Zurich)
$32,772 £16,224

One of a set of four plain oblong entree dishes and covers, by John Newburn, 1810, 245oz. (Christie's)
$485 £250

French Art Deco electroplated dish and cover, circa 1925, 17cm. wide. (Sotheby's Belgravia)
$297 £150

One of a pair of George III circular vegetable dishes and covers, 9¼in. diam., by Wakelin & Garrard, London, 1796, 64oz.12dwt.(Sotheby's)
$1,901 £980

Mid 16th century Moor's head spoon.
(Christie's) $543 £280

Elizabeth I seal top spoon, 1583.
(Clarke Gammon) $1,280 £660

Two of six scroll top dessert spoons by
Hester Bateman, 1784, 5oz. (Gray's
Antique Market) $643 £325

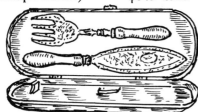

Silver fish slice and fork by Martin Hall
& Co., 1872. (Christie's S. Kensington)
                                      $228 £120

14th century Paris made spoon with
circular bowl.(Christie's)$388 £200

Guild of Handicrafts Ltd. silver butter
knife, circa 1900, 13.5cm. long.
(Sotheby's Belgravia) $329 £170

18th century Danish spoon, by Jens
Christensen, Copenhagen.(Sotheby's)
                                      $330 £170

Berry-top spoon by P. Honnoure,
Rouen, circa 1408.(Christie's)
                                  $7,372 £3,800

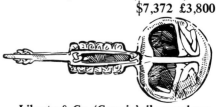

Liberty & Co. 'Cymric' silver and enamel spoon, 1901, 20.5cm. long.
(Sotheby's Belgravia) $980 £500

Part of a matched set of eighty-five
pieces of silver flatware.(Andrew
Sharp & Partners) $2,660 £1,400

Liberty & Co. 'Cymric' spoon in silver,
Birmingham, 1902, 16cm. long.
(Sotheby's Belgravia) $294 £150

17th century Norwegian parcel gilt
spoon by Jorgen Bleckman.(Sotheby's)
                                      $563 £290

17th century Scandinavian spoon, with engraved stem. (Sotheby's) $504 £260

17th century Norwegian spoon, by Oluf Jorgensen, Bergen.(Sotheby's) $563 £290

Maidenhead spoon, circa 1485. (Christie's) $3,686 £1,900

Mid 17th century parcel gilt and niello spoon, 19.5cm. long, 65gm.(Sotheby's Zurich) $1,756 £887

Part of a set of twelve close-plated dessert knives and forks by Walker & Hall, Sheffield.(Sotheby's)$235 £120

One of a set of twelve pairs of silver gilt and amber dessert knives and forks, mid 18th century.(Sotheby's) $1,552 £800

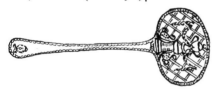

18th century Dutch fish slice, 4oz. 14dwt.(Sotheby's) $1,200 £600

Georg Jensen silver serving spoon and fork, circa 1920.(Christie's N. York) $300 £151

Rare Scottish disc-end spoon by John Kirkwood, Glasgow, circa 1600. (Sotheby's) $1,176 £600

Bubeniczek paper knife, silver coloured metal handle, Austrian, circa 1900, 32.75cm. long. (Sotheby's Belgravia) $396 £200

Scandinavian plique a jour silver spoon. (Christie's S. Kensington) $133 £70

Early 16th century Apostle's spoon, St. Philip.(Christie's) $6,984 £3,600

17th century silver gilt provincial baluster seal-top spoon by Jasper Radcliffe, Exeter, circa 1640. (Sotheby's) $1,274 £650

18th century South Italian boxwood handled knife, 33.5cm. long.(Sotheby's) $427 £220

Two from a set of twenty-four dessert knives and forks by William Chawner, London, 1829-30. (Sotheby's) $2,222 £1,100

17th century Scandinavian spoon, probably Danish. (Sotheby's) $485 £250

Set of four terminal silver serving spoons, circa 1900. (Alfie's Antique Market) $202 £100

Part of a George III crested hour glass pattern set of table silver by Wallis & Hayne, London, 116oz.10dwt. (Sotheby's) $2,828 £1,400

Cased silver gilt dessert set by Frederick Elkington, Birmingham, 1876. (Nottingham Auction Mart) $363 £180

Set of six silver seal-top spoons, 1560. (Christie's) $9,504 £4,800

Rare Mary I baluster knop spoon. (Phillips) $6,336 £3,200

Early 17th century apostle spoon, Carlisle, circa 1600. (Sotheby's) $727 £360

One of two James I apostle spoons, London, 1605. (Sotheby's)
$2,940 £1,500

Pair of George IV silver grape tongs by Mary and Charles Reilly, London, 1828, 3oz.7dwt. (Sotheby's) $282 £140

Fine Georg Jensen silver flatware service, circa 1910. (Christie's N. York)
$3,500 £1,767

Victorian silver table service of eighteen settings. (Spencer's) $4,850 £2,500

West Country 'Buddha Knop' spoon, circa 1640. (Sotheby's) $627 £320

Silver cheese scoop by Mary Chawner, 1840. (Christie's S. Kensington)
$142 £75

Early 17th century seal-top spoon, circa 1620, possibly Beccles. (Sotheby's)
$727 £360

Part of a canteen of cutlery, silver 227oz., one hundred and twenty-five pieces in all. (Phillips) £5,050 £2,500

Part of a silver gilt dessert service of sixty-two pieces. (Sotheby's)
$1,600 £800

Very rare Charles I horse's hoof terminal spoon. (Phillips) $3,564 £1,800

Silver Art Nouveau photograph frame, Birmingham, 1903, 22.5cm. high. (Sotheby's Belgravia) $294 £150

Heath and Middleton silver frame, Birmingham, 1904, 26.5cm. high. (Sotheby's Belgravia) $475 £240

Silver Art Nouveau photograph frame by J. & A. Zimmerman, 29cm. high, Birmingham, 1903. (Sotheby's Belgravia) $376 £190

One of two Liberty & Co. silver frames, Birmingham, 1905, 19.25cm. high. (Sotheby's Belgravia) $1,261 £650

WMF silvered metal mirror frame, circa 1910, 40.75cm. high. (Sotheby's Belgravia) $237 £120

Liberty & Co. silver and enamel frame, Birmingham, 1910, 27cm. high. (Sotheby's Belgravia) $435 £220

WMF silvered metal mirror frame, circa 1900, 37cm. high. (Sotheby's Belgravia) $910 £460

William Hutton & Sons Ltd., silver Art Nouveau frame, 20.5cm. high, London, 1903. (Sotheby's Belgravia) $686 £360

Ramsden and Carr silver and enamel frame, London, 1901, 23cm. high. (Sotheby's Belgravia) $686 £350

Channel Islands plain wine goblet, circa 1700, 5¾in. high, 7oz.3dwt. (Christie's)
$1,746 £900

William IV commemorative goblet, 6¾in. high, London, 1833. (Sotheby's) $543 £280

Elizabeth I provincial chalice by E. Coke, circa 1580, 6in. high, 6oz.14dwt.(Sotheby's)
$1,764 £900

Rare German gilt metal chalice dial by Marcus Purman, 1608, 12.4cm. high. (Christie's)
$46,560 £24,000

HONEY POTS

Silver mounted coconut shell goblet, 33cm. high, 402gm.(Sotheby's Zurich) $1,522 £769

One of a pair of George III campana-shaped silver goblets, by Joseph Angell, London, 1817, 23oz.6dwt., 6½in. high. (Sotheby's)
$1,300 £650

George III silver honey pot and stand by Paul Storr, 1797, 14oz. (Sotheby's)
$7,676 £3,800

Cut glass honey pot and stand with George III silver gilt mounts by Richard Cooke, London, 1800, 5½in. high. (Sotheby's)$2,000 £1,000

Silver gilt honey pot and matched stand by Paul Storr, 1798, 4¾in. high, 14oz. (Sotheby Bearne)
$7,038 £3,400

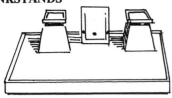

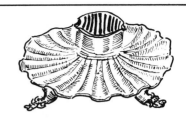

White onyx and lapis lazuli inkstand with silver mounts, London, 1922. (Alfie's Antique Market) $40 £20

George IV inkstand by Paul Storr, London, 1829, 9in. wide, 16oz.10dwt. (Sotheby's) $2,500 £1,250

Unusual silver and tortoiseshell travelling case, 18th century, 135mm. long, by Le Maire, Paris. (Sotheby's) $1,425 £720

George II rectangular inkstand, by Samuel Herbert & Co., London, 1758, 9¾in. wide, 20oz.8dwt. (Sotheby's) $1,040 £520

Silver inkstand, London, 1857, 5in. high. (Christie's S. Kensington) $285 £150

Early 19th century Portuguese inkstand, circa 1800, 1310gm., 31cm. wide. (Sotheby's Zurich) $877 £443

Small Victorian two-bottle inkstand, by Henry Wilkinson & Co., Sheffield, 1846, 12oz.6dwt., 8½in. long. (Sotheby's) $509 £260

19th century decorative desk set with boulle work. (Outhwaite & Litherland) $396 £200

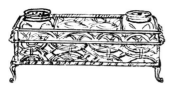

George II oblong inkstand by Samuel Herbert & Co., London, 1759, 6¾in. wide, 9oz.4dwt.(Sotheby's) $784 £400

Victorian shaped rectangular two-bottle inkstand, 11¾in. long, by Edward Barnard & Sons, London, 1872, 44oz.8dwt. (Sotheby's) $764 £390

Victorian silver inkstand, Birmingham, 1851, 19oz., 10½in. long. (Gray's Antique Mews) $762 £385

Victorian rectangular silver inkstand, 1893, 14¾oz. (Parsons, Welch & Cowell) $396 £200

Unusual silver inkstand, 8in. wide, 26½oz., 1867. (Parsons, Welch & Cowell) $1,212 £600

Mid 19th century Old Sheffield plate inkstand, 9¾in. long.(Gray's Antique Mews) $212 £105

Bronze part desk set by Tiffany, twelve pieces in all. (Christie's N. York) $1,000 £505

Oak inkstand commemorating the Battle of Navarino. (Humberts, King & Chasemore) $1,494 £740

Victorian silver vine and grape chased ovoid wine jug, 12in. high, 24oz., Sheffield, 1851. (Nottingham Auction Mart) $1,332 £680

George II silver baluster jug, 12½oz., 11.5cm. high. (King & Chasemore) $851 £430

Elizabeth I silver mounted Sieburg stoneware jug, York, 1593. (Drewatt, Watson & Barton) $10,098 £5,100

Silver jug by Abraham Pootholt and Jan van Giffen, 6in. high, 1784. (Sotheby's) $3,564 £1,800

George III silver hot water jug, 11¾in. high, by John Schofield, London, 1785, 24oz. (Sotheby's) $960 £480

George IV silver gilt ewer by Charles Fox, London, 1826, 43oz. 9dwt., 13¾in. high. (Sotheby's) $2,716 £1,400

Scottish silver vase shaped ewer by Robt. Gray & Son, Glasgow, 1841, 36oz.2dwt., 11in. high.(Sotheby's Belgravia) $871 £40

George III milk jug by Hester Bateman, London, 1777, 6½in. high, 6oz.12dwt.(Sotheby's) $831 £420

George III hot water jug, London, 1775, 8in. high, 13oz. (Nottingham Auction Mart) $291 £150

18th century Spanish silver jug, 1762, 23.5cm. high, 750gm. (Sotheby's Zurich) $1,756 £887

George III Scottish provincial covered milk jug by John Baillie, Inverness, circa 1780, 4¾in. high, 8oz.4dwt. (Sotheby's) $2,156 £1,100

George IV covered jug, by Edward Farrell, London, 1825, 28oz.17dwt., 9½in. high. (Sotheby's) $891 £450

George III baluster hot water jug by Charles Wright, London, 1777, 13oz.12dwt.(Sotheby's) $815 £420

One of a pair of silver gilt jugs by John Bache, 1705, 11¼in. high. (Sotheby's) $39,800 £20,000

Good Chinese silver ewer, 32cm. high, circa 1871, 30oz.16dwt. (Sotheby's Belgravia) $1,176 £600

George III hot water jug by Thos. Wynne, London, 1777, 26oz., 11in. high. (Messenger, May & Baverstock) $545 £270

Silver wine jug by John S. Hunt, London, 1850, 13½in. high. (Christie's S. Kensington) $1,623 £820

George I covered beer jug by John Edwards, London, 1719, 10in. high, 32oz.19dwt. (Sotheby's) $4,268 £2,200

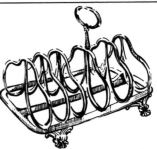

An unusual George III silver toothpick holder, London, 1817, 3in. wide, 3oz.3dwt. (Sotheby's) $1,067 £550

Georg Jensen silver cocktail shaker, circa 1927, 12¼in. high.(Christie's N. York) $600 £303

Early Victorian six-section toast rack by Henry Wilkinson & Co., 1839, 8oz. (Osmond Tricks)$114 £60

Stylish German silver mesh evening purse, circa 1910, 18cm. long. (Sotheby's Belgravia) $117 £60

Decorated and silver mounted nautilus shell, late 17th century. (Chrystal Bros., Stott & Kerruish) $5,940 £3,000

George III prize in the form of a silver gilt quill pen by John Jago, London, 1815, 7dwt., 8½in. long.(Sotheby's) $376 £190

George I censer by Anthony Nelme, London, 1722, 8¾in. high, 27oz.1dwt. (Sotheby's) $2,352 £1,200

Part of a set of twelve ballooning buttons, late 19th century, each 1½in. diam.(Sotheby's Belgravia) $316 £160

One of a pair of 20th century Persian silver coloured metal lustres, 17¼in. high, 70oz. (Sotheby's Belgravia) $595 £310

Victorian oval cradle on four feet, 17¾in. long, by H. W. Curry, 1870, 99oz. (Christie's) $2,716 £1,400

Silver plated tortoise shaped table bell. (Christie's S. Kensington) $198 £100

Late 18th century pair of cockfighting spurs, 1¾in. long. (Sotheby's) $323 £160

18th century child's rattle and whistle by Shem Drowne, Boston, 1749. (Vost's) $418 £220

Art Nouveau silver purse, 1908. (Alfie's Antique Market) $164 £80

Unusual silver screw flask, 1884. (Sotheby's Belgravia) $574 £290

One of a rare pair of George III silver spurs, London, 1784, maker B.C. (Phillips) $464 £230

Silver mounted Meerschaum pipe bowl, circa 1820, 23cm. wide. (Sotheby's) $970 £500

Enamelled silver flint lighter, 2in. high. (Christie's S. Kensington) $174 £90

MODELS

Crane with silver body and copper beak, circa 1900, 5¾in. high. (Sotheby's Belgravia) $614 £320

Part of an early 20th century Indian silver coloured metal chess set, 37oz. (Sotheby's Belgravia) $595 £310

Late 19th century silver plated kazumasa eagle, 8½in. high.(Sotheby's Belgravia) $346 £180

Statuette of a horse and jockey, 11in. long. Birmingham, 1911, 80oz. (Christie's) $1,640 £850

Bouraine silvered bronze figure, 1920's, 47.5cm. high. (Sotheby's Belgravia) $620 £320

Indian silver coloured metal boat, early 20th century. (Sotheby's Belgravia) $607 £310

Silver bronze figure of a woman, circa 1906.(Christie's N. York)$7,700 £3,850

Late 19th century silver plated Indian menagerie. (Sotheby's Belgravia) $442 £230

Silver figure of the Infant Lambrecht III, circa 1650, 25.8in. high. (Christie's) $108,887 £55,555

William III cylindrical mug by John Fawdery I, London, 1698, 9oz., 3¾in. high.(Sotheby's) $2,121 £1,050

William and Mary baluster mug, 3¼in. high, London, 1691, 4oz. 18dwt. (Sotheby's) $1,313 £650

Charles II tapering cylindrical mug by Jonah Kirk, London, 1683, 9oz.8dwt., 4in. high. (Sotheby's) $1,212 £600

Chinese silver coloured metal mug, early 20th century, 10oz.10dwt., 4in. high. (Sotheby's BElgravia) $196 £100

A pair of George I Scottish mugs, 3in. high, by Mungo Yorstoun, Edinburgh, 1717, 11oz.15dwt. (Sotheby's) $4,116 £2,100

George II silver mug, London, 1752, by Robert Cox, 7.5oz. (King & Chasemore) $316 £160

Silver mug by John Langlands, Newcastle, 1769, 9oz., 11.5cm. high. (King & Chasemore) $574 £290

William and Mary baluster mug, 5¼in. high, London, 11oz.19dwt. (Sotheby's) $3,201 £1,650

George II baluster mug, by Richard Bayley, London, 1738, 4½in. high, 12oz. (Sotheby's) $1,089 £550

George III silver drum mustard, 2¼in. high, by Samuel West, London, 1801, 6oz. (Nottingham Auction Mart) $213 £110

One of two Handicrafts Ltd. pepper casters, circa 1900, 6.5cm. high. (Sotheby's Belgravia) $426 £220

Early Victorian mustard pot by Charles Fox, London, 1837, 3in. high, 4oz. 12dwt. (Sotheby's) $336 £170

George I octagonal caster and dry mustard pot, 4½in. high, London, 1722, 5oz.13dwt. (Sotheby's) $2,020 £1,000

George I cylindrical kitchen pepper by John Hamilton, Dublin, 2½in. high, 2oz.9dwt. (Sotheby's Ireland) $646 £330

A pair of good Victorian owl pepperettes, 3¼in. high, Edinburgh, 1887, 6oz.5dwt. (Sotheby's) $744 £380

NUTMEGS

Georgian silver nutmeg grater by Phipps & Robinson, London, 1788, 2¾in. high, (damaged). (Vost's) $383 £190

George III oval nutmeg grater by Phipps & Robinson, London, 1786, 2¼in. wide. (Sotheby's)$554 £280

Silver nutmeg grater by Elkington & Co., Birmingham, 1906, 3in. long. (Gray's Antique Market) $282 £140

William III porringer by James Chadwick, London, 1697, 3¼in. high, 6oz. (Sotheby's) $970 £500

Commonwealth porringer, London, 1659, 3½in. high, 8oz.16dwt. (Sotheby's) $2,716 £1,400

William III porringer, maker's mark P.R., London, 1696, 3¼in. high, 6oz. 11dwt. (Sotheby's) $1,203 £620

Late 17th century provincial porringer, 2¾in. high, 4oz.4dwt. (Sotheby's)
$574 £290

One of a pair of Queen Anne porringers by John East, London, 1707, 16oz. 16dwt., 4in. high. (Sotheby's)
$1,862 £950

Queen Anne porringer on collet foot, 1713, 6oz. (Phillips) $505 £250

Queen Anne quaich by Robert Ker, Edinburgh, circa 1710. (Sotheby's)
$2,716 £1,400

Late 18th century porringer, 4¾in. diameter, 6oz.19dwt. (Sotheby's)
$606 £300

One of a pair of George III gadroon rim salts, London, 1818. (Clarke Gammon)　$131　£68

One of a pair of George III silver mounted salt cellars, circa 1760, 3in. diam.　(Sotheby's)　$514　£260

One of a set of four George III oval pierced salts by David R. Hennell, 1765. (Phillips)　$484　£240

One of a pair of George III salt cellars by Paul Storr, London, 1812, 4½in. wide, 12oz.6dwt. (Sotheby's)　$1,332　£680

A pair of George III silver salts by Hester Bateman, 1788. (Parsons, Welch & Cowell)　$247　£130

One of a pair of George II salt cellars by David Hennell, London, 1752, 3¼in. diam., 13oz.6dwt. (Sotheby's)　$1,274　£650

One of a set of four George III silver salts. (Phillips)　$533　£264

One of a set of four George III oval tub-shaped silver salts, London, 1808, 12½oz. (King & Chasemore)　$756　£380

One of six George III salt cellars by William Eaton, 1816, 3¾in. wide, 26oz.3dwt. (Sotheby's)　$1,010　£500

Russian silver salt with original spoon, circa 1874. (Gray's Antique Market) $370 £180

One of a pair of George III salt cellars by Edward Wood, London, 2¾in. diam., 11oz.7dwt. (Sotheby's) $712 £360

One of a pair of silver gilt salts and spoons, 23oz. (Osmond Tricks) $636 £335

One of six heavy salt cellars by Benjamin Smith, London, 1819, 5in. wide, 63oz.2dwt. (Sotheby's) $1,940 £1,000

Four silver trencher salts by John Cole, 1706. (Christie's) $3,332 £1,700

One of a pair of George III silver salts, London, 1764. (King & Chasemore) $148 £75

One of a pair of George II trencher salts by Edward Wood, London, 1724, 4oz.15dwt. (Sotheby's) $1,455 £750

One of a pair of late 18th century Dutch salt cellars by Rodolph Sondag, Rotterdam, 1780, 4oz.17dwt. (Sotheby's) $525 £260

One of four Regency salt cellars by Paul Storr, circa 1816, 61oz. (Christie's) $4,074 £2,100

SAUCEBOATS

George II Scottish cream-boat by John Main, Edin-burgh, 1739, 6½in. wide, 7oz.14dwt. (Sotheby's) $1,372 £700

One of a pair of George III silver sauceboats, London, 1800. (King & Chasemore)$653 £330

One of a pair of George III oval sauceboats, London, 1770, 16oz.15dwt., 6¾in. wide.(Sotheby's) $1,782 £900

One of a pair of George III small sauceboats by Fuller White, London, 1758, 10oz.17dwt. (Sotheby's) $3,200 £1,600

One of a pair of George III double lidded sauce-boats, 36oz. (Humberts, King & Chasemore) $2,352 £1,200

Silver creamboat by William Harrison, 1763. (Gray's Anti-que Market) $343 £170

One of a pair of George III oval sauceboats by William Skeen, London, 1769, 20oz.12dwt., 6¾in. wide.(Sotheby's) $1,568 £800

One of a pair of George III plain oval sauceboats by Alex. Johnston, 1763, 30oz. (Christie's) $2,910 £1,500

One of a pair of early 19th century silver sauceboats. (Man-chester Auction Mart) $304 £160

Small cameo glass scent bottle with silver screw cap, circa 1884, 5.5cm. high. (Sotheby's Belgravia) $386 £195

Cameo glass scent bottle with silver cover and mount by Sampson Mordan & Co., London 1887, 10.5cm. high. (Sotheby's Belgravia) $613 £310

17th century silver gilt pomander from Germany, 2½in. high. (Sotheby's) $1,067 £550

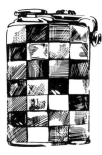

Chromed metal mother-of-pearl and abalone 'super kid' perfume atomiser, 1920's, 5.2cm. high. (Sotheby's Belgravia) $106 £55

Silver scent bottle Dutch, 5¾in. long. (Le Gallais) $191 £95

Cameo scent bottle, 1884, 10.5cm. high, with screw cap marked Birmingham. (Sotheby's Belgravia) $396 £200

Cameo glass scent bottle with silver cap, circa 1884, 6.2cm. high. (Sotheby's Belgravia) $376 £190

Cameo glass scent bottle, 1880's, 11cm. long, with hinged silver cap. (Sotheby's Belgravia) $534 £270

Ivory cameo glass scent bottle with silver screw cap by Thomas Webb & Sons, 1888, 11cm. high. (Sotheby's Belgravia) $643 £325

William IV rectangular snuff box by Joseph Willmore, Birmingham, 1836, 2¾in. wide. (Sotheby's) $1,019 £520

William IV oblong snuff box by Nat. Mills, Birmingham, 1831, 2½in. wide. (Sotheby's) $431 £220

George III snuff box with compartment at one end, by John Shaw, Birmingham, 1817, 2½in. wide. (Sotheby's) $666 £340

George III octagonal snuff box by Richard Sawyer, Dublin, 1806, 3½in. wide. (Sotheby's Ireland) $862 £440

Rare early Victorian silver snuff box in the form of a cricket bat, 9in. long, 8oz. 15dwt. (Geering & Colyer) $2,266 £1,100

Austrian oblong snuff box, 3¼in. wide, Vienna, 1840. (Sotheby's) $235 £120

George III rectangular silver gilt snuff box by Joseph Willmore, Birmingham, 1810, 2¾in. wide. (Sotheby's) $548 £280

George II cartouche shaped snuff box, 2¼in. wide, London, 1743. (Sotheby's) $784 £400

George II rectangular snuff box, 2½in. wide, London, 1732. (Sotheby's) $470 £240

William IV silver gilt snuff box by A. J. Strachan, London, 1830, 4¾in. wide. (Sotheby's)
$1,414 £700

Rare early 18th century Irish rectangular snuff box by Robert Goble, Cork, 3¼in. wide. (Sotheby's)
$1,274 £650

George IV silver gilt oblong snuff box by John Jones III, London, 1824, 3¼in. wide. (Sotheby's)
$1,019 £520

Oblong snuff box, probably Chinese, circa 1835, 2¾in. wide. (Sotheby's)
$166 £85

George IV 'Pedlar' snuff box by John Linnit, London, 1825, 4in. wide. (Sotheby's)
$2,254 £1,150

George III oblong snuff box by John Shaw, Birmingham, 1814, 3in. wide. (Sotheby's)
$313 £160

George III oblong snuff box by John Brough, London, 1814, 2¼in. wide. (Sotheby's)
$333 £170

William IV rectangular snuff box by Rawlings and Summers, London, 1834, 3¼in. wide, 6oz.11dwt. (Sotheby's)
$940 £480

George III silver gilt oblong snuff box by James Ruell, London, 1806, 2¾in. wide. (Sotheby's)
$509 £260

TANKARDS

George II cylindrical tankard by Richard Bell, London, 19oz. 6dwt., 6½in. high. (Sotheby's)$1,626 £800

George II baluster tankard by Peter Moss, London, 1747, 8¾in. high, 27oz.3dwt. (Sotheby's)$1,717 £850

Eight pint silver peg tankard, London, 1912, 80oz., 12in. high.(Nottingham Auction Mart) $1,803 £920

George III cylindrical tankard by Hester Bateman, London, 1790, 25oz.18dwt., 8¼in. high. (Sotheby's) $2,548 £1,300

George III baluster tankard, London, 1775, 30oz. 8dwt., 8½in. high. (Sotheby's) $1,666 £850

George III tapered cylindrical tankard, London, 1804, 7¾in. high, 23oz. 5dwt. (Sotheby's) $1,544 £780

James II peg tankard, 7½in. high, London, 1686, 27oz. 18dwt. (Sotheby's) $14,000 £7,000

George IV cylindrical flagon by R. Emes and E. Barnard, 1826, 61oz. (Christie's) $2,328 £1,200

Charles II tapered cylindrical tankard, London, 1679, 25oz.(Sotheby's) $7,272 £3,600

George II tankard by Richard Gurney & Co., London, 1740, 4¾in. high, 13oz.10dwt. (Messenger, May & Baverstock)$969 £480

Parcel gilt tankard made for the Haller von Hallerstein family, circa 1575. (Christie's Geneva) $23,221 £11,728

George II tapered cylindrical tankard, 7in. high, London, 1739, 24oz. 3dwt. (Sotheby's) $1,108 £560

Charles II cylindrical tankard by Marmaduke Best, York, 24oz.19dwt., 6½in. high.(Sotheby's) $8,484 £4,200

18th century Norwegian tankard, 9½in. high, circa 1750, 38oz.3dwt. (Sotheby's) $5,858 £2,900

George II plain cylindrical tankard by John Swift, 1731, 40oz. (Christie's) $2,496 £1,300

One of a pair of George III tapering tankards by Robert Sharp, London, 1794, 64oz.2dwt., 7¼in. high. (Sotheby's) $2,574 £1,300

Swedish tankard of peg type, repousse decorated with figures and fruits. (Phillips) $464 £230

Fine rare lidded tankard by Arthur Heaslewood, 23oz., 7in. high. (G. A. Key) $12,726 £6,300

TAZZAS

Georg Jensen silver centrepiece, 10¼in. diam. (Christie's N. York) $1,430 £747

A pair of Victorian tazzas by James Garrard, London, 1887, 18¼in. high, 44oz. 3dwt. (Sotheby's) $980 £500

WMF silvered metal tazza, 23.25cm. high, circa 1900.(Sotheby's Belgravia) $297 £150

Large Jensen silver coupe, London, 1922, 19.75cm. high. (Sotheby's Belgravia) $2,940 £1,500

Silver and ivory tazza by Adie Bros. Ltd., 12.75cm. diameter, 1930.(Sotheby's Belgravia) $504 £260

Attractive Guild of Handicraft Ltd. silver and enamel tazza, London, 1905, 15.25cm. high.(Sotheby's Belgravia) $2,574 £1,300

TEA CADDIES

George III oval tea caddy by Hester Bateman, London, 1784, 10oz.18dwt., 5½in. high.(Sotheby's) $2,800 £1,400

18th century Norwegian tea caddy by Jens Kahrs, Bergen, 1765, 11.2cm. high. (Sotheby's Zurich) $1,287 £650

George II oval tea caddy, 4¾in. high, by Edward Gibbon, London, 1727, 6oz.9dwt. (Sotheby's) $854 £440

George III oval tea caddy by T. Chawner, London, 1785, 5½in. high, 13oz. (Russell, Baldwin & Bright) $990 £500

George III silver tea caddy by Rebecca Emes and Edward Barnard I, London, 1809, 22½oz. (King & Chasemore) $982 £470

George III tea caddy by Daniel Smith and Robt. Sharp, London, 1786, 17oz., 5½in. high. (Nottingham Auction Mart) $1,076 £555

George III oblong tea caddy by Peter Gillois, London, 1763, 11oz. 7dwt., 5½in. high. (Sotheby's) $888 £440

George III oval tea caddy by William Vincent, London, 1785, 12oz.19dwt., 5½in. high. (Sotheby's) $1,188 £600

George II tea caddy by Samuel Taylor, London, 1755, 5¼in. high, 7oz. 16dwt. (Sotheby's) $744 £380

Early 19th century Dutch oval tea caddy, 4½in. high, 10oz. 12dwt. (Sotheby's) $1,160 £580

Victorian silver chased bombe tea caddy, 5in. high, 11½oz. (Nottingham Auction Mart) $606 £300

George III tea caddy by Hester Bateman, 1779, 10.75oz. (Hy. Duke & Son) $1,900 £1,000

Unusual three-piece electroplated coffee service, 1930's. (Sotheby's Belgravia) $156 £80

Three-piece tea service by Samuel Hennell, London, 1803, 28oz. (Woolley & Wallis) $1,939 £960

George III matching teaset, London, 99oz.9dwt., with similar coffee pot. (Sotheby's) $4,850 £2,500

Victorian Scottish teaset by Marshall & Sons, Edinburgh, 1849, 40oz.8dwt. (Sotheby's) $1,293 £660

Victorian four-piece tea and coffee set by William Robert Smily, London, 1850, 77oz.2dwt. (Sotheby's) $3,038 £1,550

Georg Jensen teaset and tray, fully London import marked.(Bonham's) $3,030 £1,500

Jensen four-piece coffee set, circa 1930. (Sotheby's Belgravia) $2,940 £1,500

George III silver teapot and sugar bowl. (Parsons, Welch & Cowell) $1,335 £675

Good Hukin & Heath electroplated picnic set in fitted wood box, 1880. (Sotheby's Belgravia) $475 £240

Victorian silver four-piece tea and coffee service, 78oz. (Russell, Baldwin & Bright) $1,881 £950

Victorian four-piece tea and coffee set by W. W. Harrison, Sheffield, 1899, 80oz.3dwt.(Sotheby's)$1,528 £780

Indian silver coloured metal teaset, circa 1900, 47oz.16dwt.(Sotheby's Belgravia) $403 £210

TEA AND COFFEE SETS

Victorian silver three-piece teaset, London, 1854, 51½oz.(Parsons, Welch & Cowell) $1,207 £610

George IV silver three-piece teaset, London, 1825, by W.S. (Biddle & Webb) $1,603 £810

Chinese silver tea and coffee service, circa 1900, 99oz.6dwt. (Sotheby's Belgravia)$1,036 £540

Mid Victorian four-piece silver teaset by Charles and Edward Fox, 78oz. (Gray's Antique Mews)
                    $2,868 £1,420

George IV four-piece tea and coffee set by Charles Price, London, 80oz. 3dwt.(Sotheby's) $2,134 £1,100

Victorian plain matched four-piece tea and coffee service, London, 1835/41, 78oz.(Russell, Baldwin & Bright) $1,940 £950

George IV Irish three-piece teaset by James Fray, Dublin, 1826, 54oz.1dwt. (Sotheby's) $1,009 £520

Victorian silver three-piece teaset by Joseph and John Angell, London, 1841, 45oz.(Parsons, Welch & Cowell)
$1,267 £640

George III teaset by Peter and Anne Bateman, London, 1798, 39oz.13dwt. (Sotheby's)$2,300 £1,150

Victorian tea and coffee service and cake basket, Sheffield, 1846, 183oz. (Christie's) $5,184 £2,700

William IV four-piece tea and coffee set by Charles Fox, London, 1830, 75oz.1dwt.(Sotheby's)$3,104 £1,600

Four-piece silver tea and coffee service by Charles Fox, London, 1833. (Spencer's) $2,619 £1,350

TEA AND COFFEE SETS

William IV four-piece tea and coffee set, by E., E., J. & W. Barnard, London, 1831-5, 84oz.2dwt.　(Sotheby's)
$2,300　£1,150

Victorian silver tea service, London, 94oz.　(King & Chasemore)
$2,280　£1,200

Tea service, circa 1900, in silver coloured metal, 60oz.16dwt. (Sotheby's Belgravia)　$422　£220

Juventa Art Nouveau electroplated metal coffee service, circa 1900. (Sotheby's Belgravia)　$194　£100

Square sectioned silver Chinese teaset, circa 1900, 62oz.8dwt.(Sotheby's Belgravia)　$557　£290

Three-piece tea service by Peter and William Bateman, London, 1805, 31½oz.　(King & Chasemore)
$1,337　£640

Victorian silver four-piece engraved tea and coffee set, London, 1839, by John Angell, 75oz. (Nottingham Auction Mart) $1,702 £860

Victorian three-piece teaset by Robert Garrard, London 1851, 38oz., sold with plated tea kettle on stand. (Woolley & Wallis) $1,292 £640

Three-piece silver tea service, London, 1900. (Sotheby's Belgravia) $776 £400

Chinese silver teaset, circa 1900, 33oz. 8dwt. (Sotheby's Belgravia) $326 £170

Silver teaset by Paul Storr, London, 1822, 120oz. (Phillips) $19,800 £10,000

Matching four-piece tea and coffee set, circa 1822, by Joseph Angell, London, 75oz.15dwt.(Sotheby's) $1,940 £1,000

TEA AND COFFEE SETS

Three-piece George IV silver tea service, London, 1822, 47½oz. (King & Chasemore) $1,171 £580

Four-piece oval silver tea and coffee service, Sheffield, 1933, 64oz. (Gray's Antique Mews) $1,313 £650

Four-piece teaset by James Ramsay, Dublin, 1913, 54oz.3dwt. (Sotheby's Belgravia) $792 £400

Victorian silver tea service, Sheffield, 1863, 67oz. (D. M. Nesbit & Co.) $1,878 £930

George IV three-piece teaset by Joseph Angell, London, 1825, 49oz.1dwt. (Sotheby's) $1,171 £580

Fine six-piece silver tea and coffee service by Charles Boyton, London, 1889, 123oz. (Messenger, May & Baverstock) $1,474 £730

Victorian tea and coffee service, 1864, 80oz. (Christie's) $2,716 £1,400

Three-piece silver bachelor teaset, Sheffield, 1905. (Gray's Antique Market) $350 £170

Six-piece tea and coffee set, London, 1947, 123oz. (Sotheby's Belgravia) $1,089 £550

George III three-piece teaset, Dublin, circa 1810, 42oz. (Sotheby's Ireland) $1,148 £580

George III three-piece teaset by George Burrows, London, 1819-20, 60oz.4dwt. (Sotheby's) $2,020 £1,000

William IV three-piece silver tea service by E., E., J. & W. Barnard, 44oz. (King & Chasemore) $915 £460

Elkington plate Victorian kettle on stand. (Alfie's Antique Market) $282 £140

Late 19th century Chinese silver kettle, stand and burner, 12¾in. high, 33oz. (Sotheby's Belgravia) $384 £200

George III Irish silver tea kettle and stand, Dublin, circa 1740, by Thos. Isaac, 68oz. (Lawrence's) $1,881 £950

Victorian silver tea kettle by Reily and Storer, 73oz. (Christie's S. Kensington) $1,843 £950

George II Irish tea kettle on lampstand by John Taylor, 13in. high, 67oz.14dwt. (Sotheby's) $2,352 £1,200

George II silver globular tea kettle, stand and burner, by Thos. Whipham, London, 1747, 61oz. (Nottingham Auction Mart) $1,115 £575

Victorian silver spirit kettle by Robb and Whittet, Edinburgh, 1837, 74oz. (King & Chasemore) $1,726 £890

Bruder Frank kettle and stand, circa 1900, in silver coloured metal. (Sotheby's Belgravia) $539 £275

George II tea kettle on stand, 14½in. high, by Peze Pilleau, London, 1755, 56oz.12dwt. (Sotheby's) $1,552 £800

Part of a Chinese silver coloured metal teaset, circa 1900, 34oz.8dwt. (Sotheby's Belgravia) $450 £230

Victorian silver teapot by Joseph Angell, London, 1847, 20½oz. (Parsons, Welch & Cowell) $495 £250

George III oval teapot and stand, Sheffield, 1778-79, 5½in. high, 19oz.7dwt. (Sotheby's) $1,176 £600

George III teapot and stand by Richard Cooke, London, 1800-01, 16oz. (Messenger, May & Baverstock) $949 £470

Silver teapot by Sanwell Green, Cork, 1805, 11in. long. (Gray's Antique Market) $1,111 £550

18th century Dutch pear shaped teapot by Jan de Vries, Amsterdam, 6in. high, 9oz.5dwt. (Sotheby's) $1,040 £520

William IV compressed teapot by Paul Storr, London, 1836, 14oz., 4in. high. (Sotheby's) $980 £500

Compressed globular teapot, London, 1836, 20½oz. (Woolley & Wallis) $721 £350

George III Scottish oval teapot, 5¾in. high, by W. & P. Cunningham, Edinburgh, 1806, 23oz.12dwt.(Sotheby's) $528 £270

George III oval teapot and stand, by Hester Bateman, London, 1788/9, 6½in. high, 16oz.2dwt.(Sotheby's) $842 £430

George III 'Drum' teapot by Makepeace and Carter, London, 1777, 4¼in. high, 13oz.14dwt.(Sotheby's) $910 £460

George III silver teapot by Hester Bateman, London, 1782, 9oz.15dwt. (Geering & Colyer) $388 £200

George II Scottish teapot by Edward Lothian, Edinburgh, 1734, 6¼in. high, 22oz.8dwt.(Sotheby's) $1,568 £800

George III octagonal teapot and stand, by Hester Bateman, London, 1787, 19oz.1dwt.(Sotheby's)$2,522 £1,300

George III oval teapot by John Denziloe, London, 1786, 15oz.1dwt., 5½in. high.(Sotheby's) $860 £430

George III oval teapot by P. & A. Bateman, London, 1796, 16oz.10dwt., 6½in. high.(Sotheby's) $892 £460

Victorian compressed teapot by J. McKay, Edinburgh, 1839, 22oz.12dwt., 6¾in. high.(Sotheby's) $333 £170

George III oval teapot by Hester Bateman, London, 1790, 13.5oz.(Woolley & Wallis) $931 £480

Victorian silver teapot, 6¾in. high, London, 1859, 21oz.5dwt.(Geering & Colyer) $485 £250

Hukin & Heath electroplated teapot, 14:5cm. high.(Sotheby's Belgravia) $633 £320

William IV compressed circular teapot, 6¼in. high, Sheffield, 1830, 25oz. 14dwt.(Sotheby's) $446 £230

Early Victorian teapot by John Angell, London, 1847, 20½oz.(Parsons, Welch & Cowell) $495 £250

Silver teapot by Peter and Anne Bateman, London, 1795, 20.5oz.(King & Chasemore) $1,411 £720

Very rare Queen Anne silver teapot, by Gabriel Sleath, 1713.(Oliver's) $5,510 £2,900

TEAPOTS

George III oval teapot by Hester Bateman, 5½in. high, 13oz.1dwt. (Sotheby's) $1,212 £600

George III oblong teapot by P. & W. Bateman, London, 1812, 21oz.8dwt., 7¾in. high. (Sotheby's) $594 £300

Irish cast rococo silver teapot by James le Bass, Dublin, 1831, 45oz. (Gray's Antique Mews) $1,262 £625

Silver teapot by Jonathan Bateman, 1790. (Gray's Antique Mews) $1,313 £650

Victorian silver teapot by James Gray, Dublin, 1841, 7in. high, 24oz.10dwt. (Sotheby's Ireland) $633 £320

Victorian plated teapot with ivory handle. (British Antique Exporters) $30 £15

Good A. A. Hebrard teapot, circa 1910, 24cm. high. (Sotheby's) $25,740 £13,000

18th century Dutch melon shaped teapot by Willem Langebeke, 10oz. 15dwt., 5¼in. high. (Sotheby's) $5,252 £2,600

Fine 19th century dressing case, London, 1838. (W. H. Lane & Son)
$707 £350

Queen Anne toilet service, London, circa 1706, 81oz.12dwt.(Sotheby's)
$15,150 £7,500

Portuguese silver and stained fish-skin necessaire de voyage, circa 1730-40. (Sotheby's) $1,050 £520

English silver gilt toilet service by various makers, late 17th/early 18th century. (Christie's Geneva) $29,115 £14,705

Charles II toilet set, circa 1680, 158oz. (Sotheby's) $38,800 £20,000

Victorian rosewood vanity box with brass stringing.(Alfie's Antique Market) $309 £150

Shaped circular salver
by Waterhouse, Hat-
field & Co., 21in. diam.,
circa 1840.(Sotheby's)
$363 £180

Enamelled silvered metal
tray, circa 1900, 11in.
wide.(Sotheby's Belgravia)
$1,574 £820

George II pie crust
salver by Edward
Cornock, London,
1734, 12in. diam.,
26oz.(Nottingham
Auction Mart)
$718 £370

Silver salver, 1667,
14in. diameter.
(Sotheby's)
$4,850 £2,500

George III Irish boat
shaped snuffers tray
by James Scott, Dublin,
8oz.5dwt.(Neales)
$707 £350

One of a pair of George
II shaped circular sal-
vers by Edward Wake-
lin, London, 1752, 7in.
diameter., 22oz.12dwt.
(Sotheby's)
$1,287 £650

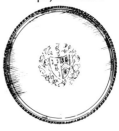

George II plain shaped
square silver salver by
Robert Abercrombie.
(Christie's)
$4,242 £2,100

George II silver salver
by Ebenezer Coker and
Thomas Hannay, Lon-
don, 1759, 11½oz.,
19.5cm. diam. (King &
Chasemore) $313 £160

George III circular
salver by Elizabeth
Cooke, London,
1771, 11½in. diam.,
35oz.2dwt.(Sotheby's)
$1,252 £620

One of a pair of George
II waiters by John Rob-
inson, London, 1745,
14oz.6dwt. (Sotheby's)
$1,120 £560

George III rectangular
salver by Simon Harris,
London, 1813, 13oz.
17dwt., 8in. wide.
(Sotheby's)$525 £260

One of twelve George
III circular dinner
plates by Paul Storr,
10in. diam., 240oz.
(Sotheby's)
$10,088 £5,200

One of a pair of George
III circular salvers by
Crouch & Hannam,
London, 1777, 19oz.
14dwt., 7¼in. diam.
(Sotheby's)$969 £480

Embossed Indian silver
tray, circa 1900, 21in.
long, sold with a teaset.
(Sotheby's Belgravia)
$883 £460

George IV shaped cir-
cular salver by John
Craddock, 1827, 24in.
diam., 206oz.(Christie's)
$5,238 £2,700

One of a pair of George
III circular salvers, 7¼in.
diam., London, 1784,
17oz.13dwt.(Sotheby's)
$776 £400

George III silver salver,
London, 1732, 10½oz.,
19.5cm. diam. (King &
Chasemore) $303 £155

**Early George III
shaped circular salver,**
14½in. diam., by
Robert Rew, 1762,
39oz.4dwt. (Sotheby's)
$1,029 £520

George III oval two-handled tray by Crouch & Hannam, London, 1792, 68oz. 6dwt., 22in. wide. (Sotheby's) $2,900 £1,450

Charles II silver gilt salver on foot, London, 1667, 14in. diam., 26oz.14dwt.(Sotheby's) $4,850 £2,500

Silver salver by Hester Bateman, London, 1790, 4½oz. (King & Chasemore) $470 £240

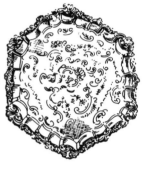

George III circular salver by Crouch & Hannam, London, 1798, 49oz. 3dwt., 15in. diameter. (Sotheby's)$1,313 £650

George II shaped circular salver by Robert Abercrombie, London, 1742, 10½in. diam., 19oz.18dwt.(Sotheby's) $752 £380

Shaped circular salver, 13in. diameter, circa 1820, engraved with crest. (Sotheby's) $198 £100

George III salver by Paul Storr, London, circa 1825, 20¾in. diam., 118oz.18dwt. (Sotheby's) $5,096 £2,600

George III silver meat dish, London, 1810, 65½oz. (King & Chasemore) $970 £500

One of twelve George III dinner plates by Paul Storr, London, 1807, 10½in. diam., 271oz.7dwt.(Sotheby's) $13,328 £6,800

Silver oval waiter on feet, 5oz. (Nottingham Auction Mart) $97 £50

Early Victorian silver tray, London, 1854, 30in. long. (Pearson's) $1,900 £1,000

Large two-handled shaped oval tray by Robert Garrard, London, 1860, 164oz., 26¼in. long. (Christie's) $3,686 £1,900

George III circular salver by John Schofield, London, 1777, 13oz.17dwt., 8in. diam. (Sotheby's) $646 £320

One of a pair of George III shaped circular salvers by Crouch & Hannam, 1765, 24oz.15dwt. (Sotheby's) $686 £340

George III shaped circular salver by Robert Abercrombie, London, 1739, 19oz.15dwt., 10¼in. diam.(Sotheby's) $901 £460

One of a pair of George II shaped circular salvers by Isaac Cookson, Newcastle, 1756, 21oz. 6dwt., 7¼in. diameter. (Sotheby's) $1,010 £500

Early 19th century American silver salver by John W. Forbes, New York, circa 1815, 11¾in. wide, 24oz. 14dwt. (Sotheby's) $707 £350

George II square shaped salver by John Tuite, London, 1730, 24oz., 10½in. wide.(Sotheby's) $1,215 £620

TUREENS

One of a pair of George III silver boat shaped sauce tureens by John Wakelin and William Taylor, London, 1786, 38oz. (Nottingham Auction Mart)
$272 £140

Robert Linzeler oval soup tureen, cover and stand, circa 1905. (Sotheby's Belgravia)
$16,830 £8,500

Victorian silver soup tureen, 88oz. (Le Gallais)
$3,030 £1,500

Oval soup tureen and cover, 17in. wide overall, circa 1830. (Sotheby's)
$1,010 £500

Circular soup tureen and cover, 14in. high, circa 1820. (Sotheby's)
$1,010 £500

Early George III oval soup tureen and cover by John Vere and William Lutwyche, London, 92oz.10dwt., 15¼in. wide. (Sotheby's)
$3,434 £1,750

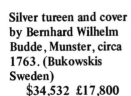

Silver tureen and cover by Bernhard Wilhelm Budde, Munster, circa 1763. (Bukowskis Sweden)
$34,532 £17,800

George III circular soup tureen and cover, 16in. wide, Sheffield, 1816, 123oz.(Sotheby's)
$3,200 £1,600

One of a pair of George III oval sauce tureens and covers by Thomas Wallis, London, 1806, 39oz.8dwt.(Sotheby's)
$2,929 £1,450

George III vase shaped tea urn, by Butty & Dumee, London, 1768, 20½in. high, 99oz. 16dwt. (Sotheby's) $2,500 £1,250

George III vase shaped tea urn by Wakelin & Taylor, London, 1783, 77oz.3dwt., 18in. high. (Sotheby's)$1,818 £900

George III spherical tea urn by George Ashworth & Co. Sheffield, 1802, 17½in. high, 88oz.19dwt. (Sotheby's)$1,800 £900

George III circular tea urn by Benjamin Smith, 16in. high, London, 1818, 135oz. 10dwt. (Sotheby's) $2,200 £1,100

Early 18th century Scottish urn, 11½in. high, Edinburgh, circa 1725, 43oz.11dwt. (Sotheby's) $1,470 £750

Plated 19th century Samovar with domed cover, 19in. high. (Nottingham Auction Mart) $303 £150

Vase shaped tea urn, 16¼in. high, by Heath & Middleton, London, 1906, 78oz.4dwt. (Sotheby's)$901 £460

French silver plated urn, circa 1830, by Balaine, Paris. (Alfie's Antique Market) $474 £235

George III tea urn by Charles Wright, London, 1771, 80oz. (Phillips)$1,292 £640

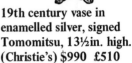

James Rogers silver
vase, 14.75cm. high,
Sheffield, 1907.
(Sotheby's Belgravia)
$194 £100

Set of three George III silver
condiment vases. (Russell,
Baldwin & Bright)
$1,980 £1,000

19th century vase in
enamelled silver, signed
Tomomitsu, 13½in. high.
(Christie's) $990 £510

One of a pair of enamel-
led silver coloured metal
vases, circa 1900, 54oz.,
27.7cm. high.(Sotheby's
Belgravia) $980 £500

One of a set of three
George III sugar vases
by Christopher Makemeid,
London, 1772, 26oz.18dwt.
(Sotheby's) $1,940 £980

One of a pair of George
III silver gilt sugar vases
and covers by Paul Storr,
8¼in. high, 61oz.7dwt.
(Sotheby's) $7,840
                        £4,000

One of two George III
sweetmeat vases by
Robert Hennell, London,
1781, 10oz.18dwt.
(Sotheby's)$1,372 £700

Japanese gold inlaid and
enamelled silver vase,
circa 1900. (King & Chasemore) $851 £430

George III silver gilt
covered vase, London,
1770, 20oz.6dwt.,
8¼in. high.(Sotheby's)
$882 £450

George III silver gilt vinaigrette, 1¾in. wide, by Phipps, Robinson & Phipps, London, 1813. (Sotheby's) $862 £440

George III vinaigrette by Matthew Linwood, 1805. (Phillips) $1,474 £760

George III purse shaped vinaigrette by John Shaw, Birmingham, 1819, 1¼in. wide. (Sotheby's)$450 £230

Silver vinaigrette depicting Newstead Abbey, by Nat. Mills. (H. Spencer & Sons) $675 £350

18th century spice box or vinaigrette, probably Danish, 3in. long, 1oz. 1dwt. (Sotheby's) $1,373 £680

George III silver articulated fish vinaigrette, Birmingham, 1817. (Bonham's) $484 £240

Silver gilt fish hinged and with a small bon-bonniere compartment. (Christie's) $940 £480

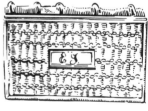

Early Victorian silver gilt vinaigrette by Nathaniel Mills, London, 1838, 1½in. wide. (Sotheby's)$862 £440

Silver vinaigrette in the form of a mussel shell by S. Mordan & Co., 1881. (Christie's S. Kensington) $484 £240

William IV rectangular vinaigrette by Taylor & Perry, Birmingham, 1836, 1¼in. wide. (Sotheby's) $294 £150

One of a pair of George IV two-handled wine coolers by R. Gainsford, Sheffield, 1823, 160oz., 9½in. high. (Christie's) $5,238 £2,700

One of a pair of George III vase shaped wine coolers by Wm. Pitts, London, 1801, 201oz. 10dwt. (Sotheby's) $12,120 £6,000

One of a pair of Old Sheffield plate wine coolers by Robert Gainsford, circa 1820, 9½in. high. (Gray's Antique Mews) $919 £455

One of a pair of campana shaped wine coolers, circa 1835, 11½in. high. (Sotheby's) $1,089 £550

Old Sheffield wine cooler, 8½in. high. (Christie's S. Kensington) $396 £200

Campana shaped wine cooler, circa 1810, 10in. high.(Sotheby's) $356 £180

One of a pair of George IV campana shaped wine coolers by M. Boulton, Birmingham, 1829, 184oz. 8dwt., 10½in. high. (Sotheby's)$5,600 £2,800

One of a pair of Catherine the Great wine coolers by Zacharias Deichmann, 1766. (Christie's) $10,450 £5,304

One of a rare pair of armorial engraved George III wine coolers by P. Cunningham, Edinburgh, 1818, 165oz.(Sotheby's) $10,890 £5,500

Georgian silver wine funnel, London, 1811, by E. Morley. (Vost's) $383 £190

George III silver wine funnel, London, 1778. (Vernon of Chichester) $260 £125

George III wine funnel by George Fenwick, 1817. (Vernon of Chichester) $115 £55

WINE LABELS

George II wine label for 'Cyder', maker's mark H.P., circa 1758. (Sotheby's)$168 £85

One of a pair of George III wine labels by R. Binley. (Sotheby's) $158 £80

George II provincial wine label by John Langlands, Newcastle. (Sotheby's)$148 £75

WINE TASTERS

18th century silver French wine taster. (Parsons, Welch & Cowell)$232 £120

18th century French silver wine taster. (Parsons, Welch & Cowell)$232 £120

Mid 17th century wine taster, 4in. diam., 1oz.16dwt. (Sotheby's) $1,500 £750

Early 18th century Scottish wine taster, 17dwt., 4¼in. wide. (Sotheby's) $254 £130

18th century French silver wine taster. (Parsons, Welch & Cowell)$136 £70

Plain 17th century silver charka with engraved frieze, 3cm. high.(Sotheby's Zurich) $3,221 £1,627

651

STONE

12th century grey stone frieze, West Indian, 16½in. high. (Christie's) $880 £453

10th century black stone stele, 23in. high. (Christie's) $770 £396

Ming dynasty sandstone head, 11in. high. (Christie's) $660 £340

11th century pink sandstone figure of Agni, 33in. high. (Christie's) $3,300 £1,701

11th century Central Indian Matrika group in pink sandstone, 33in. long. (Christie's) $1,870 £963

Grey schist stele of Kuan Yin, 26in. high. (Christie's) $825 £425

11th century redstone frieze, 17¼in. high. '(Christie's) $880 £453

11th century stone frieze of the god Vishnu, 30in. high. (Christie's) $2,420 £1,247

2nd or 3rd century figure of the Buddha, 17¼in. high. (Christie's) $1,650 £850

One of two ivory
bottles with match-
ing stoppers.
(Christie's)
$250 £128

Red overlay glass
bottle with green
glass stopper.
(Christie's)
$300 £156

One of two ivory
bottles with match-
ing stoppers.
(Christie's)
$100 £51

Red overlay glass
bottle, green glass
stopper. (Christie's)
$300 £156

Jasper bottle with
gold stone bead
stopper. (Christie's)
$200 £103

Black overlay glass
bottle with quartz
stopper.
(Christie's)
$300 £156

Famille rose Peking
glass bottle, with
jade stopper.
(Christie's)$350 £182

Red overlay glass
bottle with jade
stopper.(Christie's)
$180 £93

Famille rose Peking
glass bottle, mott-
led jade stopper.
(Christie's)$350 £182

Mottled grey and
brown agate bottle,
with glass bead stop-
per. (Christie's)
$250 £130

Grey agate bottle
with red stopper.
(Christie's)
$250 £130

Japanese gilt lacquer
bottle with soapstone
stopper. (Christie's)
$100 £51

Mottled grey and
russet agate bottle.
(Christie's)
$150 £78

Mottled grey agate
bottle with emer-
ald jade stopper.
(Christie's)
$180 £93

Rose quartz bottle
with matching
stopper, on wood
stand. (Christie's)
$160 £83

Grey agate bottle
with red bead
stopper.(Christie's)
$250 £130

Grey agate bottle
with tiger's eye
stopper.(Christie's)
$180 £93

Mottled grey agate
bottle. (Christie's)
$200 £104

Grey agate bottle
with mottled emer-
ald and white jade
stopper.(Christie's)
$200 £104

Mottled yellow agate
bottle with coral
stopper.(Christie's)
$180 £93

Flattened malachite
bottle with quartz
stopper.(Christie's)
$380 £197

Rose quartz bottle
with matching
stopper.(Christie's)
$200 £103

Light brown agate
bottle with coral
bead stopper.
(Christie's)$180 £93

Carnelian agate
bottle with carved
agate stopper.
(Christie's)
$200 £103

Purple amethyst
bottle with green
glass stopper.
(Christie's)
$400 £208

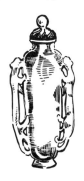

Miniature grey agate
bottle with glass
stopper.(Christie's)
$160 £83

Mottled grey and
brown agate bottle
with agate bead
stopper.(Christie's)
$160 £83

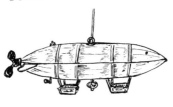

Lehmann ElI tinplate zeppelin, circa 1912, 7¾in. long. (Sotheby's Belgravia) $298 £150

Silver screen one-reel bandit by Tom Boland, Leeds, circa 1945-50. (Sotheby's Belgravia) $199 £100

Gunthermann tinplate tramcar, circa 1925-30, 10in. long. (Sotheby's Belgravia) $238 £120

Conveyor amusement machine, 3ft. high, 1945-50. (Sotheby's Belgravia) $109 £55

Lehmann 'Li-La' tinplate clockwork toy, circa 1912, 5½in. long. (Sotheby's Belgravia) $417 £210

Bryan's 'The Clock' amusement machine, circa 1952, 2ft.9in. high. (Sotheby's Belgravia) $79 £40

French hand enamelled tinplate clockwork sedan, circa 1904, 14in. long. (Sotheby's Belgravia) $298 £150

Good Kellermann tinplate clockwork frog, German, circa 1930, 4¾in. high.(Sotheby's Belgravia) $437 £220

Bing open tourer, German, circa 1918, 11½in. long. (Sotheby's Belgravia) $398 £199

Bingophone child's gramophone, circa 1925, German, turntable 17½in. diam. (Sotheby's Belgravia) $278 £140

Toy stable, German, circa 1860, 2ft.9in. wide. (Sotheby's Belgravia) $318 £160

Unusual Lehmann mechanical flying bird, circa 1910, 7in. long. (Sotheby's Belgravia) $199 £100

An Ahrems test-your-strength machine, circa 1920, 6ft.7in. high. (Sotheby's Belgravia) $636 £320

Tinplate clockwork horse and cart, by G. and K. Greppert & Keich, Brandenburg, 17cm. long. (King & Chasemore) $254 £130

Fireworks reward amusement machine, circa 1933, 2ft.8in. high. (Sotheby's Belgravia) $95 £48

Decamps mechanical ram, French, circa 1900, 1ft.2in. long. (Sotheby's Belgravia) $358 £180

Tinplate four-funnelled battleship, probably by Bing, circa 1912, 1ft.5in. long. (Sotheby's Belgravia) $696 £350

Lehmann 'tut-tut' tinplate motor car, circa 1910, 6¾in. long. (Sotheby's Belgravia) $437 £220

Lehmann 'Wild West'
bucking bronco tin-
plate toy, circa 1930,
6¼in. long.(Sotheby's
Belgravia) $338 £170

Rare child-sized model of
the Austin Seven racing
car. (Phillips) $920 £460

Orion one-armed
bandit, circa 1960,
2ft.4in. high.
(Sotheby's Belgravia)
$27 £14

Unusual child's galloper
tricycle, circa 1870, 3ft.
4in. long. (Sotheby's
Belgravia) $238 £120

French clockwork tri-
cyclist, circa 1870,
with bisque head and
original clothes.
(Phillips)$949 £470

Tinplate clockwork
horse and trap by
Greppert & Reich,
Brandenburg.
(King & Chasemore)
$254 £130

Unusual model butcher's
shop, circa 1900, 1ft.
11in. wide. (Sotheby's
Belgravia)
$1,194 £600

Gottlieb World's Fair pin-
ball machine, circa 1963,
4ft.3½in. long.(Sotheby's
Belgravia) $238 £120

Wonder's 'big wheel'
amusement machine,
circa 1950, 2ft.10in.
high. (Sotheby's Bel-
gravia) $159 £80

Rossignal clockwork
taxi and driver, 14cm.
long, French. (King &
Chasemore) $121 £60

Part of a collection
of Dinky London
taxis. (Phillips)
$161 £80

Arnold Tin Lizzy toy
car, German, 1950's,
with box. (Alfie's
Antique Market)
$42 £21

Japanese battery oper-
ated one-man band,
by Alps. (King &
Chasemore)
$111 £55

Orobr tinplate double garage
and two cars, 1920's. (King
& Chasemore) $404 £200

Scarce Toonerville
Trolley by Fischer
& Co., Germany,
13cm. long.(King
& Chasemore)
$484 £240

Self-propelled toy
steam tricycle.
(King & Chasemore)
$363 £180

Edwardian child's milk
float, circa 1900, 12in.
high. (Gray's Antique
Market) $222 £110

English carved and
painted rocking horse,
circa 1900, 7ft. long.
(Sotheby's Belgravia)
$597 £300

Unusual tinplate trolley
bus, French, circa 1905,
11in. long.(Sotheby's
Belgravia) $338 £170

Louis Marx tinplate
'Ring-a-Ling' circus,
7½in. diam., circa
1930. (Sotheby's
Belgravia) $95 £48

Mechanical tinplate
rickshaw by Lehmann,
Germany, circa 1930,
7½in. long. (Alfie's
Antique Market)
$666 £333

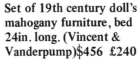

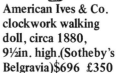

Unusual Lehmann tin-
plate 'Walking down
Broadway' couple,
circa 1896, 6in. high.
(Sotheby's Belgravia)
$597 £300

Set of 19th century doll's
mahogany furniture, bed
24in. long. (Vincent &
Vanderpump)$456 £240

American Ives & Co.
clockwork walking
doll, circa 1880,
9½in. high.(Sotheby's
Belgravia)$696 £350

Early French tricycle
clockwork toy, circa
1870, 6¾in. long.
(Sotheby's Belgravia)
$696 £350

Victorian doll's house,
completely fitted with
furniture. (Spencer's)
$2,156 £1,100

Unique Art 'Kiddy
Cyclist' toy in tin-
plate, circa 1945-55,
8½in. wide.
(Sotheby's Belgravia)
$89 £45

Tinplate clockwork 'Mickey Mouse' toy, German, circa 1930, 6¼in. long.(Sotheby's Belgravia) $318 £160

1920 tin and wood pull-along toy. (Alfie's Antique Market) $57 £29

German tinplate clockwork beetle, circa 1900, 3¾in. long. (Sotheby's Belgravia) $169 £85

Rare French tinplate push-along drummer boy, circa 1890, 5¾in. high. (Sotheby's Belgravia) $477 £240

Small Victorian rocking horse on oak stand, 29in. high. (Nottingham Auction Mart) $257 £125

Doll's house designed by Sir Wm. Clough Williams Ellis.(Christie's S. Kensington) $2,626 £1,300

Hand enamelled clockwork toy, German, 1900, 6in. high. (Gray's Antique Mews) $353 £175

Superb German toy castle made from hand-painted pinewood, circa 1850, 19in. high. (Christopher Sykes) $490 £250

Louis Marx tinplate 'Goofy' toy, circa 1945, 8½in. long. (Sotheby's Belgravia) $119 £60

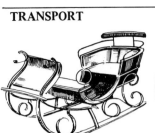

Reindeer or horse drawn sleigh, circa 1860, probably Eastern European. (Phillips) $874 £460

Penny farthing bicycle. (Christie's S. Kensington) $1,050 £520

A Victorian upholstered bathchair. (J. M. Welch) $194 £100

English bicycle, circa 1880, 5ft. high. (Sotheby's Belgravia) $1,287 £650

International Baby Carriage Store child's pushchair, circa 1900, 48in. long. (Sotheby's Belgravia) $232 £120

English ordinary bicycle, circa 1880, 4ft.8in. high. (Sotheby's Belgravia) $1,386 £700

Late Victorian Brougham, in need of restoration. (Spencer's) $4,944 £2,400

Penny farthing bicycle.(Parsons, Welch & Cowell) $779 £410

Austin heavy 12/4, first registered in 1930, in very good condition. (Andrew Sharp) $8,170 £4,300

Chinese lacquer tray,
2ft.10in. wide, circa
1820, on four bam-
boo legs.(Sotheby's)
$1,414 £700

Set of three Jennens and
Bettridge papier mache
trays, circa 1850.
(Bonham's)
$1,818 £900

Unusual Galle carved
and inlaid fruitwood
tray, circa 1900.
(Christie's N. York)
$1,160 £600

17th century early Lac
Burgaute tray, 13in.
diam. (Christie's)
$1,210 £623

Black papier mache tray,
japanned in red and gold.
(Phillips) $548 £280

Large Moreau silvered
pewter tray, 45cm.
wide, circa 1900.
(Sotheby's Belgravia)
$294 £150

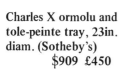

Charles X ormolu and
tole-peinte tray, 23in.
diam. (Sotheby's)
$909 £450

Edwardian mahogany
tray and stand with
painted decoration.
(British Antique
Exporters) $170 £85

One of a suite of three
Regency papier mache
trays, circa 1820.
(Sotheby's)
$707 £350

INDEX

665

669